ANTIDEMOCRATIC

ALSO BY DAVID DALEY

*Unrigged: How Americans Are Battling
Back to Save Democracy*

*Ratf**ked: Why Your Vote Doesn't Count*

ANTIDEMOCRATIC

INSIDE THE FAR RIGHT'S 50-YEAR PLOT TO CONTROL AMERICAN ELECTIONS

DAVID DALEY

MARINER BOOKS

New York   Boston

HarperCollins books may be purchased for educational, business, or sales promotional use. For information, please email the Special Markets Department at SPsales@harpercollins.com.

FIRST EDITION

Designed by Renata DiBiase

Library of Congress Cataloging-in-Publication Data has been applied for.

ISBN 978-0-06-332109-0

24 25 26 27 28 LBC 5 4 3 2 1

For Wyatt, who is the best,
With hope, joy, and lots of love

The candid citizen must confess that if the policy of the Government upon the vital questions affecting the whole people is to be irrevocably fixed by the decisions of the Supreme Court . . . the people will have ceased to be their own rulers.

—*Abraham Lincoln, first inaugural address, March 1861*

The most important thing for the public to understand is that we're not a political branch of government. They do not elect us. If they do not like what we are doing, it's more or less just too bad.

—*John Roberts, C-SPAN, October 11, 2009*

CONTENTS

PART III: THINGS HAVEN'T CHANGED

INTRODUCTION

IT WAS A line no one could see.

The invisible boundary wrapped around a new Walmart, bisected Interstate 65 in the very center of Alabama, the state at the heart of the fight for the ballot, and stretched the Calera city council district that Ernest Montgomery represented away from the growing city's downtown. Montgomery's home district was now severed from a Black church and neighborhood and pushed toward wealthy new subdivisions between Highways 22 and 31.

It would not take long for the political consequences of this line to be seen. Montgomery, just the second Black official elected in Calera's history, represented the council's only majority Black district. The invisible line— kept hidden from the Department of Justice despite the requirements of the Voting Rights Act—turned his district from 71 percent Black to nearly 70 percent white. It traded neighborhoods where double-wides sit atop makeshift concrete pillars for those with fancy homes with Range Rovers and Jeeps in the driveway. The new street names carried a *Robin Hood* theme, even though, in reality, it had the opposite effect. It stole from the poor and rewarded the elite. In the next election, Ernest Montgomery lost his council seat by two votes.

This was a line meant to divide, a line meant to turn back time. And in 2013, it became a line that, after nearly fifty years, finally broke the Voting Rights Act.

TODAY OUR DEMOCRACY teeters in a most perilous position, but we didn't get here overnight; the dangerous state of our elections in America did not come about by accident.

Over more than five decades conservatives have plotted our arrival at almost this precise point. Through a takeover of the courts, extreme gerrymanders, new voting barriers, the creation of new legal theories, and a carefully curated set of right-wing judges to rubber-stamp them, the Right has worked to refashion the nation in their image, without any concern that "elected representatives" could be removed from office by the people. America's antidemocratic slide is the product of a deliberate, long-term, and extraordinarily patient strategy, some of it behind closed doors though much of it in plain sight.

America's founders long fretted about a tyranny of the majority. Our Constitution established a representative democracy with a robust system of checks and balances, and a federal government with three coequal branches, all designed to guard against excessive partisanship and factionalism. James Madison, writing in number 10 of the *Federalist Papers*, suggested this decentralized approach created a "happy combination" of majority rule with minority protections. Alexander Hamilton, in *Federalist* 21, suggested that elections would ensure that representatives followed the will of the people. "The natural cure for an ill-administration, in a popular or representative constitution," he wrote, "is a change of men." But even elections have proven no match for the Right's antidemocratic tyranny of the minority.

There are two visions of the nation the white, male founders created. In one, best exemplified by Dr. Martin Luther King Jr.'s description of a moral arc that's long but ever-bending toward justice, America first guaranteed the vote to wealthy men, but after a civil war, the Thirteenth, Fourteenth, and Fifteenth Amendments to the Constitution that launched Reconstruction, a civil rights movement, women's suffrage, and the Voting Rights Act (VRA), that vision slowly guaranteed a more perfect union where men and women of all races and backgrounds were created equal.

The second, darker vision suggests that every step forward arrived with a backlash, that the Reconstruction dream, for example, was smothered by a Supreme Court overeager to assert that the nation had changed and equality had been achieved and, in a series of cases in the 1870s, all but guaranteed the brutal century of Jim Crow that stood until the passage of the Voting Rights Act in 1965.

This precarious moment of American history has been fueled by similar folly by the Supreme Court, and similar unease with multiracial democracy. Those federal protections within the VRA had been hard won. The brutal pillars of Jim Crow rule held strong in the former Confederacy before mass protest and principled resistance among disenfranchised Black citizens finally made the necessity and urgency of its passage undeniable on what should have marked a centennial of freedom. The regime of postbellum segregation instituted racial terror in the heart of the modern South, with a century of violence, lynchings, poll taxes, and literacy tests that derailed the post–Civil War dream of Reconstruction. Medgar Evers, John Lewis, Jimmie Lee Jackson, Lamar Smith, and countless other marchers and foot soldiers had wrested the promise of racial justice back from a federally sanctioned system of apartheid with blood or pieces of scalp left behind on Selma's Edmund Pettus Bridge.

They were gunned down by whites in broad daylight, on sunlit courthouse greens, in their homes, before frightened families. They were murdered by state troopers, faced clubs and fire hoses, tear gas and attack dogs, all for asserting their most fundamental right across southern cities and small towns. And to ensure it would never happen again in these most stubborn and resistant localities, where neither local officials nor judges could be trusted, the Voting Rights Act required the most horrific offenders, those who met the idea of equality with clubs and guns and dogs, to preapprove any changes to election laws or voting procedures with the Department of Justice or a federal court in Washington, D.C.

After the 1965 Voting Rights Act finally set a multiracial nation on a path toward multiracial democracy that had not been assured even after the Civil War and the Reconstruction amendments to the U.S. Constitution, the Supreme Court and the forces of regression pulled it backward, in part, all with that district line no one could see, in a city called Calera, located in Shelby County, Alabama.

Preclearance existed to ensure that otherwise invisible lines like these—the difference between a vote and an actual voice—were drawn fairly. It existed because stubborn pillars of resistance never truly crumbled, not in the weeks after the VRA's passage when South Carolina immediately challenged it in federal court as an infringement of state sovereignty, and not in Calera in the mid-2000s when it was lawlessly disobeyed by Alabama officials.

And so in the 2013 U.S. Supreme Court decision in *Shelby County v. Holder*, this two-mile arc shearing Montgomery's district from its historical moorings also ensnared the VRA. The ever-present American struggle over who wields power has shifted to the U.S. Supreme Court. It's there where that invisible line in Calera intersected with a five-decade conservative strategy to build supremacy in the judiciary. This line no one could see would trap, then suffocate, the Voting Rights Act and concentrate so much power over elections within the courts and gerrymandered Republican legislatures as to create dangerous ramifications for every election still to come.

THIS BOOK TELLS the story of a modern plot to undermine the most foundational of all rights, the right to vote. It is the story of a plot to advance the most antidemocratic notions of all: that not every vote should count equally, that the institutions of a free nation can be remade to sever them from the will of people, that majority rule could be subverted via election law and the courts. In the last fifty years, this plot has traveled from the fringes of the law to the heart of the Republican Party, in such dramatic measure that the party no longer pretends to care about winning elections through such old-school practices as winning more votes than the other side, or sustaining a popular mandate for its policies.

This most brazen and un-American scheme has proven staggeringly successful. These lines of money, power, and influence were nearly as circuitous and shielded from public view as the lines that pushed Montgomery's district to the frontiers of white exurbia—and they would come to shore up the same extreme agenda. *Shelby County* and the series of antidemocratic rulings by the Supreme Court led by Chief Justice John Roberts represent the hard-fought culmination of a generations-long effort to remake American law, electoral politics, and social hierarchy in the preferred image of a radicalized American Right. It emerged out of a concerted, determined effort to build and fund institutions, cultivate conservative legal thinkers, invent and empower a movement in the legal academy known as originalism, place allies on the bench, and remake the nation through the courts.

The *Shelby County* decision was chiefly the handiwork of Chief Justice Roberts—who had launched his legal career as a Reagan-era Justice Department lawyer contesting voting rights and the reauthorization of the Voting Rights Act. During his Senate confirmation hearings in 2005, Roberts famously declared and promised the American people, "I will remember that it's my job to call balls and strikes, and not pitch or bat." Named by a GOP president, Roberts was a lifelong Republican who had also served on the team of attorneys (alongside his future high court colleagues Amy Coney Barrett and Brett Kavanaugh) that had installed that same president, George W. Bush, in the Oval Office during the controversial 2000 *Bush v. Gore* decision. Yet he insisted that his approach would be objective and unassuming. "I come before the committee with no agenda. I have no platform," he said. "The role of an umpire and a judge is critical. They make sure everybody plays by the rules. But it is a limited role." Roberts's memorable metaphor has defined his image for his first two decades as chief justice. It has shaped his reputation in the press, as well, which has largely cast Roberts as a modestly conservative institutionalist whose greatest interest is in the integrity and stability of the court.

Antidemocratic proposes the opposite: that while Roberts has been praised and portrayed as a model of modest judicial restraint, his effective baseball analogy has helped disguise a quite different and much more radical approach on the bench. Each landmark decision begins with a smaller case that invites the next big question. It allows Roberts to look like an incrementalist when he is really a patient bulldozer. Precedents would be overturned, strikes would be called balls, but there would be no sudden lurch. Judicial modesty would be false, accompanied by the chief justice's carefully choreographed two-step. Roberts's actual legacy is far more powerfully grounded in *Shelby County* and other cases about voting rights, campaign finance, and the basic operations of our democracy.

Roberts endorsed Shelby County's arguments that the VRA was an outdated relic and a violation of Alabama's sovereignty in a sweeping majority opinion finding that argued, in the absence of anything resembling firm and credible evidence, that "things had changed in the South." Roberts's ahistorical reasoning overruled the VRA's calibrated formula for establishing and implementing preclearance requirements. In one astonishing blow, Roberts neutered the VRA's primary enforcement arm. Red state legislatures, having spent weeks preparing for this decision by prepping new election laws that would make it tougher for Blacks, Latinos, young people, and other Democratic-leaning constituencies to vote, began enacting these draconian new provisions that very afternoon. Nothing had changed in the South. What had changed was the ideological and partisan makeup of the Supreme Court. The most effective way to change the law—especially if the goal is to push it in a direction most citizens oppose—is to change the court, the most antidemocratic institution of them all.

As the Roberts Court has gone on to demonstrate in a series of antidemocratic and rights-abridging decisions, a pivotal Supreme Court decision can abruptly overthrow core precepts of American justice and equality. And in many ways, *Shelby County*, and the democracy decisions that followed, by virtue of its determination to enshrine a discredited and immoral regime of white electoral privilege, was a key harbinger of the high court's binge of exclusionary rulings, from *Dobbs v. Jackson Women's Health Organization* stripping women of abortion rights to *Students for Fair Admissions v. Harvard and North Carolina Universities* striking down affirmative action in college admissions.

If you want to understand the true malevolence of the Right's strategy to govern under near-permanent conditions of minority rule and judicial supremacy, you have to approach these cases as conservatives and their influential, judge-minting apparatus the Federalist Society have: together, as part of a focused, long-term effort to undo the Warren Court, and stack the courts and weaponize the countermajoritarian structures of our system to entrench themselves in power, no matter how few their numbers, no matter the election results. The conservatives in the legal wing of the backlash movement did not want to simply win cases. They wanted to change America itself—with the legal system as a powerful and profoundly antidemocratic blunt instrument for the job. The evidence is now inarguable, as the Supreme Court reliably furnishes the American Right with victories it could never achieve through the political process, and enables gerry-mandered legislatures to lock in even more.

I use the word *plot* quite specifically. This has happened because the American Right has *engineered* it to happen, patiently and deliberately, over decades. There was no checklist, no grand conspiracy, but rather a series of interlocking efforts to build and consolidate power that Democrats never noticed or fully appreciated. By disguising hardball partisan politics as constitutional theory, the Right capitalized on long-standing deferential traditions and incentives in the news media covering the courts and the academic community surrounding it. As such, many institutions meant to scrutinize the court never saw the threat it posed to American democracy until it was too late.

And so here we are: Conservative thinkers, funders, activists, lawyers, and politicians have brought about the movement capture of the legal system, while simultaneously sealing off the ability of voters to wrench the Right's hands off the levers of power through increasingly enduring gerrymanders. We cannot understand our extreme, withered politics without reckoning with this fifty-year project that has changed America, and enabled the high court's multifront assault on the preservation and expansion of American democracy. The ultimate test of what we might justly call the *antidemocratic* judiciary is the simple survival of a republic where a majority of Americans have the ability to vote out leaders they no longer wish to have in high office. It is the establishment of an American minority rule.

To understand this strategy in its full context, in other words, is to encounter a fateful series of invisible lines, all charged with currents of minoritarian power that would break America and alter the direction of our democracy.

ANY STORY OF long-term strategies and patient political planning carries the whiff of conspiracy. This is not one of those tales. Much of the story here unfolded before our eyes. It simply revealed itself so slowly that the media never captured its full dimensions, but also so suddenly that by the time hapless Democrats understood its magnitude they lacked the ability, tools, and will to counter it. Yes, some of the actors pulled strings from the shadows; some funders and foundations operated quietly and obscured the true source or agenda behind seven- and eight-figure donations. But during the great right-wing legal retrenchment, many of the key figures openly discussed these efforts and transparently admitted their agendas, tactics, and motivations. Lewis Powell, a Virginia lawyer with deep ties to the Nixon administration, wrote a 1971 private memo urging big business to work to take over the judiciary, and months later he found himself appointed to the Supreme Court. His memo helped unify and focus efforts to build and fund conservative institutions that operated in concentric circles, not private clubs or smoke-filled rooms. They spoke not in secret code but in the common language of like-minded school pals, ideological fellow travelers, and old-fashioned career opportunists.

All well-planned maneuvers, naturally, require a motive. This five-decade strategy can be traced back to the early 1970s, after the Supreme Court under the leadership of Chief Justice Earl Warren issued landmark decisions on voting rights, established the proposition of "one person, one vote," and put an end to decades of malapportioned state legislatures that enhanced the power of white rural interests and diluted the votes of cities. (Later, after Warren's retirement, many of the same justices found that a constitutional right to privacy protected abortion rights in *Roe v. Wade*.) For many Americans, the decisions of the Warren Court cemented the idea that the Supreme Court is a guardian of liberty, as is etched high above its east facade, the institution that ended segregation and ensured the principle of "one person, one vote." Today, that ideal falls sadly short of reality.

The conservative movement's successes were openly celebrated, such as at the Federalist Society's annual black-tie dinners, named in honor of Antonin Scalia, televised on C-SPAN, held just steps from the Capitol and the U.S. Supreme Court. Politicians and attorneys general and other judicial ideologues congratulated one another with champagne toasts. No less than four Supreme Court justices themselves thanked the Federalist Society for lifting them into the nation's nine most exclusive seats. No longer a mere collegiate debate club, the Federalist Society is now the most important player in the wholesale reinvention of the American court system, a credentialing society that places judges on courts nationwide. The Society's leaders, allies, and board members also control what might be called the supply side of the justice system, devoting hundreds of millions of dollars to incubate ideas, develop cases, and place them before hand-chosen friendly judges.

In 2016, when Donald Trump felt the Republican nomination in his grasp, but was still worried some conservatives viewed him as insufficiently committed to the cause, he arrived at a strategic masterstroke. Trump volunteered to choose future Supreme Court justices from a list of approved conservatives. Leonard Leo, the Federalist Society's executive vice president and the preeminent GOP court whisperer, and Donald McGahn, a longtime member and GOP election lawyer, took the lead creating the list. After Trump's surprising victory, Leo and McGahn elevated their pre-approved, prevetted favorites, Neil Gorsuch, Brett Kavanaugh, and Amy Coney Barrett, to the nation's highest court. And then after John Roberts, Antonin Scalia, and Clarence Thomas, all with long-standing Federalist Society ties, opened American elections to unlimited dark money in the 2010 *Citizens United* decision and then drove *Shelby County*, the new conservative supermajority delivered the Right's long-desired wins on affirmative action, abortion, the regulatory state, voting rights, and so much more.

"Our opponents of judicial nominees frequently claim the president has outsourced his selection of judges" to the Federalist Society, joked McGahn at the 2018 FedSoc gala. "That is completely false. I've been a member of the Federalist Society since law school. Still am. So, frankly, it seems like it's been in-sourced."

Later, Senate Majority Leader Mitch McConnell, on the edge of his eightieth birthday, struck a more serious tone. "My goal," he said, "is to do everything we can for as long as we can to transform the federal judiciary, because everything else we do is transitory. The closest thing we will ever have an opportunity to do to have the longest impact on the country is confirming these great men and women and transforming the judiciary for as long into the future as we can."

McConnell paused as he gazed out over a hall packed with 2,200 conservative luminaries rejoicing in their newfound power and influence. "I hope you are proud of what we've done."

THIS IS NOT a book about the history of the Supreme Court's antidemocratic interpretation of the Constitution since our founding, a treatise on how conservatives remade election law and redefined originalism, a biography of John Roberts or the Federalist Society, how Donald Trump transformed the Republican Party, or the story of the Voting Rights Act and every challenge to it. Many terrific books have been written on all those topics, and more will surely come.

Antidemocratic has a different goal: to narrate the broad strokes of a daring long-term plot to capture the courts, to connect dots over decades, to introduce key players who have lingered in the shadows, and to answer the crucial question of *How did we get here?* It's a question that's more urgent than ever on the eve of a presidential election that could be decided by the men and women jurists on the U.S. Supreme Court and the state supreme courts who owe their careers to the Federalist Society, and could now remake American democracy using legal theories developed by fellow members.

Some conservatives might suggest that this book simply scorns rulings that I disagree with as antidemocratic; to the contrary, this book is animated by a belief that the Reconstruction amendments represent the truest, deepest articulation of American liberty and justice for all, and that the conservative, originalist plot to control the courts is at its heart just the latest effort to unravel that vision of equality and promote a tyranny of the minority through profoundly unfair and un-American means. It begins with the belief that no democracy should concentrate this much power with any nine unelected individuals, of any political persuasion. *Antidemocratic* does not mean personally unpleasant or wrongheaded; it suggests a scheme to enshrine as law what could not be won fairly, to remake law as their own partisan politics *because they can*, to weaponize a system designed to prevent a tyranny of the majority in order to enshrine a rule of the few, to draw invisible lines that reshape our democracy one mile at a time.

In her famous dissent in *Shelby County*, Justice Ruth Bader Ginsburg argued that preclearance had restrained localities that continued to look for creative new ways to discriminate. The Voting Rights Act had stopped the worst Jim Crow tactics, she conceded in *Shelby County*, but it remained necessary to preserve those gains and prevent modernized, more subtle discriminatory practices. Tossing preclearance aside "when it has worked and is continuing to work," she argued, "is like throwing away your umbrella in a rainstorm because you are not getting wet."

That court-created downpour now threatens to drown representative democracy itself. The consequence of that line no one could see is now vividly apparent to all. This is the story of how we have arrived at this grave moment.

PART I

THE LONG GAME

CHAPTER ONE

THE TAKEOVER OF American elections began, of all places, in a memo. Specifically an attack memo written by a future Supreme Court justice that helped lay the groundwork and created the conditions for the modern war on voting rights.

The memo—drafted in 1971 for the U.S. Chamber of Commerce by Lewis Powell, a soon-to-be Nixon appointee to the high court—captured a mood of mounting panic on the American right, particularly among the corporate establishment that the Chamber faithfully represented. The U.S. Supreme Court, under the leadership of Chief Justice Earl Warren, had spent the 1960s guarding and expanding "one person, one vote" and access to the ballot box for all. The Voting Rights Act had just celebrated its fifth anniversary, and the face of the American electorate became younger and more diverse almost immediately. In Mississippi, for example, Black voter registration skyrocketed from 6.7 percent in 1965 to just under 60 percent in 1967; nationwide, some 250,000 new Black voters had been added to the rolls by the end of 1965 alone.

Not everyone celebrated this full-throated protection of small-*d* democratic principles. Fewer voters looked like Lewis Powell and his friends. Even Nixon's electoral triumph in 1968, won via racially coded appeals to a white ethnic "silent majority," did little to quell corporate America's sense that it was under siege. Powell's memo looked to describe how the genie of a changing America might be stuffed back into the bottle; liberals and young radicals might dominate college campuses, but the civil rights revolution and broader cultural change could be blunted by conquering the courts. Powell's call to arms declared that the courts could be "the most important instrument for social, economic and political change." His words awakened and inspired those who would slowly push the U.S. Supreme Court far to the right—both as a vehicle for decisions that benefited big business, and as an end run against the Warren Court's expansion of voting rights and minority protections. What Powell and his allies feared they would no longer be able to win democratically in a changing, awakened America, they set out to take by judicial fiat.

Postwar prosperity might have been built on the belief that what was good for General Motors was good for America, but that 1950s consensus could no longer be taken for granted. In the wake of an insurgent New Left and a powerful consumers' rights movement, many had lost faith that corporate values matched their own and began to see the interests of business and the public not as intertwined, but opposed. In bestselling books and headline-grabbing congressional testimony, big business took the blame for spewing toxins into the environment, cynically marketing deadly cigarettes and other products carrying serious health risks, and profiteering off the Vietnam War.

Perhaps one image captured the curdled relationship best: flames tearing through a Bank of America branch in Isla Vista, California, a university town just outside Santa Barbara, torched by a mob of student protesters in February 1970 as the nation was rocked with a fresh round of antiwar protests. A poster of the burning bank would become a dorm-room fixture on college campuses nationwide. The Isla Vista attack launched a wave of copycat threats; more than 4,440 bomb threats were called in across California alone during the ensuing ten months of 1970, including 1,052 incidents at city halls, universities, even suburban supermarkets.

Bank of America's name and ubiquitous presence made it a symbolic target for the most virulent strain of an antiwar movement determined to focus moral fury and hold banks and defense contractors accountable for their role in Vietnam. As the historian Kim Phillips-Fein writes in *Invisible Hands*, her brilliant survey of the intersection between the conservative movement and long-running business opposition to the New Deal, when Dow Chemical executives showed up for campus hiring fairs, they met a rising tide of angry protest over the company's role in producing napalm. "We are facing a real honest-to-God disenchantment, not just a passing momentary flare-up that will go away if we just keep it cool for a while," said Louis B. Lundborg, the Bank of America chairman. "There is a new value system emerging in America, starting with the youth but becoming one of the new facts of life for the rest of us to deal with." But not if Lewis Powell could offer an antidemocratic alternative via the judiciary, instead.

Public opinion polls confirmed Lundborg's analysis and heightened the stakes for Powell's well-funded allies. The ire aimed at corporate America extended deeper than Vietnam and reached far beyond radicals on campus. An annual survey by Daniel Yankelovich, Florence Skelly, and Arthur White asked Americans whether "business tries to strike a fair balance between profits and interests of the public." In 1968, 70 percent agreed. By 1970, that number had plunged to 33 percent. The discontent ran deep. A burgeoning environmental movement, inspired by Rachel Carson's *Silent Spring*, horrified by the 1969 Cuyahoga River fire on a polluted Cleveland waterway that "oozes instead of flows," accused big business of poisoning the nation's air and waterways. Consumer advocates fought back against dangerous products. Ralph Nader's *Unsafe at Any Speed* changed the way Americans thought of automobiles. What was good for General Motors suddenly seemed toxic for America.

As the tide of public outrage rose alongside the growing environmental devastation, Washington took action and created the Environmental Protection Agency. New regulations on business followed, backed up by a U.S. Supreme Court under Chief Justice Earl Warren that had steadily expanded voting, privacy, and reproductive rights. In Richard Nixon's 1970 State of the Union address, the prophet of white ethnic backlash and beneficiary of the Southern Strategy suddenly sounded like Rachel Carson himself. "The great question of the '70s," he asked, "is shall we make our peace with nature and begin to make reparations for the damage we have done to our air, to our land, and to our water?"

Business leaders, feeling voiceless, besieged, and under attack from all sides, much as conservatives did from the Warren Court, recognized they needed help. The impossible task of protecting corporate America during tumult and pushing back against the likelihood of change in a multiracial nation where everyone now possessed equal access to the ballot box fell to Virginia attorney Lewis Powell.

POWELL WAS A die-hard apostle of the 1950s consensus, straight out of central casting. He served on the founding board of Colonial Williamsburg, Virginia's prerevolutionary white Disney World—and in a perfect gloss on that imagineered vision of a harmonious national history, he also joined the board of Philip Morris, the nation's leading tobacco company. As the company's top in-house counsel, at the moment when the lethal dangers of cigarette use had come to light, Powell pioneered what would become a key bulwark of the conservative legal revolution in the Roberts era during *Citizens United*: he contorted the clear intent of the First Amendment's protections of political speech to argue that Philip Morris had the constitutional right to equal time to respond to antismoking public service announcements on TV.

When Powell appeared at Philip Morris's annual meetings, he always made sure he was photographed with a lit cigarette, even though he was not a smoker. Powell had establishment credentials nonpareil, as the former president of the American Bar Association, a founding partner of one of Richmond's leading white-shoe law firms, and a member of President Nixon's Blue Ribbon Defense Panel, a collection of corporate leaders who looked to bring an early version of McKinsey-style efficiency to the nation's military.

Powell, like many true believers on the right, was also a dedicated institution builder. According to Jane Mayer's *Dark Money*, during the tumult of antiwar protest and civil rights activism, Powell, Richard Mellon Scaife, and other wealthy conservatives formed a club they called the League to Save Carthage. The league carried a very simple mandate that might be summed up as the opposite of *noblesse oblige*: unless well-connected and lavishly resourced defenders of the faith stood athwart the wide-ranging forces of progressive subversion, the country's very future and identity were at risk. Five decades before Donald Trump descended his gilded Trump Tower escalator, Lewis Powell and his billionaire buddies also sought to make America great again, or at least to make it look more like themselves.

The memo's origins began in 1970 and 1971 as Powell chatted with his neighbor Eugene "Syd" Sydnor, the chairman of the national Chamber of Commerce's influential and increasingly active education committee. The two men lived in one of Richmond's most fashionable, old-money bastions, Windsor Farms—a stately development of country estates along the James River designed to resemble an English village. Over cocktails at the exclusive Commonwealth Club—an all-white, all-male retreat where "Mr. President" always referred to Jefferson Davis—Powell and Sydnor's talks became increasingly alarmist. They believed the time had come to defend an American republic threatened by an electorate that sought to make it more just and inclusive.

On June 30, 1970, leveraging his access from the Blue Ribbon Panel, Powell sent Nixon a private, seventeen-page memo titled "Political Warfare." It was a manifesto for what Powell viewed as a dangerously complacent business community, arguing that the nation urgently required a comprehensive strategy for "political, psychological and propaganda operations" to counter the "Communist propaganda" that is "parroted daily throughout the free world in the communications media, on campus, in literature, by the arts and theater and on the public platform."

Two weeks later, on July 15, Powell traveled to Blue Mountain, North Carolina, to deliver the opening address at the Southern Industrial Relations Conference, where manufacturers, bankers, economic development officials, and small family businesses gathered annually. Powell did not bother with parochial questions of economic growth or prospects for a recession; nor, he informed his audience of business leaders, was he there to amuse or reassure them. His mission, instead, was to send them home terrified.

"Our democracy and the values which it sustains are under broad and virulent attack," Powell warned. "For the first time in America's existence there is concern that revolution could engulf this country." Powell conceded that at first blush it might sound irrational to suggest revolution might come to the "most prosperous and freest" country in the world. Yet the "chilling fact," he thundered, is that the conspirators and their spokespeople are "as open and notorious as Hitler and his storm troopers." They could be found on campus, in Hollywood, in the news media, and delivering the nightly news. Powell must have also wondered if some sat on the

Warren Court. Powell's tone was apocalyptic and dark, but he had the ear
of the administration's most powerful men. Melvin Laird, the secretary of
defense, and General Alexander Haig, Nixon's special assistant on national
security issues, sent Powell approving notes. Haig agreed that the "creation
of a national commission such as you suggest might be advisable." Nixon
himself soon followed with a note praising Powell's speech. "I can see that
we share many similar attitudes concerning the problems we are facing in
America today," he wrote.

But Powell wasn't satisfied with grateful letters from the Nixon White
House. He wanted Nixon and the Chamber to enlist in his battle. Sydnor
and Powell knew their enemy, in short, and they believed that defeating
it would entail nothing less than a national mobilization of money, messaging, and legal strategizing. Early that summer, Sydnor asked his friend
to prepare an action memo for the Chamber's immediate consideration,
and he scheduled late-August meetings in Washington with the group's
chairman and executive vice president. Powell agreed to write a confidential memo with a blueprint for a counterassault on the academy, the news
media, and the judiciary. The thirty-four-page action plan Powell crafted
would become a road map for the rightward transformation of American
politics, setting the stage for the Supreme Court's evisceration of the Voting Rights Act, its blessing of extreme partisan gerrymandering, and the
funding of the Right's half-century campaign to remake federal courts and
state legislatures. In Powell's memo, the Right had its own *Silent Spring*.

WHEN LEWIS POWELL died in 1998, the *New York Times* memorialized the distinguished jurist as a "balancer and compromiser," a "political moderate"
who disdained "heated rhetoric and doctrinal rigidity." *Time* magazine
mourned the loss of the "marble palace's Southern gentleman," and the
Los Angeles Times praised the "middle-road course" of this "uncommonly
sweet, gentle and courteous man" who, they suggested, served the nation
only from a sense of civic-minded patriotism. They whitewashed his life
just as thoroughly as Powell burnished the reputation of Big Tobacco.

None of these obituaries mentioned Powell's manifesto for the Chamber, by far the most consequential work of a long American life, written

with a dogmatic conviction anathema to balance and moderation alike. None of them, either, mentioned Powell's many speeches during the 1960s denouncing and mocking Reverend Martin Luther King Jr. ("a prophet of civil disobedience") and his *Letter from Birmingham Jail* ("heresy," an invitation to "totalitarian rule").

The Powell Memo, titled "Attack on American Free Enterprise System," is both a declaration of war and a detailed strategy for how that war was to be waged. It helped formalize a nationwide mobilization of conservative power and wealth that has transformed voting rights, constitutional law, long-standing rights, and the country's essential political profile over the past half century.

Powell did not urge a "middle-road" course. Nor did he come anywhere close to suggesting that his conclusions were up for debate. "No thoughtful person can question that the American economic system is under broad attack," he began. He called on American business to learn how to practice "guerilla warfare" in response, and to no longer tolerate, let alone participate in, its own destruction. Businessmen owned the media that championed Nader on its covers, they served as trustees and all-important donors on campuses that indoctrinated students. "Political power is necessary," Powell exhorted. "It must be used aggressively and with determination, without embarrassment and without the reluctance which has been so characteristic of American business." Executives "have shown little stomach for hard-nose contest with their critics, and little skill in effective intellectual and philosophical debate." He wrote that the time had come, "indeed it is long overdue, for the wisdom, ingenuity and resources of American business to be marshaled against those who would destroy it."

Powell's military mindset also prompted him to remind his readers that to bend the nation back to their will they must prepare themselves for a long battle, thanks to the changing electorate now handed the vote. Individuals and corporations, he wrote, can't do this work alone. "Strength lies in organization, in careful long-range planning and implementation, in consistency of action over an indefinite period of years, in the scale of financing available only through joint effort, and in the political power available only through united action and national organizations." If you want power, Powell counseled, you have to build it—patiently and thoroughly.

To battle back on campus and in the media, he called for corporate America to make unprecedented new investments in the conservative, pro-business scholars of the future. These intellectual shock troops would serve both as professors on campus and fellows in Washington, producing op-eds, book-length manifestos, and congressional testimony to advance the Right's sacred cause. Even if these conservative-funded thinkers were outnumbered in the faculty lounge, Powell noted, they would be "stimulating teachers, and their controversy attracts student following." Powell also called for a panel of scholars to evaluate textbooks used for economics, political science, and sociology classes, envisioning the battles decades later in Texas and Florida. "We have seen the civil rights movement insist on rewriting many of the textbooks in our universities and schools," he complained. The Right must fight for an "assurance of fair and factual treatment of our system of government and our enterprise system."

Perhaps the greatest opportunity Powell identified was in the courts—a woefully neglected field of right-wing conflict, in Powell's view. An activist-minded court, Powell suggested in his memo, "may be the most important instrument for social, economic and political change." The American Civil Liberties Union (ACLU), labor unions, public interest law firms, and civil rights organizations understand this, and consequently "have been far more astute in exploiting judicial action," winning landmark victories at the high court "often at business's expense." This could be replicated, though, Powell maintained. There was no reason that a different activist-minded court couldn't be active on behalf of *business and conservatives*. To reach that goal, businessmen had to exert the same sort of influence on courts as they should be wielding on the press and the universities: they had to repopulate the courts with their kind of legal thinkers and jurists, and reimagine the kinds of arguments presented to those judges in amicus briefs. "This is a vast area of opportunity," Powell wrote, presciently, "if, in turn, business is willing to provide the funds."

POWELL WAS NOT the only conservative thinker in the early 1970s looking to galvanize a counterassault against the judiciary and the new electorate empowered by the Warren Court. Powell wrote for a private audience of

American elites and provided his counsel to presidents and CEOs behind closed doors, hoping to sway national politics at a global level.

Around the same time that Powell was finishing his Chamber of Commerce manifesto, Yale Law School professor Robert Bork traveled to Indiana University with far more modest hopes. Bork's address, bearing the anodyne title "Neutral Principles and Some First Amendment Problems," set forth a provocative vision of the Constitution and the role of the judiciary, tilted stolidly against the conservative bogey of a liberal activist court interpreting a living Constitution to address modern issues. Bork's article does not contain the word *originalism*, but the originalist movement on the legal right would come to hail it as one of its foundational texts. It is a plea, above all else, for judicial restraint, during a moment when the court envisioned a muscular Constitution that embraced putting the full vision of the Reconstruction amendments to work on behalf of multiracial democracy.

Bork captured the frustrations of conservatives who believed the Warren Court's landmark decisions on race, desegregation, reapportionment, and social issues were wrongly decided because they stitched together new constitutional rights. Among these were the dictum of "one person, one vote" and a right to privacy, soon to become even more controversial when the court decided *Roe v. Wade* two years later. As Bork and his allies would argue over and over again, none of these notions or exact phrases actually existed in the text of the document itself.

Richard Nixon had vowed to appoint "strict constructionists" to the court during his 1968 and 1972 campaigns and assailed judges who, as he saw it, made the law from the bench. When he nominated Powell and William Rehnquist as associate justices in 1971, Nixon vowed that his nominees would not "twist or bend" the Constitution to reach his preferred outcome. In the coded argot of backlash politics, Nixon's silent majority understood that he was again invoking "law and order" and all it implied in a nation just beginning to realize the transformative possibilities of the Voting Rights Act. The Warren Court had created constitutional chaos, in the eyes of conservatives. Law and order needed to be restored to the bench, as well.

Bork's lecture, reprinted that fall in the *Indiana Law Review*, might have reached a small audience, but it landed with the same force as Powell's memo. It's been said that not many people listened to the Velvet

Underground's wild art-rock in the 1960s, but everyone who did started a band. Similarly, not many read Bork at the time, but those who did found themselves inspired to join the conservative legal movement. Today Bork's piece remains one of the top-ten most cited law review articles ever, and it helped launch the originalist school of constitutional law. "The require- ment that the Court be principled arises from the resolution of the seem- ing anomaly of judicial supremacy in a democratic society. If the judiciary really is supreme, able to rule when and as it sees fit, the society is not democratic," Bork wrote. Had Bork stopped there, he would have been dif- ficult to argue with; instead, his solution provided judges with a different ideological bent with a different justification to rule as they saw fit. The clear remedy, he argued, is for justices to observe complete fealty to the language of the Constitution. "It follows that the Court's power is legiti- mate only if it has, and can demonstrate in reasoned opinions that it has, a valid theory, derived from the Constitution." If it does not have such a theory, Bork argued, "but merely imposes its own value choices," the court violates the Madisonian model "that alone justifies its power."

That theory would become known as originalism. Today there are many different variations and mutations of originalism. But at its heart, this school of thought holds that all constitutional interpretation must begin (and sometimes end) with the actual text and what the actual text meant at the time. As a corollary doctrine, conservatives *also* espoused "judicial restraint" as the proper antidote to the excesses of the activist courts of the 1960s and 1970s, arguing that judges should not interpret the law based on their own social and political beliefs. As originalism devel- oped, however, it allowed for *both* judicial activism and judicial restraint— all tied to a jurisprudential theory supposedly rooted in an impartial and disinterested reading of the Constitution.

What Bork understood is that there is no purely objective way to decide a case. A judge is always weighing competing values and ideas. So what to do? Bork's article called on the Supreme Court to uphold only rights that can be directly found in the text of the Constitution. "Where constitu- tional materials do not clearly specify the value to be preferred, there is no principled way to prefer any claimed human value to any other," he wrote. "The judge must stick close to the text and the history, and their fair implications, and not construct new rights." Judges, according to Bork, must hew to what "the men who put the amendment in the Constitution intended." They must "stick close to the text and the history, and their fair implications, and not construct new rights." Only in that way could value choices attributed to the "Founding Fathers, not to the Court" reign.

This led Bork to quarrel with much of the Warren Court's jurisprudence as unprincipled. Bork even disagreed with the landmark 1960s reapportionment cases that required legislative districts to be almost exactly equal in size—ending decades of malapportionment that favored white, rural interests over the cities—as "remarkable for their inability to muster a single respectable supporting argument. The principle of one man, one vote," Bork sniffed, "was not neutrally derived." Neither, of course, were Alabama's state senate districts that allowed one senator per county, ensuring rural whites had more power than urban Blacks; state senate maps in Alabama and Tennessee, which had not been redrawn since 1900; or population disparities in states like Nevada, where before the Warren Court's reapportionment revolution, the smallest district contained 568 people while the largest had nearly 127,000. The Warren Court sided with the principle best in line with the democratic vision of the Reconstruction amendments; originalism allowed Bork to defend racial inequality while claiming historical high ground.

Originalism didn't lead to neutral answers: it led to *different* answers, the ones Bork and the generations of conservative thinkers he inspired preferred, answers that could be swaddled in theory and the garb of the Founding Fathers, while halting and slowing the expansion of rights—including voting rights—to those the nation's founders did not include. And as those young thinkers took their places on the bench, and within the Department of Justice, Bork's opposition to "one person, one vote" would blossom into a much broader critique of voting rights and representational fairness. The Roberts Court's later attacks on the VRA, as well as its blessing of extreme GOP partisan gerrymanders, would be based, in part, on a cramped originalist embrace of "states' rights."

Decades later, when President Reagan nominated Bork to the Supreme Court in 1986, his originalist views led the Senate to reject him after a bruising twelve-day confirmation hearing. The rejecting vote was 58–42, with a solid majority finding his theories too threatening and extreme. Yet while Bork himself fell short of the high court, originalism would soon capture it anyway—largely due to Bork's evangelism, originalism's role as the organizing dogma of the Federalist Society, and the doctrine's sophisticated reinvention by young lawyers in the Reagan administration who coupled it to a whole suite of ambitious conservative political goals.

For those young lawyers, who frequently found themselves among a handful of conservatives in a law-school class, Bork's 1971 article was a thunderclap. It provided a critique that allowed them to ground their opposition to the Supreme Court's decisions in something more intellectual than just political disagreement. Right-wing legal thinkers could now say they weren't opposed to landmark rulings like *Roe v. Wade* or the apportionment cases because they differed with their substantive outcomes. No, they could conclude as dispassionate scholars that the court got it wrong because it strayed from the text of the Constitution. They weren't ideologues; they were defenders of historical truths.

"I remember vividly reading Bork's *Indiana Law Journal* article when I was in law school," says Michael Carvin, who would join the intellectual brethren at the Reagan Justice Department a decade later and work alongside a future chief justice in young John Roberts. "Bork was a voice in the wilderness. He and Scalia, they were standing on top of history shouting stop, right? It was amazing." Carvin was a Republican but not that conservative on social issues like abortion, he says. Yet under Bork's tutelage, he came to believe that the courts and his law professors were reading their political and policy preferences backward from the Constitution.

"I don't think you can justify any of the liberal decisions over the past forty or fifty years and suggest they have any connection to the statutory text of the Constitution," Carvin says. "They're just completely results-oriented, driven by the liberal justices' policy preferences. That's antidemocratic, it's authoritarian, and it's clearly wrong."

Carvin's legal awakening was replicated among thousands of other conservative-leaning law students across the country. The article "laid the intellectual groundwork for the originalism of Justices Antonin Scalia and Clarence Thomas," wrote Steven Calabresi in *National Review*. He took a class on the theory of judicial review with Bork at Yale Law School and went on to cofound the Federalist Society.

"Professor Bork's article was so important," Reagan attorney general Ed Meese told me, because "with the Warren Court and what the different justices had to say at the time, voting rights being just one of those areas, there was no question that the drift had been away from the Constitution."

YET THE STORY of both the Powell Memo and the birth of originalism is messier and darker—and steeped in the politics of race and the desire to stand athwart multiracial democracy and yell stop. If Powell's memo provided a blueprint for those who would use the courts to achieve antidemocratic goals, and originalism provided the means to install judges who would help the Right achieve them, race remained the galvanizing force. The institutions funded after Powell's memo, twinned with the promotion of originalist theories on the right, would slowly bleed the Voting Rights Act of its historic, transformative power. Make no mistake, that was the goal from the very start.

Originalism—and the battle for the ballot box—has always been about race and power. Powell, together with the men who began pushing original intent as a response to the Warren Court—specifically the court's decision in the 1954 landmark school desegregation case *Brown v. Board of Education*—effectively looked to drown multiracial democracy in America before it had a chance to draw breath. It's not only that these forces began marshaling after the passage of the Voting Rights Act and the Warren Court's democracy rulings. It's that these were the old forces that always stood against equality, wrapping the old hate in new intellectual threads, marketed to the aggrieved and those who would turn the page on injustice without the interest in remedying it.

Lewis Powell was a pillar of Richmond society, educated in all-white schools, a member of its whites-only churches and social clubs, and a founding partner of a law firm that would not hire Black attorneys. His biographer, John C. Jeffries Jr., notes that he "never met a Black as an equal." Racial segregation remained so commonplace in Richmond, the former capital of the Confederacy, into the 1960s that Powell later conceded that "it never occurred to me to question it." When the U.S. Supreme Court desegregated the nation's schools in *Brown v. Board of Education* and called

for integration "with all deliberate speed," Powell, then the chairman of
the Richmond school board, described his reaction as "shock." In letters
to colleagues and friends, he maintained that "the school decisions were
wrongly decided," misguided not only as a matter of law but as social policy
as well. "The constitutionality of segregation," he believed, according to
Jeffries, "was conclusively established by long acceptance."

While it's difficult to believe that this respected lawyer and a southern
school board chair could be caught by surprise by a ruling decades in the
making, Powell's obituaries, nevertheless, carefully praised him for arguing against "maximal resistance" to the court's order. These admiring death
notices depicted him as a crucial bridge between the old and new South.

That was anything but the truth. Powell never blockaded school doors
himself. He simply achieved the same goal through quiet inaction. Integration under Powell would occur with something close to the opposite
of all deliberate speed. When he completed his chairmanship of the Richmond school board in 1960, Powell had avoided maximal resistance but
maintained the segregated status quo. Just two of the city's twenty-three
thousand Black students had been integrated into white classrooms. Even
six years after *Brown*, Powell had helped preside over the education of two
Richmonds, separate but unequal, divided by race.

The Powell model of resistance became the standard model in the American conservative movement. With the civil rights movement gaining steady
momentum—and with Cold War liberals realizing the maintenance of Jim
Crow rule in the South was a significant blow to the prestige of American
democracy—right-wing foes of integration realized that reactionary southern leaders blocking schoolhouse doors could no longer be the public face
of their movement. "Thus, the burgeoning coalition of Southern Democrats
and conservative Republicans turned to a proactive project of constitutional
history purporting to demonstrate what Warren's opinion did not: the original intent of the Fourteenth Amendment," writes the constitutional scholar
Calvin TerBeek in a 2021 article in the *American Political Science Review*.

TerBeek and others suggest that casting Bork as the father of originalism whitewashes—an apt word here—the role of key movement conservatives in the U.S. Senate, in conservative media outlets like the *National
Review*, and in the social sciences and legal academy who all suddenly,

and simultaneously, began talking about original intent. At *National Review*, the conservative columnist James Kilpatrick not only took the lead on developing a framework of original intent, but also regularly counseled everyone from the Republican National Committee to segregationist Alabama governor George Wallace on how to talk about it. "One procedure is known to the law; it is the procedure used by the Supreme Court and by other courts from the very beginning of the Republic: It is to determine the intent of the framers," Kilpatrick wrote as far back as the early 1960s. *The Conscience of a Conservative*, Senator Barry Goldwater's 1960s mega-bestselling bible for the movement, argued that original intent provided the key to a conservative interpretation of the Constitution. William F. Buckley used the same language, describing *Brown* as "patently counter to the intent of the Constitution, shoddy and illegal in analysis."

TerBeek also identified the prime mover of originalist arguments in top law reviews during the 1960s: a professor named Alfred Avins—who would defend the constitutionality of literacy tests for voting before the Supreme Court in the 1966 *Katzenbach* case that first upheld the constitutionality of the Voting Rights Act. In a 1965 article, Avins insisted, "it was not the original intent of the framers of the fourteenth amendment to forbid English-language or other literacy tests." Writing in the *Stanford Law Review* in 1966, he maintained that when "the original intent can be established unequivocally with supporting statements by both those in favor of and those opposed to the amendment, that intent must govern interpretation." Avins and Bork knew of each other as well. After Bork wrote an article in the *New Republic* in 1963 opposing civil rights legislation in Congress, Avins sent the professor a note. "From this article," he observed, knowingly, "I gather you have an interest in race relations."

Yet that interest, like much of this history, has disappeared as modern conservatives seek to brush aside originalism's founding story. "This mythology," says TerBeek, "not only had (and has) the virtue of providing a professional claim for conservative legal elites—these were (and are) academic arguments with the demand to be treated as such—they also provided the benefit of being able to erase the uncomfortable racial origins of modern originalism."

———

ON OCTOBER 21, 1971, less than two months after he implored corporate America and influential Republicans to use their wealth and influence on behalf of big business—and to take full advantage of the neglected opportunity in the courts—Lewis Powell was appointed to the U.S. Supreme Court by Richard Nixon. Just over two months later, he would be confirmed, resoundingly, with a vote of 99–1. Oklahoma Democratic senator Fred Harris cast the only no vote, criticizing Powell as an "elitist" who had never "shown any deep feelings for little people." Powell, said Harris, presciently, "does not have the kind of exemplary record in the fields of civil rights and civil liberties that I'd like to see in a man appointed to the Supreme Court for life."

For the next fifteen years, Powell would prove Senator Harris correct, stolidly siding with business and conservative interests on the court in crucial voting rights and campaign finance cases that began to transform the relationships between wealth, speech, the ballot box, and equitable representation for all.

Meanwhile his memo would reverberate even louder and longer, as it also proved wildly influential with conservative donors and foundations. As law professor Caroline Fredrickson argues in her book *The Democracy Fix*, the Powell Memo helped shape the crucial coordination among donors, a nascent conservative legal movement, and political strategists to erect a permanent right-wing counterestablishment. The vast well-funded infrastructure that Powell sketched out in his memo—encompassing the universities, the press, the courts, and the policy world—shapes our politics unto this day. It has nurtured and propagated the war on the ballot, seeded the bench with judges opposed to voting rights, and imagined the constitutional theories on which these cramped rulings would rely.

As Fredrickson writes, Powell's call to arms pioneered "think tanks to develop proposals, media outlets to disseminate them, legislative strategies to equip their side with bills and talking points, electoral schemes to secure political advantage, and legal efforts to stack the courts with ideological judges armed with pro-corporate and anti–civil rights views."

The Powell Memo proved to be such a galvanizing force not because Powell was the first person to identify the threat—business leaders had been preaching against the rampaging socialist menace since the founding of the Liberty League at the start of the New Deal. No, Powell's message resonated precisely because it tapped into a resurgence of resentment politics on the business Right. All the movement needed was a game plan to identify the theaters of conflict and instill movement discipline.

Some conservative thinkers have sought to downplay Powell's influence, or suggest that the institution-building he called for was already underway. What's undeniable is that it catalyzed the early funders and visionaries of the modern Right, reinforced their thinking, and assured them that this was what must be done. It was neither a checklist nor a how-to manual, neither a conspiracy theory nor a top-secret plan. It inspired wealthy funders who would underwrite the institutions those thinkers dreamed of building to thrust conservative politics into the marketplace of ideas. (While originally a confidential memo, and not part of the records or writings provided by Powell to Congress during his confirmation hearings, the memo was leaked to muckraking columnist Jack Anderson in late 1972—which only served to amplify its audience.)

Those conservative activists, in turn, built the infrastructure of a movement that still exists today. Its influence can be seen everywhere from the Federalist Society to Fox News, during commercials on the Sunday public affairs shows and in ads on the op-ed page of the *New York Times*. You can find its institutional footprint everywhere as well: at the exclusive, business-funded economics conferences, elite law-and-politics gatherings rolled out like time-shares to judges and legal scholars, movement conservative confabs sponsored by the Conservative Political Action Conference and Turning Point USA. You can trace its burgeoning policy agenda five decades on in think tanks like the Heritage Foundation and organizations like the American Legislative Exchange Council, which produces model bills for state legislators. And of course you can see it in the prestigious and highly paid fellowships funded by conservative foundations for young conservative scholars that serve as one among several semiofficial pathways to today's U.S. Supreme Court.

This legacy isn't surprising when you consider the memo's initial cohort of recruits. The Powell Memo's earliest admirers read like a who's who of the architects of the modern conservative movement. In April 1974, a young midwestern industrialist addressed a meeting titled "The Anti-Capitalist Mentality" at the Institute for Humane Studies in Dallas.

Charles Koch cited the Powell Memo six different times and echoed many of its calls. Koch's speech nearly mimics the Powell manifesto word for word on several occasions. "We should cease financing our own destruction," Koch said, as he questioned contributions to universities that "encourage extreme hostility to American business." He also said, "The inept attempts of business to appease or hide from its popular critics contrast sharply with the effective offensive of its opponents."

The Colorado beer magnate Joseph Coors was convinced by the Powell Memo that American business was "ignoring a crisis" and "stirred" into action. In 1973 Coors invested the first $250,000 into a new think tank that would become the Heritage Foundation. John Olin, a midwestern heir to a chemical fortune, decided to bankroll the cause of free enterprise. He endowed an eponymous foundation that would eventually disburse hundreds of millions of dollars to support a conservative intelligentsia to counter the alleged liberal bias of American universities and the news media. In a letter to William Baroody Sr. of the American Enterprise Institute, Olin wrote that "the Powell Memorandum gives a reason for a well-organized effort to re-establish the vitality and importance of the American free enterprise system." Baroody decided to establish a new Center for the Study of Government Regulation and, just as Powell and Koch suggested, hired a bright young conservative to edit a journal. His name? Antonin Scalia.

In 1972, just months after the Chamber of Commerce distributed Powell's report to executives nationwide, two hundred CEOs of major companies formed the Business Roundtable to consolidate their political influence in Washington. As the political scientists Paul Pierson and Jacob Hacker, among others, have noted, the number of businesses with public affairs offices in the capital leapt from 100 in 1968 to more than 500 by 1978. The number of firms with lobbyists metastasized from 175 in 1971 to some 2,500 by 1982. The Chamber launched a national litigation center that helped confirm multiple Supreme Court justices. Other funders picked up on Powell's call for a nationwide network of conservative public interest law firms to counter the work of the ACLU and liberal public interest firms working on behalf of consumers, labor, and civil rights. A study by the California branch of the Chamber resulted in the 1973 creation of the Pacific Legal Foundation—a pillar of the conservative legal establishment to this day whose board members were prominent voices fifty years later in the Stop the Steal movement. Its founders cited the Powell Memo widely to sell PLF's vision to funders.

Robert Bork and Antonin Scalia, meanwhile, would become philosopher heroes for successive generations of young conservative law students. They would be the very first law professors that the nascent Federalist Society would reach out to as it looked to build a beachhead for originalism in the nation's law schools. Bork and Scalia both knew from experience how vital this new project would be for otherwise isolated and ostracized conservative law scholars in the making. The Federalist Society's launch would in turn be funded almost entirely by a robust corps of right-of-center foundations who acquired a new sense of mission under the influence of the Powell Memo. (Bork must have admired the memo as well; in a meeting with the American Enterprise Institute's trustees, Phillips-Fein notes that he said, "Business leaders will have to decide whether they are really willing to let the corporate system slide and perhaps expire without putting up a determined fight.")

Indeed, you can see all the major players in our current era of right-wing backlash and retrenchment conjured into virtual being by Powell's call to arms, as though it were a spell book from Hogwarts. The roll call is wide-ranging, and ever-growing: The Heritage Foundation. The American Legislative Exchange Council. The Federalist Society. Breitbart News. The Honest Elections Project. The Pacific Legal Foundation.

These organizations and scores of others like them midwifed and chronicled the test cases that would lead to *Citizens United, Shelby County,* and the demise of affirmative action in college admissions. They disbursed countless grants and fellowships that would invest tens of thousands in young scholars like Amy Coney Barrett—and later, they unleashed tens of millions in dark money to support her elevation to the U.S. Supreme Court. Some of them even supported Donald Trump's efforts to undo the results of the 2020 presidential election. It all begins here, with the stout military-minded action plan of a future U.S. Supreme Court justice who envisioned how America's government and elections could be dominated by wealthy white elites, even as unrepentant southern segregationists like himself dwindled into history.

CHAPTER TWO

ONCE ON THE bench, Justice Powell went about turning his memo into legal precedent, launching corporate America headlong into the battle to win back the nation—not through elections but through the courts.

A series of campaign finance decisions in the mid-1970s, including *Buckley v. Valeo* and *First National Bank v. Bellotti*, furnished a crucial first step in the fight by unshackling the monetary might of the wealthiest Americans and their corporate retainers. *Buckley* declared limits on campaign expenditures unconstitutional and *Bellotti* granted corporations First Amendment rights to free speech. Most crucially in *Bellotti*, Powell's opinion reworked the Supreme Court's precedents on campaign finance and the First Amendment by finding that corporate spending on ballot initiatives should have the same guarantees as individual speech.

Together, those cases built the legal foundation for the Roberts Court to dismantle the remaining restraints in its landmark 2010 ruling *Citizens United*. The Roberts Court ruling in *Citizens United* would quote from and cite *Bellotti* dozens of times. "We thus find no support in the First Amendment, or in the decisions of this Court, for the proposition that speech that would otherwise be within the protection of the First Amendment loses that protection simply because its source is a corporation," Powell wrote, and Justice Anthony Kennedy cited at length. That proposition, Powell and Kennedy asserted, "amounts to an impermissible legislative prohibition of speech based on the identity of the interests."

But despite having friendlier voices on the court and a handful of decisions that tipped their way, change came slower than the biggest names in right-wing philanthropy—Olin, Koch, Scaife, and Coors—desired, even as those scions poured tens of millions into a regional group of conser-

vative public-interest law firms that they hoped might counter the influence of the Nader network. Those monied donors soon came to see that
institution-building is a long, hard slog, and even a couple of judges on the
high court and some like-minded law firms would not be nearly enough to
change the power dynamic in America.

It took Michael J. Horowitz, a onetime liberal Democrat and Yale Law
graduate—who remembers shedding tears with classmate and future senator and presidential candidate Gary Hart the morning President John F.
Kennedy was assassinated—to place conservatives on a different and more
successful path. ("I may have been [teary]," Hart told me in an email, "but
not in Michael's presence.") The Horowitz Report of 1980, commissioned
by the Scaife Foundation in late 1979, delivered a damning message: The
entire right-wing offensive on the court system needed to be rethought.
The Right's legal brainpower was "appallingly mediocre," Horowitz warned.
What's more, he argued, conservatives needed to win hearts and minds and
engage in a battle of ideas. They needed to reach the members of the next
generation where their journey began, in law school.

For more than fifty years, liberals have viewed the Powell Memo as the
Right's road map to power, proof of a vast right-wing conspiracy, evidence
that the other side schemed and planned while their own complacently
snoozed. But it's the almost unknown Horowitz Report that may have been
more quietly influential. Where Powell's report laid out a master plan to
power, Horowitz showed how the conservative movement must first reca-
librate its goals from raw power to real ideas, and shift the battleground
from courtrooms to campuses. Yet its influence and Horowitz himself remain today almost entirely invisible, save an account in a 1980's law review
article by Oliver Houck, a 1993 report by the Alliance for Justice; and two
magnificent books from 2008, Ann Southworth's *Lawyers of the Right* and
Steven Teles's *The Rise of the Conservative Legal Movement*, which first
told the story of the Right's mobilization. Virtually none of it has appeared
in print.

"Young men and women are tired, as is everybody, of the old answers,"
Horowitz wrote, in a brief that quickly moved beyond its funders at Scaife
and captured the attention of donors throughout the Right. "Yet, nobody
has sufficiently offered young lawyers the sense that one can be caring,

moral, intellectual, appropriately ideological, while at the same time being radically opposed to the stale views of the left."

If Lewis Powell's message was that the American Right needed to engage in full-throated warfare on college campuses and in the news media, while using the courts as a shortcut around American elections, Horowitz argued there was little point to contesting the courts until a new generation of lawyers and thinkers could be cultivated, trained, and hired. "What is at stake . . . is not so much a battle over cases won and lost as of ideas and ideologies," Horowitz wrote. The "critical focus" must be "the law schools and bar associations." Too many on the Right, Horowitz suggested, had "little feel for the longer range potential of the movement on the legal process and as an instrument to capture youthful loyalties and to redefine what is moral in law." His report would echo throughout Washington, instruct the hiring practices of the new Reagan administration (especially at the Department of Justice), and ripple across growing conservative circles within American law schools. It would pave the way to incubate right-wing ideas on college campuses and then serve as the gateway through which conservative bona fides would be checked for GOP administrations and appointments to state and federal courts.

Perhaps most critically, the conclusions Horowitz drew would lead him to help a handful of young law students launch the Federalist Society. "Targets of opportunity abound" for the conservative movement, he wrote, "if such young attorneys can be recruited and, with popular training and leadership, can be given the chance to make their marks."

Horowitz's influence and credibility with the Right's biggest funders grabbed the attention of grant makers and unlocked the vaults. Today's Federalist Society firebrands who have reshaped American democracy through the courts, and both masterminded and green-lit the dramatic transfer of power away from the people and toward gerrymandered legislatures and rabidly ideological judges, could rightly be called the sons and daughters of Michael J. Horowitz.

According to John Miller, the biographer of the wealthy conservative donor John Olin, Horowitz "produced a devastating critique that influenced conservative grantmaking for years." Its impact, Miller writes, "was felt almost immediately." Scaife immediately shared the report with Olin and all the conservative network's philanthropic allies. This is the moment that paved the way for future Federalist Society leader Leonard Leo and conservative supermajorities to come.

The blueprint of an ascendant conservative legal movement would be designed by a young Jewish intellectual from the Bronx who had come to believe that his erstwhile allies on the left had lost their way. An early warrior for integration crafted a memo that would not only help undermine the civil rights era's most hard-fought victories, but also train and empower the lawyers and judges who would push the nation toward antidemocratic minority rule.

JERRY SEINFELD ONCE joked that when Americans root for a sports team, we're rooting less for individual players—who often change sides—than we are cheering for laundry. A similar dynamic dictates the rigid sorting of the country's political sympathies into Team Red or Team Blue. Maybe some of us have made considered, morally principled choices before choosing sides. Yet more often than not, political affiliation is a tribal proposition, grounded in an accident of birth, the vagaries of identity, the club that will or will not have us as a member, or a battery of diffuse cultural and psychosocial resentments (the "organization of hatreds," in Henry Adams's pithy definition of modern politics).

Much of Michael J. Horowitz's rightward odyssey also feels personal and cultural, producing political consequences as something of a side effect. Horowitz was born in New York in 1940 and grew up in the West Bronx, uptown from the Lower East Side sweatshops and streets where his grandfather found work as a tailor after arriving in New York at age twelve. Most of his family relations who stayed behind in Europe died during the war, but America, blessed America, vanquished Hitler.

Horowitz's upbringing was equal parts Jewish and American: Yeshiva, City College, college summers working on the railroad in Alaska, basic training in the Marine Corps, and finally Yale Law School. As a teenager, Horowitz tried to convince neighbors why the whites-only middle-class housing project in Parkchester needed to integrate, according to a 1990s feature in *New York* magazine. His hero was Eleanor Roosevelt. The famed

liberal organizer Allard Lowenstein introduced him to politics. When the
gates of the Ivy League swung open, Horowitz was admitted to that world
without really being of it. Its aura of luxury and privilege, coupled with
the reflexive contempt his classmates displayed for ordinary working-class
Americans, grated and gnawed. But he was still surrounded and swaddled
in liberalism; at Yale Law, his classmates included Hart, Eleanor Holmes
Norton, Marian Wright Edelman, Robert Rubin, and Jerry Brown. Horowitz learned to nod and fit in like anyone who'd spent his life trying to as-
similate.

"This is a remarkable class, but these are my friends," Horowitz tells
me. He's now in his mideighties, and newly divorced. As we spend an
afternoon together in Connecticut, he occasionally pauses our conversation to check his messages on Jdate. His vote for Trump in 2016 has
made it frustratingly hard for Horowitz to move from messages to actual dates. He's stared down that peer pressure for decades. "I come from
that world. I know that world. They just . . . they don't really know. They
never represented the fire officers' union in New York City. My values were
middle-class values. I was rooted in that world and saw its virtues in a way
my Ivy League classmates never could."

After graduation, Horowitz spent a dull year on Wall Street, trying to
make some money like other Yalies. But he soon grew restless, entranced
by the breakthroughs won in the civil rights movement. So he became a
law professor at the University of Mississippi. He taught some of the first
integrated classes at Ole Miss, forcing students to sit alphabetically so
whites could not ostracize their Black classmates. Horowitz actively recruited Black students from across the state to enroll at the law school. He
proved so successful that when the man later convicted of murdering Medgar Evers, Byron De La Beckwith, ran for lieutenant governor, his platform
included firing "that Jew professor."

This cultural estrangement continued when Horowitz returned to New
York and started his own one-person law firm specializing in labor law for
the city's firefighters. The increasingly brittle and bitter character of the
New Left's professionalized caste of reformers made him feel increasingly
distant from his old friends and fellow Democrats. Meanwhile, repre-

senting New York firefighters and police officers and other city employees often meant battling over affirmative action. Horowitz would meet with lawyers, judges, and New York City officials and know he was supposed to nod along, but the city's programs felt like quota systems to him. These racialized rankings of aspiring workers were imposed by wealthy Ivy League do-gooders with precious little actual benefit for minorities, he felt; if anything, Horowitz felt that the logic of affirmative action set-asides punished middle-class strivers. People like him.

Horowitz made a hard pivot. He had never felt accepted or understood by the Left, not in college, not on Wall Street, not as a young lawyer. And so, not for the first time in this story of the triumph of antidemocratic forces within American political life, personal pique and class resentment would push someone toward the right with a lifelong grudge and a determination to even the score, no matter the consequences for what they proclaimed to believe.

"At first, my disquiet at the literal madness I saw—all in the name of liberal politics and helping the poor—remained muted," he wrote in his 1979 conversion article "Why I Am a Republican." It begins: "I am Jewish, was student body president at City College, taught civil rights law in Mississippi during the sixties, now grieve at the loss of Al Lowenstein, the remarkable friend who most taught me to care about the political process. The best man at my wedding was a Democratic Congressman with a 100 percent ADA rating." But the Right captured his heart and mind, and now Horowitz wanted to nurture the moral and intellectual vision that would help future conservatives stand for a vision rather than against the Left's vision of racial progress. "As matters were posed, I had the 'choice' of being for or against blacks and the poor—even though I knew that the programs mounted on their ostensible behalf were inefficient, corrupting, often downright corrupt."

There was, Horowitz told me, "a cultural battle, a battle for moral supremacy, and a need to end this moral monopoly." The people placed on the "bad side of that moral ledger," he says, were "not able to fight, or did not know how to fight."

Michael J. Horowitz knew how to fight, especially with a chip on his shoulder. And so a scrappy Bronx striver would switch sides and teach the Right.

RICHARD MELLON SCAIFE, whose foundation funded Horowitz's report, shared Horowitz's commitment to winning a long-term battle of ideas. But that was where any resemblance between the two men ended. As Jane Mayer describes in her peerless *Dark Money,* the best telling of the mobilization of the conservative über-rich, Scaife inherited a fortune built through banking (his grandfather founded Pittsburgh's Mellon Bank) and early investments in Gulf Oil and Alcoa. Family connections won him admission to Yale, but Scaife spent most of his time in New Haven suspended for drunken behavior. He never made it past freshman year.

To avoid income and estate taxes, the Scaife family set up an elaborate network of foundations and trusts. Richard's mother, Sarah, pulled him into the family's new business of giving away their money to favored causes after his father's sudden death in 1958. When his mom passed seven years later, Richard suddenly had a free hand to make those causes his own. While Sarah favored charities that worked to end disease, Richard, fired up by anticommunism, prone to conspiracy theories, and pushed to the right during the Goldwater campaign, preferred to eradicate liberalism.

Goldwater's crushing defeat in 1964 taught conservatives that they needed to match what they considered the institutional firepower of the establishment and the Left. Scaife eagerly bankrolled the project. The Scaife Foundation became a billion-dollar lobbying arm disguised as a charity. "The result was very considerable grant making power," Scaife told an interviewer, to "advance ideas that I believe are good for America."

Scaife's unpublished memoir, unearthed by Mayer, revealed that as far back as 1964, Scaife, Lewis Powell, and other wealthy white elites who viewed liberalism as a menace threatening the nation met regularly as part of an organization called the League to Save Carthage. The group was named in a mood of acute cultural belligerence, for the ancient North African city that fell to ruin when a passive ruling class failed to recognize the threat to the thriving commercial hub it had created. When Powell penned his memo, Scaife stepped forward to fund the new institutions.

"The first idea was to copy what works," a Scaife colleague told the *Washington Post* in 1999. "We saw what the Democrats were doing and decided to do the mirror image, but do it better. In those days you had the American Civil Liberties Union, the government-supported legal corporations [neighborhood legal services programs], a strong Democratic Party with strong labor support, the Brookings Institution, the *New York Times* and *Washington Post* and all these other people on the left—and nobody on the right."

In his memoir, Scaife estimated that he bankrolled the Right to the tune of at least $1 billion. While he may have been the leading donor for the modern Right, he was hardly the only conservative heir eager to funnel inherited family wealth into right-wing politics via tax-deductible foundations and grants. The Smith Richardson Foundation, built off the Vicks cough and cold fortune, helped pave the way. Scaife and Colorado beer progeny Joseph Coors soon followed, as did the Olin family (manufacturers of chemicals, blasting powders, ammunition, and weapons) and the Bradley Foundation (which soared in prominence and capitalization after defense conglomerate Rockwell purchased a family-held Milwaukee electronics company).

David Brock, the onetime conservative activist who pursued Bill Clinton in the 1990s with Scaife's support, wrote in his memoir *Blinded by the Right* that he "saw how right-wing ideology was manufactured and controlled by a small group of powerful foundations," naming Scaife as first among equals with Coors, Bradley, Olin, and Smith Richardson. Scaife, in Brock's estimation, was "the most important single figure in building the modern conservative movement and spreading its ideas into the political realm."

"These guys individually and collectively created a new philanthropic form which was movement philanthropy," the late Rob Stein, a former Democratic Party official and progressive activist, told Mayer. Stein caught on to the importance of "the conservative message machine's money matrix" after the 2000 elections and built the left-leaning Democracy Alliance to help his side catch up to what he saw as the GOP's strategic and institutional advantages. "What they started is the most potent machine ever assembled in a democracy to promote a set of beliefs and to control the reins of government."

Coors, "stirred" by the Powell Memo into greater action of his own, inherited wealth and extreme politics from his father. He launched the conservative think tank the Heritage Foundation with $550,000 in gifts in the early 1970s. Scaife then became its largest donor; by 1998 he'd stuffed its coffers with $23 million. Charles Koch launched the Libertarian-leaning Cato Institute in 1977 with upward of $10 million, and perhaps as much as $20 million, over its first three years. Scaife, along with the conservative activist Paul Weyrich, also began the American Legislative Exchange Council in 1973, providing the bulk of its budget over the next ten years.

Much of this media delivered immediate, as well as long-term, rewards when it came to incubating conservative thinkers. The conservative foundations knew power when they saw it, so they set out to mimic the Left's model of ambitious reform won through the courts. Scaife, Olin, Bradley, the Alcoa Foundation, and Exxon/Mobil built the National Legal Center for the Public Interest. That was the first blow in the creation of a right-wing legal counterestablishment; soon afterward, Scaife, Olin, Coors, Bradley, Koch, and the Scaife-inspired Carthage Foundation poured millions into a regional network of conservative public interest law firms. Here, they fell short. This was the failure that Horowitz seized upon.

Too many of the regional legal foundations were producing streams of amicus briefs but few tangible victories. They struggled to hire and inspire the same bright young lawyers attracted to the left; few idealists freshly matriculated from high-profile law schools wanted to work on what seemed like the wrong side of environmental and regulatory issues. Defending DDT and padding the bottom line for big business failed to fire many imaginations.

"No, that didn't work," says Michael Greve, who began his career as a program officer at the Smith Richardson Foundation before founding the free-market litigation boutique Center for Individual Rights and later was a professor at the Scalia Law School at George Mason University. "And it was sort of a misunderstanding to my mind. The idea was, 'If Ralph Nader can do this, we can do it too.' Think again. That just shows you have no idea how American politics works, or for that matter, litigation."

The conservative foundations dumped tens of millions in a failed effort to create a conservative public interest movement. They tried to copy the

Left without studying it. If they had, they would have quickly realized that you can't build a grassroots effort from the top down. Money matters, but an idealistic, intellectual buzz is something else entirely. That's where Michael J. Horowitz's insights proved pivotal.

AS THE 1970S pushed to a close, Gary Hart had chaired George McGovern's presidential campaign and been elected to the U.S. Senate from Colorado. Jerry Brown succeeded Ronald Reagan as the governor of California. Marian Wright Edelman helped organize the Southern Christian Leadership Conference and founded the Children's Defense Fund. Robert Rubin was on his way to leading Goldman Sachs. But Horowitz believed his most powerful and influential classmate was not a murmured presidential candidate or a future Treasury secretary but rather Charles Halpern.

Halpern, the founder of the Center for Law and Social Policy, one of Washington's first public interest law firms, wasn't a household name. Still, he made headlines and altered public policy. Halpern leveraged the social and political agenda of '60s activists into a potent legal and regulatory playbook, scoring key victories for the burgeoning field of public interest law. In March 1970, the fledgling CLASP operation, which was then just a handful of lawyers working from a cramped, run-down Dupont Circle office, halted construction on the Trans-Alaska Pipeline, defeating the far richer and more influential interests of Big Oil. Two years later, as counsel for the Environmental Defense Fund, Halpern won the case that banned DDT. By 1975 he'd created the Council for the Advancement of Public Interest Law, soon renamed the Alliance for Justice, an umbrella for a coalition of some 120 progressive groups fighting for civil rights, the environment, reproductive rights, child welfare, and other legal breakthroughs.

Halpern celebrated the tenth anniversary of what had become the liberal public interest law movement with a spring 1979 conference at Yale Law. Horowitz, still a sole practitioner in New York, decided to attend. What he heard both horrified and inspired him. "It was this grand fellowship of God's chosen," he says now. Horowitz believed that the chummy gathering confirmed all his hard-won insights about the hypocrisies of the Left and the rampant collusion among activists, government agencies, and the courts. At the same time, he realized his side had to fight the same way—in Washington, from a moral high ground, based on a theory of justice that attracted people to the cause. Without that critical infusion of genuine faith in what the Left called the long march through the institutions, the Right would continue to lose ground even if they won elections.

"All these appointees of the Carter administration were there. Some of them were general counsels of agencies. Others were public interest litigators. They would joke about cutting corners, because after all, it was for the public good that they were in business," he says. "These general counsels would get up and say in front of everyone, 'My door is always open to the Environmental Defense Fund. We plot and we scheme.'" Horowitz suddenly saw a key way that the Left advanced its policy desires: Activists made demands on agencies, threatened lawsuits under new rules and regulations, while friendly agencies provided what support they could. At the end of the process, sympathetic judges awarded ever greater and higher-profile victories. Horowitz "thought that was a wonderful model—and not at all what conservatives had even considered."

"I can't remember how he got in there, but it's not surprising to me," Charles Halpern says now. "He liked to see himself as one of us in a certain sense, fighting for the public interest and civil rights. I think he recognized that we were having some major accomplishments and he wanted to learn what he could from us. I'm sure it was an open public event. We were not operating in the dark. We didn't feel we had a great secret."

That's not how it seemed to Horowitz. To him, it looked as if the Left had unlocked a secret inside game that it could not lose. They were proud of it! In his report, Horowitz quotes from the keynote speech delivered by Harvard Law professor Abram Chayes, who also served in the John Kennedy administration. "I think all of us know that there is an ideological element in public interest law and thank goodness there is," Chayes said, as reported by Horowitz. "This is not a neutral enterprise. We are for social change. We are for social change in a particular direction." They'd built themselves an iron triangle: government agencies, the courts, and outside "public interest" organizations. All three sides hired from the same pool of do-gooders, then promoted like-minded allies from one group to another. The courts, the litigants, the government officials—they were all teammates. Horowitz watched them all admit it, with growing incredulousness but also jealousy. "A movement comprised of small numbers of people can influence national policy when policy is essentially fixed at one place and by a small group of decision makers against whom pressure can be applied," Horowitz wrote, and one can imagine Leonard Leo nodding along. "One example of the traditional movement's concern with matters beyond litigations," Horowitz continued, "is the recent success which it has achieved in the area of judicial appointments."

This was what had to be replicated on the other side. His ticket to acceptance with his new team would be to bring them this powerful idea. It would fuel the Right's gameplay on voting rights and elections for decades to come, as they built their own triangle within the Federalist Society, the courts, and conservative litigants and foundations.

When Horowitz got back to New York, he called Richard Larry, the executive director of the Scaife Foundation. The two had never spoken before; Larry told Horowitz that no one had ever just picked up the phone and pitched him on a grant. But as Horowitz kept talking, Larry realized he was onto something big. "In general, there was a sense that the foundations had not gotten their money's worth," Michael Greve says. "There had for a long time been a lot of dissatisfaction." Horowitz's cold call paid off: Scaife wrote the check. "It didn't make me rich, but it gave me the ability to devote all my time to it. And I got into it," Horowitz says.

"Here was Charlie, placing the Supreme Court law clerks, hiring the best and brightest young people, who felt morally fulfilled and charged to do the right thing—and they were kicking the pants off the system! Charlie Halpern and Ralph Nader, just look at what they were doing!

"It was such a learning experience just sitting there. Then I saw what the conservatives were doing. They were effectively just writing amicus briefs, having no effect, focusing on litigation rather than regulations. They didn't affect what was happening in Washington at all. It was a waste of money. It was a waste of time."

HOROWITZ'S KEY MESSAGE to the Right was that they'd built the wrong infrastructure. Mountains of cash produced an avalanche of business-friendly amicus briefs; program officers could weigh them to justify the work in reports to the movement's donor base, but these were largely exercises in paper-pushing. They certainly didn't add up to any kind of movement to alter the law. If anything, the public interest push to generate right-wing legal reform turned off potential recruits and allies. "All too often, conservative public interest law firms serve as mere conduits by which monies contributed by businesses and foundations are given to private law firms to assist it in the prosecution of its cases," Horowitz wrote. "No practice presently engaged in by conservative public interest law firms is more inappropriate."

What Horowitz saw as the conservatives' surrender of the center of legal and regulatory power could be fixed by redressing its woeful strategic disadvantages on campus and in the broader battle of ideas. Here, too, "Charlie was doing it right," Horowitz told me. "We weren't looking to win hearts, minds, and souls." Halpern and Nader placed their efforts "on a higher moral plane than those of its adversaries and has thus engaged the loyalties of young attorneys" as well as the news media, he wrote. Conservatives weren't bothering to compete in this arena at all. As a result, "The conservative public interest law movement will at best achieve episodic tactical victories, which will be dwarfed by social change in the infinite number of areas beyond its case agendas."

Horowitz suggested building from the bottom up, beginning with the nation's law schools. Halpern and Nader nabbed bright, idealistic law students and trained them to follow their sense of justice and morality toward Democrats and the Left. Universities were often the forcing bed for the great network of interlocking directorates that made up modern regulatory law. The pipeline between elite law schools and coveted clerkships and jobs flowed leftward. The New Right's intellectual energy counted for virtually nothing in such crucial career-shaping networking and job-placement efforts. The movement has "had essentially no impact on the still-prevailing notions of law students and young attorneys," Horowitz bemoans, because its leaders "have neither the background nor capacity to attract and train first-rate young lawyers, or to build permanent relationships with law schools and bar associations." Horowitz dismissed the brainpower of staff attorneys and conservative lawyers at these firms as "appallingly mediocre."

If conservatives wanted to win converts, they needed to nurture their own intellectuals, their own incentive structure, and their own networks. They needed to appeal to idealism, Horowitz exhorted. "The very decline in power of the American business community over the last decade, and the corresponding growth of a government-growth oriented anti-business, traditional public interest movement is perhaps the best evidence that the skills in the business community are not well correlated with the skills involved in generating idealism and enlisting the intellectual loyalties of bright young men and women," he wrote. Only such a forceful rebranding of the Right's legal and intellectual agenda, and the "fellowship of like-minded people, with whom to share ideas, debate principles and from and with whom real teaching and learning can take place," Horowitz wrote, "would . . . be useful for attracting idealistic young lawyers."

As Horowitz wrote his report, several of those young soon-to-be law students moved into a group home just outside Washington and intern-ships on Capitol Hill and elsewhere. The Horowitz Report would be cru-cial in helping them found—and fund—something those students would soon name the Federalist Society.

"That's exactly right," says Judge J. Michael Luttig, who often lunched with Horowitz and Michael McConnell, a Federalist Society superstar scholar who would become a federal judge on the U.S. Court of Appeals for the Tenth Circuit and director of the Constitutional Law Center at Stan-ford Law School, during their days in the Reagan administration. "Michael had the intellectual vision surrounding all the various pieces of a conser-vative legal movement that was about to take off."

TO FULLY GRASP the Horowitz Report's thunderclap effect on conservative funders and the broader movement, consider this: When Horowitz filed his conclusions to the Scaife Foundation, he was a little-known solo prac-titioner in New York. Little more than a year later, when Reagan took office in January 1981, Horowitz had a prime White House perch as one of those general counsels himself—not just at any agency, but the most powerful and wide-ranging position of them all, the Office of Management and Budget. In his new D.C. role, Horowitz sat at the intersection of everything: OMB not only produced the federal budget, but patrolled the agencies, ensuring that every department's policies hewed tightly to the president's agenda.

The report "certainly helped everything," says Greve. "Foundation officers needed somebody else—a voice of respectability—to say it's not just us thinking this, we're not crazy."

"Before Mike's report, a few people had that view but they didn't have the vehicles to push their ideas," says Ed Meese. "The Horowitz Report—and very soon after that the Federalist Society—provided that opportunity."

Federalist Society cofounder Lee Liberman Otis remembers that Horowitz "found us" almost immediately after the Society started in 1982.

"I called up funders early in the game and said, give money to the Federalist Society," Horowitz told me. "I did that. That's absolutely right. Absolutely."

Horowitz all but demanded the Right's leading foundations act. "Scaife Foundation is to be commended for its active support of the movement, although that support must clearly be increased," he wrote, "if, as is surely the case, the directors of Scaife are interested in effecting fundamental change." Other foundations, he wrote, naming Olin, Smith Richardson, and Lily, "have a striking, present responsibility and opportunity to substantially increase and in some cases initiate support for the conservative public interest law movement, under circumstances where dollars invested . . . can yield remarkably high dividends."

Part general counsel and part movement talent scout, Horowitz identified the young students clerking for Robert Bork and other conservative judges and invited them over to OMB for lunch, to plot out their careers and offer assistance. "It was just a handful of us, and handful of funders," Horowitz told me. "They understood that by funding a few students, a few writers, a few chairs, that they could make a huge difference." By 1992, Bork sounded the same message in a fundraising letter for the Society, arguing that FedSoc was the bulwark against liberal judges. "Restoring the primacy of the Constitution must begin with the education of law students and lawyers, an ongoing task that cannot be completed overnight. Each year it requires exposing thousands of new law students to these ideas while they are forming their views about the courts and the legal profession."

Horowitz shared Yale ties with the Federalist Society's founders, and as the group launched, Horowitz promptly contacted them with ideas and connections he wanted to share, both inside the new administration and with foundations. "He made the introductions and put us in touch with the foundation people," Liberman Otis told me. Many of them, she said, "seemed to have adopted and internalized his views. He knew everybody. He understood the power of friendships. One really big insight he had is that the ideas come first."

Greve awarded the Federalist Society a Smith Richardson grant that, he told me, "I know was one of the very, very first meaningful grants that the Federalist Society received." James Piereson, of the Olin Foundation and later the vice chairman of the conservative consortium DonorsTrust, remembers Liberman Otis and the other founders coming to visit in 1982. He'd read the Horowitz Report and knew the law schools and had fully absorbed its central message, that the federal courts were the prime testing ground for a resurgent right-wing intellectual and legal movement.

"As conservatives, we had really nothing else going in the judicial world," he says. "We didn't have a voice in the law schools, and we didn't have much of a judicial philosophy with which to oppose the liberal outlook. We were aware, more or less, that the federal courts controlled public policy in the United States, in the sense that no one could do anything of any importance in the United States without sign-off by the federal courts. So we were aware that they were extremely important and that this is an area where we ought to work. And so we had few other opportunities." Olin wrote a sizable check.

In turn, "without Olin," says Federalist Society executive director Gene Meyer, "we might not be here."

The Federalist Society, says Horowitz, "became the model we countered Charlie [Halpern]'s public interest groups with" and how we "tried to shatter the caricature of who we are."

One connection at a time, and one clerkship at a time, conservatives forged a foothold in Washington and in law schools. It didn't take long for a new generation to arrive.

CHAPTER THREE

TO MANY PEOPLE, the Voting Rights Act flourished, largely unharmed, for decades until John Roberts took an axe to it in 2013. This version of history elides a much more complicated reality: the right wing was trying to undo its impact from day one.

The sustained legal assault began mere days after Lyndon Johnson signed it into law in August 1965. By late September, the state of South Carolina filed a complaint directly to the U.S. Supreme Court. The state asserted that the VRA unfairly singled out the "sovereign state" of South Carolina, created an unequal system of voting between the states, and punished South Carolina for racial misdeeds when, the state argued, a tiny county in Idaho and a sparsely settled county in the northernmost corner of Maine had also used a literacy test. Chief Justice Warren, in an 8–1 decision in March 1966, quickly affirmed its constitutionality.

"Congress had found that case-by-case litigation was inadequate to combat wide-spread and persistent discrimination in voting, because of the inordinate amount of time and energy required to overcome the obstructionist tactics invariably encountered in these lawsuits," Warren wrote, in a full-throated judicial endorsement of the necessity for Congress to use its constitutional powers in the face of willful southern roadblocks. "After enduring nearly a century of systematic resistance to the Fifteenth Amendment, Congress might well decide to shift the advantage of time and inertia from the perpetrators of the evil to its victims."

Yet even this decisive decision would not end the lawlessness and obstinance of southern whites. Southern legislatures continued to blithely ignore the Voting Rights Act and the U.S. Supreme Court. In Mississippi, for example, almost immediately after the court issued its ruling, the state legislature delivered its backlash: an overhaul of state election law with hundreds of minor changes all designed to reduce the power of newly enfranchised Black voters. One of them would have allowed counties to elect boards of supervisors at-large—ensuring the white majority would select every member—rather than from districts. Legislators refused to submit the new laws for preclearance, insisting they did not need to because the state's attorney general, a white man, knew of the changes and raised no objection.

In 1969's *Allen v. State Board of Elections*, the court rolled up four cases of seemingly deliberate defiance across two southern states, and Warren restated that preclearance applied to any change, period. The VRA, he wrote, "was aimed at the subtle, as well as the obvious, state regulations which have the effect of denying citizens their right to vote because of race." Moreover, the chief justice reasserted that the "legislative history lends support to the view that Congress intended to reach any enactment which altered the election law of a covered State in even a minor way."

These were not the first challenges to the VRA and they would not be the last. Southern resistance continued unabated and ultimately outlasted Warren and his allies on the court. By then, the Powell and Horowitz projects to remake the judiciary gave new oxygen and allies to these antidemocratic arguments that had previously lost at the high court. That long-term success, however, followed a carefully crafted antidemocratic playbook. John Roberts's 2013 ruling that the VRA singled out sovereign Alabama required Powell's plan to win the court, Bork's intellectual vision, Horowitz's appeal to hearts and minds of the next generation of lawyers and judges—and all the funders and activists that those conservative visionaries inspired.

From his seat on the U.S. Supreme Court, Lewis Powell would urge on these forces—including those looking to take down the still nascent VRA. It was a strategy rooted not in memos and position papers, but also in good old-fashioned racism. This challenge did not emerge organically, but grew from more than a decade of racist strategies designed to counter the gains of the civil rights movement. And it is here that the GOP project to weaponize the courts to control American elections collides with voting rights.

With Powell flexing his muscle on the court, a little-known but crucial

U.S. Supreme Court case, 1979's *City of Mobile v. Bolden* (decided in 1980), would signal the beginning of the court's retrenchment on voting rights, and the ascendance of new theories about race neutrality and a color-blind Constitution that, twinned with originalism, would blossom into the faux-legal concepts that conservative activists and academics would use decades later to undo the Voting Rights Act in the *Shelby County* case as well as affirmative action. This notion—historical fiction in a nation where race has never been neutral—was incubated in the activist conservative foundations Powell's memo had urged into the vanguard of the conservative movement.

What's so shocking—and important—about the *Mobile* case is how close the conservative legal movement came to unraveling the effectiveness of the Voting Rights Act so long ago, how quickly the dream of multiracial democracy nearly perished, before it even had a chance to breathe.

MOBILE SITS AT the confluence of the Mobile River and Mobile Bay. It's the oldest city in Alabama, founded in 1702, some 117 years before the Cotton State first joined the union. By the late 1970s, the Port City had grown into the second-largest city in Alabama. As it rose to prominence, however, Mobile became a symbol of urbanized Jim Crow rule, as one of the ten most-segregated cities in the nation. Whites lived in the city's wealthier southern and western neighborhoods. Blacks resided almost entirely in the central city and the impoverished neighborhoods to its north. Many of Mobile's neighborhoods were either 100 percent white or entirely Black.

Another city fixture that was 100 percent white: Mobile's city council. Blacks made up one-third of the city's population, but because Mobile elected its three-member council via at-large elections, the white majority had controlled the mayor's office and every seat on the council for one hundred years. Mobile's white communities had their divisions—chiefly between working- and middle-class whites, many of whom worked in the shipyards, and the old-money, landholding elite. Yet they could agree on one thing: when they voted together, this method of government kept whites in power and Blacks out.

The at-large elections Mobile relied on were one of the oldest tricks in the Jim Crow playbook. In an at-large election for a five-seat board, for example, each voter would be able to select five candidates. As a result, a unified majority bloc can hold all the power and share none. Long banned for federal elections—originally halted by Congress in 1842, then ended once and for all with the VRA in 1965—they were nevertheless allowed in local jurisdictions. Unsurprisingly, they exploded in popularity across the South after the Civil War as the easiest way for whites to band together as a bloc, thereby ensuring that they wouldn't share any political power with Blacks or other minority communities. With that power base established, all the familiar machinery of southern segregation swung into action: those 100 percent white neighborhoods would budget themselves the vast majority of city resources from park budgets to schools, public works, and public safety provisions.

"This heritage of white supremacy effectively blocked electoral reform in Mobile, which became one of the last cities in the United States to retain the city commission form of government," notes James Blacksher, one of the three attorneys who represented Mobile's voters all the way to the U.S. Supreme Court in his survey *Voting Rights in Alabama*.

Alabama established its at-large council elections in 1911, not long after the state adopted a new constitution in 1901 with its stated goal to "establish white supremacy in this State . . . by law—not by force or fraud." The new setup worked beautifully—so much so that some state residents forgot the original intent of at-large elections; it faded into the background, just another taken-for-granted feature of a bitterly unjust social order, rooted in the nation's original sin.

When Blacksher and his colleagues filed litigation challenging this system, they hoped to piggyback off a 1973 Supreme Court decision in *White v. Regester*, where the court created a new "totality of circumstances" standard and allowed current and historical discrimination to be considered when assessing a voting rights claim. For its part, Mobile's defense played ignorant to history: Blacks could not vote when the system was devised, they claimed, so how could it discriminate against them?

In *Mobile v. Bolden*, the court was charged with deciding whether historic racism and systemic inequality had played a role in creating Mobile's entirely white power structure. The central question opened on to a series of others: Did decades-old racial intent still matter in modern times? Or had things sufficiently changed in the South that it was unfair to blame anyone now for an electoral system that had been designed by others so long ago? Did the Voting Rights Act simply guarantee Blacks and other minorities the formal right to vote—or did it also make a promise that those votes ought to be translated equitably into seats and political power, in places where both had been long denied? What did the Fifteenth Amendment and "one person, one vote" mean when guarding against the systematic dilution of minority votes?

As the court waded through such quandaries, it narrowed its focus on a pivotal point of inquiry: whether Mobile's at-large system had a racial *intent* or simply a race-based *effect*. In other words: Did Mobile intend to keep Blacks out of power? Or did it simply work out that way, even though Blacks had the same opportunity to vote as whites? The decision was eagerly anticipated by a wide range of conservative thinkers in politics and the legal academy, who were now seeking to redefine civil rights as "race-neutral."

Yet in Alabama, as in so much of the South, the past never really disappeared. In Mobile, it formed the public face of the city, in neighborhoods and school districts that remained separate and unequal. The past even contaminated the very air people breathed on the Black side of Mobile. Some of this history was submerged, some of it was invisible. But for anyone with eyes to see, it was undeniable—so long as they weren't blinded by the rhetoric of color blindness.

THE "TOTALITY OF circumstances" that the court was called on to weigh in *Mobile v. Bolden* could well start with a close look at Timothy Meaher, one of the leading lights of antebellum Mobile. His sordid history shows how intent and effect have always been intertwined in Mobile.

In the days before the Civil War, Mobile's wealthiest men spent weekends in style aboard riverboat casinos, steaming back and forth to Montgomery along the Alabama River. Cards were dealt, brown liquor flowed, the air turned toxic with cigar smoke and drunken boasts. One evening in 1859, on a steamship named after Roger B. Taney, the chief justice who delivered the infamous *Dred Scott* decision that ruled slaves were property under the Fifth Amendment, conversation turned to the slave trade. Congress had banned the international market in slaves in 1807 and 1808, much to the grumbling dismay of these men who remained unhappy they could not continue to buy new, younger slaves overseas.

Meaher, a second-generation Irishman, had moved from Maine to Mobile with his brothers in search of riches. He quickly amassed a fortune in sawmills, shipbuilding, cotton plantations, and the lumber trade—and, of course, slaves. Timothy Meaher sent lumber all over the world and believed he could import most anything and get away with it. As the story goes, in the spring of 1860, a fellow high roller took him up on that challenge and bet $100,000—nearly $3 million today—that Meaher could not bring a hundred new slaves to Alabama. "Inside two years, I can myself bring a shipful of n***ers into Mobile Bay under the officers' noses," Meaher bragged.

Meaher tasked one of his finest captains, William Foster, with the journey and bought him a speedy schooner called the *Clotilda*, complete with a false deck, phony papers, and an eleven-person crew who did not know the journey's actual purpose. Foster departed with $9,000 in gold to buy his human cargo. His destination was West Africa, where warring tribes often held captured fighters who might then be purchased by slave traders.

The story of Meaher, the *Clotilda*, and the families of the men he kidnapped and enslaved is passionately narrated in Margaret Brown's documentary *Descendant* and Ben Raines's *The Last Slave Ship*. Federal agents lurked in Mobile Harbor as the *Clotilda* made the ten-week voyage home with 110 men in chains. As rumors spread of Meaher's daring gambit, almost every arrival would be met and searched. Foster docked on the nearby Mississippi side and rode horseback to meet Meaher. Together, they transferred the smuggled slaves from the *Clotilda* to one of Meaher's riverboats and made the craft look like just another good-time vessel carrying tourists and travelers. Then they lit the *Clotilda* on fire and allowed it to sink in the muck just north of Mobile Bay. (It was not discovered offshore until 2018.) Everyone suspected what Meaher had done, but he eluded charges, as wealthy white men often do.

Meaher won his bet, but the South would soon lose the war. He sold some of the slaves to friends, kept some for himself, but with the Confederacy's defeat, the Africans he brought to America as chattel won their freedom. They barely spoke English and had little time to acclimate to their new home, so they settled in a swampy neighborhood three miles north of downtown Mobile, almost exactly where they had first come ashore in Alabama. Meaher owned the land and refused to give it to the people he trafficked to America. Instead he sold them small parcels, while retaining much of the surrounding land. He endeavored to stop them from voting, as well. When residents attempted to cast a ballot, Meaher physically blocked them himself. When they tried to cast ballots at a nearby precinct, Meaher galloped off via horseback and beat them there.

The neighborhood soon became known as Africatown. It's considered the first all-Black neighborhood in America, though in the 1980s, much of its downtown was bulldozed for a highway connector. By then, however, many residents had contracted cancer, largely believed to be connected to the steady belching of chloroform, dioxins, and other deadly poisons from the chemical plants and International Paper Company plants that operated on leases from the Meaher family on hundreds of acres encircling Africatown. (International Paper and local citizens settled a lawsuit in fall 2020; the company continues to deny all allegations.) New pastors would arrive at the local Baptist church and find themselves conducting dozens of funerals each year. New cars would rust almost immediately. Vegetable gardens would fill with ash, soot, and other airborne pollution.

With this history in view, how does one assess intent and effect in a place like Mobile? How much time must pass before history fades and intent gets lost? The Meahers brought these men and women to Mobile in chains. Their descendants filled their air with toxins. And if you were Black in Mobile during all this time, with decades of neglect and injustice just woven into everyday life, city councillors still didn't bother pretending to represent you at all.

IF IT WAS hard to be color-blind in Mobile, it was much easier for conservative academics whose everyday lives never brought them in proximity with Africatown. It was easier still when those academics used the language of the civil rights movement against its clear objectives, in an effort to essentially declare that doing the work of equality was itself racist.

"Our Constitution is color-blind and neither knows nor tolerates classes among citizens," wrote Justice John Marshall Harlan in his brave dissent in the 1896 *Plessy v. Ferguson* case that enshrined "separate but equal" as Supreme Court doctrine until it was overturned some sixty years later in *Brown v. Board of Education*. It did not take long after the passage of the Voting Rights Act and the Civil Rights Act for the enemies of racial progress to turn the aspirational color-blind dream back on itself and suggest that the very means of creating multiracial democracy itself echoed the sin of segregation.

The prominent sociologist Nathan Glazer, who became a leading voice among the neoconservative thinkers opposed to busing, affirmative action, and other government-enforced programs to promote racial equity, was among the pioneering voices who advanced this critique, and an important early influence on Antonin Scalia. "In 1964 we declared that no account should be taken of race, color, national origin or religion in the spheres of voting, jobs and education," Glazer wrote. "Yet no sooner had we made this national assertion than we entered into an unexpected enterprise of recording the color, race and national origin of every individual in every significant sphere of his life."

Glazer would become a mentor for Abigail Thernstrom, who would later partner with Edward Blum during the battle over the Voting Rights Act reauthorization in 2006, before the master conservative matchmaker took *Shelby County* to the Supreme Court. Thernstrom leaned heavily into Glazer's color-blind gospel, contending that the only true goal of the VRA was to fix the problem of uneven registration rates among Blacks and whites. It had nothing to do, she argued, with leveling results or transfers of political power.

That was not what Chief Justice Earl Warren had in mind when his court was hearing challenges to the VRA. "The Act gives a broad interpretation to the right to vote, recognizing that voting includes 'all action necessary to make a vote effective,'" he wrote in the 1969 case *Allen v. State Board of Elections*. "The right to vote can be affected by a dilution of voting power, as well as by an absolute prohibition on casting a ballot."

———

THE PASSAGE OF the Voting Rights Act in 1965 had indeed helped increase Black voter registration in Mobile. It set Black and white registration levels on a road to parity. But is parity in registration the same as equality if the rules have been fixed in advance to ensure one side wins? In Mobile, the century-long exclusion of Black representatives from the city council continued even after the passage of the VRA. Blacks still made up about one-third of Mobile's population. Yet because every councillor was selected at-large, because whites demonstrated that they remained unlikely to vote for a Black candidate, and because any white candidate with crossover, coalitional support from the Black community didn't generate enough support to win, the shutout continued.

If time clouded the memory of how white supremacy took deep structural root in the city's modern history, one might get a quick refresher course by paying a visit to the public library. There you'd find a written confession from Frederick Bromberg, who wrote a letter to the editor of the Mobile newspaper in 1909 while representing the city in the state senate. The senator made it clear that the purpose of at-large elections for city commissioners was to eradicate any possibility of Black voting power.

"We have always, as you know, falsely pretended that our main purpose was to exclude the ignorant vote when, in fact, we were trying to exclude not the ignorant vote, but the Negro vote," he wrote. "This is fully recognized by all statesmen."

Bromberg's candid admission was painful common knowledge among generations of Black voters in Mobile and across Alabama. As a result, the immediate legacy of the VRA a decade after its passage translated into more of the same when it came to political representation in Mobile. So two longtime civil rights activists decided it was time to test equality's true reach in court.

These activists, Wiley Bolden and John LeFlore, became the named plaintiffs in the federal lawsuit challenging the at-large districts as an unconstitutional vote dilution scheme. They alleged the system violated not only Section 2 of the Voting Rights Act—which authorized challenges to the electoral system that predated the act's passage in 1965—but also the equal protection promises contained within the Fourteenth and Fifteenth Amendments.

"If you were Black in Mobile, you had a vote, but it was worthless. It didn't count for anything. But the whole state was like that," says Larry Menefee, one of Blacksher's partners representing the plaintiffs.

THE *MOBILE* CASE seemed tailor-made for a "totality of circumstances" argument. Virgil Pittman, the U.S. federal judge who would hear *City of Mobile v. Bolden,* set out to discover those circumstances—even though he was born in an Alabama town where baldly racist justifications such as the ones that made up Mobile's defense held sway for decades.

Pittman, a Lyndon Johnson appointee to the federal bench, set out to transform the skewed racial reasoning that governed Mobile. In return, there would be crosses burned on his lawn, Ku Klux Klan marches through town, and many months where Pittman stopped attending church, fearful that his presence would place fellow parishioners in danger. Pittman's courageous decision required leaving not just his house but his courtroom and taking a hard, close-up look at everyday life in Mobile. Pittman made the uncommon, even radical decision to conduct several days of the *Mobile v. Bolden* trial walking across Mobile itself to see how political power was wielded and shared across white and Black neighborhoods.

No detail escaped Pittman's eye. Mobile, he observed, was subject to torrential downpours totaling more than sixty inches of rainfall each year. "All temporary relief in critical areas has been in the white areas," the judge wrote. "Somehow the white areas get relief with little temporary relief given the black areas." An in-person visit also revealed that the "resurfacing and maintenance of streets in black neighborhoods significantly suffers in comparison with the resurfacing of streets in white neighborhoods."

When it came to the construction of "first class roads, curbs, gutters and underground storm sewers," Pittman found, "there is a significant difference and sluggishness in the response of the city to critical needs of the blacks compared to that in the white area." Pittman visited Black elementary schools in densely populated and heavily trafficked areas, noting that they lacked sidewalks. In the white neighborhoods, kids strolled safely on new sidewalks.

The Mobile Fire Department, Pittman wrote, had only fifteen Black employees out of a total of 435. Desegregating the city police department required a court order in 1972. In the midst of the *Bolden* trial, white Mobile police officers arrested a Black suspect near a burglary scene and attempted a "mock lynching" that resulted in five indictments. Some two dozen cross burnings followed, without sufficient investigation or protection of the Black community, Pittman wrote. "The lack of reassurance by the city commission to the black citizens," Pittman wrote, indicated "the pervasiveness of the fear of white backlash" and "a failure by elected officials to take positive, vigorous, affirmative action in matters which are of such vital concern to the black people."

The Mobile County Commission operated under a court order enjoining racial discrimination. It also required federal litigation, the judge noted, to desegregate the municipal golf course—as well as public transportation and the Mobile city airport. The Educational Board, the Air Conditioning Board, the Architectural Board, the Board of Electrical Examiners, the Board of Examining Engineers, the Codes Advisory Committee—all of them were entirely white. "The city commission's custom or policy of appointing disproportionately few blacks to committees is a clear reflection of the at-large election system's dilution of blacks' influence and participation," Pittman ruled. A different system would "open parts of the governmental process to those to whom they have for so long been denied."

The totality of circumstances could only point in one direction. "The purposeful excesses of the past are still in evidence today," he concluded, finding both intent and effect in the concerted exclusion of Black citizens from Mobile's political life—as well as in an electoral system that minimized their ability to win any political power. Pittman ordered that Mobile create a new electoral system—instead of three councillors, elected citywide, he called for a mayor and a nine-member council to be represented from neighborhood districts, offering everyone a chance to win a seat at the table.

Mobile's white leadership howled. City officials and the *Mobile Press-Register* editorial page accused the judge of being power-mad—a black-robed tyrant who wanted to turn Mobile into "Pittmanville." They had one last recourse: the U.S. Supreme Court. There they would find a powerful ally in Lewis Powell.

CITY OF MOBILE v. Bolden reached the U.S. Supreme Court in October 1979, in between the United States' return of the Panama Canal to the government of Panama and the first march on Washington on behalf of gay and lesbian civil rights. The decision would eventually be written by Justice Potter Stewart, who famously observed in an earlier case that he could not define pornography but knew it when he saw it.

Stewart apparently lacked Pittman's recognition skills for racial discrimination. Stewart's and Powell's papers, maintained at Yale University, reveal that Powell was the key driver behind the decision. The junior justice was the member of the court who was most skeptical of Pittman's ruling and most eager to undo it. Again and again, in private memos and letters, Powell urged Stewart to go further and write more boldly—especially after the court's only Black member, Thurgood Marshall, circulated a powerful dissent that Powell believed should be attacked straight-on.

Powell simply did not know the history of at-large elections. As the moneyed southern lawyer saw things, at-large balloting was just another neutral tool of political representation. "The commission government per se has never been viewed, so far as I know, as a more effective means of depriving negroes of equal voting opportunities than any other form of government," Powell wrote in saucer-eyed historical ignorance reminiscent of his surprise over the *Brown v. Board of Education* decision. "Although discrimination certainly was a way of life in every southern community until 1954, and continued with respect to voting until well into the 1960s, I doubt that anyone thought of the commission form of government—or any other particular form of government—as a means of effectuating discriminatory intent. The government obviously had been satisfactory to the people of Mobile for more than half a century."

In the most detailed note any justice involved in this case sent to a clerk, Powell forwarded an eight-page missive on February 26, 1979. In that communiqué, Powell expressed grave concern over Judge Pittman's "judicially imposed" decision and "unprecedented action, as far I know," while conspicuously downplaying the invidious decades of racial discrimination that led to it. "Unless the judgments below are reversed, the second largest city in Alabama will have had imposed upon it a form of government never considered by any elected representatives," Powell complained. An unelected judge, Powell wrote, would have undone the unbeatable white supremacy secured to Mobile's white voters in 1911. Indeed, that judge would have gone along with every finding of discrimination against Mobile's Black voters as could possibly be imagined. They'd even done so, Powell added snidely, "with obvious enthusiasm."

In private letters found in Powell's papers—correspondence that the junior justice informed Stewart he was not circulating to other justices—he pushed Stewart to draft a stronger opinion that advanced the notion of race neutrality, in an early echo of what would become commonplace GOP talking points in years to come. Powell argued for a decision that insisted the Constitution and the Voting Rights Act offer citizens only a vote, not actual representation. He also demanded a bolder strike against a "radical" and "extreme" Thurgood Marshall dissent that Powell feared would create a strong historical legacy in the annals of the court.

Again and again, as Stewart's opinions moved through multiple drafts, Powell set out to drive the majority opinion in his direction. Stewart added language exactly mirroring suggestions from both Powell and his clerk, David Stewart. Indeed, Powell helped ensure that language was added to the decision that went against the basic facts of the case. "The answer to the appellees' argument is that they have not been denied the right to vote by anyone and there has been no finding that the city commission elections in Mobile have been designed intentionally to abridge the voting rights of negroes," Stewart's opinion held. Powell, meanwhile, celebrated the real-world impact of the ruling with a handwritten note on one draft, proclaiming that "if this becomes a court opinion it will reverse a trend toward guaranteeing that certain categories of citizens will be elected to office."

In yet another private letter located in Stewart's papers at Yale, Powell left little doubt as to which citizens will not be elected. "Apart from my interest in having 'my side' prevail in a case, I view this case as crucial to the successful governance of our cities," Powell wrote to Stewart. "If a decision by this Court required wards, and that they be shaped to assure proportional representation of identifiable 'political groups,' our cities could become jungles." That shocking, racially charged language is a stark reminder of the kind of power Lewis Powell confidently wielded from the bench—and the kind of backlash politics he was urging on the chief funders of the conservative movement just prior to his elevation to the high court. It says everything about the success of Powell's campaign to reimagine right-wing political combat in America that he drafted it on Supreme Court letterhead to the attention of a fellow high-court justice.

This letter, never before published, is Powell's memo to control the courts—and therefore American elections—in action from the bench. Eight years earlier, he had advised the Chamber and President Nixon to fight harder through the courts to control American politics, and he even earned his own appointment to the high court. "The judiciary may be the most important instrument for social, economic and political change," he counseled. "Labor unions, civil rights groups and now the public interest law firms are extremely active in the judicial arena. Their success . . . has not been inconsequential." Here was Powell, from the Supreme Court, rolling that success backward, breathing new life into conservative arguments about how power should be shared in a democracy that Congress and a previous court had considered settled with the Voting Rights Act. Now, with frightening language about different categories of citizens, and cities becoming "jungles," he was upholding Jim Crow from the bench. The very best way to control American elections? Powell knew the answer: control who could vote—and how.

The court's final decision in *City of Mobile v. Bolden*, written by Stewart with Powell pulling the strings, found that "[r]acially discriminatory motivation is a necessary ingredient of a Fifteenth Amendment violation" and that the Fifteenth Amendment "does not entail the right to have Negro candidates elected, but prohibits only purposefully discriminatory denial or abridgment by government of the freedom to vote."

A saddened Marshall, in dissent, mourned that this emerging consensus on the jurisdiction of the VRA left Blacks with just the "right to cast meaningless ballots." He noted further that this crabbed interpretation of the central Reconstruction amendment converted its revolutionary call for liberty and equality into "language illusory in symbol and hollow in substance."

Justice Byron White—who wrote the decisions in both *White v. Regester* and the racially discriminatory purpose standard in *Washington v.*

Davis—studied the totality of evidence that Pittman, as well as a federal appeals court, found convincing in Mobile. He agreed with Thurgood Marshall and William Brennan that Pittman's ruling was entirely within the bounds of the court's established standards of VRA jurisprudence. Yet in this case, White found himself in the minority writing a dissent for a 6–3 court that had decided to create an entirely new precedent and burden.

In this respect, *City of Mobile v. Bolden* underlines a key truth of Supreme Court jurisprudence: when the court changes, so does the law. You might even say there is no law, only justices. The Supreme Court in 1980 was far different from the Warren-era court that decided previous cases relating to the VRA. What we proclaim to be "the law" actually matters far less than the nine people seated on the Supreme Court. From 1979 onward, that lesson would never be lost on conservatives.

Justice White's decisions in *White v. Regester* and *Washington v. Davis* had opened courts to minority communities to bring discrimination claims in cities where citizens lacked power commensurate with their numbers, and where long-standing structures made it unlikely for their voice to be heard at all. In the *Mobile* case, everything changed. The court did not simply uphold Mobile's discriminatory at-large districts; it rewrote the standard to require racial discrimination claims under the Fourteenth and Fifteenth Amendments to show proof of discriminatory intent. It then made that standard nearly impossible to meet—since the lawmakers who had designed those systems several decades earlier typically did not leave "smoking gun" testimonials.

And even when they did—as in the case of the Mobile state representative who forcefully said the quiet part out loud in touting the discriminatory effects of the at-large system—the court arbitrarily ruled that such evidence simply did not count. Stewart and Powell went so far as to deny that any lawmakers or experts, at any time, could have possibly imagined creating a system with this intent, let alone been cognizant that this would be the effect. The simple fact of the system's existence across the decades, in so many cities, the court insisted, didn't demonstrate a determined white power grab but its opposite. It should be taken as proof of good faith.

Just fifteen years after the Voting Rights Act and the court's landmark 1960s cases that enshrined equal protection and the doctrine of "one person, one vote," it's startling to behold the speed and the potency of the legal backlash. This was grounded in Powell and Stewart's cramped, ideologically driven reading of the VRA cases in order to strategically downgrade the need to safeguard the vote—and to uncritically accept a Mobile electoral structure that created a permanent white power establishment as somehow "race neutral."

"Their freedom to vote has not been denied or abridged by anyone," the court ruled of the Black plaintiffs in the case. "The Fifteenth Amendment does not entail the right to have Negro candidates elected. . . . That Amendment prohibits only purposefully discriminatory denial or abridgment by government of the freedom to vote 'on account of race, color, or previous condition of servitude.' Having found that Negroes in Mobile 'register and vote without hindrance,' the District Court and Court of Appeals were in error."

This round of the voting rights war would go to Powell—an early and telling victory for "race neutrality" and a color-blind Constitution. The decision in *City of Mobile v. Bolden* was also a clear sign that many forces within the judiciary and the American political establishment had grown restive and impatient with the expectation that true racial equality should be a permanent feature of American life. They continued to hail the unambiguous success of the VRA in increasing Black registration and turnout rates. But they also made a point of drawing a clear line between the right to vote, reluctantly granted, and the right to hold power, stubbornly opposed.

The court's decision in *City of Mobile v. Bolden* also highlighted the importance of the upcoming congressional debate over the VRA's reauthorization, which would be required in 1982. Congress and civil rights activists would be ready to add new language that overrode the court's decision and reiterated that the VRA was intended to police racial discrimination in voting wherever it is found—whether in intent or effect. But a new generation of conservative activists would be prepared as well; after all, look at what Powell had managed to achieve after a few short years on the bench. And one young conservative lawyer in particular would find himself right at home in Ronald Reagan's new morning in America.

CHAPTER FOUR

"THIS WOULD BECOME John Roberts's life work," says Charles Fried, a Harvard Law School professor who served in the Reagan administration as solicitor general, the government's lead voice before the U.S. Supreme Court, "undermining voting rights and the Voting Rights Act."

Conservatives had a mission: use the courts to advance policies that could not be won at the ballot box. By the time Reagan took office, they had placed the architect of the original plan directly onto the U.S. Supreme Court, where he promptly delivered resounding rebukes to voting rights. They had used hard-won lessons to refine the original playbook and focus on building influence within law schools, elevating promising young thinkers into prominent roles in GOP administrations, and seeding the next generation of conservatives on the bench. Decades later, John Roberts, the most consequential piece to emerge from this cynical system, would arrive at a hearing before the Senate Judiciary Committee as if from central casting, a sunny, heartland optimist born on third base, but easily portrayed as a meritocratic striver.

During his 2005 confirmation hearings, Roberts charmed the Senate Judiciary Committee, and the nation, with tales of a midwestern upbringing straight out of a John Cougar Mellencamp song. "I think all of us retain from our youth certain enduring images," he recalled before the senators. "For me, those images are of the endless fields of Indiana stretching to the horizons, punctuated by an isolated silo or a barn."

It's certainly possible, of course, that Roberts gazed upon rural Indiana farmland during his 1960s boyhood, perhaps from the back seat on a Sunday drive. But the rustic, mythic Americana Roberts described before the committee didn't have much relation to his actual childhood. The future chief justice who would determine that race was no longer a problem in American life—who would grow up to roll back the historic legislation that truly began America's march toward multiracial democracy—spent his most formative years up in Long Beach, Indiana, a lily-white suburban enclave on the shores of Lake Michigan, home to some of the wealthiest Chicago entrepreneurs. As Joan Biskupic, Roberts's terrific biographer, explains in her illuminating *The Chief,* Roberts's boyhood consisted of prep schools, country clubs, and waterskiing; there were no cow-milking chores or early mornings aboard a John Deere combine. Everyone looked much like he did. While John Lewis was beaten in Selma, while Freedom Summer Riders died registering voters in Mississippi, while Lyndon Johnson muscled the Voting Rights Act through Congress, the boy who would grow up to eviscerate it rode bikes along tree-lined suburbs and was cosseted in private schools in a town built for whites only.

As Biskupic details, Roberts learned loyalty as the son of a company man. He was born in Buffalo in 1955, and his family moved to Long Beach in time for fourth grade, when Bethlehem Steel transferred his father to manage the opening of a new plant in Burns Harbor, about twenty miles away. The family spent its initial years in Long Beach among the waterfront summer homes of the Chicago elite. But by 1965 John Jr., his parents, and three sisters moved several blocks away to a lovely five-bedroom yellow mock Tudor split-level in a neighborhood with expansive, manicured front lawns and quiet streets perfect for bike-riding.

Long Beach and the ritzy lakefront environs surrounding it remained one of the most segregated areas of the nation even in 1965. Decades after the federal government put an end to official housing discrimination, early twentieth-century brochures advertising Long Beach real estate touted a vacationland in a "highly restricted home community" where "all residents are Caucasian Gentiles." Roberts devoured history and math at the local Catholic school, Notre Dame.

Then, in 1968, as debates over Vietnam and the civil rights revolution raged elsewhere, he stepped up to a new private Catholic, all-male high school, La Lumiere, in nearby La Porte. Roberts's high school resembled a luxury campground on a bucolic lakefront estate. The estate's former chauffeur's quarters were turned into a classroom, after the school had been founded in 1964 by local elites, including the future chairman of Mc-Donald's. La Lumiere was an enclave within an enclave, a "haven of formality" along the woodsy Indiana coastline. Families spent nearly $7,000 a year—the equivalent of $61,000 annually today—for their children to be educated in tiny classes of twenty where they would attend daily Mass in mandatory blazers, gray flannel trousers, and ties. They also would have four years of Latin and change into suits before dinner. "I've always wanted to stay ahead of the crowd," a thirteen-year-old Roberts wrote in his application essay. "I won't be content to get a good job by getting a good education. I want to get the best job by getting the best education." La Lumiere did recruit two Black brothers from Chicago for diversity, Paris and Neil Barclay, but that brought the number of Black students to three. "No one ever called me the N-word," remembered Paris Barclay, who went on to direct *Sons of Anarchy*. "They were a little too sophisticated for that," he told the *Los Angeles Times*.

When George W. Bush introduced Roberts as his nominee for chief justice, he suggested that the young preppie had working-class roots because he had spent at least one summer working at Bethlehem Steel. But this gig, too, was an inside job: the company reserved specific summer positions for the sons of executives. According to a 2005 *Washington Post* article, Bethlehem paid between $12 and $16 an hour in the early 1970s; that's the equivalent of a summer job's wages at between $88 and $117 an hour today.

In any event, Roberts would not be long for Long Beach or Bethlehem Steel. Roberts became the first La Lumiere graduate to matriculate at Harvard, and then at Harvard Law. His years in Cambridge overlapped not only with Vietnam and Watergate, but also with the Supreme Court's 1973 decision in *Roe v. Wade* that legalized abortion nationwide. While protests often filled Harvard Square, Roberts ventured there only for Mass every Sunday morning at St. Paul's. While fellow students knew his politics, whenever classmates and professors are asked about Roberts in those days, whether for books or profiles of the chief justice, they insist that he simply didn't engage in any of the momentous battles of his time.

"He was really very good at being thoughtful and careful and not particularly conspicuous," says Laurence Tribe, who taught Roberts constitutional law at Harvard. "He was very lawyerly, even as a law student."

Tribe, one of the great constitutional law professors of his generation and a devoted liberal, still struggles to understand how someone as thoughtful and curious as Roberts could confuse the difference between using race to segregate and using it to integrate. Tribe told me that "I only wish I had a plausible explanation for how a fellow as bright, decent, and seemingly devoid in the kind of racism that even the first Justice Harlan displayed in his justly celebrated *Plessy v. Ferguson* dissent—a dissent in which Harlan reassured white readers that their racial dominance 'in prestige, in achievements, in education, in wealth and in power' would 'continue for all time'—as John Roberts could have come from the earliest stages of his career to be so deeply committed to a view that amounts to a belief that any effort to eradicate racial discrimination is itself racial discrimination."

Tribe says that his classes have always focused on issues of how to properly account for race in public decision-making, and related questions of formal equality versus practical equality. He adds that such questions, and others like them, "no doubt were very much in the air when Roberts was at HLS."

At the same time, one of the signature issues of conservative jurisprudence on race—the question of racial effects versus racial intent—was prominently in play during Roberts's law school days. In the 1976 Supreme Court case *Washington v. Davis*, a 7–2 court found that Washington, D.C.'s personnel test—which Black applicants failed at a dramatically higher percentage than their white counterparts did—was perfectly constitutional. The court contended that the testing apparatus in Washington lacked discriminatory intent and gauged qualifications in what the court—then made up of eight white men and one Black man—held to be racially neutral terms.

Then, in 1978, in a 5–4 decision in *Regents of California v. Bakke* in which Lewis Powell wrote the controlling opinion, the court allowed affirmative action in college admissions to remain, but transformed its purpose. Allan Bakke, a white man, had twice been denied admission to the medical school at the University of California, Davis, and maintained his rejections were the result of a university policy that held 16 of 100 seats for Black applicants. Affirmative action, Powell wrote, held its virtue not as a remedy for prior racial discrimination but in providing diversity that would benefit the cultural makeup of predominantly white institutions. The decision upended several key court precedents addressing the Fourteenth Amendment and equal protection under the law. Congress had explicitly drafted such provisions to help minority groups who had been historically disadvantaged achieve some measure of redress and social justice. Under the diffuse diversity mandate now enshrined in *Bakke*, those protections were turned on their head.

The fallout from the Burger Court's central race decisions, Tribe suspects, in *Bakke*, *Washington v. Davis*, and *Mobile v. Bolden*, crystallized young John Roberts's understanding of race, and the proper state-sanctioned remedies for racial discrimination. As Tribe puts it, his formerly taciturn conservative student "became . . . fanatical about the race-blind ideal as the end-all and be-all of equal protection."

Several of Roberts's Harvard Law classmates honored the court's most prominent and outspoken conservative, William Rehnquist, by founding the Rehnquist Club in his honor. Roberts declined to join the new society. Instead, the striver who wanted to stay ahead of the crowd and get the best job became part of an even tinier and more exclusive group: he became Rehnquist's clerk at the U.S. Supreme Court. As a future chief justice clerking for another, Roberts got a close-in opportunity to develop his views on race and American society, learning at the feet of a justice who had clear ideas about how the GOP could use the courts to gain power through elections.

WHEN ROBERTS TESTIFIED before the Senate Judiciary Commission during his 2005 nomination hearings, he emphasized his judicial modesty and insisted that he viewed the judge's role as akin to that of a home plate umpire in a baseball game. To drive that point home, he cited his first clerkship for Judge Henry Friendly, a universally esteemed Eisenhower appointee, as a key ethical tutelage in the virtues of humility and restraint. He said he found it admirable that the news media and public could not determine Friendly's politics, and Roberts highlighted his boss's "essential humility" in deferring to elected officials rather than legislating his own agenda from the bench. By any account, the warmth between the judge from another era and the young law school graduate on the verge of a new partisan age was real.

Yet Roberts's praise for Friendly also served as rhetorical misdirection. For even as Roberts scrupulously cultivated the image of a humble caller of balls and strikes, his résumé told a very different story. Throughout his career, Roberts had attached himself to deeply conservative Washington mentors. Roberts may have had a closer relationship with Friendly, but his jurisprudence as chief justice hardly reflects respect for restraint, precedent, or elected officials. Instead, it comes closer to mirroring Roberts's next intellectual mentor, Rehnquist, for whom he clerked from spring 1979 until the summer of 1980.

Mentioning Friendly allowed him to dial back the significance of his Rehnquist clerkship while he was priming himself to claim his mentor's job, a smart play if Roberts wanted to sell the umpire metaphor. In Rehnquist, Roberts had a chief justice mentor who had personally worked to block Black and Latino voters from the polls in Arizona in the years preceding the passage of the Voting Rights Act. This history would become an unmistakable line of influence on Roberts's career when he wrote the majority opinion in *Shelby County v. Holder*, the 2013 high court decision that effectively disemboweled the VRA.

Between 1958 and 1964, Rehnquist led a brigade of white Arizona conservatives—calling themselves "flying squads" and nicknaming their battle plan "Operation Eagle Eye"—who used literacy tests and "voter caging" tactics at Phoenix precincts. Eyewitnesses said that these efforts overtly harassed and intimidated minority voters. During his 1971 and 1986 confirmation hearings, multiple onlookers, both Democrats and Republicans, in sworn testimony before Congress and interviews later unsealed by the FBI, remembered Rehnquist himself—already a well-known figure in Arizona political and legal circles—aggressively demanding that voters read and interpret a passage from the Constitution. Rehnquist insisted that he had never himself challenged anyone's right to vote, and that he was simply one among a group of GOP attorneys who provided legal advice to citizen activists seeking to preserve the integrity of the ballot. "Operation Eagle Eye," he said, with a deflection that would echo to the present day, simply protected against voter fraud.

Nixon's nominations of Powell and Rehnquist to the court, on the same day in October 1971, would have deep repercussions for American elections. During his confirmation hearings, Rehnquist danced carefully through the allegations with a barrage of memory-defying euphemisms— "As I recall" and "my recollection is" and "I do not think I did." But his accusers had more vivid memories.

Some onlookers even remember that Rehnquist got involved in a shoving match. Lito Peña, a Democratic poll watcher, recalled seeing Rehnquist at the Bethune School precinct in 1964, quizzing minority voters about where they lived and for how long, and demanding anyone who spoke broken English analyze a reading from the Constitution before they could vote. "He knew the law and applied it with the precision of a swordsman," Peña told the *Pittsburgh Post-Gazette* in 2000.

Dr. Sydney Smith, a university professor, testified that she remembered Rehnquist rapidly emerging from a car at a southwestern Phoenix precinct with at least two other men, brandishing a white index card at Black voters, and telling them: "You can't read. You're not qualified to vote. You should leave here." Many did leave. At other times, the challenges from Rehnquist and his flying squads created longer lines at minority precincts, further discouraging voter participation.

Perhaps the most damning testimony before Congress came from a former assistant U.S. attorney in Phoenix who was charged with investigating any potential civil rights violations at the polls. James Brosnahan told the Senate Judiciary Committee that GOP challengers were, without any basis, aggressively challenging minority voters. "Based on my interviews with others, polling officials, and my fellow assistant U.S. attorneys, it was my opinion in 1962 that the challenging effort was designed to reduce the number of black and Hispanic voters by confrontation and intimidation," he said.

This alleged voter intimidation by Rehnquist, however, was not the only indication that he was averse to the causes of civil rights and racial justice. During his 1971 confirmation hearings, *Newsweek* discovered a memo that Rehnquist wrote during his own days as a clerk, for Justice Robert H. Jackson, during the high court's internal debates over *Brown v. Board of Education*, the landmark school desegregation case. Rehnquist, writing in the first person, pushed Jackson to uphold one of the court's most notorious decisions, *Plessy v. Ferguson* from 1896, in which the court ruled that "separate but equal" accommodations for Blacks and whites were constitutional. "I realize that this is an unpopular and unhumanitarian position for which I have been excoriated by 'liberal' colleagues," Rehnquist wrote, "but I think *Plessy v. Ferguson* was right and should be re-affirmed."

FOR ROBERTS—"A CONSERVATIVE looking for a conservative ideology in American history," as Morton Horwitz, one of his Harvard history professors, told Ari Berman in his essential history *Give Us the Ballot*—a clerkship with Rehnquist was the perfect incubation. The three clerks working for Rehnquist shared a fifteen-by-twenty-foot room with three desks and worked in such close quarters that they became lifelong, and history-making, friends. (Roberts would be the best man at the wedding of fellow clerk Dean Colson. Then in 2000, as a renowned Miami attorney and friend of Florida governor Jeb Bush, Colson, according to the *Washington Post*, helped connect Roberts to Jeb Bush's team. They invited him to Tallahassee to offer the governor private counsel during the disputed recount that ended with the Supreme Court—and William Rehnquist—installing Bush's brother George W. in the White House.) Berman called it "the closest place to the center of an emerging conservative legal movement," in an office that "functioned as a federalist society before there was a Federalist Society."

Rehnquist adopted so many "states' rights" positions on civil rights and other issues that Roberts and the other clerks presented him with a figurine of the Lone Ranger, which remained on display in his chambers for decades. Roberts would long describe the stimulating intellectual effect of the long walks that Rehnquist would take alongside his clerks in and around the Supreme Court building. Sometimes the four men would tour the Capitol Hill area late into the night, working out the finer points and specific phrasings of the justice's opinions.

"There were three or four really conservative clerks at the Court that year, but he was certainly very, very conservative," says Paul Smith, then a recent Yale Law graduate who clerked alongside Roberts that term for Powell and went on to argue twenty-one cases before the Supreme Court. Smith and Roberts would lunch together some days in the court's basement cafeteria.

"John was certainly in sync with his justice," Smith wryly told the *New York Times* in 2005 after his nomination was announced. Rehnquist's other clerks were conservative but lacked "the ideological edge" that Roberts had, Smith later told Berman. "Rehnquist reinforced John's pre-existing philosophies. . . . He was definitely in sync with Rehnquist. John was not a believer in the courts giving rights to minorities and the downtrodden. That was the basic Rehnquist philosophy."

The court did not have a hot-button race case during the year Roberts and Smith clerked—"It was not a very interesting term, frankly," Smith told me. But the high court was already well down the path of revising the basic precepts of racial discrimination and voting rights law in Rehnquist's preferred image. In both the *Mobile v. Bolden* decision and the same year's ruling in *City of Rome*, a Section 5 case involving a Georgia town that annexed white neighborhoods sixty times between 1964 and 1975 without bothering to obtain preclearance, the court endorsed Rehnquist's fervent states' rights opinions. Roberts would again lean on those same glib race-neutral fallacies in the landmark *Shelby County* decision overturning preclearance some thirty-five years later.

Preclearance, Rehnquist wrote in *City of Rome*, placed Rome, Georgia, in a "straitjacket." His concern was not that Rome had never elected a Black official and that the city had repeatedly violated the Voting Rights Act to keep it that way. No, Rehnquist was troubled by the specter of federal overreach that deprived state and local officials of power and liberty. "The enforcement provisions of the Civil War Amendments were not premised on the notion that Congress could empower a later generation of blacks to 'get even' for wrongs inflicted on their forebears," he wrote.

Rehnquist wanted to move the law in a conservative direction, regardless of precedent. In 1982, the conservative columnist Charles Krauthammer issued a blistering evaluation of his tenure, writing that Rehnquist "repudiates precedents frequently and openly, and if that is impossible (because the precedent represents a tradition that neither the Court nor society is prepared to abandon), then he distorts them." One could draw a straight line from that critique to Roberts's approach in *Citizens United* and *Shelby County* several decades later, when he based his ruling on a doctrine of state sovereignty that he created by editing a court precedent so that it had the opposite meaning. It's as if Roberts wanted it all: Friendly's gold-plated reputation but Rehnquist's hard-right results.

As Roberts ended his clerkship, the presidential election of 1980 was in full swing. The young conservative cemented his partisan preferences during his clerkship—his roommate Richard Lazarus, later to become a liberal law professor at Georgetown, remembers taping a Democratic donkey to their television set during election coverage, only to have Roberts affix a Republican elephant. Apart from the election's outcome, however, the fledgling conservative legal establishment took its measure of Roberts and cemented its trust with him. When Reagan won that fall, conservatives needed to quickly staff up federal agencies and the Department of Justice. By now, the young Indiana native and Harvard Law graduate who won the highest plaudits from the court's most conservative member was in line for "the best job."

"Reagan came from nowhere to beat Carter and suddenly the conservative legal movement blossoms and builds on itself," Paul Smith told me. "As in most things in this country, the energy came from race and racial resentment."

Roberts would quickly dedicate himself to sorting out questions about racial intent and effect, working to defend the Supreme Court's racial recidivism as the Reagan administration prepared for the next reauthorization of the Voting Rights Act in 1982. The civil rights community, alarmed by both the court's ruling in *City of Mobile v. Bolden* and the rise of the Reagan Right, undertook an all but existential battle for voting rights and the prospects for multiracial democracy as the debate in Congress commenced. For his part, Roberts would be the principal architect of the conservative legal movement's intellectual case against congressional action. It was a battle that would define Roberts's life's work for decades to come, reshaping American democracy along the way.

An excited Roberts, newly hired by the administration, sent his old mentor Friendly an appreciative note. "While I suspect you may be displeased that I have not yet found my way to a litigator's table in the courtroom, the legal issues surrounding the President are fascinating," he wrote. "I am delighted to have the opportunity to explore them and serve an Administration whose objectives I share."

CHAPTER FIVE

ELECTION NIGHT 1980 delivered a thorough rout that John Roberts could scarcely have imagined when he affixed his lucky elephant to the TV set and settled in to watch Walter Cronkite and John Chancellor deliver the returns. Reagan captured 44 states and 489 electoral votes. An anxious nation weary of energy crises, gas lines, and recession fears, as well as embarrassed and exhausted by the Iranian hostage crisis, embraced a conservative revolution. Republicans captured the Senate for the first time since 1954, and the twelve-seat swing included the defeats of some of the chamber's most stalwart liberal lions. The new chairman of the Senate Judiciary Committee would be the staunchest segregationist of them all, South Carolina senator Strom Thurmond.

Voting rights advocates had ample reason to be worried as the calendar turned and the congressional debate over the 1982 reauthorization of the Voting Rights Act stood only a year away. With Powell and Rehnquist on the bench turning conservative position papers and talking points about race into law, the U.S. Supreme Court appeared far less friendly to voting rights and newly inclined to place limits on protections for minorities. The immediate impact of *Mobile v. Bolden* proved devastating and justified the *New York Times*'s contention that the ruling had been "the biggest step backward in civil rights to come from the Court." What seemed relatively clear to anyone reading through the court's decision was that firmly establishing the racial intent of the long-dead officials who had created the prejudiced systems in the first place was nearly impossible. Meanwhile most modern-day vote suppressors were wise enough not to leave a paper trail.

This new intent standard didn't just chill VRA cases—it made them so difficult to prove that it brought all pending Section 2 enforcement litigation from the Justice Department to a screeching halt. Cases DOJ lawyers had won under the older standards were vacated and remanded now that at least five, and possibly six, justices appeared to require the intent standard. A once clear-cut voting rights enforcement case against South Carolina, which hadn't elected a single Black candidate to any seat in the state senate since the end of Reconstruction despite being 30 percent Black, had to be dropped entirely.

Decisions on voting rights and affirmative action handed more momentum to those influential law professors and thinkers within conservative legal circles to expand their embrace of "race neutrality" and a "color-blind Constitution." Some felt so emboldened to suggest that they were the true intellectual heirs of the civil rights leader Dr. Martin Luther King Jr.'s vision of a nation where children would be judged not "by the color of the skin but the content of their character." (This same King quotation, wrenched out of context, would become a standard talking point among crusaders against critical race theory and other purported excesses of a power-mad race-identity industrial complex, in the Trump era.)

Special protections based on race, these insurgent conservative thinkers suggested, were themselves unfair racial entitlements. When Justice Harry Blackmun wrote in one 1970s case that to get beyond racism, the nation first needed to account for it, a young law professor at the University of Chicago wrote a stinging dissent in the influential *Washington University Law Quarterly*. In a 1979 article titled "The Disease as Cure," Antonin Scalia argued that the current legal framework establishing remedies for past discrimination "is based upon concepts of racial indebtedness and racial entitlement rather than individual worth and individual need."

"That is to say," Scalia concluded, "it is racist."

Reagan knew an ideological ally when he saw one. In 1982, he appointed Scalia to the U.S. Court of Appeals, and then elevated him to the Supreme Court in 1986.

The new president, meanwhile, had opposed the Civil Rights Act of 1964, the Voting Rights Act in 1965, and, during his 1966 campaign for governor of California, promised to eliminate the Fair Housing Act. "If an individual wants to discriminate against Negroes or others in selling or renting his house," Reagan said then, "he has a right to do so." Nor were these beliefs outmoded artifacts of Reagan's career as a '60s Goldwater conservative. During the 1980 presidential race, Reagan again voiced his opposition to the Voting Rights Act, calling it "humiliating to the South." He'd launched his victorious campaign at the Neshoba County Fair in Philadelphia, Mississippi, surrounded by Confederate flags, mere miles from where the mutilated bodies of three Freedom Summer Riders were found some fifteen years earlier. "I believe in states' rights," Reagan told the crowd, and the prominence of the traitors' flag ensured that his southern audience would not mistake his meaning.

The Voting Rights Act had been reauthorized twice before under Republican presidents, under Nixon in 1970 and then again under Ford in 1975. But 1982 represented an entire new set of unknowns: a White House with an ideological opposition to laws that used race to help reverse a nation's sordid history of racial discrimination.

"We were in real trouble," says Don Edwards, the California Democrat who chaired the House Judiciary Subcommittee on Civil and Constitutional Rights, in an oral history archived at the University of North Carolina at Chapel Hill. "Initially, not many people in the Capitol agreed about the need for a legislated extension of the 1965 law. There was a general attitude that we don't need (it), people can vote."

Edwards and the full committee chairman, Peter Rodino of New Jersey, had before them the challenging task of shepherding the reauthorization of perhaps the most important and successful legislation Congress had ever passed. The VRA also needed to be modernized to address *City of Mobile v. Bolden*: prior to that decision, most experts agreed that in view of the VRA's legislative history, the law required that its federal enforcers simply needed to demonstrate that a given election law or electoral system had a discriminatory effect. With intent entering the picture after *Mobile*, this requirement became far murkier.

The battle lines were drawn: On one side were the civil rights leaders who wanted to use the 1982 reauthorization to address the Supreme Court's ruling and obtain explicit language saying that the Voting Rights Act banned discriminatory effects regardless of intent. On the other side

were officials in the Department of Justice and other Reagan administration figures who embraced the *Mobile* decision and did not want to see the
statute changed at all.

Everyone prepared for battle. The Leadership Conference on Civil
Rights, a coalition that represented 165 different organizations, hired its
first full-time executive director to develop and execute a winning strategy
on the Hill. They turned to thirty-six-year-old Ralph Neas, a white male
Catholic Republican—"I was zero for four in some people's eyes," he says
now with a laugh. But Neas was a longtime civil rights activist, a canny
Capitol Hill connector, and a veteran Senate counsel to Ed Brooke—the
liberal Republican senator from Massachusetts and the first Black candidate elected to the U.S. Senate via the popular vote.

They knew that the road ahead was steep. What they didn't know was
that the chief intellectual strategist among the Reaganites, and their most
determined foe, was a newly hired twenty-six-year-old assistant in the Justice Department.

"It was John Roberts leading the charge on the Voting Rights Act,"
Neas says. "The counteroffense started with considerable force from John."

TWO WEEKS AFTER Ronald Reagan's inauguration, John Roberts sent his résumé to Kenneth W. Starr at the Department of Justice along with a cover
letter written on Supreme Court letterhead. "Thank you for arranging to
meet with me on Friday to discuss my interest in serving as a Special Assistant to the Attorney General," Roberts wrote, later adding that he had
heard a "call to action" in Reagan's inaugural speech. He listed Rehnquist
and Friendly as references and noted on his résumé not only clerkships at
the court and for a firm in Honolulu, but also a litany of Harvard awards
for "the best dissertation submitted in the English language" and "the out-
standing essay submitted by a Sophomore concentrating in History."

While it would take six months to get Roberts to the DOJ, the "Reagan
Revolution" was already working its way into the atmosphere. If Rehnquist's chambers had been a lonely outpost for a still-budding conservative
legal movement, Ronald Reagan's Department of Justice would become its
intellectual headquarters for the next eight years. A small cadre of bright,

young true believers were determined to move the law in their direction. They would form fast friendships as they made history together and rose to the summit of their profession.

"There were 180 career lawyers and they hated everything we did, particularly on race and affirmative action," says Michael Carvin, with a laugh. Carvin would serve in several top jobs at the DOJ before working with Roberts to install George W. Bush in the White House during *Bush v. Gore*, then becoming one of the go-to Supreme Court litigators for conservative causes on voting rights, Obamacare, and more. Such shared antipathy only forged tighter bonds among the revolutionaries. "The band of brothers!" exclaims Bruce Fein, a fellow assistant to a deputy attorney general; at thirty-four he could have been Roberts's older brother.

Bork and Scalia might have defined originalism, but these DOJ masterminds, assistants, and deputies were the shock troops of the conservative legal movement. Their number included Kenneth Starr (who would later win wide acclaim and notoriety for running, along with a young Brett Kavanaugh, the Special Counsel's investigation into Bill Clinton's White-water dealings and various sexual dalliances). There was also a corps of future master litigators, movement builders, and federal judges including Carvin, Samuel Alito, Stephen Markman, Carolyn Kuhl, Roger Clegg, and Charles "Chuck" Cooper. Together, this close-knit group of Washington players transformed the formerly fringe academic theory of originalism into a self-evident badge of belonging in the conservative movement.

"This is an exciting time to be at the Justice Department," Roberts wrote in a letter to Friendly. "So much that has been taken for granted for so long is being seriously reconsidered."

Much of this reappraisal had to do with race. The young DOJ brigade believed in race neutrality and a color-blind Constitution as uncritically as they endorsed the dogma of originalism. Reagan wanted to do away with affirmative action quotas. School busing, college admissions, and workplace quotas remained hot-button issues. The Justice Department had been tasked with enshrining Reagan's thoughts on race and affirmative action into law—in part by providing the theories and the arguments to change the law and move the courts in Reagan's direction. Voting rights might not have been the first issue anyone wanted to take on. Roberts and his band of brothers knew full well that in the broader terms of political debate, voting rights was right up there with baseball, motherhood, and apple pie, making full-throated opposition all but impossible.

Still, the Justice Department brain trust on the issue enjoyed a critical advantage in Washington: timing. The 1982 reauthorization fell early on the administration's calendar. And the key fight—on intent versus effects, after the *Mobile v. Bolden* decision—was exactly the one the young conservatives were spoiling to pick.

"I was steeped in color blindness when I came to Washington. Our bible was the dissent of Justice Harlan in *Plessy v. Ferguson*: 'The law takes man as man and has no regard for his color,'" Fein says. "Obviously, if you can prove discrimination, you should get a remedy. But other than that? What is an effects test except a runaround when you can't prove intent?"

Fein invoked Thurgood Marshall and Martin Luther King Jr. as allies in this fight. "This was Marshall's argument in *Brown* against the Board. He said we want race-neutral student assignments. He didn't want race-conscious student assignments. So our argument was hardly, you know, a throwback to Jim Crow. This is not the racism of the post–Civil War era."

Marshall, of course, saw both intent and effect in *City of Mobile*, but no matter. The effects test in the VRA reauthorization, Carvin says, was just "quotas for Congress." Carvin and other conservatives inside and outside DOJ viewed it as affirmative action to award Blacks a fixed number of seats in Congress, a new race-based entitlement. Left unsaid, usually, is that those seats would then be taken from duly elected white members.

"There was a basic moral principle enshrined in the Civil Rights Act that you shall not treat people differently," Carvin says, claiming Dr. King's words as his own. "The content of their character, not the color of their skin."

It was only the band of brothers at DOJ, however, who really wanted to dig in on the addition of the effects test to the 1982 reauthorization. "We were the only ones," Fein remembers, who said, "Wait a minute. This is not good."

Carvin says he gives Reagan's attorney general, William French Smith, a lot of credit for backing the deputies and assistants on an issue so politically controversial. Republicans "get nervous about civil rights issues because they don't want to be called racist. The path of least resistance was just to reauthorize it. Smith took a principled stance—largely with John [Roberts]'s strong support. He completely analyzed it. And John's been really good on voting rights stuff ever since. Because he gets the game: If you're helping Blacks, go for it. If you're discriminating against an eighteen-year-old Italian in Brooklyn? Then it's fine to judge him based on his skin color."

With Ronald Reagan in the White House and the Department of Justice swerving toward originalism, the federal government's stance on how voting rights should be enforced—just sixteen years after Selma and the passage of the VRA—was in the hands of those who saw it as a zero-sum political game to boost Blacks at the expense of ethnic whites. This was no longer the stuff of second-tier, midwestern law review articles. These were the discussions inside the Department of Justice—involving the future chief justice of the United States—ahead of a 1982 reauthorization debate where the stakes were nothing less than whether white-run state and local governments across the South, and much of the nation, that had ferociously resisted multiracial democracy should now be trusted to help build one.

YET EVEN AS the idealistic conservative ideologues at DOJ bristled for a fight over effects and intent, few Republicans in Congress or inside the Reagan White House shared those pugilistic interests. They knew that the VRA represented a hard-line "principle" that could cost the party critical support from minority voters.

The administration's first year was hectic and crazed. Ten weeks after his inauguration, Reagan would be shot and nearly killed after a speech at the Washington Hilton; he'd spend the next twelve days in the hospital. That summer brought a tax-cut battle on Capitol Hill, an ultimatum to striking air-traffic controllers to return to work or be fired, and the nomination of Sandra Day O'Connor to the court. The fall included the assassination of Egyptian president Anwar Sadat, the announcement of a new generation of nuclear weapons and delivery systems, and the controversial sale of advanced fighter planes to Saudi Arabia.

In this roiling political atmosphere, top Reagan aides like James Baker, Lyn Nofziger, and Michael Deaver were perfectly content not to pick a fight with Black voters over the VRA. Nofziger told Reagan that full support for the VRA would be a strong way to win back Black voters. A significant number of Black Americans still chafed at the president's stances on race during the campaign and had been hurt by budget cuts to popular welfare and social safety net programs.

Among those on the right who wanted to fight over the reauthorization, there was a range of positions on how aggressive to be. Within the Justice Department, conservatives wanted to hold the line on principles like state sovereignty, federal deregulation, racial quotas, and race neutrality. Meanwhile other students of right-wing realpolitik, including Michael Carvin, recognized a political advantage for the GOP in VRA provisions that required more majority-minority districts, because that would concentrate Black voters into fewer overall seats, creating more lily-white and Republican-leaning districts around them. Some savvily pushed for a straight renewal of the VRA, recognizing that across an increasingly solid Republican South, Powell and the Supreme Court had coated the dirty work in high-minded legalese in *Mobile v. Bolden*. Whites across the South would now reap political advantage with VRA enforcement that much more difficult. Others wanted to go even further, citing rising Black voter registration rates across the states covered by the VRA and declaring, as John Roberts would fatefully do from the bench in 2013, that things had changed in the South and it was time to turn the page.

William French Smith, Reagan's first attorney general, came to DOJ following a career in both corporate law and as Reagan's personal attorney. His "courteous demeanor, conservative clothes and gray hair made him look the very model of a lawyer," wrote the *New York Times*. Smith's wealthy Boston upbringing and Harvard Law training made him equally at home in the boardroom or the Oval Office. Yet his politics were formed not in the moderate clubs of New England noblesse oblige but out west with Reagan.

The Civil Rights Division at the DOJ was run by William Bradford (Brad) Reynolds. Neas says that a moderate Republican senator, Charles Mathias of Maryland, guaranteed him that Reynolds was a Dupont and a Rockefeller Republican—someone whom everyone could work with. "Wrong, very wrong," Neas says now. "What I did not know," he says, is that Chuck Cooper "and two people who are now on the Supreme Court would quickly take hold of Brad and turn this moderate Republican into someone who four years later was defeated by the Senate Judiciary Committee controlled by the Republicans, because he wasn't enforcing the Voting Rights Act, among other important civil rights priorities."

But while Smith and Reynolds took the lead, according to Carvin, Roberts's colleague at DOJ, "Voting—that was John's fight. Always John's fight."

THE LEADERSHIP CONFERENCE on Civil Rights strategy—developed in weekly Friday meetings that often stretched toward midnight—was to stall the White House, sideline any early opposition, and build unstoppable momentum with a strong bipartisan bill through the House. Neas provided letters, notes, and many private papers. (The other essential contemporaneous history is a 1983 *Washington and Lee Law Review* article by Neas foe and future Federalist Society/Reagan DOJ intellectual masterminds Stephen Markman and Thomas M. Boyd.) The reasoning here was simple: the House was the one chamber Democrats still controlled, and by digging in there, the VRA's defenders could rely on the leadership and strategic savvy of Edwards and Rodino. In a perfect world, the White House would not take a position until the House acted and defined the debate. Neas articulated three crucial priorities for the VRA reauthorization: maintaining preclearance, extending the bilingual ballot provisions for another decade, and amending Section 2 to counteract the decision in *Mobile v. Bolden*, making it clear that discriminatory effects violated the VRA regardless of whether discriminatory intent could be proven in court.

"We were trying to buy time," Neas told me. "If we could not win on the Voting Rights Act, we probably could not win on anything. While the bills were introduced in the first week of April of 1981, the decision was made well before that to first get out of the House as soon as possible with the strongest bipartisan majority possible."

The bill Rodino introduced on April 7 addressed *Mobile v. Bolden* head-on: it effectively overturned that decision and codified the effects

standard. Section 2 now prohibited any qualification, prerequisite, or practice that led to the denial or abridgement of any citizens' right to vote due
to race or color. Congress reiterated that judges had the power to weigh
all the evidence—the full totality of circumstances—when examining the
impact and effects of voting practices on communities of color. "We had to
reverse *Mobile*," says Representative Edwards, the cochair of the House Judiciary Committee that would hold the first hearings on reauthorization.
"Had to. That was a must."

Henry Hyde, Edwards's GOP counterpoint on the civil and constitutional rights subcommittee, had different ideas. Hyde put forth his own
bill that eliminated Section 5 preclearance because it unfairly singled out
specific states. In an unfortunate metaphor, he compared preclearance to
making certain states "sit in the back of the bus." Hyde wanted to replace
preclearance with a national plan that he said would treat voting abuses
everywhere with the same intensity. Things had changed in the South over
the previous fifteen years, Hyde argued—another near-universal talking
point for supporters of today's backlash Right. Black voter registration had
improved nationwide. The number of Black elected officials had multiplied as well.

But when the subcommittee traveled to Austin, Texas, and Montgomery, Alabama, for field hearings to gather testimony from actual voters in
states covered by preclearance, not much seemed to have changed after all.
Members heard such shocking stories of brazen, present-day voter suppression that many minds were changed, including Hyde's. "The plight of
the deep South and Southwest, our sessions in Montgomery and Austin,"
says Edwards in his archived oral history, "it was like going back 100 years."
Edwards, a veteran of civil rights marches in Montgomery, observed that
"it's still tough down there. I marched in Montgomery and let me tell you
we didn't get a white smile. They just looked at us with daggers in their
eyes."

Hyde experienced something close to a full-conversion moment as
he listened. Dr. Joe Reed testified that while Alabama now allowed each
county to add deputy registrars to speed Black registration, only a dozen
had actually done so. Polling places, Reed explained, remained located in
"white private establishments" such as churches and private businesses,

creating a chilling effect while also forcing Black voters to travel a longer distance to the polls. In rural Choctaw County, members learned that not only did voters need to reregister every year, but that the county also only allowed registration between 9 A.M. and 4 P.M. During those hours, most Black citizens in the state worked in the fields, often thirty or forty miles away from the town offices.

"I want to say that I have listened with great interest and concern, and I will tell you, registration hours from 9 to 4 are outrageous. It is absolutely designed to keep people who are working and who have difficulty in traveling from registering," Hyde said. He was only getting started. "If that persists and exists, it is more than wrong. . . . The lack of deputy registrars, only 12 counties have them, demonstrates a clear lack of enthusiasm for getting people registered, obviously. The location of voting places, if what Mr. Reed says is true—and I don't doubt that it is—is a subtle intimidation of black people and is also wrong. The lack of blacks working as polling officials is wrong."

Hyde went before reporters after the hearing and made a shocking admission for a politician. "I was wrong," he conceded, "and now I want to be right." Days later, he revised his bill accordingly, moving much closer to the Leadership Conference's position. It was the crucial conversion that all but removed any serious opposition in the House—especially since DOJ officials wouldn't testify at all. "The Justice Department wouldn't answer our phone calls. They refused to testify. About 80 career lawyers, people who had been filing their cases for 15 years almost had a revolt down there," said Edwards, "because Justice was not enforcing the law."

When Hyde returned to Washington, he agreed to protect Section 5 but suggested an easier route to allow localities to "bail out" of coverage. Democrats pushed to make those standards tougher. Rodino offered language to assure Republicans that the new effects standard would not lead to quotas—a flashpoint for the new administration on race—or proportional representation for minorities. The compromise cleared the committee 23–1 and then went for debate on the full House floor.

Hyde urged his old friend Reagan to support the bill. In a letter Hyde sent to the president on July 20, he advised Reagan that "[i]f you move quickly you may be able to broaden your constituency by eliminating a fear that plagues the black community most, that the time will soon return when they [are] literally unable to vote or . . . made to feel that they have no meaningful impact whatsoever on their destiny."

Reagan seemed to listen. In June 1981, the president went before the National Association for the Advancement of Colored People (NAACP) annual convention in Denver. He was greeted with stony silence for calling government affirmative action programs "a new kind of bondage"—but he also vowed that he would make "equal treatment of all citizens" his "primary responsibility," and never "permit a barrier to come between a secret ballot and any citizen who makes a choice to cast it."

On October 5, 1981, the reauthorized VRA cleared the House with a stunning bipartisan mandate, 389 to 24.

Yet despite the conversion of key Republicans on the Hill, and the reluctance of the administration to take an aggressive stance, one person would not yield that easily: John Roberts.

ROBERTS STARTED AT the DOJ as a special assistant in the Civil Rights Division on August 14, 1981, just weeks after completing his clerkship with Rehnquist. The DOJ hired him at $46,685 a year. He still lived with Richard Lazarus in the brick Capitol Hill row house at 602 North Carolina Avenue, but he didn't spend much time there.

Ken Starr threw Roberts right into high-profile work. He immediately took over responsibility for preparing Sandra Day O'Connor for her Senate confirmation hearings. After O'Connor took her seat on the first Monday in October, voting rights became Roberts's central focus. Fein remembers the DOJ as the hub of opposition to overturning the intent test from *Mobile v. Bolden*, and the headquarters for the only conservatives inside the administration willing to fight for race-neutral principles. Roberts, he told me, was the architect of it all.

"The Justice Department was the only one who went to the White House and said, 'Listen, this is not necessary. It's going to be a huge mess legally. No one knows what the hell this intent stuff means,'" Fein told me. But Reagan's closest advisers thought this was a fight they should avoid,

almost impossible to win given the numbers in Congress, and a loser politically should they pull out an unlikely win.

"Some people," Fein adds dismissively, "never think long range."

That wasn't the case with the DOJ's crew, particularly Roberts, whose
DOJ tenure probably marked the first time since high school that he was
surrounded by like-minded peers. The effects test became his personal
bête noire. Roberts became a man obsessed, driven to have his viewpoint
carry the day. As the Voting Rights Act debate moved to the Senate, Roberts worked ten- to twelve-hour days, sometimes longer, often through the
weekend; in his papers at the National Archives, Roberts says he worked
more than sixty-hour weeks. He drafted memos and talking points, scripted
draft answers for his bosses to deliver in meetings or during congressional
testimony, and assembled presentations for senators and other staff on the
Hill. Roberts also devoted himself to publicizing the war on the effects test.

In a foreshadowing of the strategy Roberts would display on the court
with voting rights and democracy issues, the memos show that he crafted
strategies that allowed DOJ to undermine voting rights without looking
like extremists. His files at the National Archives, released after his 2005
nomination to the high court, show how Roberts devised messaging strategies that made it possible for the administration to thread the savvy line
of supporting reauthorization, while rendering the VRA practically neutered by opposing any change from an intent to an effects test. He crafted
his own op-eds to run in newspapers, offering them under the byline of
anyone in the department who might want them published, as well as longer pieces for more academic publications. He also engaged in the rising
right-wing obsession with alleged liberal media bias, distributing news
clips on the issue and critiquing individual stories and editorials that ran
in the *New York Times* and *Washington Post*.

"He was intimately involved in that. Definitely, intimately involved,"
says Fein now. "John, more than anyone, was very familiar with the voting
rights stuff."

But Roberts's long hours, voluminous memos, and relentless lobbying
started from a tough position. Before Roberts joined the DOJ, pragmatists
inside the White House who wanted to avoid the political messiness of any

fight over voting rights appeared to hold the winning hand, particularly after the lopsided House reauthorization vote. Over the summer, Reagan had slowly moved toward embracing reauthorization that included the House's language on effects and walked back *Mobile v. Bolden*. He told Black leaders that he finally understood why extending preclearance nationally—stretching the limited resources of the DOJ's Civil Rights Division thin and forcing lawyers to review every change, rather than simply those in the states with the most damaging histories—would actually weaken Section 5 enforcement where it was needed most. Hyde told Reagan that his former proposal of equal-intensity enforcement would actually "hug the Voting Rights Act to death." Reagan told Black leaders that he "did not want to do that."

The DOJ had pushed back, and anonymous sources told the media that Reagan actually hadn't officially made up his mind about reauthorization. But as Roberts arrived in August the real fight was on: Reagan had just told the *Washington Star* that he would back a ten-year reauthorization and that he would oppose national preclearance because it "might make [the VRA] so cumbersome as to not be effectively workable." (Roberts, relentlessly committed to the long game, would revive the idea of national preclearance as chief justice with his decisions in both *Northwest Austin Municipal Utility District Number One v. Holder* and *Shelby County*.)

That left the question of intent versus effects as the last significant hurdle. At first, Roberts and the DOJ appeared to lose here as well. Smith delivered a report to Reagan in October, reiterating the DOJ's opposition to the results test and its desire to hold fast to *Mobile v. Bolden*. Even this push seemed to be fruitless. In early November, the White House prepared a statement that would have announced that Reagan would support whatever Congress decided to do on the VRA and released it to the *New York Times*. The statement effectively conceded to the VRA's backers on the new results standard and abandoned the court's decision in *City of Mobile v. Bolden*.

A furious Smith raced the six and a half blocks up Pennsylvania Avenue and demanded a meeting with the president. He'd been prepped with fresh talking points from John Roberts. They worked. A new battle was joined. After that meeting, the *Times* would need to rewrite its story. Reagan embraced two of Smith's proposals: making it easier for southern localities to escape preclearance and "bail out" of coverage, and retaining the intent standard. "The statement was issued," the *Times* noted, "after last-minute skirmishing between White House aides and Attorney General William French Smith, who fought to make the statement more conservative than originally planned."

Reagan now declared the effects standard "new and untested"—a position that clearly hewed almost word for word with Roberts's talking points. In his end-of-the-year news conference, Reagan channeled Roberts and his DOJ allies again. "We believe that the intent was a useful thing in that bill because there have been communities and areas of the country who have proven, without question, their total adherence to voting rights for all their people, and yet the difficulty of them then escaping the provisions of the law which impose a burden on them are still denied," Reagan said. "The effect rule could lead to the type of thing in which effect could be judged if there was some disproportion in the number of public officials who were elected at any governmental level, and so forth. And we don't think that that was what the bill intended or that that would be a fair test. You could come down to where all of society had to have an actual quota system."

This was almost exactly what Roberts wrote in his December 1981 memo, "Why Section 2 of the Voting Rights Act Should Remain Unchanged." "The House-passed version of Section 2 would in effect establish a right in racial and language minorities to electoral representation proportional to their population in the community," Roberts claimed. "Incorporation of an effects test in Section 2 would establish essentially a quota system for electoral politics."

John Roberts had helped orchestrate a shift on the Voting Rights Act at the highest level of the administration. And he was now scripting the president's statements on the year's most crucial civil rights debate. The Voting Rights Act had just celebrated its fifteenth anniversary, yet the combination of Powell's decision in *Mobile v. Bolden* and Roberts's crafty, determined work inside the administration created the most direct and consequential effort from the Right to undo the promise of multiracial democracy and wrestle control of elections and election law back toward white conservatives and the GOP. Roberts had placed the administration into a fiercely pitched intent-versus-effects fight that Reagan's wisest political counselors thought unwise and unnecessary. Yet at every step of the battle, Roberts refused to concede a rhetorical inch and muscled onward. This fight would define his tenure at DOJ; indeed, combined with his patient jurisprudence on the Supreme Court that has pushed election law inexorably in the same rightward direction, it is easy to call it John Roberts's lifework.

The next front would be before the U.S. Senate. Roberts would write much of the script again. And the team in DOJ would find themselves aligned with the most stubborn southern segregationists and senators from the whitest states in the nation.

CHAPTER SIX

JOHN ROBERTS HATED the idea of White House papers being released to the public. When young Roberts worked as a counsel to Ronald Reagan, he took a vociferous stance against turning over internal documents to a Senate committee as part of the confirmation process. He described the Presidential Records of Act of 1978—which governs when White House files become available in presidential libraries—as "pernicious." In an August 1985 memo, he expressed concern that "By 2001, Hill staffers need only go to the Reagan Library to see any internal White House deliberative document they want to see." Ten days later, he warned that the act could have a chilling effect on White House debate.

"Twelve years is a brief lifetime in public life," Roberts noted. "Many of the personalities candidly discussed in sensitive White House memoranda, and certainly many of the authors of the memoranda, will be active 12 years from now."

The force of his opposition suggests that the ever-cautious and ambitious Roberts, then just thirty, wondered whether his own memos might someday become public, perhaps even as part of a future confirmation hearing. The young lawyer proved prescient. It's these hundreds of pages of Roberts's own writings from his early days at Justice that reveal the deep roots of his issues with the Voting Rights Act as well as the outsize role he played during the 1982 reauthorization. They provide a portrait of a young ideologue despite his carefully curated image of scarcely having been touched by ideology at all.

More important, they show an ideology—even a zealotry—that has already been fully formed: the John Roberts who battled to immobilize the

VRA in 1982 contains an eerie echo of the chief justice who would have the final word four decades later.

WHEN JOHN ROBERTS opened his newspaper on November 16, 1981, he discovered a column by Vernon Jordan, the head of the National Urban League, titled "Diluting Voting Rights." Like so many debates about race and voting rights, the last round of the battle over intent versus effects would begin on the op-ed page of the *New York Times*.

Roberts could not have liked what he read. Jordan opened his argument sounding much like the pragmatic Reagan aides. Reagan's endorsement of the intent standard "was not only a political mistake," Jordan wrote, but a "disservice" to a conservatism that "venerates constitutional rights, individual freedom, and protection of civil rights from Government abuse." A muscular Voting Rights Act, he argued, is "in essence a deeply conservative law."

Then the Black civil rights leader lowered the boom. Intent to discriminate, he wrote, is impossible to prove. "Local officials don't wallpaper their offices with memos about how to restrict minority-group members' access to the polling booth," Jordan wrote. "Discriminatory effects are clear to all." Proving intent, he argued, shifted and required the burden of proof and required evidence that "would be virtually impossible to assemble."

"The President's endorsement of the Voting Rights Act," he concluded, "is a sham."

Jordan's op-ed sent the Department of Justice into a tizzy. Roberts and his colleagues convened multiple meetings to discuss how they might respond. The following morning, Roberts drafted a response and circulated it to Smith, Reynolds, Fein, and Starr, "if anyone is interested in appropriating all or parts of it."

In a pugnacious response, discovered in Roberts's papers at the National Archives, Roberts insists that the intent test would make a "radical change" to the Voting Rights Act and slams the congressional version that included the broader effects test as an "untested piece of legislation" and a "radical experiment" in a law that "has been so widely praised for its effectiveness." Roberts conceded that local officials might not wallpaper racist memos in their offices, but he insisted that "circumstantial evidence" would still suffice, "as Mr. Jordan presumably knows." Roberts reached for an old saw in his conclusion: "As the old saying goes, if it isn't broken, don't fix it."

It's hard to believe that this argument even convinced its author, since it does not grapple at all with the near impossibility of enforcing claims after *Mobile v. Bolden*. And as Roberts presumably knew, in blithely asserting that intent was readily provable, he ignored how *Mobile v. Bolden* had actually been tried. Bolden and his attorneys had presented decades of historical evidence, circumstantial evidence, and firsthand testimonials of widespread and devastating racist rigging of Mobile's civic and political life, all of which lower federal courts found convincing. And yet the Supreme Court, and his mentor Rehnquist, brushed it all aside.

"The only ones who could be disappointed by the President's actions," Roberts held, "are not those truly concerned about the right to vote but rather those who, for whatever reason, were simply spoiling for a fight that never materialized." Thus did a twenty-six-year-old Justice official who launched his career in conditions of segregated privilege dismiss Jordan's long-established integrity as an advocate for voting rights and racial justice.

Of course, this fight materialized due in no small part to Roberts's own persistence and determination. Roberts would pen almost two dozen additional memos urging the DOJ to stand firm behind *Mobile*'s intent standard. Meanwhile, while Roberts simmered, his chief legislative foes— Ralph Neas and the Leadership Conference—were quietly reconstituting a majority in the U.S. Senate that the DOJ's brothers would be hard-pressed to overcome.

DECADES LATER, WHEN Roberts used his influence as chief justice to unravel much of Section 2 and freeze Section 5 of the Voting Rights Act, he only needed to command a majority of five. The Senate had a much higher magic number: sixty, the number of senators necessary to stave off the filibuster. Opponents of civil rights had long mastered and refined this obstructionist parliamentary tactic to "talk bills to death" and prevent legislation with majority support from reaching the floor for a vote.

South Carolina senator Strom Thurmond held the record for the longest filibuster in Senate history for his twenty-four-hour-and-eighteen-
minute marathon against the Civil Rights Act of 1957. By the time the VRA
came up for reauthorization in 1982, Thurmond had risen to serve as the
chair of the Senate Judiciary Committee. Opponents of the VRA's effects
provision felt confident that they could engineer a host of obstructionist
feints and amendments to block its passage, up to and including another
filibuster.

So it meant something when Senators Ted Kennedy and Charles
Mathias, the bipartisan cosponsors in the Senate, filed their bill—including
the effects test—with sixty-one cosponsors. If the coalition of forty Democrats and twenty-one Republicans held, not only would the reauthorization pass easily but it would also overcome any filibuster. Neas remembers
that when NPR reporter Nina Totenberg informed Thurmond that sixty-
one senators introduced the reauthorization together, the old segregationist sputtered in disbelief. "They must not have read the bill!"

An equally stunned John Roberts prepared to fight on regardless. "Do
not be fooled by the House vote or the 61 Senate sponsors of the House bill
into believing that the President cannot win on this issue," Roberts wrote
in a January 1982 private memo to the attorney general. Roberts's allies
were dubious, his math was bad, and his political instincts worse, but he
urged his troops onward, confident in his own assessment of Congress.
"Many members of the House did not know they were doing more than
simply extending the Act, and several of the 61 Senators have already indicated that they only intended to support simple extension," he wrote.

"Once the senators are educated on the differences between the President's position and the House bill, and the serious dangers in the House
bill," Roberts insisted, "solid support will emerge for the President's position."

THE DAY BEFORE the Senate Judiciary Committee was set to begin its hearings,
the administration abruptly asked to delay the attorney general's testimony
for a week. Roberts, however, remained focused. On January 21, 1982, he

sent Attorney General Smith six pages of draft questions and answers to help vet Smith's testimony.

The memo bears vivid and shocking testimony to the crusade that would shape Roberts's career—an Inspector Javert–style obsession with clawing back the central provisions of the Voting Rights Act. In his behind-the-scenes brief to his boss, it's clear that there's simply no improvement to the VRA that Roberts is willing to countenance. At one point, he advises Smith that if the Senate committee questions him about the role of results-based patterns of discrimination in determining violations of the VRA, the attorney general should push back firmly. That posture should even hold, Roberts wrote, in cases such as the lower-court ruling in *City of Mobile v. Bolden*, which affirmed such a pattern going back to Alabama's 1901 Jim Crow state constitution—a document whose own conveners readily admitted was drafted to enshrine white supremacy. "It would seem odd to legislate against existing practices more stringently now, after there has been so much progress, than Congress did in 1965," Roberts wrote.

When he detailed his objections to the effects test, Roberts supplied a tendentious account of supposed open-minded inquiry that pointedly ignored the testimony of experts and misrepresented the words of civil rights leaders. He counseled Smith to tell Congress that "In reviewing the Voting Rights Act last summer in the course of preparing recommendations to the President, I met personally with scores of civil rights leaders." Roberts wrote, "The one theme from these discussions was clear: the Act has been the most successful civil rights legislation ever enacted and it should be extended unchanged. As the old saying goes, if it isn't broken, don't fix it." Here Roberts was merely parroting an earlier talking point he'd circulated during the House debate; it had nothing to do with the actual views of civil rights leaders who, in fact, were determined at all costs to repair the defective *Mobile* decision.

Roberts's rhetorical counsel didn't end with dubious paraphrases from civil rights leaders, which would have been contrary to everything they said in public. His memos encouraged Smith to double down on loose talk of racial quotas before Thurmond's committee, contending without any empirical backing that the effects test "would establish a quota system for electoral politics"—here he underlined quota system—which "we believe is fundamentally inconsistent with democratic principles."

Five days later, on January 26, Roberts again urged Smith to stiffen his resolve on the effects question as the attorney general prepared to begin his testimony the next day. The same day, Roberts also attended a crucial meeting at the White House where DOJ officials sought to shore up Reagan's opposition to the effects test—"once and for all," as a seemingly frustrated Roberts wrote.

In this final prehearing memo, the young aide exhorted his boss as follows: "I recommend taking a very positive and aggressive stance." Roberts followed the same counsel in the White House meeting; he had clearly grown weary of all the bureaucratic skirmishing with Reagan's political team who still disagreed with the DOJ, and he demanded that the White House "actively work" to enact the DOJ's policy. He insisted his position could be sold politically. "The President's opinion is a very positive one," Roberts wrote, repeating his pet mantra. "If it isn't broken, don't fix it."

In the White House confab and his memos, Roberts further maintained that the effects test would "throw into litigation existing electoral systems at every level of government nationwide when there is no evidence of voting abuses nationwide supporting the need for such a change." Roberts also again sought to tie opposition to the effects test to the administration's overall stance on race and affirmative action. "Just as we oppose quotas in employment and education, so too we oppose them in elections."

"It is very important that the fight be won, and the President is fully committed to this effort," Roberts concluded. "His staff should be as well."

No one could question Roberts's own commitment. That day he sent Smith yet another memo, a two-page response to an editorial in the *Washington Post* that endorsed the effects test and again enraged Roberts. Throughout the reauthorization fight, Roberts took a personal role in directing the DOJ's communication strategy. He edited op-eds under the names of several different DOJ officials and even ghost-wrote opinion pieces aimed at small regional newspapers.

In early February 1982, in a memo to Brad Reynolds, Roberts offered extensive handwritten edits on a draft op-ed that he thought needed to strike a more muscular and aggressive tone in opposition to the results test. "I do not agree with the Attorney General that it is necessary to 'talk down' to the audience," Roberts proclaimed, before demanding that the DOJ strike back quickly. "The frequent writings in this area by our adversaries have gone unanswered for too long," he wrote. In the piece, Roberts now claimed that "no one" has "shown any need whatsoever" for an effects test, and that if Congress enacted one, that action would polarize the nation along racial lines. "Too much progress has been made for Congress now to countenance such a backward step."

ROBERTS MUST HAVE known that no matter how many op-eds he wrote, he'd never change the tide of elite opinion. He would also come to learn that no matter how cleverly he reframed the argument, he'd never bring minority voters around to his pinched views on the Voting Rights Act. Still, he remained hopeful that his position would prevail in the Senate, the least democratic branch of the national legislature.

In one scenario, Roberts could pick off at least two senators from the cosponsor list and put the filibuster back in play. In another, the Senate might pass the bill with fewer than sixty-seven votes, putting a presidential veto in play if the DOJ could convince the White House to disown the effects test as a politically unpopular racial quota system being applied to the voting process. In still another encouraging prospect, Roberts might bank on the Senate's own penchant for prolonged legislative inertia; the VRA could be bottled up in the Judiciary Committee or a subcommittee, with progress slowed to a crawl as expiration dates for crucial provisions approached. With much of the VRA slated to expire in 1982 without reauthorization, such a procedural slowdown could give DOJ and its Senate allies a powerful negotiating cudgel.

Whatever obstructionist vision beguiled him most, Roberts seemed determined to make some slowdown or reversal happen, and he worked the Senate hard. He assembled clip packages of anti–results test op-eds for senators and their aides. He sent friendly offices his essay called "Why Section Two of the Voting Rights Should Be Retained Unchanged." He ran this offensive by Starr, with a handwritten note on the attorney general's letterhead: "Ken, possibilities to distribute to senators. John."

Recalcitrant senators hit the brakes. Orrin Hatch's subcommittee, after six weeks of hearings, focused almost entirely on intent versus effects—restored the original language on intent and rejected the House revisions. Hatch hailed the vote for forestalling a nightmarish turn in American life "in which considerations of race and ethnicity intrude into each and every policy decision," and predicted America would continue to move toward "a constitutional color-blind society."

The Senate bill then moved to Thurmond's kingdom, the full Judiciary Committee. Nine senators backed the House language on effects, seven opposed it, and two had not announced an intention either way. Senator Jesse Helms, a longtime civil rights opponent, spotted his opportunity to maneuver the Senate's confusing procedural rules and grind everything to a halt.

Senator Bob Dole, however, a moderate Republican from Kansas, one of the two undecideds, had seen enough. Dole was determined that his party preserve its image as the party of Lincoln and not the party of Thurmond. "It was a no-brainer," Dole said in a 2015 interview. He quietly forged a bipartisan compromise with Kennedy and Mathias. Section 2 would carry a results standard that rolled back *Mobile v. Bolden* and codified the exact "totality of circumstances" language from *White v. Regester*. The language of the accompanying Senate report could not have been clearer. A "finding of the appropriate factors showing current dilution is sufficient, without any need to decide whether those findings, by themselves, or with additional circumstantial evidence, also would warrant an inference of discriminatory purpose." In case there was any lingering doubt over what that meant, the senators added this: "The main reason [for rejecting the intent test] is that, simply put, the test asks the wrong question." Dole went to the White House and informed Reagan that he and the DOJ, of course, were welcome to continue the fight—but they'd lose because he had eighty votes in hand.

"I didn't always agree with Dole," former Connecticut senator Lowell Weicker told me, "but on this occasion, he stood up to the right people in a wonderful way."

Thurmond knew that eighty was an insurmountable number even in the majority-averse Senate and declined to filibuster. "Strom Thurmond came over. He can count Black votes," Representative Edwards added.

"As I've said before, the right to vote is the crown jewel of American liberties, and we will not see its luster diminished," Reagan said days later at a White House signing ceremony for the freshly reauthorized VRA.

BACK OVER AT the DOJ, the band of brothers didn't seethe so much as they threw up their hands in politically chastened resignation. They'd won big intra-administration battles. But in the end, they recognized what they were up against.

"The Reagan administration took the principled view over the politically advantageous," says Carvin, "and then they eventually caved. They got the Dole compromise and caved."

"William French Smith came over to us and said we lost [Reagan]," says Fein. "We were the only ones fighting. So we just moved on. Smith, Brad, John, we lost."

They consoled themselves with realpolitik, convinced that elected officials just didn't have any incentive to destroy the status quo—especially when the price of opposition was being labeled a racist.

"Whether you agree with them or not, we didn't have dumb people. They're not racist," Fein says. "They're people who are Harvard and Yale and think and they write books and they're philosophical and deep. John, Scalia, racist? Are you kidding?" Fein laughs out loud. "They don't have a racist bone in their body. But they understood what happens. That's why John used to say it was a racial spoil system."

Judges, however, didn't have to worry about politics. Judges could interpret and enforce statutes based on legal principles without having to worry about fielding hostile op-eds, confronting a skeptical news media, or winning reelection. If conservatives were serious about unwinding what they viewed as special racial preferences wrapped up in the Voting Rights Act, it made no sense to keep fighting in Congress. The lesson was obvious to all: the road to granting the GOP increased dominion over elections would come through the courts. After all, it was the Supreme Court that had nearly brought the VRA to its knees; if there was one branch of government strong enough to withstand the political blowback from such seismic change, it was the Supreme Court. This change, though, required an effort to put conservatives on the bench, and to arm them with a clear legal philosophy, tricked out in the enabling fiction of a race-neutral, color-blind Constitution.

In the months to come, Stephen Markman would move from Hatch's team on the Senate Judiciary Commission to the Justice Department. There, he'd join the alliance in a drive to extend the Reagan Revolution to the federal judiciary. And from the legal academy, still more help was on the way. That April, as the lonely DOJ warriors battled fiercely if quix-otically, young conservative law students, joined by mentors such as Rob-ert Bork, Antonin Scalia, and Ted Olson, had the very first meeting of the conservative legal clearinghouse that would become the Federalist Society. The merry band would have reinforcements, a new strategy, and, soon, friends in high places.

"John has seen this [special racial preferences] seep into the culture and knows that if the court doesn't end it then it will never end," Carvin says. "I do think our strong feelings about all this comes from the fact that we were dealing with these arguments in 1982 and 1983."

When Roberts and Alito arrived at the Supreme Court in 2005, the same arguments would carry the day—not because things had actually changed in the South or the underlying terms of intellectual engagement had shifted, but because the arena and the players moved from Congress and the White House over to the judiciary. The lesson was simple: if you want to change the law, change the judges. In the courts, you didn't need 60 senators or 218 representatives, or to sway a presidential team look-ing at public opinion polls. There, five like-minded conservatives would be more than enough.

CHAPTER SEVEN

BY APRIL 1982, Washington's conservative revolution seemed to be in abeyance. Unemployment approached 10 percent for the first time since World War II, and the sour economy pulled Ronald Reagan's approval ratings underwater for the first time in his presidency. A frustrated John Roberts had struggled to convince a Republican Senate to hold strong on the intent test. Conservatives emerged from this yearlong battle more convinced than ever that Powell and Horowitz were right: the path to power and the surest way to control American elections did not run through Congress, but the courts.

Conservatives would never be able to rewrite something as popular and consequential as the Voting Rights Act through the legislative process. A frontal assault on the Voting Rights Act was simply bad politics even for many conservatives. They needed conservative judges—true believers who would not shrink from making unpopular decisions, who pledged fealty to a clear judicial ideology, and with the backbone and temperament to defend that approach even when it ran contrary to elite Washington thinking or the op-ed page of the *New York Times*. This required a religion of sorts, the comfort of a text, and a Sunday morning gathering where the like-minded held one another responsible: call it the hymnal of Originalism, combined with the community swaddling of the Federalist Society.

This was not a simple lift. Reagan swept into the White House talking about a transformed judiciary, but in the nation's law schools, it still felt like Carter won a massive electoral mandate and Earl Warren still presided over a liberal-minded court. A small cadre of conservative law students— fulfilling the vision of the Horowitz Report—dared to imagine a radically different future. The nascent Federalist Society would be devoted to wiping out these liberal legacies.

"There was no forum at the law schools for discussion of those ideas. They weren't taken seriously," says one of the Society's founders, Lee Liberman Otis, a first-year law student at the University of Chicago, where Professor Antonin Scalia taught before Reagan nominated him to the federal bench.

To be a conservative law student in 1982, particularly at one of the nation's elite schools, was to feel outnumbered and surrounded. In much of your daily life, you could be expected to be treated as an oddball figure, subject to amused contempt. The television sitcom *Family Ties*, starring Michael J. Fox as a young Reaganite high schooler never understood by his liberal, hippie parents, wouldn't debut until the fall, but it would have felt immediately familiar to Liberman Otis, Steven Calabresi, Gene Meyer, Spencer Abraham, David McIntosh, and Gary Lawson, among other young right-wing legal thinkers who would together launch and lead the Federalist Society and build what has become perhaps the most consequential political organization in modern American history.

Liberman Otis, Calabresi, and McIntosh could hardly imagine that they would remake America's judiciary in their image and have a profound effect on the nation's elections when they met as undergraduates at Yale through the Political Union, a campus debate society. They came from different backgrounds and (initially) diverse political persuasions. Calabresi, whose uncle would become dean of Yale Law and a liberal judge appointed to the bench by Bill Clinton, voted for Jimmy Carter in 1976 before the nation's late '70s malaise brought him under Reagan's spell. Liberman Otis had been a student volunteer for Reagan as far back as 1976. Meyer, meanwhile, another Yalie, came from conservative royalty; his father, Frank, was a senior editor at *National Review* and an influential New Right political philosopher. The Yale friends spent the summer after graduation living together in a group house just across the Potomac from Washington, D.C., and holding down a variety of internships. But they forged their most enduring ideological bonds at home, as they came of political and intellectual age: debating, arguing, persuading, first with each other—and then after arriving at law school, realizing the kinds of discussions they had over drinks and dinners, about issues and ideas, simply weren't happening in Cambridge and New Haven.

The day after the 1980 presidential election, Calabresi later told CNN, his torts professor at Yale Law tossed his prepared lecture aside to console a shell-shocked class. When he asked if any of the ninety students had backed Reagan, only Calabresi and one other classmate raised their hands. In Noah Feldman's audiobook *Takeover: How a Conservative Student Club Took Over the Supreme Court*, Gary Lawson, another Yale Law student, told the author that "any time a student in class said anything that could remotely be considered right of center, a good chunk of the class would hiss."

In response to what they experienced as a stultifying preserve of intellectual conformity, Calabresi, Lawson, and a handful of other exotic Yale Law school conservatives started a club where they could discuss these ideas. Liberman Otis and McIntosh did the same at the University of Chicago. That spring, they planned a weekend at Yale where they could talk about originalism and the proper role of judges. They invited their intellectual heroes, like Bork and Scalia, to lecture, along with prominent conservatives from the Reagan administration, including Ted Olson and veteran grassroots mobilizer Morton Blackwell.

Together, they crafted a mission statement for what they called "A Symposium on Federalism: Legal and Political Ramifications." Law schools and the legal profession, they wrote, "are currently strongly dominated by a form of orthodox liberal ideology" and "no comprehensive conservative critique or agenda has been formulated in this field. This conference will furnish an occasion for such a response to begin to be articulated."

The young scholars crafted a set of founding principles that still guide the Society to this day—principles that have the ring of objectivity even as they plainly advance the ideological aims of the conservative legal movement. That agenda came across forcefully in the group's founding apothegms: "The state exists to preserve freedom," one typical flourish went; another held that "the separation of governmental powers is central to our Constitution." Most important was the claim—borrowing from Chief Justice John Marshall in *Marbury v. Madison*—that "it is emphatically the province and duty of the judiciary to say what the law is, not what it should be." Or, as Gary Lawson, who had a hand in writing all these maxims, told Feldman in *Takeover*, "A pompous way of saying just get the law right. Don't make up crap."

What the Federalist crew lacked in campus camaraderie they more than compensated for with ambition and smarts. The *National Review* promoted the gathering with a brief listing. Liberman Otis, already a skilled networker and fundraiser, leveraged an introduction from Scalia into a grant from the conservative Institute of Economic Affairs. The Olin Foundation and other conservative donors—primed by the Horowitz Report to look favorably on opportunities to cultivate conservative thought inside law schools—picked up the rest of the $25,000 needed to seed the weekend. "I think this will be a lot of fun," Liberman Otis wrote Bork, "particularly watching the reaction of Yale, which will think it has created a Frankenstein monster."

It's hard to imagine a greater return on investment in the history of movement politics. or a university symposium so momentous. By 2023, six members of the U.S. Supreme Court would be Federalist Society members or close intimates. And that institutional takeover was but the crowning flourish of a networking and fundraising combine that remade the legal profession from the ground up. Well before Amy Coney Barrett, the most recent high court member bearing Federalist Society credentials, took her seat, Society membership had become the crucial credential for any young law student hoping to advance in the conservative legal movement. That credentialing status reflected still another facet of the Federalist Society's power: since the midaughts, members had routinely vetted—and effectively wielded veto power over—every major appointee to the bench by a Republican president.

"Steve Calabresi, at least, if not all the founders, had a vision for a broad conservative counterelite, not just a group in a law school. That was always in the DNA of the organization," says Amanda Hollis-Brusky, author of the masterful *Ideas Have Consequences*, a 2015 history of the organization and its influence.

"It just took a little while to develop the resources, and then they attracted the kinds of patrons and supporters who had access to power, who credentialed the organization and started placing their members in the

Justice Department and the White House counsel's office," she says. "And that's when you get the pipeline to clerkships and judgeships and ultimately the Supreme Court."

The ambition was there from the beginning. To host the founding conference, Calabresi booked the biggest room at Yale law school: room 127, a lecture hall out of a movie like *The Paper Chase*. No one really dreamed the group could fill it. The *New York Times* sent a reporter to Yale Law that weekend to cover two debut conferences, the Federalist Society and a Black alumni gathering. The *Times* reporter wrote with astonishment that the young conservatives drew nearly twice as many people. Lawson, who worked the registration table that weekend, couldn't believe it either.

"I'm sitting there . . . expecting a couple dozen people, maybe," Lawson told Feldman. Instead, hundreds arrived who had not even preregistered. "I'm asking them, do you have any place to stay? No. Do you have a sleeping bag?"

Young attendees traveled miles and slept on floors for the chance to listen to Scalia, Bork, and others. It was a golden opportunity to chat with thinkers who had fueled their own awakening—and perhaps most important, to surround themselves with fellow iconoclasts eager to think and argue as they all had hoped they'd be encouraged to do in law school.

Antonin Scalia encouraged the young law students to find intellectual courage in numbers. He read from *Federalist* 49: "The reason of man, like man himself, is timid and cautious when left alone, and acquits firmness and confidence in proportion to the number with which it is associated."

Ted Olson made a bold prediction: "I sense that we are at one of those points in history where the pendulum may be beginning to swing in another direction."

For his part, Robert Bork focused on a pet theme of the modern legal Right: a high court that he claimed was legislating morality based on their own "middle-class values." He insisted—as the Roberts Court would later help codify—that certain issues, including privacy, voting rights, contraception, and abortion, were best left to state legislatures, not federal judges.

Morton Blackwell, meanwhile, urged the new cohort of young legal conservatives to "study how to win." The special assistant to the president told them that "you should be the prime source of expertise" on topics including "how to succeed as a conservative in law school," "how to get a good clerking job," "how to become a judge," and "how to make sure the right people get to be judges."

The young people in room 127 that weekend would heed Blackwell's counsel closely. In short order, they'd fan out to the Justice Department, to the bench, to law school faculties nationwide.

Spencer Abraham had recently cofounded the *Harvard Journal of Law and Public Policy*; it became the Federalist Society's own law review, at a time when very few reputable law reviews would publish an article suggesting the Constitution should be interpreted according to its original public meaning. (Olin and the conservative Institute for Educational Affairs stepped in to fund the journal after Harvard Law's administration declined to fund a FedSoc chapter, believing it would be too political.) "That becomes an outlet to publish Federalist Society conference transcripts that are then refined into law review articles. And it's Harvard—so you have that immediate brand recognition," Hollis-Brusky says. It's now one of the top-circulated law reviews in the nation.

"The vibe was really one of excitement. This was a genuinely grassroots organization, started by students coming out of nowhere with lots of exciting and important ideas," says Michael McConnell, who would become a circuit judge on the U.S. Court of Appeals and later the director of the Constitutional Law Center at Stanford Law School, in Feldman's *Takeover*. "I think many people there really did have the sense that this was an organization that was going to make a difference."

LIBERMAN OTIS, MEYER, and Calabresi weren't the only conservatives who felt isolated in the early 1980s. Edwin Meese, Reagan's attorney general during his second term, felt that way in the Oval Office. "It was very lonely," Meese told me. Meese had been one of the original recruits to Reagan's unvarnished brand of backlash politics, going back to his tenure as his chief of staff in California. Like the leading lights of the Federalist Society, Meese wanted to remake the judiciary with a conservative tilt. Yet he learned during his years by Reagan's side in Sacramento that a well-organized network of liberal judges, law professors, law students, and public interest law firms could thwart conservative policies even when Republicans took office.

"We were interested in getting back to what the Constitution actually said," Meese says. "That meant changing ideas, changing the way judges were ruling, and also doing something to set an example for other lawyers and professors to make constitutionalism the thing to do. Which, of course, it should have been."

Meese wanted a well-organized network of his own. Reagan wanted to put conservatives on the bench. The trouble, Meese said, was identifying them. After all, Richard Nixon had made the same vow to transform a liberal Supreme Court. But even though Nixon had named four justices over three years, the court maintained a stolidly liberal profile on social issues and other hot-button topics—such as abortion, school busing, and capital punishment (business and race were another matter, with Powell rapidly helping to move the court rightward on those fronts).

"The Left has historically taken the view that we control the law schools and the curriculum. That's their pipeline," former Reagan administration economic adviser Bruce Bartlett told me. "They never understood there are alternative systems out there." The Right had a long-term plan to build those networks, generate academics, and credentialize lawyers and experts. "They understood that this is a multidecade process and they were willing to do that. Now they are reaping the benefits."

"That's what the Federalist Society has done over years and years and years," says Judge Michael Luttig in an interview. "I mean, even over years by *individual*. I'm not just saying that they've done this for more than forty years, I'm saying they've done this for forty years *individual by individual*. The rest of the world would call them a bunch of nerds. No one would ever want to sit there and listen to their conferences or seminars. But this is what they do. It's not dishonest. It just takes work, and a desire to sit down years and years and years in advance so you know what someone thinks and how he thinks.

"If you take the time, as the conservative movement has, they know that person better than anything in the world."

MEESE PROVIDED THE intellectual home. The Department of Justice—first under William French Smith with young stars such as Roberts and Alito, and then under the second-term leadership of Attorney General Meese— became the signature incubator of conservative ideas and conservative talent. In 1985, both Meese and his top assistant, T. Kenneth Cribb Jr., arrived at Justice with a clear ideological mission. If Smith managed the department with an eye toward meeting its pressing daily needs and often overwhelming caseload, his successors sought the headier game of institutional revolution. They wanted to transform the DOJ, the courts, and the law for decades to come. Steven Teles's 2009 article "Transformative Bureaucracy: Reagan's Lawyers and the Dynamics of Political Investment," first detailed the story; Patrick Gallagher filled in important additional details in his 2017 paper "The Conservative Incubator of Originalism."

They adopted the heretofore fringe academic doctrine of originalism and promoted it as a crucial part of that strategy. Originalism became the method to screen judges, the means of connecting the Right's policy agenda to the Constitution. For Meese, the originalist movement provided the platform that allowed him and his allies to reimagine the very nature of the department. Meese says he wanted to create a "think tank" within the department that could further develop originalist ideas. "It was a bit like a conservative legal think tank," Calabresi told Hollis-Brusky. "There was a very academic atmosphere to the department." Meese hired Liberman Otis and Calabresi, two cofounders of the Federalist Society, and in their wake, a stream of brilliant young conservatives poured into the DOJ.

Before the Federalist Society launched, staffing a revolution wasn't easy. Earlier Republican administrations typically relied on veteran blue blood business types to fill senior positions. But Reagan's DOJ wanted movement conservatives—and the stockpile of résumés for those candidates was much thinner. So Meese and Cribb created a career pipeline and mentored a rising generation of conservative lawyers. That pipeline was maintained and reinforced with the additional help of first-term Reagan officials and DOJ assistants who had now advanced at Justice or moved to the White House. "I thought the Federalist Society was the best damn idea that had come along in 20 years," said Brad Reynolds, Roberts's boss in the Civil Rights Division, to Jonathan Riehl in a 2007 graduate dissertation on the Federalist Society.

"Ed Meese asked me to hire experienced people, 'gray hairs,'" Cribb told me. "Well, there were no conservatives among the gray hairs." The true movement conservatives were younger and less experienced. The DOJ made a long-term investment in them; meanwhile Meese, Reynolds, Cooper, Cribb, and others in turn spoke at Federalist Society meetings, both sharpening the debate and building the network. "The typical assistant in the Meese Justice Department was in his mid-30s. We did the same thing with judges, we put a lot of young judges on the bench. We filled up those slots all across the Department with people who were in the Federalist Society . . . and it made a difference," Cribb told Riehl. "For the period from 1986 to 1987 the spark of the whole administration was at Justice, because that's where the brainpower was."

At the same time, the DOJ rebranded originalism, not as some fringe academic theory or out-of-left-field notion, but as a commonsense approach to the law that came across in popular discourse as a studiously nonpartisan school of interpretation, grounded in historical wisdom. The leaders of Reagan's Justice Department understood that originalism could well furnish the most direct avenue to the wholesale ideological makeover of the courts.

In public and when questioned by reporters, officials denied that originalism was a Trojan horse designed to create outcomes desired by conservatives. But private memos that circulated among the DOJ brain trust, many with Federalist Society ties, made the subtext clear: conservative legal activists embraced originalism as the best way to turn longtime right-wing priorities—especially when it came to race, voting rights, the regulatory state, and state control of elections—into settled law. Just as important, the originalist school supplied a ready-made intellectual framework for identifying movement-aligned candidates for the judiciary, promulgating law review articles that advanced conservative legal aims and supplying conservative professors with tenured academic gigs.

The Reagan Justice Department, like the conservative foundation world, was now investing in ideas. And because of their prominence in the newly networked right-wing legal universe, the Federalist Society's acolytes and allies helped ensure that the notions and themes refined in their debates would go on to transform the American judiciary, and then American elections. (Teles's article, "Transformative Bureaucracy," tells the story in great detail.)

"These ideas slowly became established," Meese told me. "The Federalist Society was catching on in the law schools. It was a combination of appointing judges, having this new organization really taking over in the law schools, all of this. And that in turn stirred the jurisprudence that people were writing about and talking about. It was a combination of several things that all came together at the right time."

In addition to reinventing his public affairs team as de facto propagandists for the agency's new right-wing mission and building a muscular Office of Legal Policy, Meese began stuffing the DOJ's work schedule with activities very much in line with his vision of the department as a uniquely high-powered think tank. "One of the things that I was particularly interested in was to increase the opportunities for intellectual activity by the people in the Justice Department, particularly the appointed people that I had brought in," Meese says. He held regular seminars at breakfast and lunchtime, even over the weekends. "We wanted to provide intellectual stimulation. We thought that the Justice Department should be a leader in the legal profession." These lunches attracted a host of legal luminaries aligned with the conservative movement, and soon became the stuff of movement lore.

But Meese was also overseeing far more consequential realignments within the heart of the DOJ bureaucracy. James "Mit" Spears, the new acting assistant attorney general for the Office of Legal Policy, had already proposed that his division serve as a center to help identify "judicial conservatives whose philosophy is well-defined and who are capable of exercising intellectual leadership on the bench." In March 1985, Spears sent Meese another memo detailing a more robust strategic approach to policy development and implementation. Such far-seeing directives are essential, he wrote, if "we are to rise above the tugs and pulls of daily business and achieve our long-range policy goals."

In his report, Spears laid out a public relations plan for the new originalist movement within Justice, as well as a behind-the-scenes lobbying effort to win wider acceptance for originalism among the general public and the legal world alike. After Reagan's campaign managers had sold him to the public as a stolid mainstream conservative leader, his legal team turned to the task of promoting originalism as the new face of conservative legal thinking—and packaged the product accordingly.

When we discussed his work at OLP, Spears downplayed any role he might have played in executing an overarching strategy to make originalism a signature Reagan franchise. "I'm just the country lawyer from Texas," he said, in a Roberts-style flourish of heartland modesty. Then I read him his memo.

"Well, yes," he conceded in abrupt backtracking mode. "I mean, you know, we had a plan."

In his March 18, 1985, memo, Spears first proposed testing the originalist message with a series of focus groups. "Meeting with leading conservative academics will help sharpen the development of our own constitutional doctrines and the arguments that must be made to obtain their acceptance," Spears wrote. "Also, it can help get the debate started in the academic community, which is of great help in paving the way for acceptance of new ideas by the courts." OLP would pitch in with a series of legal memoranda explaining why this new doctrine "represents the correct interpretation of the Constitution." At the same time, the originalist gospel had to be sold to the public. The next step, Spears wrote, was to "raise these issues in speeches and articles by the Attorney General, thus starting the debate in the political community and the editorial pages."

Farther down Pennsylvania Avenue, similar conversations, including Pat Buchanan, Bruce Fein, and John Roberts, were underway in the White House. According to White House documents, Fein, now an assistant deputy attorney general, had proposed that the administration make a full-throated frontal assault on activist judges and the theory of a "living constitution" that each generation might adapt to changing times. Roberts, a new Reagan assistant counselor and ever the incrementalist, jumped in with both support and caution. He proposed that the White House focus "on the more important articulation of the President's view of the proper role of the Federal judiciary," rather than on criticism of specific cases or justices. But when European terror attacks took over the news cycle, Attorney General Meese delivered the speech instead.

The forum for Meese's high-profile speech was an audience then viewed as enemy territory: a conference of the American Bar Association in July 1985. The *New York Times* called it the speech of Meese's career and credited it with "helping lay the foundation for the judicial wars that continue today." The *Times* later suggested Meese's broadside may have influenced young John Roberts—unaware that the lines of influence here actually ran in the opposite direction. The July speech helped preside over the reinvention of modern originalism as a first-order allegiance of the conservative movement. Meese proclaimed that the only constitutional jurisprudence is one of "Original Intention." In line with the rhetorical tactics of the movement's founders, he framed originalism and the founders' words as neutral and nonpartisan—but also as a ready-made response to the legal Right's judicial activism. The high court cannot "govern simply by what it views at the time as fair and decent," the attorney general warned. Instead, "by seeking to judge policies in light of principles, rather than remold principles in light of policies, the Court could avoid both the charge of incoherence and the charge of being either too conservative or too liberal."

Meese received some unexpected help in raising originalism's profile. Justice William Brennan—perhaps the court's most liberal member—engaged the debate in a speech of his own at Georgetown. Brennan pushed back forcefully against Meese's sweeping claims. He called the idea that justices could divine the founders' intent on "specific, contemporary questions" many centuries later "little more than arrogance cloaked as humility." Brennan warned that Meese's originalist pitch was simply a warmed-over version of familiar right-wing political objectives. Operating under originalism's broad dictums, conservative jurists would simply select the history that aligned with their own preconceived values and notions. They would then pretend it was the straightforward verdict of history that led them to the decision, rather than their own subjective opinions. "While proponents of this facile historicism justify it as a depoliticization of the judiciary," he said, "the political underpinnings of such a choice should not escape notice."

Brennan's critique saw through originalism from the beginning, but for Meese and his colleagues at the DOJ, when he joined the battle they knew their message had hit its target. "All of a sudden, we're being taken seriously," says Michael Greve. The more liberals objected, the more conservatives within the Federalist Society and elsewhere mobilized to refine their arguments. "It took on a life of its own, in a way," Greve says.

"That was the best, best thing that ever happened," Meese told me, chuckling years later. "If my speech had been given with no rebuttal by the other side, then it probably would've been forgotten as most speeches are. But by having Brennan take this on, wow, he actually made it a debate. The fight was on."

ORIGINALISM'S LONG CON might be the Right's niftiest trick. "It is almost unknown for a general theory of constitutional interpretation to itself become a site for popular mobilization," write Yale Law School professors Robert Post and Reva Siegel. Meese pulled off the impossible, repackaging what Calvin TerBeek identified as segregationist ideas as a modern theory of constitutional interpretation accepted by the masses. "During the Reagan Presidency, however, 'originalism' emerged as a new and powerful kind of constitutional politics in which claims about the sole legitimate method of interpreting the Constitution inspired conservative mobilization in both electoral politics and in the legal profession. In this form originalism has flourished ever since."

Meese carried the battle flag of originalism far and wide. He introduced, popularized, and weaponized terms that would soon become well-worn entries in the nation's political lexicon—from original intent and activist judges to the idea of legislating from the bench. He spoke before Federalist Society gatherings in Washington and throughout the country. He traveled to colleges and universities. And the DOJ put together a busy schedule of breakfast and lunch seminars, both at the Justice Department and before legal groups nationwide, where officials would tie originalism's ideals to current cases before the courts.

Here, Meese was playing a long game every bit as savvy as the ones laid out by Powell and Horowitz. His appearances before Federalist Society clubs elevated a wonky collective into the place to be for anyone serious about a career in conservative legal circles. It was an investment in the people who would become the future litigators, judges, and even Supreme Court justices. The Federalist Society provided the ticket. Originalism became the password. And taken together, one lunch meeting or campus chat at a time, conservatives fired up young hearts and minds and encouraged them to enlist in the battle of ideas. If the Reagan administration lacked enough reliable conservatives to push the law rightward from the bench, Meese and the Federalist Society ensured that future administrations would not lack for appointees. And if Robert Bork's nomination would stall because too many senators—including Republicans—believed originalism led to results dangerously beyond the mainstream of American politics, it would be entirely mainstreamed as a legal and political idea by 2016, championed by a triumphant Federalist Society, defended by conservative scholars, and embraced by large numbers on the right from Fox News to talk radio.

Conservatives understood that the law is not fixed: it is a product of those placed on the bench and the values those justices hold. Change those people, change the values, and you can change American political life and alter its elections forever, from the inside—even when large majorities disagree with the results. Indeed, that was the entire idea.

The great originalism offensive may have presented itself as a key front in the battle of ideas. But most people inside the DOJ and the movement understood the quarrel over the court and the Constitution to be a battle of *political* ideas. Meese and others would claim for decades that originalism wasn't partisan at all; it simply revealed the right framework for judges to adopt in interpreting the text of the Constitution.

Internal Reagan White House memos tell a different story. They show that the administration's embrace of originalism had a political purpose right from the start. In a 1985 memo to Meese laying out his agenda for the second term, Spears highlighted the importance of "identifying candidates who share the President's philosophy of judicial restraint . . . [and seeking] judicial conservatives whose philosophy is well-defined and who are capable of exercising intellectual leadership on the bench."

"When we came in with the Reagan administration, it was like, we're pulling these threads together, Bork and others, and making them operational," Spears told me. "In other words, it was just not something to be discussed at the faculty lounge anymore. We were going to give these concepts some breadth. We're going to apply them. And the courts—that was the most important part of the deal."

His March 18, 1985, memo to Meese spelled out the five-step plan:

Step 1: Address selected issues in the IOP [Intellectual Outreach Program]. Meeting with leading conservative academics will help sharpen the development of our own constitutional doctrines and the arguments that must be made to obtain their acceptance. Also, it can help get the debate started in the academic community, which is of great help in paving the way for acceptance of new ideas by the courts.

Step 2: Draft memoranda crystalizing [*sic*] our doctrine and why it represents the correct interpretation of the Constitution. OLP has prepared draft memos analyzing some of these issues.

Step 3: Raise these issues in speeches and articles by the Attorney General and Solicitor General, thus starting the debate in the political community and the editorial pages.

Step 4: Look for favorable litigation opportunities to challenge such doctrines in the courts. The Litigation Strategy Working group (composed of the political DAAGs [Deputy Assistant Attorneys General]) is probably the most creative and aggressive group to pursue this.

Step 5: Prepare a handbook for Department trial lawyers on litigation issues faced by AUSAs [Assistant United States Attorneys] and attorneys in more than one division. These include justiciability issues, such as standing, ripeness, mootness, abstention, exhaustion, and preclusion, as well as other issues like requests for and defenses to attorneys [*sic*] fee shifting. This would be best done under the guidance of the LSWG, with the work split among the divisions and staff offices; OLP and some divisions have previously worked on specific issues.

Meese would insist for decades, even when we talked in 2023, that originalism was purely a legal idea and had nothing to do with politics at all. It was merely a method of constitutional interpretation that provided a neutral methodology, he insisted, not a conservative results generator machine, a right-wing wolf dressed up in garb of the founders and the guise of objectivity. "What is at issue here is not an agenda of issues or a menu of results. At issue is a way of government. A jurisprudence based on first principles is neither conservative nor liberal, neither right nor left," Meese told a Federalist Society gathering in 1987. "A jurisprudence that seeks fidelity to the Constitution—a jurisprudence of original intention—is not a jurisprudence of political results. It is very much concerned with process, and it is a jurisprudence that in our day seeks to depoliticize the law."

In the same vein, Federalist Society founders and members would long insist the group simply functioned as a debate club that took no political stances at all. But once they spoke to one another, that fond conceit soon vanished. Steve Calabresi, a cofounder, told Riehl, the doctoral student writing in 2007 from a conservative perspective, that "part of Reagan's policy was to build up forces in 105 battleground nations in order to help topple enemy regimes, and I thought of us as kind of the same equivalent in law schools."

Michael Greve, meanwhile, says Meese's aides knew perfectly well that Operation Originalism was always much more about politics than the law. Years later, those who worked alongside him at the DOJ still expressed surprise that anyone could think otherwise. They seemed particularly amazed that the political media and the law school establishment would fall for such an obvious misdirection: How could any credulous person believe that there would be nothing political about a new school of thought that also happened to provide a convenient way to identify and confirm conservative judges and produce broadly unpopular policy outcomes that Republicans nevertheless desired but struggled to achieve?

"A very close friend of mine worked on (Meese's) speech on original-ism," says Greve, referring to the game-changer Meese delivered before the ABA, "and you know, some years ago we sat in some restaurant or bar in North Carolina, and the conversation is about 'How on earth did this hap-pen?' The guy says, 'You know, I wrote that speech. It was supposed to be a joke. How was I supposed to know that we were taking this seriously?'"

Antonin Scalia became Greve's good friend as well. Greve now says you can sense in Scalia's own scholarship and opinions that even the man con-sidered originalism's leading jurist himself didn't really buy what he was selling.

"I mean, you can sort of sense a version of this in Justice Scalia's writ-ings. In his public utterances he sometimes said, 'Look, it's not a serious jurisprudence. It's just better than anything else out there. If somebody else has something better, that's fine.' He had very, very little patience for all these refinements that came in later years. I think he would have gagged at the modern-day tendencies. *Corpus linguistics.* Excuse me? What's that supposed to be? Again, you know, people became really, really invested in it. I think that accounts for a lot of what happened."

Nobody really took this seriously. That the legal theory that conquered America seemed like a joke, or an intellectual puzzle at best, feels like a wild admission from the grant officer who helped launch the Federalist Society and who now works as a law professor at the law school that bears Scalia's name. So I asked him if people really didn't believe this idea could take hold at the time—and on that, Greve corrected me. They knew they could sell it to the academy and the public. They knew they had true be-lievers who would buy most anything. But no one thought the originalist gospel was handed down on a tablet. They just recognized it as useful.

"No, no, no, I'm not saying nobody thought it could take hold. There were quite a few people who wanted to sail or march under that banner: Judges should read the law and interpret the law and not make it da da da da da," Greve says. "But a lot of serious people—not just on the liberal side—said, 'Uh, this is just sort of a conservative agenda in drag.'

"We tried the judicial restraint stuff. Good luck. So you need a Plan B, and that was this. A lot of people knew that. It doesn't take a cynic to re-alize that. On the other hand, it developed a lot of intellectual oomph and respectability. I guess it's a mixture of both." In other words, somewhere along the line, the grift became reality.

YET PRECISELY BECAUSE it did take hold—because originalism reworked the way both conservatives and liberals approached the Constitution—it's important to understand both how it was created, as well as the long-term strategy that elevated it to the level of received legal doctrine.

While Ed Meese received the credit, Mit Spears and Stephen Markman did much of the heavy lifting. Markman was especially influential, as something of a Where's Waldo figure on the rising legal right: he led the Federalist Society chapter in Washington, D.C., worked with Senator Orrin Hatch as a key Senate Judiciary Committee aide during the 1982 VRA reauthorization, and arrived at Justice to run OLP in fall 1985 at the age of thirty-six. It was Markman who turned Meese's vision of a DOJ think tank into reality—and who focused on translating originalism's ideals into policy and litigation strategies focused on long-term results. Spears, meanwhile, with help from Markman and others at the White House and DOJ, including John Roberts, Bruce Fein, and Fred Fielding, focused on the Judges Project.

Markman's memos to Meese and to Solicitor General Charles Fried, first uncovered by University of Chicago doctoral student Patrick Gallagher, make it abundantly clear that no one in the orbit of Reagan's DOJ was simply bowled over by the intellectual might and explanatory power of originalism. Instead, as Markman forcefully argued, they endorsed originalism as the most effective way to package the conservative legal agenda as commonsense jurisprudence. In a January 1986 memo that Markman sent to Meese, titled "Random Thoughts on Original Intent Debate," the OLP director laid out a brilliant political strategy to maximize the benefits of originalism. Originalism, Markman recognized, gave conservatives an advantage in any debate because it aligned them with a legible actual theory and interpretative approach. That platform put their adversaries instantly on the defensive, since most liberals in the legal world eschewed fixed doctrine in favor of case-by-case decision-making easy to deride as "legislating from the bench" when it led to progressive wins.

The current legal wars, Markman went on to suggest, pitched, on the conservative side, a specific method against a more far-flung corps of judges who would "wing it" based on their own sense of fairness and justice. "The contemporary debate," he wrote, "divides those inclined toward any serious effort at interpretation and those who believe such interpretation to be either unknowable or irrelevant . . . the present debate is between believers and non-believers."

Originalism, he suggested, packaged correctly, could be "camouflage." Markman writes that "Our most sophisticated adversaries recognize that, to the extent current debate is accurately characterized, public opinion is probably predisposed to our point of view."

The nonbelievers, Markman wrote, should be pressed to identify a theory of their own. Most of the time, he wrote, it would sound vague and appeal to "translating the national will into constitutional terms," developing "moral standards" or ensuring the "dignity of full membership in society." All of that, he said, sounds like the judge really wants to impose his or her own moral view. Force them into articulating a worldview, he suggested. If they failed, they'd court the image of intellectual and legal unseriousness. Whatever they came up with was almost certain to sound as if activist judges just wanted to make it all up.

Yet the reality, of course, was that originalism handed conservatives a permission slip to claim original intent on any number of issues—voting rights, gun access, abortion, affirmative action, the regulatory state, the funding of religious schools—on which the Constitution remained silent. The conservative decisions had far less in common with any original intent of the founders and much more with the modern-day platform of the Republican Party and the economic interests of its major donors. And what it failed to recognize, perhaps most damningly, was that American democracy in the 1980s was a vastly different place, as it is today.

Hugging the original document so closely was really an ideological sleight of hand: it justifies the kind of institutional bigotry that the Constitution's actual intent was to protect against. Moreover, it prevents modern ideas about race, diversity, and representation from claiming constitutional legitimacy. The better and more useful question to ask, of course, would be how the Constitution might be interpreted to advance a

modern, multiracial democracy, and how to find the proper balance between majority rule and minority protections in a pluralistic nation.

The beauty of this rhetorical feint, Markman intimated, is that "original
intent" could both check progressive activism while opening the door to
conservative activism. "Our case can perhaps be presented most emphatically by placing the burden on our adversaries to suggest an appropriate
theory of jurisprudence in place of 'original intent.'" Meanwhile, he argued,
originalists can go on offense and claim that "no other articulated theory"
creates any check on judicial activism. Original intent, he writes, "must not
be marketed as simply another theory of jurisprudence; rather it is an essential part of the constitutional framework of checks and balances."

When it came to judicial nominations, he wrote, originalism allowed
conservatives a better way to talk about placing friendly judges on the
bench. "We are not choosing judges who will impose a 'right-wing social
agenda,'" he wrote. "We would choose a 'pro-choice' jurist who understood
that *Roe* was not part of the Constitution."

When I read Markman his memo, almost forty years later, he chuck-
led and admitted that, naturally, conservatives wanted to push the courts
in their direction. "Well, you know, that wasn't something that turned off
conservatives. Yes. It was something that had some appeal and some en-
ticement to conservatives. But I think it was not because this was achieving
results by camouflage, but because we thought that restoring traditional
approaches to constitutionalism would better facilitate the kind of values
that most conservatives held."

Markman also touted his own long-term vision of a Right-captured
court system. He actually advised that DOJ look to lose some cases—even
those that might have fit short-term GOP policy preferences—"in order
to emphasize the depth of our commitment" to originalism. And he suggested that "a more explicit connection could be drawn between our views
on jurisprudence and the mettle of the people that we are nominating [to]
the judiciary." Again, another masterful sleight of hand. "Contrary to allegations, we are not choosing judges who will impose a 'right-wing social
agenda,' upon the Nation," he writes, alchemically turning his politics into
history and law, "but rather those who recognize that they, too, are bound
by the Constitution."

Markman, now retired as a justice on Michigan's state supreme court, said that he and Meese's other lieutenants at Justice were fixated on the originalist cause in part as a marketing challenge: Could they turn a theory of constitutional interpretation into a commonsense rallying cry that spurred Republicans and connected with average Americans? "We were trying to turn around an understanding of the supreme law of our land," he told me, "and it's very difficult to do that."

When he offered similar counsel to Solicitor General Fried, Markman was even more direct: he didn't mind Fried losing on originalist grounds at the court, especially if opponents were to start using originalist examples of their own, legitimizing the theory while they tried to appeal to conservative justices. "If we are serious about supporting a jurisprudence of original intentions, we should be prepared to acknowledge that history in the relatively few cases where it would be adverse to the government," he wrote in a December 1985 memo. "As a practical matter, though, it is reasonably clear that history would be more supportive of our position than that of our adversaries in the vast majority of cases." (Fried, for his part, has come to understand the entire project was a political game from the beginning. "I think textualism and originalism are a fake," he says. "It's a propaganda tool. It's a slogan.")

As Markman looks back on the originalist wars four decades on, he's happy to declare victory. Originalism clearly prevailed, he says, noting Justice Elena Kagan's admission that "we are all originalists now," because conservatives and liberals alike feel obliged to approach the law through that lens. "It has given conservatives a leg up," he tells me. "It's important that the particular justices that are on the court now are people who are placed on the bench because it was understood that they already brought to bear an originalist or an interpretivist or a historical view to the Constitution."

He might well have added a critical takeaway from his body of DOJ memos: By virtue of a canny marketing campaign spanning the legal academy, the courts, the Justice Department, and the press, originalism has become the skeleton key for procuring legal power on the American right. That key would ultimately unlock rulings that would reshape elections in America, and it was only a matter of time before that key would unlock the doors to the highest court in the land.

CHAPTER EIGHT

THERE ARE AT least three different versions of the Federalist Society. Its conferences and panels, campus chapters, and addresses by the attorney general and other luminaries fulfill a classic educational role. "They do put on very interesting programs in law schools. I've had fun debating some of their people," says former senator Russell Feingold, who also has taught at Harvard, Yale, and Stanford Law schools and who now runs the American Constitution Society, a recent attempt by progressives to match the Federalist Society.

But that's just part of the iceberg that surfaces for public view. Feingold calls them a "Dr. Jekyll and Mr. Hyde organization." Dr. Jekyll is a respectable, sometimes even brilliant legal academic. The evil Hyde, he says, "is what they do behind the scenes. Leonard Leo and the Koch brothers' money and the deal that we will move your career along. They're trying to control what is supposed to be an independent judiciary. They're trying to lock it down for political reasons." Students know the deal from the day they enter law school, he says. "There's an element of the selling of the soul. For success." Jekyll thrives in the marketplace of ideas; Hyde runs the money-laundering project in the basement.

That *sub rosa*—and more consequential—part of the Federalist Society operation moves a select group of activist judges like William Pryor, Brett Kavanaugh, Neil Gorsuch, and Amy Coney Barrett—and increasingly most every GOP nominee for state supreme courts—through a process of vetting, vouching, and auditioning. If all goes well, they're finally ushered past the great federal judicial turnstile (or nominated as GOP candidates for state supreme courts) and into a lifetime appointment. The Federalist Society itself need not take any official stances, let alone on voting rights.

It simply credentials and shepherds lawyers and judges whose ideological bona fides are known to them and can be trusted to stick into positions where they can push not only the law but our politics in a rightward direction. The Federalist Society develops friendly judges for the cases that conservatives develop to diminish the right to vote. One couldn't happen without the other.

"It's a student society, which it has every right to be. And I welcome that it's a D.C. think tank, and it's really not much grosser than any other D.C. think tank," says Senator Sheldon Whitehouse of Rhode Island. Whitehouse has used his position on the Senate Judiciary Committee to painstakingly track the Federalist Society's channels of influence—as well as the megamillions bankrolling the group and Leonard Leo's broader organizational network. The problem, Whitehouse says, is that the Federalist Society sits at the heart of an untrackable dark money network that fast-tracks conservative judges and promotes conservative politicians as part of the same great rightward counterrevolution in the courts.

This funnel of judges into federal courts and state supreme courts is the ultimate, if whispered, goal of the Federalist Society. The conferences and the crowded calendar of regional meetings provide both social support and peer pressure for lawyers whose ideas, in many ways, remain in the minority of their profession. But the real purpose is to cultivate the judges of tomorrow and whoosh reliable conservatives onto influential benches— the implementation of the crucial lesson that conservatives took from the Powell and Horowitz reports: The law is whatever judges say it is. Remake the law, remake the nation—elections and democracy be damned.

"It also became the venue where Supreme Court nominees were chosen in a dark room while the entity was taking huge dark money contributions," Whitehouse says of the Federalist Society. "Imagine that a judicial delegation went to some weird, bizarre corrupt republic. In that republic, a private organization that had very strong views about judicial matters was secretly picking the members of the Supreme Court—and [it] was taking big contributions while it was picking the members of the Supreme Court. I think our judicial delegation would say, 'You know, this is terrible practice. This is an open invitation to corruption and this will put the whole judicial system into disrepute.'

"Of course, we can't say that now," Whitehouse says, closing out the hypothetical. "Because that's precisely how we did it for this horrible period of time. And then again, here they all are pretending that there was nothing wrong with that, that it was okay. That it was normal, that it was legit. It was none of the above."

NOT THAT ITS members would ever say so outright. The standard talking point whenever any FedSoc leader faced questioning from skeptical lawmakers, reporters, or citizens was simply that the group continued to operate just as its original founders intended: as a collegial debate club, a place for legal nerds to argue, with all sides welcome. The group doesn't take positions or file amicus briefs. But the alliance between the right-wing political world and the self-styled debate club has been entrenched ever since the Society's founding.

Veterans of Reagan's Justice Department, the nerve center of the conservative legal movement, laid out how it all happened. As the new cadre of Reagan legal strategists scoured the landscape for dedicated new talent, the Federalist Society eagerly stepped in to serve as a credentialing network for the conservative legal revolution. Even during the salad days of the 1980s, the young hires that the Federalist Society brokered were ushered into exciting jobs with power and authority. The group's fledgling track record quickly underlined a central truth: this was the club to join if you wanted power and influence within the new conservative legal movement.

"Personnel is policy," says James "Mit" Spears. "If you go back to Nixon and Ford, and forward perhaps to George H. W. Bush, there were a lot of people running around with great credentials. But they weren't the kind of people who were thinking about *why are we here?* and *what [should we] be focusing on?*"

Come Reagan's second term, Meese's DOJ showed how membership in the Federalist Society could provide a fast track to the sanctums of federal legal power in Washington. When Meese used a Federalist Society meeting in D.C. to set out a vision of originalism as political orthodoxy on the right, or when top-ranking DOJ officials showed up at the group's lunches, word got around. Gaining status as a Federalist Society recruit meant that you'd get to know the important people—and they would get to know you. As Meese speechwriter Gary McDowell told Steven Teles, "The Federalist Society was an integral part of the Meese Justice Department. . . . It's not like the Federalist Society was some sort of distant organization. The founders were on board with us on a daily basis."

A long-term revolution, however, is not won by staffing the Justice Department for a single administration. The clearest endgame of this strategy was winning the courts via lifetime appointments of Federalist Society–blessed judges. In this regard the story of William Pryor is both a typical example of Federalist Society benefits and an exceptional example of its success.

By the mid-1980s, Pryor—a new student at Tulane Law School in New Orleans who had been radicalized at the age of ten when he learned about *Roe v. Wade*—found a listing in his old copy of *National Review* for a Federalist Society event at Yale and called the number. Gene Meyer answered the phone. The following year, young William Pryor was elected president of the Tulane chapter and coordinated with the D.C. office on booking speakers at his campus. Ed Meese delivered one of his important 1985 originalism speeches at Tulane—and, then, in his Federalist Society tie, hosted a reception afterward with Pryor and the other members of the Tulane club.

"The only thing he wanted to talk about was the Federalist Society," Pryor told *Slate* many years later.

Meese agreed to let Pryor publish his speech in the campus's *Tulane Law Review*. Meese brought Calabresi along—marking the first time Pryor met the Society's cofounder. Meese, Pryor, and Calabresi became friends. When Pryor graduated from law school, his Federalist Society connections helped him earn a prestigious clerkship with Judge John Minor Wisdom—an awkward name for a judge—on the Fifth Circuit U.S. Court of Appeals.

By thirty-four, Pryor was elected attorney general of Alabama. Seven years later, President George W. Bush—who had his judicial appointments vetted by two other Federalist Society members, Brett Kavanaugh and Viet Dinh, with Federalist Society vice president Leonard Leo directing all conservative support from outside the administration—named Pryor to a seat on the Eleventh Circuit. A dozen years later, Pryor was one of the original eleven names on a list of judges for potential Supreme Court seats that Leonard Leo and Donald McGahn compiled at the request of Donald Trump.

Over all those decades, Pryor's Federalist Society connections pushed him along the judicial escalator. And the embrace was mutual: even though Pryor's views hadn't been suitable for prime-time airing in the Senate during his appellate appointment, the Federalist Society recognized he was a faithful foot soldier in a shared cause. And Trump's ascendancy meant that the Society's vetting strategists no longer had to worry so much about how a given candidate performed before the Senate. Still, the shared trajectory of the bellicose appellate jurist and his FedSoc mentors dated all the way back to that first reception on the Tulane Law campus. Meese, Pryor told *Slate*, "helped me at various points of my career—particularly when I entered public service, when I became a state attorney general. In many ways, the Federalist Society made that possible."

FAR FROM BEING just another avenue of interest for the Federalist Society, stories like Pryor's were precisely the point.

"The other point that I think has to be understood—and I think is really, really important—was the process that Steve Markman and I were involved in," says Spears. "Because unless you start changing the face of the judiciary, none of this makes any difference."

After conservatives had been disappointed with many of the Nixon and Ford appointees to the bench, many of whom drifted toward the center on social issues, Meese charged his team with developing a more "sophisticated understanding" of the appointments process. The aim was to ensure those mistakes were not repeated, according to Markman.

Originalism helped there as well. Ambitious conservatives in the legal sphere recognized in short order that originalism and the Federalist Society forged a speedy shortcut to wielding power in and around Washington, without all the messy back-and-forth entailed in an inquisition on abortion rights. Far easier and more high-minded to discuss constitutional interpretation and originalism. "We were trying to identify people who understood these new principles," Markman explains. "But it wasn't, 'Forget the interviews, get his name before the president tomorrow morning by 8:30.'" Except sometimes it was.

In those days it wasn't always easy to line up suitable talent on the fly. An assistant attorney general, Richard Willard, remembers trying to fill a vacancy on the Eighth Circuit and struggling to find a true believer rather than a political appointee or donor to some midwestern senator. "In my desk I had a full-page ad," he told Steven Teles. It bore the headline "Law Professors and Deans for Reagan/Bush."

"I looked at it, and noticed this guy from the University of Missouri," he says, "put his name in the hat, and he was appointed." Luckily for Willard, the candidate turned out to be a committed conservative named Pasco Bowman. But the larger point here was unmistakable: blind dart-throwing in search of an originalist for the federal circuit courts wouldn't do. The lack of any truly deep bench on the right played no small part in the Supreme Court nominations of Anthony Kennedy and David Souter. Both names became virtual curse words on the legal right, as they became centrist swing votes who often lined up with liberal jurists on key hot-button issues like abortion and affirmative action. Over time, it was clear that it made far more sense to put forward the names of Federalist Society members, duly vetted by other Federalist Society members.

"There was a complementary relationship between the Justice Department, the values of the president, and, of course, what the Federalist Society was trying to do," says Markman, himself a former head of the D.C. Federalist Society chapter.

Bork and Scalia, the group's two original faculty advisers, earned nominations first to the powerful U.S. Court of Appeals for the D.C. Circuit and then nods for the U.S. Supreme Court. (Bork's Supreme Court nomination would be defeated by the Senate in 1987.) Even though "Borked" has since become a synonym for politicized rejection of conservative candidates for the bench, Bork's record wasn't distorted, and his character wasn't maligned. Rather, his tactical mistake was intellectual arrogance and answering questions too honestly and clearly about where originalism would lead—no right to privacy, a much more limited conception of equal protection, a curtailed First Amendment for anything other than political expression. Other Federalist Society judges landed on the appellate courts during the Reagan and Bush years. Society member Clarence Thomas joined Scalia on the Supreme Court in 1991, and Society cofounder Lee Liberman Otis moved to the White House counsel's office under Bush the elder to lead the White House's judicial selection initiative as the "ideological gatekeeper for the Bush Administration's process for selecting judges."

"The bottom-up story is really important, the one that the Federalist Society helps build," says Amanda Hollis-Brusky, the author of the Fed-Soc history *Ideas Have Consequences*. "But also the top-down matters as well. Scalia's suddenly on the bench. He's the first faculty adviser to the Federalist Society, and he immediately starts making people take originalism seriously because he's doing it. He's not winning in the beginning. O'Connor, Kennedy, they might dabble in originalism, but they had their own jurisprudence that was not necessarily patently originalist.

"Then those kinds of justices get phased out," Hollis-Brusky continues, "and they're replaced by folks who openly practice originalism in ways that are consistent with what's been going on in the Federalist Society and in the academy. And they're bringing all of these ideas into opinions, which then further legitimates them."

These were ideas spelled out in DOJ's two-hundred-page reports and white papers, all directing the movement faithful onward toward a bold, redemptive future. The torrent of briefings, memos, and strategy papers all laid out what narrow constitutional guidelines to follow, which decisions needed to be overruled, and the optimal strategies to permanently enshrine the conservative reign over the courts.

Few noticed or read these reports at the time. It took more than a decade for the rest of the country to mark the rapid transformation of legal thought, doctrine, and practice. By then, of course, a great deal of the legal Right's lofty ambitions for the federal justice system had been realized. The detailed blueprints lovingly crafted by Markman, Meese, and the Office for Legal Policy were museum pieces, documenting a sweeping revolution-in-the-making. Poring through them, one unmistakable lesson stands out: conservatives and the Federalist Society have always seen the courts as political actors, regardless of their professed fondness for ivory tower debate or balls-and-strikes-calling judicial neutrality.

In 1988, Markman's office released a report titled *The Constitution in the Year 2000*. The document spanned 199 pages, covering fifteen issues that could create constitutional controversies likely to arrive before the high court. Markman's report also thoughtfully supplied potential resolutions to each crisis—depending, that is, on the philosophies of the justices. "The constitution of the United States is what the judges say it is," the report notes, quoting FDR-era chief justice Charles Evans Hughes. The central takeaway of the exercise was clear: control the courts, change the nation.

Markman's report set the agenda for the great antidemocratic rollback enacted by the Roberts Court, spelling out how the Right's selective menu of judicial appointments would produce greater restrictions in civil rights law and voting rights law, and tamp down congressional efforts to bolster and expand Fourteenth Amendment guarantees of due process and equal protection. "The meaning of the constitution in the year 2000 will be determined largely by the people who sit on the court over the next decade," Markman's report concluded. You can say that again.

BY THE TIME the next Republican administration set up shop in Washington, any conservative who didn't quite understand who wielded the power when it came to judicial appointments quickly learned their lesson and fell in line. Alberto Gonzales arrived from Texas as George W. Bush's White House counsel and right-hand man in 2001, a buzzed-about Supreme Court selection and future attorney general.

"He did not know the Federalist Society. Perhaps more importantly, the Federalist Society did not know him. He feels like this group that he's never heard of is attacking him, and he's told that this group is very important to his judicial nominations," Tim Flanigan, Gonzales's deputy counsel at the White House, told *The New Yorker* in 2017. "We used to have a staff meeting of about a dozen lawyers, and at one of the early meetings Al started to vent a little bit about the Federalist Society, saying, 'Who is this Federalist

Society?' And, finally, he's getting frustrated and he says, 'How many of you here are members of the Federalist Society?' And every hand in the room went up, except for Al's and mine."

Gonzales, you might have noticed, never made it to the Supreme Court. He did not clear the turnstile. Neither did Harriet Miers, another White House counsel and longtime Texas friend who didn't win the FedSoc's trust when Bush nominated her to take Sandra Day O'Connor's seat. "The Federalist Society had created a signaling mechanism within the conservative movement," adds Hollis-Brusky. "The message Leonard [Leo] and others had sent was: if you want to rise through the ranks, we need to know you." The message came through loud and clear about Miers: "She is not one of us." With almost no support in conservative circles, Miers withdrew from consideration. She was replaced with Samuel Alito. "I had always been a big Sam Alito fan," Leo told *The New Yorker*. You can almost imagine the kingmaker saying it with a big wink.

Perhaps in that very moment, long before Donald Trump's fateful ascension to the presidency, Leo codified the conservative pipeline connecting the Federalist Society, the White House, and the U.S. Supreme Court. Republicans knew both who they'd be nominating to future vacancies and the go-betweens they'd rely on to shepherd the nominations through. No president would risk nominating anyone unknown or unpredictable. There would be no more surprise moderates. No ambitious judge desiring a promotion would turn down the opportunity to speak before the Federalist Society or be anything less than transparent, with fellow members, about their strong conservative credentials. Leo would be the consigliere and the conductor rolled into one. He orchestrated the talent network dedicated to grooming judges and justices from law school to clerkships to the bench and sometimes even 1 First Street NE.

Crucially, the Federalist Society monitored the turnstile. To be certain, there have long been credentialing societies on the left. The difference is that the Left is more diffuse and internally divided. There are dozens of smaller organizations aligned with liberal advocacy causes, but no single group wields veto power over nominees to the federal bench. On the right, things are far simpler and more efficient: it's the Leo network, and a billion-dollar war chest.

"Republicans come into office with a list, ready to go," says Bruce Bartlett, the former Reagan adviser. "Democrats constantly reinvent the wheel
from scratch, study résumés, look for the best-qualified person—and end
up with people on the courts who don't move the ball. They're not de-
pendable. These conservatives get on the court and they never leave. It's a
lifetime appointment, and they make every minute of it count."

From 1991 forward, Leo built the Federalist Society's Lawyers Division as the key testing ground for all federal judiciary hopefuls. Leo spent
months on the road visiting Federalist Society conferences and getting ac-
quainted with conservative lawyers and thinkers. And when a Republican
president had a nominee to put forth, Leo would provide the key counsel,
oftentimes working with other FedSoc veterans inside the White House
and DOJ, and for major seats like a Supreme Court justice, would step
briefly aside from FedSoc to manage the nomination. This meant he had to
know the conservative bona fides of absolutely everyone, which isn't that
difficult, Leo told the *New Yorker*—"In the sense that when you've been
working in this vineyard for twenty-five years, you know everybody."

Steven Teles of Johns Hopkins University, author of *The Rise of the
Conservative Legal Movement*, told the magazine that the idea behind
the Lawyers Division was to build "a network . . . with Leonard Leo at the
center to give conservatives a chance to meet one another and check one
another out." It's the opposite of speed dating; the more apt comparison
would be the patient advisory work of a baseball scout who needs to know
the strengths of every hitter coming out of high school and college. Leo
would spend much of the year on the road, at conferences and campus
gatherings, gripping, grinning, and always assessing. "The one thing all
the lawyers have in common," Teles says, "is that they all know Leonard
and he knows all of them."

Leo has been part of the FedSoc pipeline since the very beginning. As
a young college intern for Senator Orrin Hatch and the Judiciary Committee in the mid-1980s, Leo had a front-row seat as Democrats browbeat
a young conservative judge, Alex Kozinski, President Reagan's nominee
for the U.S. Court of Appeals for the Ninth Circuit. During the hearings,
which concluded in November 1985, Democrats had spent hours interro-
gating Kozinski, alleging that he had "demeaned" and "abused" his staff,

that he lacked "judicial temperament," that he was "too arrogant and insensitive" to sit on the federal bench. Now Democrats wanted to reopen the hearings and call further witnesses. Leo delivered Hatch lunch after the hearing, and the Utah senator accepted the sandwich fuming, with a vow that Democrats would never do this to a GOP nominee again.

On Judiciary, Leo also worked with then–chief counsel Stephen Markman. Markman, the president of the D.C. chapter of the Federalist Society's Lawyers Division, would bring the young conservative to the group's soon-to-be-legendary Monday lunches at the Golden Palace in Chinatown. "He clearly shared the values," Markman told me. The guest at the second lunch Leonard Leo attended would be the attorney general, Edwin Meese, who delivered a speech on originalism. Fired up, Leo went back to his studies at Cornell. Soon afterward, he enrolled at Cornell Law and decided he would join the Federalist Society. No chapter existed at the school, so Leo founded one himself. Markman and Kozinski accepted his invitations to address the new chapter. After getting his law degree, Leo landed a prime clerkship at the U.S. Court of Appeals in Washington. A friendship blossomed with a young judge named Clarence Thomas. All the while, Orrin Hatch's words stuck with him: *They will never, ever do this to one of our nominees again.*

Leonard Leo—already an expert networker and devout conservative, whose suburban New Jersey high school yearbook shows him waving a fistful of cash and lists his teenage nickname as "Moneybags Kid"—took Hatch's vow and made it a conservative movement mandate.

IF ONE MOMENT offered proof of concept for the conservative strategy to control American elections via the courts it arrived on Election Night 2000 when Texas governor George W. Bush and Vice President Al Gore ended a marathon evening practically tied in the state of Florida. The presidency hung in the balance; the Sunshine State's electoral votes would determine the winner of the 2000 election. Just as soon as anyone could determine who deserved them.

On election night, just 1,784 votes separated the two men, and an automatic recount began. After just one day, Bush's lead dwindled to 900 votes.

The next day, it tumbled to just over 300. Gore requested a recount in four counties; the Bush campaign tried to shut the recounts down. A two-year race for the White House would come down to the courts, as the Gore team sprinted to get recounts in counties they believed most favorable to them while the Bush team sought to pump the brakes and keep the tight certification process on track. Among those who sprinted to Florida were three future Supreme Court justices who solidified their movement bona fides by working to turn a presidential election in the GOP's favor during a moment unlike any other in modern American politics.

John Roberts was among the very first Bush lawyers to make the trek to Florida. Roberts, then one of the nation's top appellate lawyers, had a case before the U.S. Supreme Court to prepare, and also details to handle over the adoption of his son, who had just been born. Yet he flew to Florida several times during the thirty-six-day standoff, first to advise the candidate's brother, Florida governor Jeb Bush, on his responsibilities during a disputed presidential election, and then to brief his former DOJ brother Michael Carvin, who would be arguing the finer points of Bush's constitutional argument to stop the recount in Palm Beach County and allow the GOP secretary of state to declare Bush the winner, before the Florida Supreme Court.

"It was bedlam," Carvin remembers. "Just crazy."

"I really appreciate your input on my role in this unique and historic situation," Governor Bush emailed Roberts on December 6, 2000. During the 2016 presidential campaign, Bush called the constitutional lesson he received from Roberts a "very arcane discussion." Later, according to Texas senator Ted Cruz, Roberts would write and line edit the future president's briefs to the U.S. Supreme Court. Cruz also remembers Roberts playing a crucial role in drafting the Bush team's most important briefs and then suddenly announcing he had to go back to Washington.

"Distraught, I asked where he was going—we were in the middle of an enormous legal battle. Quickly, he replied, 'I know, but I've got a Supreme Court argument tomorrow morning,'" Cruz, who was also working on the case, wrote in his memoir. "He flew back to D.C. Tuesday night, argued a complicated trademark case Wednesday morning, and returned immediately to Florida to continue helping us represent the president."

Amy Coney Barrett, meanwhile, all of twenty-eight, arrived in Martin County, just south of Palm Beach, to defend thousands of Republican absentee ballots that Democrats claimed had been tainted when a Republican official was allowed to take them and fill in missing voter identification numbers.

While the top GOP minds in the nation scoured the Constitution looking for every advantage, an aide in the Florida state house noticed the Elections Clause and the Electors Clause. There the Constitution held that elections were to be administered in the states by "the legislature thereof." As unmovable Electoral College deadlines neared, Bush and the Florida state house worked through the ultimate break-glass-in-case-of-emergency move: using that single word, *legislature*, to award the state's electors to Bush.

Democrats never imagined such an obscure notion and hypertextual reading of the Constitution would fly with the U.S. Supreme Court. But then, during oral arguments for *Bush v. Gore*, GOP lawyer Ted Olson (who hosted annual summer FedSoc barbecues at his Virginia home) gave it a go. "The Constitution specifically vested the authority to determine the manner of the appointment of electors in state legislatures," he argued—an early attempt to articulate what would later become known as the independent state legislature doctrine, which would appear before the Supreme Court and these *Bush v. Gore* alums some two decades later.

The Bush lawyer who exited the court that day, only to be cornered on live television by CNN's Wolf Blitzer, was thirty-five-year-old Brett Kavanaugh.

"The real issue is what does Article II of the Constitution mean in the first instance. And it delegates authority directly to the state legislatures. And the textualists on the court, led by Justice Scalia, are paying close attention to that language," Kavanaugh told Blitzer. He then added that the high court was concerned about "whether the Florida Supreme Court had so departed from the election code previously established by the legislature that it had violated the United States Constitution, which after all delegates the power to the legislatures of the states."

A 5–4 court decision, in an unsigned opinion following drearily predictable partisan lines, awarded the presidency to Bush. The GOP majority did not embrace the novel interpretation of the Elections Clause. Instead, it ended the recount under the equal protection provision in the Constitution, on the grounds that only some of the state would be recounted and not all of it. Proceeding along these lines, the court implausibly held, would abridge Bush's heretofore unsuspected Fourteenth Amendment right to be elected president. Then the court admitted the speciousness of its reasoning by declaring the decision a one-off and not binding precedent. The conservative majority knew it didn't want the federal government reaching into every state election—only the ones where it suited their needs.

The so-called principled originalists and textualists revealed their truest colors: they were partisans, twisting the Constitution toward their desired outcome.

Lewis Powell would have nodded along. The law? The Constitution? It was what they said it was. It was what they wanted it to be. The courts were the ultimate arbiter and the ultimate backup plan in case of a disputed election. Control the courts, win the tiebreaker. The Supreme Court looks quite different under a President Al Gore. It's possible that Roberts and Alito never join the bench, possible that all the antidemocratic decisions of the next decade never happen at all. Instead, that three GOP veterans of this case became three Leonard Leo–approved justices only shows how long a shadow this case would cast, and how clearly its lessons would be imprinted on a FedSoc judiciary.

ONE WAY TO understand what Leo built, and how deeply the Federalist Society and the White House were linked on judicial issues and appointments, is to read a revealing set of White House emails from the early aughts. They were all submitted to the Senate Judiciary Committee during Brett Kavanaugh's confirmation hearings, and they all concern Leo and the Federalist Society. Back then, Kavanaugh served in George W. Bush's White House as associate counsel, and judicial nominations were an important piece of Kavanaugh's portfolio.

Leo and the Federalist Society come up again and again in Kavanaugh's emails; in one of them, Leo is described as the person who drives "all outside coalition activism regarding judicial nominations." Already in the early 2000s, the ambitious White House staffer was concerned that the Society had become controversial enough that he ought to try and maintain a distance from it for optics' sake.

Sometimes Leo seemed to think he and the Federalist Society were actually the ones in charge. Emails show that when Kavanaugh and the White House planned a spring 2003 rally to call attention to a growing number of judicial nominations now bogged down in the Senate, Leo had a special VIP seat reserved for him. But then the Federalist Society went ahead and invited its own list of Hill staffers to the White House event. "Federalist Society should not be calling people in government to invite them," Kavanaugh emailed Leo at his Federalist Society account. Yet they did with no pushback from the White House. And it didn't take long before Kavanaugh was currying favor with the group once again. "Can we talk about President possibly speaking at Federalist Society National Conference in November?" he asked in another email. "The Vice President spoke last year."

Leo was already known inside the White House as the moneyman. When Miguel Estrada's controversial 2001 appointment to the D.C. Court of Appeals collided with a Democratic filibuster, the White House needed someone to foot the bill for a media campaign to try and save the embattled nomination.

"Leonard Leo will know where to find money to hold a presser for a failing nominee," a Bush adviser wrote in another email discovered by the *Washington Post.* "We probably don't want the fed soc paying for it, but he might know some generous donor." He might indeed: Leo could always be counted on to know a fabulously wealthy funder eager to underwrite something useful to the greater cause.

Kavanaugh's Federalist Society credentials and close ties to Leo mattered because Kavanaugh himself—along with Leo—had President George W. Bush's ear as he prepared to fill Supreme Court vacancies created by O'Connor's retirement and Rehnquist's death. "Brett told me that Luttig, Alito and Roberts would all be solid justices," Bush wrote in his memoir. "The tiebreaker question, he suggested, was which man would be the most effective leader on the Court—the most capable of convincing his colleagues through persuasion and strategic thinking."

That strategic thinker would be John Roberts.

Bush might have made the call. But Leo and Kavanaugh's inside-out game narrowed the list to three vetted and preapproved candidates. And then Leo went to work to ensure Roberts's victory. The "Moneybags Kid," alongside other well-connected lawyers, launched a nonprofit called the Judicial Confirmation Network, which served as a rapid-response campaign arm for the Roberts nomination, a full-service shop that produced positive thirty-second TV spots in support of the nominee and helped burnish his image in the press. No direct line connected the JCN and FedSoc. It wasn't needed. The dotted one represented by FedSoc executive Leonard Leo and many of the same funders ensured that regardless of any official ties, everyone who mattered knew the real deal. "Leonard was the guy," top Bush adviser Steve Schmidt told *ProPublica*. "A hundred percent."

The JCN would play the same role for Alito. And by the end of 2005, the Federalist Society caucus on the bench of the U.S. Supreme Court had multiplied exponentially. The pipeline churned. It wouldn't be long before those judges had a majority to remake American elections.

PART II

CONTROL THE LAW, REMAKE THE LAND

CHAPTER NINE

THE TINY TOWNS across Mississippi's hill country feel disconnected from time. But when you walk them as a stranger, it's easy to feel the menace of history. Some of that history is commemorated, like the sign in Kilmichael that claims blues legend B.B. King as a native son. As a young boy picking cotton here, the child then known as Riley first heard fellow farm workers singing the blues in the fields, and he told himself he'd make his living in music. But there's not much commemoration of this region's violent racial past. Kilmichael's desolate town square, made up of dusty white-brick buildings set along wide roads, offers little hope for dreamers. Today, there are mostly empty storefronts whose former owners left behind signs advertising pecans for sale, and old-school soda machines that once dispensed quarter Cokes with the press of a giant button.

When the Voting Rights Act came up for reauthorization in 2006, and then immediately faced renewed challenges to its constitutionality before the U.S. Supreme Court, its opponents sang the familiar hymn of progress and toasted a nation that had come so far since the 1960s that its protections had become archaic. Throughout these hearings in the halls of Congress and hallowed sanctums of justice, those insisting that the nation could safely turn the page repeated the same mantra: *Things have changed.* Perhaps the calendar had rolled over. But places like Kilmichael, Mississippi—as well as Pleasant Grove, Alabama; Prairie View, Texas; or dozens of small towns and suburbs across Georgia, Louisiana, and South Carolina—remained stubbornly the same, so much so that it almost required either disingenuousness or indifference to argue otherwise, let alone to claim some sort of moral imperative to declare victory over race-based barricades to the ballot box.

If Chief Justice John Roberts truly believes things have changed in the South, as he would so infamously claim in his decision in *Shelby County v. Holder,* he ought to spend an afternoon on state highways 51 and 82, driving through towns so forgotten you need to buy the newspaper to remember the year. The menace here really isn't in the past at all. It can be felt everywhere. In this stretch of former Jim Crow country, long-ago attitudes have hardened into the soil as an unquestioned legacy of the way things always had to be.

In 2015, these rural communities elected funeral director Karl Oliver to represent them in the state house. Oliver freely invokes the region's history as if no burden weighs on him at all. When New Orleans leaders ordered the removal of statues honoring General Robert E. Lee and other Confederate soldiers in 2017, Oliver exploded with rage on Facebook. "If the, and I use this term extremely loosely, 'leadership' of Louisiana wishes to, in a Nazi-ish fashion, burn books or destroy historical monuments of OUR HISTORY, they should be LYNCHED!"

That's a word with particular resonance here. Oliver's hate-filled response would have been shocking under any circumstances, but it seemed all the more so in a district that included Money, Mississippi. That was the town where fourteen-year-old Emmett Till was brutally murdered for the crime of talking to a white woman in a grocery store. Oliver's district also includes Duck Hill, just fourteen miles from Kilmichael, where in 1937 a white mob lynched and burned alive two Black men who attested their innocence of charges that they'd killed a white store owner. Some three hundred men surrounded sheriffs as they transported the Black men for arraignment, overwhelming officers who later insisted they did not recognize any of the unmasked men. "It was all done very quickly, quietly and orderly," a deputy sheriff testified.

The savage murders that followed were anything but. The howling men were hustled onto an awaiting school bus and rushed to Duck Hill, as the mob followed in thirty to forty automobiles. Another five hundred townsfolk, women and children among them, watched as the men were dragged off the buses and chained fast to pine trees. The *Madera Tribune* tells the horrifying story in detail. "A mobster produced a blow torch and struck a match," and in a minute the blue-white flame "was roaring above the pleadings of the doomed men." The lynch mob tortured the two men with the plumber's torch until they finally produced phony confessions. They then riddled one of the arraigned men with bullets and doused the other with gasoline. The mob gathered brush and then someone struck a match. Pictures taken at the scene later appeared in *Time* and *Life* magazines as well as some newspapers—the first lynching photographs published by the national press. On that very day, Congress debated antilynching legislation but failed to pass it once more, in part due to the Senate filibuster that had protected white supremacy for so long.

It was the bitter and violent resistance to civil rights in places like Kilmichael, Grenada, Clinton, and Duck Hill that made the Voting Rights Act of 1965 necessary. And it's the continued efforts since its passage to build even newer obstacles to prevent Black people from voting and holding office that demonstrate, time and again, why Congress created preclearance. Mississippi's state legislature waited only until its 1966 session to enact a massive package of election law changes designed to constrain the political power of the state's newly enfranchised Black voters. Lawmakers then ignored Section 5 and refused to submit the changes for preclearance. Only the intervention of the U.S. Supreme Court in 1969's *Allen v. State Board of Elections*, a 7–2 opinion written by then chief justice Warren, made it clear to the white leaders of the state that any changes to voting practices without preclearance were invalid and unenforceable.

Not that *Allen* ended Mississippi's resistance. Between the *Allen* decision and the VRA's reauthorization in 2006, the Department of Justice objected to 169 changes in Mississippi voting procedures. The enforcement actions encompassed everything from tainted congressional and state legislative maps to county governing boards and local school committees. The objections actually accelerated over time: 112 of them were lodged between the 1982 and 2006 reauthorizations. Mississippi also led the nation in the allotment of federal elections observers charged with ensuring the core provisions of the VRA were being honored. But numbers only tell part of the story. Perhaps there's not lynching here any longer, just clueless politicians talking tough with Bull Connor cosplay. But there are white politicians who simply cancel elections they think they won't win, and state judges who allow it—some of the very reasons why

Congress enacted preclearance in 1965, all on display in our twenty-first century.

In May 2001, when white officials in Kilmichael realized voters might elect the town's first Black mayor and council members in spring elections, they simply decided to call the elections off, less than three weeks before voters were scheduled to go to the polls. The story of Kilmichael's canceled election is so audacious, so absurdly racist on its face, so impossible to believe, that it seems like it must come from another era altogether. But it was so unexceptionable here that it barely received a ripple of coverage in the local weekly papers that cover these towns, let alone in the national media.

This was happening. It is still happening. And while one can find the occasional reference to Kilmichael in the 2013 *Shelby County* briefs, Chief Justice John Roberts doesn't mention what happened there in his majority opinion. How could he? There's no place for it in a didactic ruling organized around the central claim that Kilmichael baldly refutes: that things have changed in the South.

MARY YOUNG WASN'T expecting the knock on her door. But with fewer than three weeks remaining before the June 2 election, friends were coming and going at all times. Young's house doubled as a makeshift campaign headquarters for the volunteers who believed they could make change happen and elect her Kilmichael's first Black mayor. For decades, Blacks had made up at least 40 percent of the population in the town, but the five-member council was elected at-large. That meant whites only voted for whites, and so none of the four Black candidates who'd ever sought election had won, much as things had been for so long in Mobile. This year looked to be different. The 2000 census found that Kilmichael was now majority Black. Four Black candidates qualified for the city council race. Young suspected that Kilmichael's white leaders would look to knock her off the ballot, or disqualify her over something picayune if they could. So the veteran community organizer and lifelong resident kept her mayoral candidacy quiet until the last moment. Her under-the-radar strategy worked. Young qualified for the ballot. If Kilmichael's white establishment wanted to stop her, it would need to come up with a different plan—fast.

And so in the United States of America, in 2001, a Mississippi town simply decided not to hold an election that whites feared would produce a Black mayor and even a Black-majority council. The council met with zero advance notice to the community and voted unanimously on May 15 simply not to have the June election. The town's election board and then a state circuit court allowed it to happen.

"We were amazed," said Young, who had been involved in Mississippi politics long enough not to be stunned by much of anything. She'd seen too many elections where officials visited Black voters who could vote and told them that they couldn't, or residents harassed into moving a mobile home just over the town line to ensure they were no longer qualified to partici- pate in an election. But this was something far more brazen. "It was right at the election—and they canceled it."

Young said that a city official called the candidates to a meeting down- town. There, he announced that the town leaders feared that federal liti- gation filed the month before regarding the census and localities that used single-member districts needed to be studied and addressed. Except Kil- michael elected council members through an at-large system, not districts. The litigation in question did not name or mention them at all. "It wasn't our situation. It wasn't us," Young said. "It didn't answer why we had our election canceled. We didn't buy that one."

Neither did the Department of Justice. After four months of investiga- tion, the DOJ used Section 5 of the Voting Rights Act to officially object to the election's cancellation. In a letter that made it clear the department believed the only motivating factor in Kilmichael was race, DOJ officials insisted that the town failed to prove the lack of a discriminatory purpose and also could not prove a lack of discriminatory intent.

"The town has not established that its decision was motivated by reasons other than an intent to cause retrogression in minority voting strength," the letter says. The town's "purported non-racial rationales" for the decision "do not withstand scrutiny." The board did not consider any changes to the method of the election, they wrote, "until it became clear that the minority community potentially could win the mayoral seat as well as four of the five" council seats. As for concerns about litigation elsewhere over single-member districts, the official noted, drily, that "election-related federal litigation has been occurring in Mississippi for approximately 30 years."

It took two years, but Section 5 forced Kilmichael to hold an election. And while it happened two years later than it should have, Mary Young was finally elected Kilmichael's first Black mayor in 2003. Her term only lasted two years instead of four. But the VRA, even in twenty-first-century America, was still required to hold off race-based election inequality enacted by white officials and allowed by southern courts. "Well," Young said, "the years might change, but you still have those who want to remain in control, dominant in control. Those things happened—and they're still occurring."

HAPPENED AND STILL occurring. That could be the motto of Waller County, Texas, just to the east of the Brazos River, where Confederate soldiers regrouped in March 1865, as Sherman's army scorched a path across the South, with dreams of one final stand among the cotton plantations of Hempstead. A division of eight thousand men arrived from Louisiana and awaited the arrival of Jefferson Davis, but the president of the Confederacy never came, and likely never intended to fight there. When he was captured in Georgia, disguised in his wife's dress and dark shawl, many accounts suggest he intended to flee overseas. The soldiers dispersed by early June. Hempstead became the county seat of Waller County, where a historical plaque at the courthouse, erected during the 1960s, imbues that befuddled surrender with poignance, honor, and brotherhood.

In Waller County, the conflict remains recent. Little has changed from the times when officials romanticized the Lost Cause at the height of the civil rights movement. During the century between the end of the Civil War and the passage of the Voting Rights Act, the early Reconstruction dream flickered there, only to be crushed by the Ku Klux Klan. More lynchings took place in Waller County between 1877 and 1950 than in any other county in Texas. What violence and racial terror could not attain, the Texas whites-only Democratic primary achieved, shutting Black voters out of the only election that actually mattered in what was still then the Democratic solid South. More recently, the county jail in Hempstead is where Sandra Bland died in 2015, after a routine traffic stop for failing to signal a lane change led to her arrest and, according to police, her suicide (an account adamantly disputed by her family).

Bland was about to begin a new job at Prairie View A&M University, established in 1876 when this was a Black-majority county—one of the first Texas colleges to admit Black students and the first funded by the state. This predominantly Black university, which reclaimed the old Alta Vista plantation for a higher purpose, has provided a pathway for more than seventy thousand students to earn a college degree. Yet Waller County being Waller County, the white political and legal establishment has worked tirelessly to build creative barriers to the ballot box that make it far more difficult for the eighty-one hundred students to cast a ballot than it is for the county's white residents.

Name a trick and Waller County has tried it. The Voting Rights Act—and Section 5's preclearance protections—provided the best defense, all the way through the early 2010s.

During the 1970s, if a Prairie View student tried to register to vote in Waller County, officials put them through a circuitous and burdensome application process that included lengthy questionnaires. The process culminated in an administrative hearing to test whether they were "bona fide" residents. It required a 1979 decision by the U.S. Supreme Court to end that chicanery in Waller County and affirm the right of college students nationwide to vote where they attend school.

Waller County responded with decade after decade of racial gerrymanders that diluted student voting strength for county elections by scattering the campus across multiple districts. After Waller County redrew maps in 2001 and limited the ability of Black voters to elect candidates of their choosing yet again—lowering the percentage of Black voters from 52 percent to less than 30 percent in one district that had just elected a Black councillor by two votes—the Department of Justice sent officials a stinging June 2002 letter that disallowed the maps for a third consecutive decade.

Waller County's defiance appeared never-ending. In the mid-2000s,

the county's district attorney—again openly disregarding the 1979 Supreme Court decision—published an open letter in a local newspaper
that threatened to prosecute students who voted in violation of his own
interpretation of the residency laws. A Justice Department investigation
forced him to back off from those warnings, but in the meantime, he was
taken seriously; after all, a dozen students had been charged with voter
fraud for participating in a 1992 runoff election. The charges were later
dropped, but few college students wanted to fit arraignments and court
dates around exams.

Then, in the months before the 2008 elections, and the first presidential election with a Black major-party nominee, the county violated federal
law—both the Voting Rights Act and the Civil Rights Act—by setting up
a more difficult approval process for voter registration applications from
Prairie View students. Hundreds of students had their applications rejected
for something as minor as a missing ZIP code. That was a clear violation of
election law—and to compound the offense, the county enacted its own new
registration criteria. This, too, they did without preclearance. DOJ brought
litigation against the county under Section 5 on October 9, 2008. Eight
days later, on October 17, the county backed down completely, admitted
that it had violated the Voting Rights Act, and agreed to end these discriminatory practices. Under the consent decree with the government, Waller
County also agreed to conduct voter registration drives on campus, and to
justify any rejection of an application to vote to the DOJ through 2012.
That is, up until 2013, when Chief Justice Roberts gutted preclearance.

Waller County is not ancient history. The same animus drives our politics today. What began as a white primary, a literacy test, or a poll tax is
now a litany of disproportionate burdens and inconveniences. The goal
is the same, and the impact will profoundly reshape the meaning of representative democracy everywhere and for us all. What begins in Waller
County—or in Maricopa County, Fulton County, or hundreds of other voting jurisdictions throughout the country—will not stay there.

THINGS HAVE CHANGED *in the South.* Perhaps, if you choose not to listen to
the stories. Mississippi led the way with 112 Section 5 objections between

1982 and 2006. Texas finished a close second, with 107—but the state had more Section 5 withdrawals than any other, in which the threat of denial served as a deterrent. Ten of those objections were to statewide laws or redistricting plans, but 97 of them were for local changes—affecting just under 30 percent of the counties in the state, where nearly three-quarters of the state's minority voters live. In addition, there were at least 54 election changes that Texas or its localities decided not to enact simply because the Department of Justice sent a letter of inquiry seeking additional information.

Contrary to the opinion of John Roberts, the story of Mississippi and Texas *is* the story of the South. In Louisiana, the number of Section 5 objections rose from 50 between 1965 and 1982, to 96 between 1982 and 2006. Without Section 5, says voting rights attorney Debo Adegbile, "the Voting Rights Act might have represented little more than an occasion for another change in the strategy by which white officials perpetuated barriers to political equality." In Pointe Coupée Parish, for example, just one of the tiny towns where preclearance was the only shield, the DOJ objected to local, decennial redistricting plans for three consecutive decades—in 1983, 1992, and 2002. In the 1980s and 1990s, officials tried to pack all minority voters into one district. In the 2000s, they simply did away with that district altogether. And thirteen times, the DOJ came back to Louisiana localities with the objection that officials were simply resubmitting the same plan without any actual changes.

Again and again, preclearance prevented white officials from moving polling places out of Black neighborhoods. In 1994, a white alderman in St. Landry Parish complained that some white residents felt uncomfortable voting in the Sunset Community Center, in a Black part of town. The board moved the precinct from the community center to Sunset Town Hall—the site of a lynching and other historical racial discrimination. "It appears that the decision making process considered the presumed desires of white voters, but made no effort to consider the desires of black voters," the Justice Department wrote. What's more, the board did not seek any public input, hold a public hearing, or even advertise the change in any way. Without preclearance, Black voters here would have had no idea the polling place had moved at all.

Alabama had another forty-six Section 5 objections during this period;
the civil rights attorney James Blacksher, who brought the *Mobile v. Bolden*
case to the U.S. Supreme Court, observed that "though there has been
significant progress in electoral access and equality for Alabama's Black
citizens, it has largely been as the result of extensive voting rights enforcement." Perhaps one of the boldest defenses came from Pleasant Grove,
which dubs itself the "Good Neighbor" community. In 1985, a federal court
found that the town had "an astonishing hostility to the presence and the
rights of black Americans." Perhaps that's because even in the mid-1980s,
it did not have a single Black resident. When Pleasant Grove attempted
to annex two parcels of land in the early 1980s—one for a wealthy new
subdivision, and another, smaller piece where white families wanted their
children to attend the town's all-white schools—the DOJ refused the request using Section 5, because the town had denied petitions to annex a
nearby Black community. Pleasant Grove's defense echoed the ludicrous
argument in *Mobile v. Bolden*. Officials insisted that the town couldn't be
hostile to Black voting rights if no Blacks lived there.

SPEND SOME TIME with the Justice Department files from this era and two
things become immediately clear: First, across small-towns in the South,
the VRA helped to promote parity in voter registration numbers, but preclearance prevented the adoption of many new-school methods of voter
suppression designed to keep the past alive in little locales where no media
played watchdog and officials could be not trusted. And second, the five
Supreme Court justices who declared that preclearance should have been
a vestige of the past spent little time examining these stories.

They likely knew nothing of the majority-Latino town Seguin, Texas,
about a half hour east of San Antonio, where the white population accounted for a third of the population but two-thirds of the city council.
That imbalance persists because officials simply refused to redistrict for
more than two decades, after both the 1980 and the 1990 census. Latino
leaders filed a lawsuit using Section 5 and won—only to see the city respond by rushing the filing deadlines forward for candidates so that no

Latino candidates could qualify. To stave off that latest scheme, the Latino majority had to rely on preclearance—and another successful lawsuit.

Back in Mississippi, former Kilmichael mayor Mary Young has spent years wondering what she would say to the chief justice, who would cheerfully assert in *Northwest Austin* and then *Shelby County* that things had changed in the South, and that preclearance was a dusty relic of another time in a nation that had long turned the page.

"No," she said sadly, and then repeated "no" when I asked her whether Roberts was right and racial discrimination was a thing of the past where she lived. "It's not gone. It's not gone. It's not gone. They should be the ones protecting the civil rights, not gutting it. They should have been investigating some facts before they went and changed it, because the evidence is there that things had not changed."

CHAPTER TEN

VIEWED FROM A comfortable distance, and judging by the final votes of 390–33 in the House and 98–0 in the Senate, the near-unanimous reauthorization of the Voting Rights Act in 2006 looked like a halcyon moment for civil rights. It was a forceful—and rare—moment of bipartisan accord seeking to strengthen and continue these core protections for another twenty-five years. Political pundits still hail that lopsided vote as a reminder that it wasn't so long ago that both parties supported voting rights—and that the consensus around those issues crumbled both suddenly and surprisingly. In fact, the opposite is true.

The landslides in Congress are deceptive; a closer look reveals that the bipartisan kumbaya moment on voting rights was always a facade. Just as in the 1982 reauthorization fight, Republican political leaders didn't want to risk undermining something as American as jazz. But even as the hallelujah chorus of bipartisan self-congratulation faded on Capitol Hill, the strategy to smother the Voting Rights Act in the courts was well underway.

Republicans knew they could ill afford the political cost of challenging the Voting Rights Act head-on. Instead, they adopted the long-term strategy of appointing judges with the approval stamp of the Federalist Society who would do it for them. For that reason, it's not enough to simply tell the story of the VRA's 2006 bipartisan reauthorization by itself. It needs to be understood in the context of another crucial moment in the Senate, one that took place shortly before the eighteen senators on the Judiciary Committee considered the markup of the House VRA reauthorization. Eight months before the Senate Judiciary Committee debated reauthorizing the VRA, it hosted the Supreme Court confirmation hearings for John Roberts. Indeed, the man who had worked so hard to end the VRA in 1982, and who would go on to be the chief architect of its demise, found himself sharing a stage with the piece of legislation that would entangle him for decades to come.

And yet, for all the animosity Roberts had shown the VRA in the early 1980s, for all that he would do to unwind it in the coming years, the proximity to the reauthorization fight did little to spur a Senate interrogation on his actual beliefs on voting rights. It was a telling convergence of the venerable past struggle for democratic self-rule in the former Jim Crow South and the new order of brazenly ideological electoral control on the legal right.

THE SIMPLEST TELLING of this story looks like a hero's tale. In 2005, Representative James Sensenbrenner, now the GOP chairman of House Judiciary, decided that he would lead a bipartisan reauthorization effort in Congress. Sensenbrenner, a rock-ribbed conservative lawmaker from Wisconsin, seemed like an unlikely champion for this historic civil rights cause, but the battle for equal ballot access was a lifelong crusade for him as well.

Sensenbrenner was first elected to his state's assembly during the tumultuous year of 1968. He vividly recalled Black constituents in Milwaukee's poorest neighborhoods describing to him the many obstructions that stood between them and the ballot box. Sensenbrenner, whose relationship with Reagan dated back to his own law school days at Stanford in the 1960s, went to the White House during the 1982 battle and told the president that of all the civil rights legislation that emerged from that era, the Voting Rights Act had been the most transformative. He helped defeat the voices inside the administration—John Roberts foremost among them—who sought to burden the VRA with Lewis Powell's intent standard.

Then, in 2005, having risen to chair the House Judiciary Committee, Sensenbrenner looked over his shoulder and saw a restive Right. Important pieces of the fifteen-year reauthorization signed by President George H. W. Bush in 1991 would soon expire. Sensenbrenner's chairmanship also faced term limits; Lamar Smith of Texas stood next in line for the chairmanship. "He was opposed to the Voting Rights Act because so many Texas jurisdictions fell under it," Sensenbrenner told me. "I made a conscious decision to reauthorize it early, basically to have this a done deal before Mr. Smith ascended."

Sensenbrenner approached his longtime colleague John Conyers, a Democrat from Michigan, with an idea. He proposed a twenty-five-year reauthorization, the longest yet. But it had to be done now. Sensenbrenner and Representative Mel Watt, the North Carolina Democrat who chaired the Congressional Black Caucus, struck a deal. "I would fight off the people on the left who wanted to do substantially more than reauthorize," Watt told me. "He would fight off the people on the right who wanted to do nothing. We would stand back to back and fight this battle all the way through."

Sensenbrenner, Watt, and Conyers all knew that fight could end at the U.S. Supreme Court. The chairman assigned Representative Steve Chabot, an Ohio Republican, the task of building an incontrovertible record demonstrating why the VRA remained crucial—and most important, showing why Congress had to preserve the preclearance provisions contained within Section 5.

Over twelve hearings, some forty-six witnesses described ongoing, discriminatory efforts to deny minority voters full participation in the political process. All the old techniques were very much alive: from Sunset, Louisiana to Waller County, Texas, and across all the states covered by Section 5, the full suite of schemes to suppress Black and other minority votes was in play: gerrymandering, annexation, precinct closures, secret deals between white political leaders that pivoted on sham public considerations.

The committee members noted the hundreds, if not thousands, of potentially discriminatory voting changes that localities subject to preclearance briskly withdrew when it became clear that the Department of Justice was about to take a closer look. The case they built in favor of reauthorization was staggering.

The one Republican in the House willing to challenge Sensenbrenner and the GOP leadership on the Voting Rights Act and Section 5 was the conservative Georgia lawmaker Lynn Westmoreland. The lifelong Georgian, then in his first term, bristled that civil rights leaders would admit that progress had been made on race in the South but still demanded that his state and its neighbors remain under the thumb of the federal government, as if it was still 1964. "We have repented, and we have reformed, and now, as Fannie Lou Hamer famously said"—and here Westmoreland invoked the name of the legendary Mississippi civil rights activist whom the 2006 VRA reauthorization would be named after—"'I am sick and tired of being sick and tired.'"

Westmoreland tried to rally House conservatives to push for changes to the Sensenbrenner-Conyers bill. His arguments echoed the central organizing theme of John Roberts's opinion in the *Shelby County* decision several years later: things had changed in the South.

These days, he suggested, voting rights were being trampled in the North as well. Perhaps preclearance would benefit those states just as they had Georgia and Alabama. Or perhaps the preclearance formula could be modernized so it wasn't still based on presidential election statistics from 1972 and earlier. "Nineteen seventy-two! That was a long time ago," Westmoreland tells me. "Things have changed. That was a big issue to me."

Westmoreland visited Sensenbrenner in his office—"I called him Smiley," Westmoreland cracks—and noticed the photos on the wall. Sensenbrenner with Reagan signing the 1982 VRA reauthorization and with John Lewis. For Westmoreland, Sensenbrenner's commitment to voting rights looked like mere legacy-buffing and posturing—an excuse to paper his walls with photos and honors.

"Milwaukee had more voting rights violations than Georgia. Yet we were still under Section 5 and they weren't," he says. "Sensenbrenner being from a state that was not under Section 5 didn't give him a good view of what it was like, you know, if you wanted to change a voting precinct and then needed to get federal approval. I just thought it made sense that if we were gonna be under Section 5, all states should be under Section 5." This was the old rallying cry of equal-intensity enforcement of the VRA that conservative Illinois congressman Henry Hyde raised to galvanize opposition to the effects test in the 1982 reauthorization battle—only to relinquish it once he heard testimony from Black southerners about the brutal, unjust obstacles to voting they still faced.

Sensenbrenner was part of that fight as well, so he knew that such rhetoric just represented the latest effort to love the VRA to death by hugging it so tightly it suffocated, as Hyde himself once put it. Modernizing the formula could take years. Extending it nationwide would drain resources and make it harder to regulate the localities with the most serious issues. Under the Supreme Court's 1980 ruling in *City of Boerne v. Flores*, civil rights legislation had to be congruent and proportional to the evil it attempted to remedy. National preclearance without proof of national need would certainly catch the court's attention.

Sensenbrenner, Watt, and others also worried that making no change at all could invite the court's inspection as well. But given the timing and the political issues, the cosponsors and a national coalition of civil rights organizations decided together to work within the bounds imposed by *Boerne*. They would develop the extensive record supporting reauthorization with the aim of showing that Section 5 remained an essential response.

Westmoreland knew he was being stonewalled. House leaders and party officials told them they wouldn't budge. "They made it clear," Westmoreland says. "It was all about not wanting to stir the pot. It was about not wanting to get Mel Watt and the Black community upset about voting rights. It was political expediency from folks who weren't living under it and didn't have any interest in living under it."

Still, Westmoreland set out to stir the pot one last time. Under what had become known as the "Hastert rule," the Republican conference required all legislation that went to the floor to have the support of a "majority of the majority." Since the VRA reauthorization bill hadn't yet cleared that threshold, House leaders had to pull it for a day and agree to votes on four key amendments. They would have modified the preclearance formula to a rolling average of turnout and registration over the last three presidential elections, made it easier for covered localities to escape preclearance, shortened the extension from twenty-five years to just ten, and eliminated assistance for multilingual voters.

All four amendments went down in defeat. But there, too, the final score disguised the real story. A majority of the Republican members backed three of the four amendments—a sign that bipartisan support for the VRA was slipping, not solidifying.

"We knew we didn't have a chance to change it," Westmoreland told me. "But we wanted to point all of these things out, and create a record if it was ever taken to the high court. I knew that if we got to the high court, we would win."

For his part, Sensenbrenner described it as "one of the most extensive considerations of any piece of legislation that the United States Congress has dealt with." The GOP-led House responded with a resounding reauthorization vote of 390–33. When the U.S. Senate didn't take it up immediately, Sensenbrenner and Representative John Lewis made some good trouble and wheeled more than twelve thousand pages of the committee's report over to the Senate side and demanded action.

A jubilant Lewis bestowed his Republican partner with an honorific he never imagined. "Here I was, this white conservative Republican from the Milwaukee suburbs, called 'bro' by a Black Democratic civil rights icon," Sensenbrenner marvels. "It felt good."

Meanwhile a defeated Westmoreland went to the House floor and predicted the victory to come. "We came up short today of the votes we needed to modernize and strengthen the Voting Rights Act, largely because of partisan posturing, ignorance of the act's details and lingering prejudice toward Southerners. We lost on the vote board in the House, but we won in the grand scheme of things," he insisted.

"We created a public record that will be cited when there's an inevitable court challenge to Section 5. We needed 218 votes in the House but we'll only need five votes on the Supreme Court. Justice will prevail. The honor of Georgia will be restored."

WHAT WESTMORELAND CERTAINLY understood—even if it frustrated him at the time—was that, in reality, the GOP leadership in the House and the Bush administration, as well, was solidly on his side. Republican leaders knew it was in their long-term interest to erode the Voting Rights Act. They simply didn't want to be blamed for the demise of popular legislation, so they appointed judges who would do it for them.

In 2005, just as Congress began considering the VRA reauthorization, Bush made his two most consequential court appointments. When

O'Connor announced her retirement, he nominated Roberts. Bush certainly had to be aware of the 1981 and 1982 memos in which the young Roberts so stridently suggested that the reforms proposed by Congress were radical, extreme, and threatened "existing electoral systems at every level of government." Bush also would have certainly known how forcefully Roberts exhorted his bosses to oppose results tests and other revisions to the VRA.

But, when Rehnquist died, Bush nudged Roberts into the chief's chair. Roberts would now be replacing the justice he clerked for—another diehard opponent of an expansive vision of voting rights who talked through conservative legal thought with his clerks as they strolled the Supreme Court grounds. Then, after caving to Federalist Society pressure to jettison his first choice for the Rehnquist vacancy, Harriet Miers, on grounds of insufficient conservatism, Bush rubber-stamped the Right's strongly preferred known quantity: Samuel Alito.

"A significant motivation in all these appointments seemed to be to use them to secure conservative voting rights objectives that the president had cherished but declined to advance legislatively so as to maintain the party's standing both with citizens of color and with moderate whites," writes Jesse Rhodes, a voting rights scholar and political scientist at the University of Massachusetts, in *Ballot Blocked*.

That stratagem is also almost the very definition of antidemocratic behavior. Conservatives had no interest in fighting a direct attack on the Voting Rights Act. So they mounted a rearguard assault. Conservatives would empower the courts to achieve their long-desired goal of dialing back the federal government's role in preserving the right to vote. The man at the center of the strategy would be John Roberts, the same person at the heart of the strategy in 1982. But this time, Democrats would barely see it coming.

AS JOHN ROBERTS sat before the eighteen-member Judiciary Committee, Roberts charmed Senate lions such as Orrin Hatch, Ted Kennedy, Charles Grassley, and Joe Biden with fictional images of his Indiana boyhood while pledging that he would be a modest jurist. He proposed to serve as a humble umpire calling balls and strikes, always remembering that Congress made the laws, not him.

Roberts had been a full-throated Republican for decades and his strategic genius sought out by multiple Bushes in 2000 when the all-hands alarm sounded for all prominent GOP lawyers—especially those who hoped to be appointed to top positions by the next administration—to coalesce and ensure that George W. Bush prevailed in the courts. But Democrats were woefully ineffective when it came to pushing Roberts on such questions.

They were even more anemic in engaging with Roberts's views on voting rights. They largely preferred to keep the tone of courtly badinage going during Roberts's testimony—even though there was an extensive public record for them to explore on the nominee's voting rights record. The National Archives had released memo after memo documenting Roberts's scorched-earth views in the 1982 reauthorization fight. And a wide array of scholars and lawmakers alike well understood that the Federalist Society's originalist takeover of the courts—which counted Roberts as an early recruit—meant that the VRA was bound to face grave judicial threats even as Congress reauthorized it.

"I was very impressed with Roberts, and I voted for him," Russell Feingold, the Democratic senator from Wisconsin, told me. "Look, Bush was going to make the choice. Roberts was a modest, thoughtful guy who struck me as somebody who understood what his place in history would be."

The Democrats on the Judiciary panel failed to prod Roberts away from a single talking point, or challenge the nominee's carefully cultivated image of himself as a humble yet high-achieving midwestern choirboy. They also sat on their hands as the nominee told his version of the 1982 reauthorization fight, in which the future chief justice dramatically underplayed his own leadership role that's clear from his memos, insisted that he was a junior official implementing the policies of others, and danced awfully close to the line of misleading Congress.

Roberts spent seventeen hours in the witness chair answering questions from senators. Very few of them had to do with voting rights. Only

Ted Kennedy, and once Feingold, truly dug into the Roberts memos and tried to divine where he might take the nation now on voting rights.

Kennedy did not mince words:

> You wrote that violations of Section 2 of the Voting Rights Act, and I quote, "should not be made too easy to prove since they provide a basis for the most intrusive interference imaginable by Federal courts into State and local processes." You also wrote, and I quote, "it would be difficult to conceive of a more drastic alteration of local government affairs, and under our Federal system such an intrusion should not be too readily permitted."
>
> And you didn't stop there. You concluded that Section 2 of the Voting Rights Act was, quote, "constitutionally suspect and contrary to the most fundamental tenets of the legislating process on which the laws of this country are based." I am deeply troubled by another statement that you made at the time, and I quote, "there is no evidence of voting abuses nationwide supporting the need for such a change."
>
> No evidence? I was there, Judge Roberts; both the House and the Senate had the extensive hearings. We considered detail-specific testimony from affected voters throughout the country. But you dismissed the work of Congress out of hand. "Do not be fooled," you wrote, "by the House vote or the 61 Senate sponsors of the House bill. Many members of the House did not know they were doing more than simply extending the Act, and several of the 61 Senators have already indicated that they only intended to support simple extension."
>
> Judge Roberts, Republicans and Democrats overwhelmingly supported this legislation, but you thought we didn't really know what we were doing. Newt Gingrich and James Sensenbrenner voted for the House bill. Dan Quayle was an original Senate cosponsor of the bill. We held extensive hearings, created a lengthy record, yet you thought there was no evidence of voting abuses that would justify the legislation.

Roberts remained calm under repeated questioning from Kennedy over both days. He came prepared for this line of investigation. Over and over, Roberts maintained that he was simply a young aide in the Department of Justice executing the administration's position. He also implied, without stating outright, that his views had evolved, by reiterating that the debate had been twenty-three years ago. Roberts elided the question of effects versus intent and said that it was the position of both the Reagan administration and the attorney general that the "Voting Rights Act should be extended for the longest period of its extension in history without change."

"The articulation of views that you read from represented my effort to articulate the views of the administration and the position of the administration for whom I worked, for which I worked, 23 years ago," Roberts said, leaning into his talking points.

He then dismissed Kennedy's concerns about whether his past writings reflected any personal opinion, waving away his 1981 and 1982 memos as the work of a young, low-level staffer just doing his job. But when he'd reach the high court, the throughline would be clear to all.

"Oh, well, the existing Voting Rights Act, the constitutionality has been upheld," he said, before noting, presciently, that "[t]here is a separate question that would be raised if the Voting Rights Act were extended, as I know Congress is considering."

Roberts told Kennedy that he saw no constitutional issue with the 1982 VRA and that he was "not aware of any constitutional issue that's been raised about it." Yet in one of his 1982 memos, he had written to his Civil Rights Division boss, Brad Reynolds, that "on the issue of [imposing] the effects standard nationwide on the strength of the record will be constitutionally suspect, but also contrary to the most fundamental tenets of the legislative process on which the laws of this country are based."

Feingold reminded Roberts what the stakes had been in *Mobile v. Bolden*: Blacks had been unable to elect a single city commissioner in seven decades because the at-large voting method allowed the white majority to choose every single member, every single time. "The evidence was very clear that, as a practical matter, although African-Americans could register and vote, they couldn't elect anyone. But to get relief under the Supreme Court standard which you appear to have supported, they had to go to enormous effort and financial expense to prove discriminatory intent, including hiring a historian who could piece together the motivations of city officials who had designed the electoral system almost a hundred years earlier."

Feingold then asked the obvious question: "In this situation, the administration was not bound by a Supreme Court decision in deciding what position to take under the proposed Voting Rights Act amendments. So why at that point did you want to make Section 2 cases so difficult to prove?"

"Senator," Roberts replied, "you keep referring to what I supported and what I wanted to do. I was a 26-year-old staff lawyer. It was my first job as a lawyer after my clerkships. I was not shaping administration policy. The administration policy was shaped by the Attorney General on whose staff I served. It was the policy of President Reagan. It was to extend the Voting Rights Act without change for the longest period in history at that point, and it was my job to promote the Attorney General's view and the President's view on that issue. And that's what I was doing."

Roberts not only ducked the specific question, he also appears to have rewritten history, whitewashing his own prominent involvement in the fight to erect greater obstacles to the enforcement of the VRA. Recall that the position of the Reagan administration and the position of Smith, Reynolds, Roberts, and the DOJ differed at crucial times throughout the 1982 reauthorization fight. In the summer of 1982, and again in the fall, the Reagan administration said that it would sign whatever reauthorization Congress passed. It was Roberts's own DOJ that pushed back, over and over, driven by the young attorney's memos. Despite his protestations before the Judiciary Committee, Roberts was in fact driving the DOJ's intransigent position on the effects test and other key bulwarks of the VRA. Instead of blindly doing the bidding of William French Smith, Roberts had drafted the talking points Smith had used at the White House to persuade Reagan to reverse himself on the intent question.

There was no unified Reagan administration position. Indeed, Roberts and the DOJ at key junctures were on quite different sides from the White House. Roberts elided the truth and grossly understated his actual role. The memos show, again and again, that Roberts was among those crafting the policy, leading the charge, and often on the opposite side of the president in the reauthorization fight.

"What I am interested in doing is asking now whether you believe that the effects test is constitutionally suspect," Kennedy continued. "Is it suspect today or whether you find that it is settled law. . . . This is the backbone of effective voting in our country and our society, and I think the American people are entitled to know whether you believe or suspect that that particular provision, which has passed just overwhelmingly by the House and the Senate, signed by President Reagan, and has resulted in this historic march to progress, is constitutionally sound. That is what I am interested in."

"I have no basis for viewing it as constitutionally suspect and I don't. If an issue were to arise before the Supreme Court or before the Court of Appeals, if I head back there, I would consider that issue with an open mind in light of the arguments."

"I gather—you've had an extensive answer—that from that answer, I did hear that it is not constitutionally suspect as far as your view today."

"Yes."

The Judiciary Committee sent Roberts's confirmation to the full Senate with a 13–5 vote in favor. The Senate confirmed with a vote of 78–22.

Four years later in *Northwest Austin*, and then another four years after that in *Shelby County*, the chief justice would make it very clear that he found key provisions of the Voting Rights Act to be much worse than constitutionally suspect.

When Feingold and I talked, he maintained that in 2005 the committee wasn't much exercised over the voting rights entries on Roberts's résumé. "Voting rights wasn't an issue then," he said. "The Voting Rights Act, when he came before me, was still a big bipartisan thing. People weren't talking about voting rights."

Feingold's position didn't make a great deal of sense, especially in view of all the attention he and Kennedy paid to the Roberts memos during his confirmation hearings. So I asked him why Democrats missed the larger Republican play to unwind the VRA through the courts, given that the Roberts DOJ memos made his intentions to gut the act clear.

"We weren't concerned that it's ever going to become an issue," Feingold insisted. "Yes, maybe it's something to be discussed. But I don't think any of us felt that he was really going to try and undermine the Voting Rights Act, which of course is one of the worst things he could have possibly done. Then he did."

THE GOP'S LONG-TERM judicial strategy to control elections would get another crucial assist when the 2006 reauthorization went to the U.S. Senate. Senate Republicans, like their House counterparts, had no interest in actually opposing the VRA. But they did want to build a legislative record to support the court battle they knew would be imminent. The basic math had already tilted their way.

Unlike the House, which welcomed committee testimony from only the friendliest of expert witnesses, the Senate Judiciary Committee held nine hearings during the spring of 2006 that turned deeply contentious.

The GOP efforts in the Senate clearly arose out of a concerted strategy. Conservatives did not trust the committee chairman, the moderate Republican Arlen Specter from Pennsylvania. To keep relations cordial, Specter was told he needed to hire a top conservative lawyer and strategist, Michael O'Neill, a Federalist Society member and former Supreme Court clerk to Clarence Thomas, as chief counsel. The chief counsel played an important role in preparing Supreme Court and other judicial nominees and in scripting committee hearings. And in this case, the script Republicans were looking to write for the VRA committee hearings was very specific.

Republicans in the Senate reached out to a collection of elite law professors, largely liberal-leaning, who would typically field invitations to testify from Senate Democrats. "I was specifically called by Republicans. Every other time I've been called to testify before Congress, I've been called by the Democratic side," says Richard Hasen, a professor of law and political science at UCLA and director of the Safeguarding Democracy Project. This time, the invitation came with an entirely different agenda. "It was primarily to make a record that the Voting Rights Act's constitutionality was in danger."

The danger, of course, came from the Supreme Court. If this had been a horror film, the call would be coming from inside the house. The truth of the matter was this: Like so many other products of political compromise, the Voting Rights Act resembled a hot-wired Rube Goldberg contraption that couldn't be put back together if someone started messing too closely under the hood. Start picking it apart, and it couldn't be reassembled again. And so step one of the conservative plot to undo it in the courts required getting liberal law professors to admit that some of the problems with the VRA were real. Did Section 5 miss the abuses in Tennessee and Arkansas? Sure, it did. Should the formula be updated, when states like Ohio and Florida had seen the most issues in 2000 and 2004? Absolutely.

Those same congressional Republicans who wanted those issues on the record, however, had no interest in actually remedying them. Conservatives had zero political appetite to bring two big Republican states like Ohio and Florida into the preclearance regime. Republican lawmakers in Arkansas and Tennessee weren't interested in joining either. And the solution that some Republicans professed to back—extending preclearance to the entire nation—would never pass muster with a conservative Supreme Court increasingly focused on federalism and states' rights. A massive overhaul of the VRA would introduce even more potential avenues for challenges before Federalist Society judges.

It was a brilliant strategy. Get experts to articulate the issues with the VRA on the record, so that future litigants could make the case that "even liberal law professors" believed the law should be changed. Then have those same experts propose solutions that would never make it through Congress, let alone withstand scrutiny from John Roberts and his allies.

In subsequent years, this Senate testimony would help set up briefs from the right-wing judicial apparatus arguing that Congress simply lacked the will to do the heavy lifting required to modernize the act. It was a nifty act of political jujitsu, given that the GOP's own opposition to the necessary changes is what made effective legislating on the issue so impossible.

"The groundwork was being laid," Hasen says. "There was a political and legal strategy being made. It would take from 2006 to 2013 for it to bear fruit, but it's laid out there. The path was pretty clear." What the Republicans sought to do was introduce all this doubt into the official record.

Hasen still marvels at the strategic savvy. "These guys are patient," says Hasen, "and they've got a long-term strategy." The expert testimony built a record that they could—and would—use in dozens of future briefs that argued Congress understood that the VRA reauthorization had potential constitutional issues, yet moved it along anyway.

But the tactical, long-term planning went even deeper than this. Senate Republicans invited former Texas solicitor general (and onetime Clarence Thomas clerk at the Supreme Court) Gregory Coleman to testify before the Judiciary Committee. Coleman used his testimony to drop a crucial statistic into the congressional record. Preclearance, he claimed, cost states and political subdivisions "tens or hundreds of millions of dollars" in legal fees to prepare DOJ submissions, Coleman declared in his opening statement. He offered no proof. He did not cite any study. He provided no evidence whatsoever that his numbers were accurate. In the written statement that he provided the committee, his already vague and unsubstantiated numbers became inflated again—by a huge margin. "Preclearance compliance has over the past decade required the commitment of state and local resources easily valued at over a billion dollars," Coleman claimed.

Once again, Coleman did not provide any supporting evidence or show how he arrived at this figure. Nor did he explain how it got revised so dramatically upward from the guesstimate he floated in his opening statement citing a range of "tens or hundreds of millions." No senator on either side asked him for sourcing or about this wild incongruity. The statistic that Coleman got introduced into congressional record soon became a mantra on the legal right. It would become a crucial part of the briefs and amici filed in the high court's evisceration of the VRA in *Shelby County*. It would also be featured in questions that Supreme Court justices posed from the bench, citing language in the briefs before it that in turn cited the congressional hearings. No party in this tightly closed epistemic circle revealed that Coleman was the source—and that he never provided any source of his own.

That was hardly the only misleading entry in the Senate committee's official record. The legislative history included in the Senate report—a tranche of documents considered crucial to federal judges and Supreme Court justices working to divine lawmakers' intent—itself played fast and loose with the facts. The Senate had approved the reauthorization unanimously, as did the Judiciary Committee. But the legislative report—released six days after the Senate vote, and the day before the president signed the bill into law—reads as if the senators had opposed legislation that they all actually backed. Right-wing senators are on record in the documents complaining not only about the substance of the bill, but also about the process—even though the GOP enjoyed full control over that process in both the House and Senate. They noted an "artificial rush" to approve the bill a year before it expired, passed as a "foregone conclusion" and without deliberation.

The unprecedented report provided a road map for future judges to contest the VRA's continued constitutionality.

"That's right: while the Voting Rights Act reauthorization in 2006 passes on a ninety-eight to zero basis, at the same time, the Senate Judiciary Committee issues a report saying it's probably unconstitutional," says Hasen, still shaking his head over it all. "These guys are very patient. And they were playing a very long game."

CHAPTER ELEVEN

TWO MEN WHO quietly remade American democracy work from offices with completely different views. Edward Blum's study overlooks Penobscot Bay in Maine, and if the floor-to-ceiling windows look like they open onto a real-life Andrew Wyeth watercolor, it's because the great American realist spent seven decades capturing the beauty of this New England island coastline. Meanwhile James Bopp's law office sits alongside a quiet, wide midwestern intersection in downtown Terre Haute, Indiana, amid bank branches and medical offices and local pizza chains—none of which can be observed from his waiting room because its window is covered with a giant American flag.

Yet both men look as if they could have been chiseled from the local landscape. Blum, affable and kind, wears a light-blue shirt and khakis as naturally as if he were born in them, a lighthouse twinkle in his deep-set eyes. The determined Bopp sports a slight center part in his dome of gray hair, almost as if he woke up in his suit and tie.

Neither man originally set out to remake the nation's campaign finance laws or to use the rhetoric of race neutrality to halt the progress of voting rights and affirmative action. But as the visionaries behind *Citizens United* and *Shelby County*, Bopp and Blum, respectively, recognized that the right litigation, patiently crafted through multiple cases over the better part of a decade, could rewrite the American social contract on campaign spending and multiracial democracy.

Blum never attended a day of law school but earned his fortune and stunning coastal views in finance. In 1992, he mounted a losing bid for Congress from a Houston-area district drawn as a majority-minority seat. That experience propelled him into activism. Before long, he'd joined

forces with many of the Right's best-known, and best-resourced, foundations and carved out a critical role as what might be called a Supreme
Court whisperer—trying to match up strong test cases with viable majorities on the high court.

Bopp had intended to join a long line of family doctors until he wound
up in an organic chemistry class he could not ace. He studied law and set up
a practice in his hometown of Terre Haute so that he could keep expenses
low, while advancing his pro-life and free speech arguments on behalf of
tiny conservative nonprofits. Neither man loses often. And neither Blum
nor Bopp allows any defeat to be more than a bump on a long journey.

Bopp and Blum have both made a point of staying out of Washington. Bopp even found himself replaced on *Citizens United* and *Bush v.
Gore,* even though he'd been the intellectual architect for both cases, in
favor of D.C. insider (and former solicitor general) Ted Olson. Like many
working on the vanguard of the legal Right, they became Republicans, in
part, because they felt alienated by the Left during the tumultuous 1960s
and 1970s. But that's not to say they viewed the opposition as unworthy—
indeed, they both freely borrowed rhetoric and strategies from the NAACP
and ACLU that those organizations had successfully used in winning civil
rights cases even as they worked to unravel them.

They also both made a virtue out of their D.C. exile: by attacking the legal and regulatory scene from outside, they had far more success than they
would have from an office on K Street. Blum and Bopp advanced ideals
that claimed their deep personal allegiance, meaning that they remained
uninterested in party-line doctrine—or compromise. Instead, they tapped
their own supreme confidence in their beliefs to wrench our politics in
their direction.

They know they court the image of readily caricatured villainy. Blum
once boarded a flight to Washington and heard a well-dressed man dis-
cussing his challenge to the Voting Rights Act. It turned out to be Armand
Derfner, whose 1960s victories at the Supreme Court preserved and advanced the Voting Rights Act. They disagreed politely and Derfner walked
away confused, wondering, as he recalls, "How can a nice person be doing
such awful things?"

In many ways, they see themselves as inheritors of the true mission of building a stronger, freer nation. And now we are all living in Bopp's and Blum's America.

THE MOST EFFECTIVE conservative Supreme Court savant of the last generation believes he might be the first Republican his mother ever met. Edward Blum grew up in a lefty household with framed pictures of Franklin Roosevelt, raised by Jewish parents deeply invested in the fight for civil rights. His father was the rare enlisted man who spoke Yiddish and so he remained in the military through 1946 helping resettle Jews rescued from concentration camps. When his dad returned home, the family settled first in Florida, then Texas, with his father selling shoes or anything else he could. Blum remembers traveling with his dad to North Carolina textile towns where he'd buy women's underwear at wholesale prices and sell them at coffee shops and motels for twice as much along the road home.

His parents' experiences informed Blum's sense of race, religion, and ethnicity: equality mattered deeply. Yet he also believed that such personal concerns ought to have no bearing on public life. His high school yearbook from Bellaire High in Houston, where then "Eddie" Blum graduated in 1969, shows a serious-looking student with a long, floppy haircut casually parted to the side. He can't be found in the pictures for any politics clubs, but he did participate in three others: Bellarama (drama), Cinemakers (movies), and Entre Nous (French). Blum's classmate Randy Quaid, who would go on to star in *Midnight Express* and *National Lampoon's Vacation*, joined him in the drama and film clubs.

Blum says he was a campus liberal at the University of Texas, where he joined the Taskforce on the Improvement of Minority Education, opposed the Vietnam War, and studied African literature. A literature professor from Nigeria encouraged him to do graduate work, so Blum enrolled at the State University of New York in New Paltz to study fiction from Nigeria, Ghana, and Sierra Leone, and he thought he might have found his niche. A life in the academy beckoned, but to the chagrin of many liberals, Blum says with a laugh, "You know, I am not on the faculty at Purdue teaching West African literature." After college, he returned home to Houston, taught school, and opened a bookstore that specialized in thrillers. Nothing stuck. A professor who liked Blum's taste in mystery novels brought in a stack of conservative and libertarian magazines for him. Between back issues of *Commentary* and *Reason*, his political transformation began.

But how—without a staff, a real office, even a day of law school—did Blum become the unquestioned master of turning the ideas behind the conservative civil rights counterrevolution into real-life litigation? His timing certainly helped. Blum would bring cases espousing color-blind, race-neutral ideals at exactly the time that the Federalist Society and the broader quest for court capture represented the Right's true policy arm.

"I'm a one-trick pony. I really do recognize that I'm a one-trick pony," Blum says. "If you remember *Fiddler on the Roof* or *Hello, Dolly!*—my role is to identify an area of the law that I think needs changing, or identify a policy that needs revisiting. Then I recruit a plaintiff to do that, hire a legal team, raise the funds, and then try to keep the train on track. Really, I just know one area of the law fairly well. I don't know any other areas of the law at all."

Blum's true journey begins after the bookstore collapsed and he endured bankruptcy. He landed a very different job as an investment banker selling municipal bonds. The finance world solidified his move to the right. For years he commuted downtown from Houston's outer suburbs, but when his daughter went to college, he and his wife, an insurance executive, bought a town house in the thriving Museum District. When he registered to vote as a Republican, Blum was dismayed to learn that the GOP had not fielded a candidate for this U.S. House seat for years.

"I always think there should be a choice," he told me. That's how, in 1992, Blum found himself the GOP nominee for Texas's Eighteenth Congressional District. Republican friends warned him that he was wasting his time. Blum hired a national pollster who delivered the same message with more statistics: a white investment banker, they told him, stood precisely zero chance of beating Texas's only Black congressman in a majority-Black district long represented by the trailblazing civil rights icon Barbara Jordan. Yet Blum persisted. "If the people of Russia and Czechoslovakia can rise up and replace their leaders," he said on the campaign trail, "so can the people of the Eighteenth District."

The activists in Prague might have had a simpler task. Blum had to overcome gerrymandering. Houston's Black and Latino populations grew during the 1990 census. The 1982 reauthorization of the VRA mandated that states draw "opportunity districts" for minority communities where possible. In many parts of the South, the practice favored both groups, racial minorities and Republicans. Drawing a majority-minority seat often meant packing Black or Latino voters, most likely to support a Democrat, into a single district, and bleaching surrounding districts with whiter and more Republican constituents. Both patterns produced rapid results. In 1994, the Congressional Black Caucus reached its largest membership since Reconstruction. But that same year, the GOP took the House for the first time in fifty years and began to lock down the Solid South.

It did not favor Blum. The Texas legislature, then controlled by Democrats, created a new Latino seat by contorting the Eighteenth into a radical racial gerrymander that hopscotched over some seventy-five miles, from Houston's Intercontinental Airport to the old Astrodome. Along the way, it collected housing projects and some of the city's wealthiest enclaves. The neighborhoods shared nothing in common. But the district was not designed to represent communities; it was carved to be exactly 49 percent Black and ensure the election of a Black Democrat, while preserving as many Democratic votes as possible to elect white incumbents in nearby seats.

Blum worked as many traditional levers as he could. He produced position papers on the economy, attacked the incumbent for not supporting Houston's billion-dollar space industry, and published a forty-nine-page book that the *Houston Chronicle* called "an effort unmatched by the congressional candidates throughout Southeast Texas." As an overmatched, underfinanced Republican, Blum and his wife hit every neighborhood in the sprawling district. By Election Day, they'd banged on some twenty-five thousand doors. "This was long before GPS," Blum says, "so we would have to map out our routes in advance. I'd take one side of the street and my wife would go down the other." Blum's aggressive retail strategy worked, to some extent: he lost, but earned 34 percent of the vote. That outpaced Houston's native son George H. W. Bush, who won the presidency but just 23 percent in Texas's Eighteenth.

As Blum reflected on the experience, what bothered him wasn't the defeat, which he'd expected. It was walking the district and seeing how law-makers pulled apart multiracial neighborhoods where Blacks and Latinos lived side by side for the purpose of creating a specific racial outcome.

"The state of Texas, block by block, harvested individuals based on their race in order to create these racially homogenous districts," he says. "That is not what electoral districts are supposed to be about." Traditional re-districting principles, such as compactness and continuity, kept neighbor-hoods together, he argues. But as they rang doorbells, Blum and his wife would walk down an average Houston block and discover that the Black apartment complex on one side of the street would be in the Eighteenth while the Latino building across the way had been drawn into an entirely different district. "It happened dozens and dozens of times."

Splitting voters into white, Latino, and Black districts felt like a new form of political segregation. It rankled his ideals of equality and fair representation. "We used to have separate drinking fountains for blacks and whites, and separate schools for blacks and whites," Blum told *Texas Monthly* in 1994. "We said that was wrong and got rid of it. So why, today, should we have separate congressional districts for blacks and whites?"

The answer, of course, depends on how you define the problem. After the 1990 elections, Texas's twenty-seven-person congressional delegation was all men, including twenty-two whites, four Latinos, and one Black member. The 1990 census showed that Latinos and Blacks accounted for nearly 40 percent of the state's population, yet white lawmakers drew dis-tricts that kept themselves entrenched in power. Growing communities were correspondingly locked out of political power and denied the re-sources and influence that come with elected office.

The VRA looked to fix that. From Blum's perspective, ensuring all these groups had representation in politics came at the cost of slicing apart multi-ethnic neighborhoods and making the insulting judgment that people only wanted to be represented by someone who looked like them. But from the perspective of groups who had been locked out of power for decades, and represented by whites for years, *that* was the insult. They tended, with no small justification, to view traditional redistricting principles as code for white power as usual.

In North Carolina, Mel Watt became in 1994 the first Black elected to

Congress from the Tar Heel State in ninety-four years. The district he represented forms a meandering, slicing work of cartography that resembles a coiled snake. He bristled when whites brought litigation protesting a district drawn intentionally to elect a Black member. "They said my district was political apartheid," Watt told me, still fuming about the phrase thirty years later. "What was North Carolina before that?"

At home in Houston, Blum had read a *New York Times* article about the suit claiming that Watt's seat was a racial gerrymander. It seemed to him that if there was a good case in North Carolina, brought by law professors at Duke, he might be able to mount one just as good in Texas. He found a small-town lawyer in Louisiana who would take the case. The following year, Blum sued Texas, claiming that its new congressional map represented an unconstitutional racial gerrymander. A three-judge panel in Houston agreed and overturned the map. Texas appealed to the U.S. Supreme Court. In 1996, the high court also found in Blum's favor: the Texas map had to go. An amateur armchair litigant had won at every step, culminating in a precedent-setting Supreme Court decision. It was a high that Paine Webber couldn't compete with.

"My business associates back in Houston," says Blum with a laugh, "recognized that date as the date in which my interest in public finance and investments started to wane."

He didn't stop in Texas. Not when he could see a path toward changing the rules of the game everywhere. "It was the triumph of ordinary citizens," he said after the victory. "And we did it because we believe so deeply in a color-blind society." After the Supreme Court delivered that first win for Blum and his team in *Bush v. Vera*, and then forced changes to North Carolina's map in *Shaw v. Reno*, Blum's operation compiled a list of equally vulnerable racially gerrymandered districts in the country, including seats in New York, South Carolina, and Virginia.

"One by one we went after the others," he says, "and you know, we just knocked off all of them."

Just like that, Edward Blum understood his path to making change. He would use litigation to restore what he believed to be the original objectives of the civil rights movement: race and ethnicity should not be used to help anyone and should not be used to hurt anyone.

In 2005 Blum founded the Project on Fair Representation as an advocacy organization, hopeful he could offer the GOP-controlled Congress a framework that he believed would update and modernize the VRA. Blum and his then-partner Abigail Thernstrom spent nearly four months on Capitol Hill lobbying their cause before congressional lawmakers. Most of his meetings ended the same way that Lynn Westmoreland's had.

While the VRA had become a rite of faith on the Democratic side, there were also conservatives who had come to believe "these provisions actually benefited them in the drawing of their safe districts." Blum recalls one meeting with a confused Republican congressman, "a good old boy, back-slapping type," who interrupted the presentation at the beginning and says, "Now, you've got to help me on this. I'm kind of confused. Do we like Section 5 or do we not like Section 5?" Blum throws his hands in the air and laughs two decades later. "That question alone made clear that people thought Section 5 was good for Republicans. Those safe Black districts make all the other ones white and more Republican. And that's good for us." This was just Blum and Thernstrom's third meeting on the Hill, but already, "I'm saying to myself, 'This is over.'"

Blum knew Karl Rove from Texas, and George W. Bush's top strategist agreed to meet. Blum and Thernstrom settled into Rove's West Wing office, steps from the president, and encountered the same story. No one, on either side, had the political appetite to oppose the VRA. "Karl was pleasant and funny, a little sardonic," Blum says, but Rove hardly wanted the president to make any case that could be seen as hostile to voting rights during the midterms.

The entire meeting lasted about fifteen minutes. Blum offered to come back and provide any additional statistics the White House might want. Rove politely demurred. "He said, 'Well, you know, thanks for coming in.'" Blum understood what that meant. "At this point, I realize this is not going to happen," he says. "The only way these provisions were ever going to be modified or struck down would be through the courts."

JAMES BOPP MIGHT not have followed the family medical tradition, yet much the same reverence for life shaped the choices of this midwestern Catholic.

Bopp graduated from Indiana University in 1970. In his college years, he was repelled by the antiwar and countercultural activists on campus and became the head of IU's chapter of Young Americans for Freedom—the organization launched by William F. Buckley to train and network a generation of collegiate conservatives. While in Bloomington, Bopp also wrote for a campus publication that ultimately became the long-running and influential conservative hell-raising journal *The American Spectator*. But journalism was merely a way station, he told *Mother Jones*—"another way to fight the left, and that's what I was into." He earned his law degree at the University of Florida, then returned home to Indiana in 1973, just as the U.S. Supreme Court handed down its decision in *Roe v. Wade* and legalized abortion nationwide.

Five years later, Bopp had risen from Indiana Right to Life to general counsel of the nationwide National Right to Life Committee. During the 1980 presidential election, the rising pro-life and religious Right went all in for Ronald Reagan. The National Right to Life voter guides, distributed to millions via state groups and religious activists, played a crucial role in building grassroots support for the former California governor.

The voter guides walked a fine legal line: Were they advocacy for a specific candidate or issue-driven voter education manuals from a protected nonprofit? When liberal litigants tested the question in a suit, Bopp defended them as protected First Amendment speech. His victories won him a national reputation as the young conservative lawyer with the intellectual vision and persuasive power to fight election law and campaign finance cases.

This work taught Bopp something else as well: these groups supplied a megaphone for everyday citizens to amplify their voices in American politics. Elites and incumbents might view their rise as a threat. But for Bopp, nonprofit advocacy organizations represented civic involvement at its best and embodied the purpose of First Amendment protections. Campaign finance laws, he believed, were an elite tool to limit the ability of advocacy groups to get their message out.

"What's at stake is the ability of average citizens to participate in our democracy," Bopp told *Frontline*. "Rich people have the money and under our laws, and under the Constitution, can spend the money. People of average means don't have the money. They have to pool their resources. They have to join a group. So when these laws attack groups, then they are attacking people of average means. They are not attacking the rich."

That characterization is something of a stretch for an activity generously subsidized by federal tax law. The ability of groups like National Right to Life to participate at such a high level arose from a loophole in the liberal-minded Tax Reform Act passed by Congress in 1976. It allowed groups formed with a tax-exempt educational purpose to use as much as 20 percent of their budgets for direct lobbying and political activity, all while protecting their special tax status. That, in turn, was a strong incentive for them to raise much more money. National Right to Life claimed eleven million active supporters across some three thousand chapters nationwide. Many of those supporters might have been people of average means. But as Rick Perlstein reports in *Nixonland*, Bopp's boss at the time, the National Right to Life executive director Dr. Mildred Jefferson, admitted that the idea that they represented some grassroots movement— rather than a top-down organization taking advantage of a change in the tax law—was so much "romantic noise."

In 2002, Congress returned to campaign finance reform with the Bipartisan Campaign Reform Act—the most significant package of election reforms in the four decades since Watergate. (It became known more popularly as McCain-Feingold, after the two senators who sponsored it and returned to the issue again and again.) McCain-Feingold looked to close the so-called soft-money loophole that allowed donors, unions, and corporations to write blank checks to political parties for party-building and get-out-the-vote drives.

But those activities proved so amorphous, so prone to savvy manipulation, and easy to funnel toward support of individual candidates, that soft money became an end run around restrictions on donations to candidates themselves. McCain-Feingold tightened another loophole as well, around so-called issue-advocacy ads. These saturated the airwaves before elections, purported to take a stance on an issue, but really served as personalized attack spots. They carefully tiptoed the increasingly meaningless line between an issue-themed commercial and a campaign ad: "Baseball, puppies, and the flag make America great. Senator X hates baseball, puppies, and the flag. Call Senator X and tell him to stop voting against baseball, puppies, and the flag." McCain-Feingold created a new restriction that sought to fortify that line with barbed wire: it prevented outside donors, corporations, or labor unions from airing ads that mentioned candidates within sixty days of the general election (and thirty days before a primary).

Bopp eagerly awaited an opportunity to challenge the new law as a violation of the First Amendment. In 2004, he found his client in Feingold's home state: Wisconsin Right to Life (WRTL) wanted to run issue ads during Feingold's reelection bid to the U.S. Senate. Feingold served on the Judiciary Committee, the first stopping point for judicial nominees, and had opposed many of the judges nominated by President George W. Bush. So WRTL produced a barrage of spots designed to highlight the senator's record and call attention to the importance of the federal bench and the Supreme Court. However, the law prevented these ads from airing within the sixty-day window before Election Day.

Bopp had his case, but he also had a problem. Just a year earlier, in 2003, the Supreme Court upheld nearly the entirety of McCain-Feingold as constitutional in *McConnell v. FEC*. Justices O'Connor and John Paul Stevens coauthored the 5–4 decision that upheld both the new rules regarding third-party electioneering advertisements and the ban on unrestricted "soft money" contributions to political parties, often used as a vehicle to elude limits on donations to candidates from individual or corporate political action committees. "It was not unwarranted for Congress to conclude that the selling of access gives rise to the appearance of corruption," according to the majority decision.

Now, Bopp brought a narrower claim: he did not argue that the entire McCain-Feingold law was unconstitutional—only that the sixty-day ban violated the free speech rights of Wisconsin Right to Life. Still, challenging a barely year-old precedent seemed quixotic—except for one thing. The Supreme Court had been radically remade in 2005. Roberts had replaced the late chief justice, William Rehnquist. More importantly, Sandra Day O'Connor, the swing vote on the 5–4 2003 decision, retired, and her seat had been taken by Samuel Alito.

The law hadn't changed—the court had. Bopp and Blum were ready to take full advantage. So, too, was the conservative legal movement that funded them, created the intellectual framework for their cases, and helped place the judges who would decide them on the bench.

BOPP AND BLUM had crucial roles to play. Yet they were not lone wolves. Rewiring the nation's campaign finance laws in favor of corporations and the wealthy required a full-team effort. Litigators and matchmakers needed to bring airtight cases. But conservative judges also needed to be grounded in the arguments and constitutional theories to navigate breaks from precedent that would push the law in a new direction and ensure—in the name of what the Federalist Society called freedom and liberty—that the government play no role in equalizing political speech. When lawmakers put limitations on the ability of corporations or wealthy individuals to spend during political campaigns, conservative thinkers argued, it unconstitutionally redistributed political power. Campaign finance reforms, in the eyes of these Federalist Society members, added up to an effort to entrench legislative majorities and a scheme by liberals to realign political power.

With campaign finance, the Federalist Society would perform the most crucial roles—just as it did in future landmark challenges to national health care, regulatory reform, and gun control. Its members would frame the cases, bring the cases, then rule on them—all to the benefit of their side of the political aisle. As Hollis-Brusky has demonstrated better than anyone, the legal strategy depended on the Federalist Society network every step of the way, even as the Society purported to take no issue stands at all.

The Federalist Society earnestly took up the cause of reversing campaign finance regulation in 1996, with the launch of the Free Speech and Election Law Practice Group. The timing here was far from accidental. Congress had just launched a fresh set of measures to reform campaign finance, building toward the eventual passage of McCain-Feingold. In fall 1996, the Practice Group launched a journal, and the Senate's most stalwart opponent of campaign finance reform, Senator Mitch McConnell, wrote its most prominent piece. "Freedom-loving Americans of all ideological persuasions should be horrified by the professional reformers' ambition to force a takeover of the American political process," he wrote, calling the

proposed legislation "an unprecedented power grab." Bopp published a
piece as well, a jeremiad against the Federal Election Commission's "assault on the First Amendment."

As Hollis-Brusky shows, during the journal's first five years, from 1996
through 2000, the Practice Group published some thirty-eight pieces re-
thinking campaign finance from the Right. It would go on to host keynote
presentations at every subsequent Federalist Society national convention.
In articles and in panel discussions, prominent lawyers and thinkers broke
down the many ways they saw campaign regulation blocking the cause of
citizen advocacy. They argued that mandating disclosure of donors' names
violated the First Amendment, and that transparency and spending limits
would chill free speech. They argued that the government should play no
role in equalizing free speech among groups and individuals with different
levels of resources. They also contended that campaign finance restrictions
gave an unfair advantage to the liberal opposition, whose allies in Hollywood and the news media enjoyed full First Amendment protection. This
was the argument from the Powell Memo, advanced by Powell himself
from the bench in *Bellotti*, and now honed by the conservative institutions
inspired by Powell and Horowitz. Finally, they urged the Supreme Court
to abandon judicial restraint and overturn precedent as necessary to bring
the law in line with conservative thinking.

"Taken together," Hollis-Brusky suggests, "these arguments helped to
arm the Supreme Court majority with both the intellectual capital and the
judicial bravado necessary to abandon judicial restraint and *stare decisis*
and radically reinterpret the constitutional framework for campaign finance in *Citizens United*."

By the time the court decided *McConnell v. FEC* in 2003, narrowly
upholding the constitutionality of McCain-Feingold's limits on corporate
spending, union spending, and soft money donations, Justices Thomas,
Scalia, and Kennedy were already echoing Federalist Society arguments in
their dissent. They also clearly signaled that, given the right case and the
right justices, the next decision could go the other way.

Bopp not only developed the right case with *Wisconsin Right to Life v.
FEC*, but the Federalist Society appeared joined at the hip. Indeed, the
district court opinion that first allowed the antiabortion group's ads was

authored by Federalist Society member David Sentelle. Ten other Federalist Society members—including Ted Olson, Chuck Cooper, and Jay Sekulow—affixed their names to amicus briefs in the case. At the Supreme Court, the four members claiming a Federalist Society pedigree wrote three crucial opinions upholding the lower court's decision to upend the law. And, as Hollis-Brusky notes, twelve different law clerks relied on the Society's intellectual resources to aid the justices writing those opinions.

"Federalist Society network amici all urged the Supreme Court to uphold Federalist Society member David Sentelle's District Court ruling that Section 203 of the BCRA [Bipartisan Campaign Reform Act] was unconstitutional," argues Hollis-Brusky. "Their briefs supplemented Sentelle's opinion with intellectual capital from Federalist Society network scholarship [and] the originalist canon."

Even so, some Federalist Society members bemoaned that the Supreme Court only took a half step toward reworking the constitutional issue— allowing the group's ads to air but not taking on the larger question. But Alito's decision made it clear that he and Roberts were on the lookout for future opportunities to go further. "We will presumably be asked in a future case to reconsider" the bigger picture issue, he wrote.

A different court had again produced a different 5–4 decision. A long game put that court in place. There was no rush. The next case—*Citizens United*—was just around the corner.

EDWARD BLUM HAS long been portrayed as a solo operator, a distinguished, kind gentleman battling the establishment all the way to the Supreme Court from his house in Maine, the David of Penobscot Bay taking down the liberal Goliath armed with nothing but a laptop and a Wi-Fi link.

The reality doesn't make for such good copy. But it does drive home the organizational depth and long-term vision behind the conservative legal movement. Blum is really the front person at the nexus of a powerful constellation of conservative lawyers, wealthy donors, and right-wing foundations. All these players have used their financial might—and their allies on a captured court—to deliver victory after victory that likely could not have been won any other way.

Just follow the money. Between 2006 and 2011, Blum's one-man organization was funded largely by a little-known but staggeringly powerful
organization called DonorsTrust—to the tune of $1.2 million. Two other
major conservative foundations, the Bradley Foundation and the Searle
Freedom Trust, contributed $100,000 and $597,500, respectively. Post-
Shelby, between 2015 and 2020, Blum's Project on Fair Representation
and Students for Fair Admissions pulled in $11.2 million. This haul again
mostly came at the behest of a handful of foundations, including Searle,
Bradley, and the Scaife Foundation, together with another $3 million from
DonorsTrust.

DonorsTrust, in turn, has been described as the "dark-money ATM for
the Right." The group has distributed more than $1.7 billion in funds to con-
servative organizations since its founding in 1999. Where does the money
come from? It's almost impossible to track—which is a big reason for its
clout and influence. DonorsTrust is not a family foundation like Searle,
Bradley, or Scaife. It's a donor-advised fund, run by a tiny board from a
nondescript office building on Diagonal Street in Arlington, Virginia—an
appropriate address for a group dedicated to tilting politics rightward.

Its board—which controls the group's grantmaking—includes some of
the most powerful conservative interests in the nation. Much of it has been
bankrolled by the Koch Brothers, the Bradley family, and the DeVos family. These lions of right-wing giving can filter millions into DonorsTrust
and then funnel it to preferred organizations with almost total anonymity.

Its founder, Whitney Ball, launched DonorsTrust to keep conservative
money in conservative hands. "Over time, we have too often witnessed
philanthropic capital stray from an original donor's free-market ideals,"
the fund's own history drily notes. The rough translation here is that the
rich guy's kids didn't like his politics and later donated their inheritance
to liberal causes. But DonorsTrust does much more than write checks. According to a victory lap DonorsTrust took in an internal document not
long after the Supreme Court heard another of Blum's cases, "Our DNA
floats in the bloodstream" of his work. "If non-profits had parents, then
DonorsTrust would act as mom and dad."

"What many may not realize," the memo continues, "is that over the
years DonorsTrust has also worked closely with individual donors and pri-

vate foundations to help grow institutions that contribute to the overall 'marketplace of ideas' by putting those ideas into actionable projects or institutions."

In that extremely cozy stretch of the marketplace of ideas, Blum's organization appears to have become an all but wholly owned subsidiary of DonorsTrust. It was listed as an internal program between 2006 and 2012, and was then spun into something called Project Liberty, which had no employees but shared top officers with, yes, DonorsTrust. Project Liberty, in turn, began to pay the seven-figure legal bills for the law firm Wiley Rein, which handled the *Shelby County* case.

But dig deeper into Project Liberty's IRS paperwork and something interesting emerges. The IRS's Form 990 requires public charities to reveal "related" tax-exempt organizations. A related organization is defined as "organizations that stand in a parent/subsidiary relationship, brother/sister relationship, or supporting/supported organization relationship." DonorsTrust, the parent, is listed first, followed by the Heritage Foundation. Turn the page, and another "related organization" is the Federalist Society. That's right: the supposed debate club that does not take policy stances, whose officials vet the list of Supreme Court justices, is "related" to Blum.

Because once you've taken over the courts, you need to tee up some cases for them to decide.

Blum knew all along where he was headed. The license plate on his old Toyota minivan? It's 1FRSTNE. That's the address of the Supreme Court: 1 First St. Northeast.

BALLS, STRIKES, WHATEVER. When Bopp's *WRTL* case was decided by the Supreme Court, the only question that mattered to the umpires was which team was pitching. The strike zone changed with the judges.

Roberts, in his confirmation hearings just two years prior, had emphasized his respect for precedent. "Judges have to have the humility to recognize that they operate within a system of precedent shaped by other judges equally striving to live up to their judicial oath," he said in his opening statement. Under questioning from senators, Roberts noted that even flaws in a decision were "not enough . . . to justify revisiting it," and emphasized "the values of respect for precedent, evenhandedness, predictability, and stability."

And then, just two years after settling into the chief's chair, Roberts proceeded to eviscerate a four-year-old precedent on a question central to the nature of a democracy. Roberts wrote the decision himself and cast himself in the role of a cautious moderate even as the umpire rewrote the rulebook. "The First Amendment requires us to err on the side of protecting political speech rather than suppressing it," he wrote in his 5–4 decision. He insisted the court was not overturning the decision in *McConnell v. FEC*. "We have," Roberts wrote, "no occasion to revisit that determination today."

This, too, was false modesty. Roberts was not showing deference to precedent. He was taking a first bite of the apple. The key word in that sentence was *today*. This would be just another example of the Roberts two-step. That decision sent a clear signal that five justices stood ready to address the larger constitutional issues in voting rights law the next time. It didn't require a mind reader to decode the chief justice's message. James Bopp took today's victory back to Terre Haute and began to prepare for tomorrow.

CHAPTER TWELVE

GAME RESPECTS GAME. When the veteran conservative provocateur David Bossie first watched *Fahrenheit 9/11*, Michael Moore's savage documentary on the George W. Bush White House and the invasion of Iraq, released into the heart of the 2004 presidential campaign, he knew his side needed to push back. "It was incredibly powerful, incredibly well-done," Bossie says. "In my opinion, he didn't let the facts get in the way of a good story. But as a political guy? We needed to have an answer for this."

Bossie's concern only deepened when he saw the thirty-second TV spots advertising the film. They almost seemed to double as support for Bush's opponent, Senator John Kerry. Moore had figured out what seemed to Bossie like a triple bank shot: he was in theaters with a film pressing the case against Bush's invasion of Iraq, he was giving interviews on cable news and late-night comedy shows, and the film's commercials seemed to air everywhere else. "They were a lot better than Kerry's commercials," Bossie admitted to C-SPAN at the time.

Few understood the power of a well-timed thirty-second spot like the president of Citizens United. Though Bossie was only in his midthirties, he was already a veteran of political dark arts. Bossie didn't invent "owning the libs," the cynical game of generating outrage, media attention, and small-dollar donations off culture wars and tawdry allegations about one's opponents, but he elevated ratfucking to near-classical elegance.

Bossie's early mentor, Floyd Brown, deployed the infamous Willie Horton ad against 1988 Democratic presidential nominee Michael Dukakis—a brazen, racist dog whistle that portrayed the former Massachusetts governor as weak on crime through Horton, a Black man who raped a white woman while released on a furlough program. Many believe that ad helped change the way race could be deployed in campaigns, paving the way for Donald Trump's explicit talk about Mexican rapists, violent Black men, and "shithole" nations. Bossie later signed on as Brown's "chief researcher," which really meant chief peddler of sleaze about Bill Clinton, and he would go on to become the committee investigator for an Indiana congressman convinced that the Clintons had murdered their friend Vince Foster.

At Citizens United, Bossie watched enviously as Moore funneled his liberal, anti-Bush messages throughout the mainstream media. The documentary was produced by Miramax, which in turn was owned by Disney. Why was the film not an illegal corporate contribution? McCain-Feingold had put an end to "electioneering communications" paid for by corporations during the window before elections. Didn't that disallow these brutally effective ads from running on TV?

Bossie took the question to the Federal Election Commission. But the film's marketers short-circuited his challenge; uninterested in the fight, the studio vowed it had no intention of advertising the film before the conventions or general election. Nevertheless, a genius triple bank shot of his own began to percolate in the master troller's mind. He'd transform Citizens United into a maker of documentary films. Bossie and his allies would get their message out and raise money through DVDs and screenings. More importantly, they'd also produce thirty-second ads. And unlike Michael Moore's team, Bossie and Citizens United would not shy from directly challenging the McCain-Feingold blackout period as an unconstitutional violation of free speech.

Bossie pitched his case to every well-known conservative lawyer in Washington. "They laughed at me when I came up with the concept," Bossie says. "They said there is no way to do that."

Bossie moved ahead, undeterred. *Hillary: The Movie* premiered during the Democratic primaries and did not last long in theaters. When Barack Obama defeated Clinton for the Democratic nomination, the movie seemed unlikely to have much influence at all—let alone that it would upend the nation's campaign finance laws and allow for a torrent of unregulated, untraceable dark money to flood elections and remake American democracy.

The story of how this happened begins with Bossie. It blossoms with Bopp, the one lawyer who immediately recognized the possibilities in

Bossie's vision. Both men knew where it would end: the U.S. Supreme Court. Yet it goes nowhere without the eagerness of the Roberts Court to eradicate precedent, steamroll Congress, and remake legislation designed to level the electoral playing field into something wholly different that advantages their own political benefactors. The real audience wouldn't be conservative moviegoers. It would be five conservative justices. "I certainly was hoping," Bossie says. He was able to get his project before a dream audience who helped write an ending Bossie barely dared imagine, but for which the conservative legal movement had long prepared.

"*Citizens United* was the first indication of how far the Roberts Court was willing to go. It showed us that Roberts was willing to drive a truck through precedent and manufacture cases," says Trevor Potter, a former head of the Federal Election Commission and a Republican lawyer. "It was a case where they reached results at many levels that they did not have to reach. And the only explanation for that is they were not being conservative. They were being radicals. Five of them wanted to get rid of the corporate ban. So five of them did."

RADICALISM, OF COURSE, comes in many varieties. Roberts's radicalism is that of the incrementalist, slowly turning up the heat while the oblivious frog boils.

When *Citizens United* arrived at the U.S. Supreme Court in 2009, the Roberts Court had already charted a new pro-business direction on security fraud, corporate misconduct, the regulatory state, punitive damages limits, and much more. These rulings were often 5–4 decisions that aligned on a partisan basis. Between 2004 and 2007, the court accepted fewer than 2 percent of the ten thousand petitions for a case to be heard. But petitions filed by the Chamber of Commerce were granted at an astounding rate of 26 percent. It was a trend that would only accelerate. A 2017 study by three legal scholars, including the conservative judge Richard Posner, found that when business came before the court (in cases where corporations were plaintiffs or defendants, but not suing each other), corporate interests prevailed 61 percent of the time.

Yet none of those cases tipped the scales in favor of monied interests and the billionaire class quite like *Citizens United*. Roberts, cautiously but decisively, began to remake the complex patchwork of campaign finance laws with the very first cases that came before him, as early as 2006–07. This early series of decisions incrementally made it more difficult for the government to regulate a variety of campaign contributions while also expanding the nature of protected political speech under the First Amendment. "He was suspicious of government attempts to target the effects of wealth in elections. He did not think money was naturally corrosive, and he felt government had gone too far in curtailing the ability of corporations to engage in political speech," writes Joan Biskupic in *The Chief*. During a moment when large numbers of Americans—worried about the corrupting influence of big money, frustrated at the high cost of campaigns, turned off by a ceaseless barrage of negative ads—pushed big majorities in Congress into action on an issue politicians preferred to avoid, Roberts steered the Supreme Court in the opposite direction.

The new chief justice, despite his professed commitment to precedent during his confirmation hearings and his vow to modestly call balls and strikes, would slowly unravel a century of laws designed to protect citizens from the undue influence of wealth on elections, including the court's own barely dried precedent from 2003's *McConnell v. FEC*. Again, it's not that the laws changed. It's that Roberts soon had the all-important fifth vote, when Alito replaced O'Connor before the court's fall 2005 calendar began. "Different justices," Feingold tells me. "That's the only thing that changed from *McConnell* to *Citizens United*. Then it's unconstitutional. It's completely ridiculous. It's the opposite of precedent. It's pure whim—political whim."

But just as Roberts's incrementalism is radical, his whims are calculated to protect the appearance of judicial modesty. As chief justice, Roberts knows exactly where he is going but feels in no hurry to get there. He's calling his own balls and strikes—but is also fully aware how the entire at bat will go before the pitcher has begun his windup.

Roberts perfected the rightward glide path on campaign finance before the court took up voting rights. His colleagues could see right through him, much to the annoyance of all sides—whether liberals frustrated with the court's direction, or conservatives who wanted to arrive faster. First, in the case Bopp brought from Wisconsin Right to Life, Roberts added a new test to McCain-Feingold. That law prohibited any "express" electioneering within the window before a primary or general election—but Roberts blessed the WRTL ads as long as they had "no reasonable interpretation other than as an appeal to vote for or against a specific candidate." While Roberts added a new loophole—a "reasonable interpretation" standard that he and the court's conservative majority could apply as it wished—he declined to take on the bigger question about McCain-Feingold's constitutionality. Scalia, writing a concurring opinion along with Kennedy and Thomas, torched Roberts for going halfway and for a decision that both liberal and conservative justices agreed "effectively overrules *McConnell* without saying so."

"This faux judicial restraint," Scalia wrote, "is judicial obfuscation."

Souter, writing for the liberals, recognized both the judicial obfuscation as well as the way Wisconsin Right to Life disregarded the purpose of the law to put the test case before the court, when a simpler, more modest fix could have kept the group on the right side of the statute. "The Court (and, I think, the country) loses when important precedent is overruled without good reason," he lamented, "and there is no justification for departing from our usual rule of *stare decisis* here."

Unless, of course, overruling precedent is the point.

CITIZENS UNITED IS a most unusual case. The Supreme Court was originally asked to decide a fairly narrow question. The filmmakers, like Wisconsin Right to Life, asked not to be bound by the McCain-Feingold advertising blackout, since they had made a documentary film that was not "express advocacy." Nevertheless, Bossie, Bopp, and the conservative foundations who supported this lawsuit were veteran court watchers. They understood that there were five justices primed to deliver much more. "If we do it right, I think we can pretty much dismantle the entire regulatory regime that is called campaign finance law," Bopp told the *New York Times*, hardly disguising his ambitions as the court prepared to hear the case.

Roberts was finally ready. A conservative majority on a court that ordinarily operates under rules of constitutional avoidance—steering clear of sweeping constitutional decisions where they are not necessary—used its power to shred the campaign finance rulebook. They turned *Citizens United* into a vehicle to reexamine the broader laws that restricted corporate campaign spending. They took a case that could have been decided on narrow grounds and demanded that it be rebriefed and reargued to take on the larger questions the five conservatives wanted to answer instead. The justices widened the scope of the case and transformed *Citizens United* from something narrow into an earthquake that opened the door for unlimited campaign spending by corporations and unions. An exchange between Alito and Deputy Solicitor General Malcolm Stewart provided that opening.

Alito hit Stewart with a barrage of difficult hypotheticals. He wanted to know whether McCain-Feingold might regulate more than just electronic communications. "Do you think the Constitution required Congress to draw the line where it did, limiting this to broadcast and cable and so forth?" Alito said. Would it be possible to restrict the same material, for example, from being published in a book?

Stewart agreed, shockingly and incorrectly. "Those could have been applied to additional media." The conservatives sensed blood. Broadcast commercials had been regulated in one form or another since the dawn of television. Books, however, were something else entirely.

"That's pretty incredible," Alito replied. "You think that if a book was published, a campaign biography that was the functional equivalent of express advocacy, that could be banned?"

"I'm not saying it could be banned," Stewart said. "I'm saying that Congress could prohibit the use of corporate treasury funds." But the damage had been done.

Kennedy joined the fray next. "Suppose it were an advocacy organization that had a book," he asked Stewart. "Your position is that, under the Constitution, the advertising for this book or the sale for the book itself could be prohibited within the sixty- and thirty-day periods?" Once again, Stewart agreed.

Finally, Roberts interjected with his own hypothetical about a one-line endorsement in a five-hundred-page book, and by the time Stewart botched another answer, the case about campaign finance had been wholly reworked into something different. The central question was no longer whether Citizens United could advertise its film, or about whether Congress was within its rights to regulate corporate spending on elections. It was a hypothetical about whether the federal government could effectively ban a book during the weeks before an election. And the government's own representative before the court wouldn't simply say no.

According to accounts by Jeffrey Toobin and others, when the justices met in conference, it was immediately apparent to all that the five conservatives were ready to deliver a sweeping decision on the largest constitutional questions. This outcome had been almost preordained ever since O'Connor retired and Alito took her seat. Nevertheless, the court's liberal wing howled: the larger First Amendment issues had not been argued before the court. They were part of the disastrous mauling of the deputy solicitor general but weren't included among the issues briefed for the justices or argued before the lower courts. A furious Souter confronted Roberts and vowed that his dissent would call out a shoddy process that impugned the integrity of the courts. And so the chief justice, concerned about maintaining the image of modestly calling balls and strikes, touched the brakes. The justices ordered that the case be reargued and rebriefed, this time on the larger questions, making it clear that they would now directly consider overturning *McConnell*. The liberals won only the briefest reprieve. The court's timeline emphasized that the conservative justices were in a rush. The new case would be heard in early September 2009, almost a full month before the court's usual first day of the first Monday in October.

With the votes in hand, tradition could be dispensed with. Precedent would soon follow.

WHEN SEPTEMBER ARRIVED, and the Supreme Court opened *Citizens United* arguments for the second time in just six months, little mystery remained. The government had a new solicitor general, Elena Kagan, less than a year before her own nomination to the court. This would be her very first appearance, and she knew she was playing a bad hand. It's not a good day at the court if an answer begins, "If you are asking me, Mr. Chief Justice, as to whether the government has a preference as to the way in which it loses, if it has to lose, the answer is yes."

In the end, oral arguments did not change any minds. Once again, the vote at conference divided 5–4, along the same ideological fault lines. Roberts, having orchestrated a four-year path to achieve a certain result, assigned the majority opinion to Kennedy, himself the son of a lobbyist, long sympathetic to the pet causes of corporations. The decision effectively affirmed that corporations enjoy the same First Amendment rights as citizens. "Speech is an essential mechanism of democracy, for it is the means to hold officials accountable to the people," Kennedy wrote. "The right of citizens to inquire, to hear, to speak, and to use information to reach consensus is a precondition to enlightened self-government and a necessary means to protect it."

That's certainly a lofty theoretical argument for what ensued: unlimited, untraceable billions flooded into elections and campaigns from the superwealthy, without citizens having any right to inquire about the source. Souter retired between the two cases, and was replaced by Justice Sonia Sotomayor, so it was left to John Paul Stevens to write a long and stinging dissent. At ninety pages, it was the most voluminous opinion Stevens composed in his five decades on the Supreme Court. He read it from the bench, an unusual event ordinarily reserved for the most disappointed dissents in the most crucial cases. He took his colleague's decision apart relentlessly, reviewing corporate speech rights, corruption, the influence of money on politics, the nature of censorship, the role of the First Amendment, and the differences between corporations and individuals. Perhaps most sadly, he castigated the way the court on which he had served for so long had mangled precedent and shredded its credibility in pursuit of a result. Thus did the last of a breed of moderates appointed by Republican presidents, dating back to an era less nakedly ideological, now deeply worried about the institution's corruption by politics, say his goodbye.

"Five Justices were unhappy with the limited nature of the case before us," he began, "so they changed the case to give themselves an opportunity to change the law." In the end, Stevens wrote, "the Court's rejection of *Austin* and *McConnell* comes down to nothing more than its disagreement with their results. Virtually every one of its arguments was rejected in those cases, and the majority opinion is essentially an amalgamation of resuscitated dissents.

"The only relevant thing that has changed since *Austin* and *McConnell*," he emphasized, "is the composition of this Court."

As Stevens's voice shook and wavered, he realized his years on the court were coming to an end. He would step down days later; his dissent registered deep disenchantment with the court he was leaving. "At bottom, the Court's opinion is thus a rejection of the common sense of the American people, who have recognized a need to prevent corporations from undermining self-government since the founding," Stevens wrote. "It is a strange time to repudiate that common sense. While American democracy is imperfect, few outside the majority of this Court would have thought its flaws included a dearth of corporate money in politics."

THE DECISION'S AFTERSHOCKS and repercussions arrived quickly. President Obama, himself a former constitutional law professor, criticized *Citizens United* for having green-lit "a new stampede of special-interest money." It amounted to "a major victory for Big Oil, Wall Street banks, health insurance companies and the other powerful interests that marshal their power every day in Washington to drown out the voices of everyday Americans." Six days later, in his first State of the Union, as six of the nine justices sat before him, Obama furthered his critique, warning that the court had blithely overturned a century of precedents in order to "open the floodgates for special interests."

Citizens United not only liberated corporate treasuries to be spent freely in support of candidates, it did something far more damaging: it created the newest campaign-finance Frankenstein, the super PAC. A standard political action committee had operated under the usual campaign finance regulations, including limitations on donations and transparency requirements. On the other hand, super PACs, which are not associated with campaigns, use their money only for expenditures—and the *Citizens United* decision stated, for the first time in the U.S. Supreme Court's history, that expenditures could not be regulated by the government. That was because the court insisted—naively, and indeed almost fancifully—

there was no anticorruption interest at stake. Two months after the decision arrived, in March 2010, a lower court required to follow the Supreme Court's lead found itself forced to strike down limits on the money these super PACs could raise from any individual donor. Forget about opening the floodgates—this was a tsunami. In the first decade after the Supreme Court decided *Citizens United*, super PAC spending soared past $3 billion.

Yet the Roberts Court wasn't finished upending the old regulatory order. The following year, in 2011, the same five conservative justices declared an Arizona law unconstitutional that allowed for public financing of candidates who voluntarily agreed to spending limits and provided them with additional dollars if they faced a wealthy self-financing opponent. Roberts, again inverting common sense, found that it was the rich candidates who deserved additional protections instead. One year later, in 2013's *American Tradition Partnership v. Bullock*, the same five conservatives struck down a Montana law that banned corporate political spending. This ruling put an end to efforts to block corporate dollars in campaigns at the state level. Finally, in 2014's *McCutcheon v. FEC*, the court put an end to federal contribution limits for the first time, declaring any aggregate contribution limit unconstitutional.

In the bizarro world of inverted causation and nonexistent corruption by the same five conservative hardliners, the court declared that access and influence for donors was an essential and protected constitutional right. Roberts wrote, "'Ingratiation and access . . . are not corruption.' They embody a central feature of democracy—that constituents support candidates who share their beliefs and interests, and candidates who are elected can be expected to be responsive to those concerns."

Justice Stephen Breyer, in a dissent he read from the bench, derided the majority decision as one "that substitutes judges' understandings of how the political process works for the understanding of Congress; that fails to recognize the difference between influence resting upon public opinion and influence bought by money alone." Breyer had it right, but he could have gone further: the Right had bought even this influence on the court as part of a careful, patient strategy to win through the judiciary what could not be won at the ballot box. This strategy complemented the steady hollowing of the VRA. If American elections could be seen as a scale, eroding voting rights lessened the weight on one side, while allowing corporations and the wealthy unlimited speech to frame political debates brought the thumb down harder on the other.

Yet Roberts understood the political process, and the court's role in it, perfectly well. "The most important thing for the public to understand," he told C-SPAN in a rare interview, "is that we are not a political branch of government." No, his court was something else entirely—something that put itself knowingly beyond the reach of the public in a democracy, and once insulated, turned the law into something of its own choosing. "They don't elect us. If they don't like what we're doing, it's more or less just too bad."

CHAPTER THIRTEEN

THE MOMENT COULD not have felt more triumphant. On July 27, President George W. Bush signed the 2006 Voting Rights Act reauthorization surrounded by bipartisan congressional leaders and the families of Martin Luther King Jr., Rosa Parks, and Fannie Lou Hamer. In a South Lawn ceremony drenched in summer sun, Bush proclaimed that Congress had reaffirmed the nation's most basic belief that all men are created equal. "In the four decades since the Voting Rights Act was first passed, we've made progress toward equality, yet the work for a more perfect union is never ending," Bush vowed.

Some of the foot soldiers who marched over Selma's Edmund Pettus Bridge four decades earlier might have hoped the victories they earned would be safe for another quarter century. In reality, though, a new phase of the fight was just getting started—in the right-leaning judiciary. The battleground shifted from Congress to the courts, from Selma to the suburbs. The key players were no longer elected leaders striving for greater equity but unelected judges asking when all this work might finally be complete. The highly networked forces on the American right had been preparing for this moment for decades.

No one will ever confuse Canyon Creek Elementary School in Austin, Texas, where four hundred K–5 students are welcomed under a grand brick entranceway, with that infamous Selma bridge that still carries the name of a Klan grand master. It plays a dramatic role in kick-starting the counterrevolution, nevertheless.

Don Zimmerman spent Election Day outside the school in March 2002, trying to convince his neighbors in this well-heeled Austin neighborhood to support his bid for the board of the local municipal utility district, or

MUD for short. The position didn't come with much power. The MUD did not produce water or electricity. Each of five board members was paid $100 annually to collect taxes for the municipal bonds that funded the neighborhood's original water and sewer infrastructure, while also managing a local park. Zimmerman was convinced—correctly—that residents were being taxed twice, illegally, by both the city and the MUD.

He campaigned on a promise to fix that—but his neighbors did not turn out in high numbers, perhaps because voting in the MUD race required walking an additional three blocks from the school and casting another ballot in Jack Steuber's garage. The state and county elections were held at the school. But Northwest Austin Municipal Utility District Number One existed in an odd netherworld. It was a hyperlocal body governed neither by the state of Texas, nor Travis County or the city of Austin. It oversaw its own elections. "Nobody wants to go vote twice," Zimmerman told me. "Especially if they have to go to someone's garage."

On election morning, Steuber backed his two cars into the driveway and placed a makeshift ballot box atop a card table. He didn't have many visitors, even though Zimmerman spent hours approaching voters at the school and distributing hand-drawn directions. This board seemed so inconsequential to Canyon Creek's thirty-five hundred residents that multiple meetings could go by with only the commissioners themselves in attendance.

Zimmerman, an engineer who moved to Austin for a job in the region's thriving computer industry, recognized the dual-site voting arrangement made little sense. He decided one of his first goals—in addition to installing security cameras to keep teenagers out of the park after dark—would be to combine the utility district's elections with the county's. Yet because Texas fell under Section 5 of the Voting Rights Act, even this minor change needed to be precleared with the Justice Department. Zimmerman and his fellow commissioners completed twenty pages in paperwork, paid about $1,250 in legal fees, and waited the two months for approval. It was granted.

Few would have imagined that this well-intentioned effort to make a low-turnout community election in an overwhelmingly white suburb just a little more efficient would end at the U.S. Supreme Court with a decision that jeopardized the heart of the Voting Rights Act. Still, there were two people who understood the possibilities right away: Edward Blum and Gregory Coleman.

PRIOR TO THE passage of the VRA reauthorization, Blum had left his White House meeting with Karl Rove certain that Republican leaders had no interest in his arguments, and even less enthusiasm for taking on something as popular as the Voting Rights Act. "This is politics," Blum says with a shrug.

So Blum left the inside Beltway game to the politicians. He returned to his true calling: identifying the perfect plaintiff for a fight in the courts. The U.S. Supreme Court had a new chief justice who had already expressed skepticism about both the VRA and racial preferences. Blum expected a much more receptive audience for his arguments at 1 First Street NE than he had received across the street at the Capitol.

He started hunting for the perfect locality to make his case. One of his first calls went to Gregory Coleman, the former clerk for Clarence Thomas at the Supreme Court who had been the solicitor general for Texas. Coleman, of course, had also testified for the Republicans in the Senate hearings on the 2006 VRA reauthorization, but previously he'd been Blum's counsel on his successful challenge to race-based admissions at a Houston charter school, as well.

"You just can't pick up the phone and call the state of Alabama and say, 'Hey, do you want to sue?'" Blum says. "Greg and I chatted about this and he said, 'You know, I think I know a guy.'"

The guy was Don Zimmerman.

In addition to Coleman's unsubstantiated allegation during his Senate testimony about how much money preclearance was costing states, he had dropped another dubiously sourced nugget into the official record. While rattling off a list of those jurisdictions "bitter" over the "shuffling paperwork," Coleman had mentioned states, counties, cities—and then, interestingly, "*municipal utility districts.*" On the surface it seemed quixotic, a throwaway phrase. But as with so much of the Right's legal groundwork, it was highly deliberate and carefully crafted.

Zimmerman and his little MUD board had hired Coleman for their lawsuit against Austin that charged the city with unlawfully taxing Canyon Creek residents twice for the same water and sewer service. They'd met through the Republican Club of Austin, shared a quixotic libertarian streak, and bonded over memories of college days at Texas A&M.

When Blum updated Coleman on his quest for a strong plaintiff in a VRA test case, the Texas lawyer recalled Zimmerman's annoyance with the paperwork and expense involved in moving the utility district's polling place those three blocks.

"He's very astute," says Zimmerman of Coleman. "Section 5? I didn't even know what it was. In hindsight, I want to say that when he heard me talk about that election being put in the garage, I think that's why he took the taxation case."

Coleman told Blum he might have the dream plaintiff: a tiny water district with no history of racial discrimination or any complaints over voting at all. They'd sought to dismantle the nonsensical two-venue voting arrangement and been marched through the byzantine Washington bureaucracy, even though the neighborhood had been nothing but ranchland during the insidious reign of Jim Crow. So how was it that, in the early 2000s, a neighborhood water board needed the Justice Department's permission to make its elections more convenient?

Blum couldn't believe his luck. "I know everything there is to know about MUD districts because that's what I did for a living. I traded MUD bonds!" Blum saw the entire case unfold before him: the tiny district, the handful of voters, the lack of any racial animus—and, not least by a long shot, how silly it would all seem to judges and the public that this board would need to seek federal permission to do anything. "They had to get a lawyer and do all this? Rather than pick up the phone and say, 'Is it OK to move the election from Charlie's garage to Eisenhower Elementary?' It just seemed a little wacky."

Coleman approached Zimmerman and the board with a deal: He'd handle the tax issue. He also wanted to represent the board in a challenge to the constitutionality of Section 5. "I'm, like, 'Heck, yeah. We should do something with this.' But of course, I can't justify spending the money. We're a tiny neighborhood here. We can't afford to fight the Department

of Justice," Zimmerman says. Coleman assured the board that wouldn't
be a problem, The Northwest Austin Municipal Utility District wouldn't
have to pay a dime. Blum's Project on Fair Representation would cover the
fees. "All we have to do is be the plaintiff and other people cover the legal
expenses?" Zimmerman recalls. "Let's go!"

And that was how Blum and Coleman convinced this small community
board to push the U.S. Supreme Court to rule on a weighty issue that would
affect all Americans: the very future of the Voting Rights Act. The United
States Congress had spent fifteen months creating a sixteen-thousand-
page record documenting the continued need for preclearance due to determined, creative efforts to block minority voters from the ballot box in
covered states such as Texas. Blum and Coleman's stealth challenge was
launched so quietly that few in Canyon Creek even realized what the MUD
board's 4–1 vote had authorized while they skipped another dull meeting.

"Those little districts!" Blum marvels now, still appreciating the genius
of his legal handiwork. "They may have only had eight hundred or nine
hundred people. But they elected a board, you know, even if maybe thirty
people showed up for that election. Maybe."

And so it came to pass that, just one week after President Bush signed
the Voting Rights Act reauthorization among that bipartisan and multiracial celebration, Coleman and the Northwest Austin Municipal Utility
District Number One filed suit in federal court. Their argument was the
inverse of Bush's, and yet in some ways, no less optimistic. Whereas Bush
exulted in decades of progress and looked to the work still to be done, Coleman and the board wanted to declare victory because the work had been
completed. "The people here have no history of discrimination. None!"
Zimmerman says. "So why should we automatically be presumed guilty?"

Race neutrality had arrived in Canyon Creek. In an eight-page complaint filed that August, which closely followed the arguments Coleman
and other opponents of reauthorization made to Congress, the MUD
claimed to be a political subdivision that should have the right to bail out
from preclearance. If the board was denied that right, the complaint continued, Section 5 should be declared unconstitutional, a dusty relic of another day.

"Congress cannot forever rely on findings of conditions that existed thirty years ago to continue to justify the use of its Fifteenth Amendment enforcement power in a way that infringes on the rights of an entire generation of voters who were not even alive when the discriminatory practices were ended," Coleman wrote in the board's complaint. In reauthorizing Section 5, he argued, Congress "incongruously and irrationally" continued using an "ancient formula" that punished states that addressed historic ills and did not cover localities where new problems had emerged.

It no longer mattered that the nation's elected political leaders saw it differently. Blum and Coleman had set their challenge on a collision course for the Supreme Court. Blum's wealthy backers would not only fund the litigation; they'd also spent decades and megamillions priming the high court with friendly justices who'd popularized theories of a "color-blind Constitution" for precisely this case. But first, an old-school judge with no interest in ideological gamesmanship would see through it all.

THE VIEW FROM Judge David Tatel's chambers high above Constitution Avenue was sweeping and magisterial; from this angle it's as if one peers down on the U.S. Capitol and the very top of the U.S. Supreme Court. Turn the other direction and it's the splendor of the National Gallery of Art. But for Tatel, blind since his early thirties due to the rare genetic disease retinitis pigmentosa, this was merely another room to do his life's work. His decaying eyesight didn't stop him from playing baseball in the 1950s as a teenager in suburban Maryland. He simply focused harder to catch fly balls. As an adult, his blindness never kept him from running marathons and skiing. He simply uses a radio transmitter as he heads down his favorite Aspen slopes, one of his four children behind him calling out the turns— and he's jogged thousands of miles with a neighbor, keeping pace, the two men linked at the forearms via a long, ultrastrong shoelace.

Here in his chambers, his seeing-eye dog, Vixen, at his feet, Tatel wrote careful, clear opinions—demanding habeas corpus for Guantanamo Bay prisoners, upholding a subpoena to require *New York Times* reporter Judith Miller to testify about a source that misled her on the Iraq War. He also drafted majority decisions in the *Northwest Austin* and *Shelby County* cases before they went to the Supreme Court—using a Braille computer.

Tatel's command of every nuance became the stuff of legend; while lawyers scrambled during trial to find the right page to answer a question, or when there was a dispute over the exact wording of a statute, he could direct everyone to the exact page of the brief or cite a complicated statute from memory.

When President Clinton appointed Tatel to the D.C. Circuit Court in 1994, to take the seat of Supreme Court nominee Ruth Bader Ginsburg, he praised him as one of the nation's leading education and civil rights lawyers, well-respected for his work on desegregating public schools in Chicago and St. Louis. An appointee of President George W. Bush, however, later applauded Tatel as the court's "model conservative," a judge who always played it straight, never letting politics interfere with his judgment, as he remained true to rational argument and thoughtful persuasion.

When Tatel was named to the three-judge panel that would first hear the *Northwest Austin* case, he knew that the U.S. Supreme Court was its ultimate destination. He also instantly understood that this case could be a vehicle for eroding the VRA. So Tatel immersed himself in the sixteen-thousand-page congressional record from 2006, reviewed the debates over the 1982 reauthorization, and studied the actual statutory language with great care, determined to write an authoritative and persuasive opinion. He knew his audience even if he could not glimpse the Supreme Court itself from his window. "You're looking at one of the few people who's actually read the whole thing," says Tatel. "It took me almost a year to write the *Northwest Austin* opinion. I've never taken that long to write an opinion, and I've never written one as long as that."

Tatel's meticulous opinion, written for a unanimous three-judge panel, dismissed the MUD board's complaint and took apart Coleman's arguments one by one. Over 133 pages, Tatel disembowels the board's smallest claims and its larger constitutional argument. The opinion provides a virtual graduate seminar in Supreme Court precedent in the relevant VRA cases, narrates the history of Reconstruction and Jim Crow, and condenses the tens of thousands of pages in the 1982 and 2006 VRA with the skill of a screenwriter turning an epic novel into a blockbuster film script.

Could the utility district bail out of preclearance as a political subdivision with a clean record? The board claimed that it qualified as a political subdivision under the VRA and argued that Congress intended a "political subdivision" to mean any board that conducts any governmental business. But Tatel went back to the Senate debate in 1982, in which Congress explicitly rejected that definition and chose to define "political subdivision" in a far narrower way. The language of the bill made it clear that a political subdivision meant only a county, parish, or other subunit that actually registered voters. The utility board did not. "In the end, deciding which entities may seek bailout is a question for Congress, not the courts," Tatel concluded. He was clearly reckoning that this exactitude and consistent legislative intent would catch the attention of the Supreme Court's conservative textualists.

Tatel also dismantled another central claim of the plaintiffs: the notion that the courts should strike down preclearance as unconstitutional under the Tenth, Fourteenth, and Fifteenth Amendments because Congress, as the board charged, "irrationally and incongruously" imposed "disproportionate" burdens and a "badge of shame" on covered states and localities. In his opinion, Tatel clarified that four decades of Supreme Court precedent on Voting Rights Act cases bound him to apply the court's own standard of greater deference to Congress in a case involving Congress's constitutional authority to remedy racial discrimination in voting. Tatel then patiently detailed the findings that led both chambers to reauthorize the VRA almost unanimously. Here, as well, Tatel looked to appeal to tradition-minded, high court conservatives, noting that when the 1975 reauthorization was challenged in *City of Rome*, the court found that congressional record sufficient to justify another twenty-five-year period. The correct comparison, Tatel wrote, ought to be the evidence that the court accepted as sufficient in 1975 versus the body of evidence compiled in 2006. "Viewed from that perspective, the racial disparities revealed in the 2006 legislative record differ little from what Congress found in 1975," he concluded.

In 1975, he pointed out, Alabama, Louisiana, and North Carolina had racial disparities in voter registration spanning from 16 to 24 points. In 2006, three covered states, Virginia, Texas, and Florida, had the same gaps. Nine of the thirteen states covered by preclearance had received more Section 5 objections from the attorney general between 1982 and 2006 than they had between the passage of the VRA in 1965 and the Reagan era re-authorization—a sign that preclearance remained a necessary tool against new barriers.

Again and again, Tatel noted, Section 5 prevented—and courts upheld—electoral changes that showed clear evidence of intentional racial discrimination. Section 5 was especially valuable in smaller localities, he found. To make that case, he cited that canceled election in Kilmichael, Mississippi, the repeated annexations in white enclaves to prevent Black political power, and admissions that the state of Louisiana had aimed "to diminish Black electoral opportunity in order to increase the electoral opportunity of white voters." Tatel took special care to point out that three Texas utility districts—boards just like the Northwest Austin commission bringing this suit—received objections, one for drawing "grossly malapportioned" districts in which minority voters "appear effectively to have been frozen out." Tatel even dismissed the argument that preclearance placed any real burden on the Northwest Austin board at all, let alone an unconstitutional one. He noted that the district had in fact filed eight preclearance requests over twenty years, all of them granted, at a "modest" annual cost of $223 a year, and never identified any voting change it might want to make but chose not to pursue.

"In view of this extensive legislative record and the deference we owe Congress," Tatel concluded, "we see no constitutional basis for rejecting Congress's considered judgment."

The blind judge couldn't imagine that anyone else could confront the evidence and the record honestly and come to any other conclusion. He also lacked faith that the record would get an honest reading at the U.S. Supreme Court. Indeed, he worried that it might not be read at all.

"The reason it's so long," Tatel says, with astonishing and almost frightening frankness for a distinguished judge who could have easily sat on the nation's highest court, "is I had no confidence that the Supreme Court would ever look at the record."

As it turns out, Tatel's fears were justified.

CHAPTER FOURTEEN

BARACK OBAMA INHERITED in 2009 the deepest economic meltdown since the Great Depression and two wars in the Middle East. He spent his first hundred days in office negotiating the $831 billion American Recovery and Reinvestment Act and hammering out the details of a $9 billion bailout of an automotive industry teetering on the edge of bankruptcy.

Amid these deepening crises, few in the administration paid a second thought to voting rights. "To be honest, when I was sworn in, I didn't think protecting the franchise would be at the top of my agenda," says Eric Holder, President Obama's attorney general. "I came into office thinking that there was going to be some maintenance that we needed to do, but that we were not going to be in a full-blown fight for the protection of the franchise—that it would be fifth or sixth on my agenda as opposed to what it turned out to be, top one or two."

What Holder didn't yet know was that the U.S. Supreme Court had a different plan. On exactly Obama's one hundredth day in office, April 29, 2009, as the new president touted his achievements, took questions on the safety of Pakistan's nuclear arsenal, and briefed the nation on preparations for the deadly H1N1 flu, the Roberts Court heard oral arguments in *Northwest Austin* and began to turn Obama's victory inside out.

Judge Tatel was right about one thing: the lengthy record developed by Congress did not interest this court at all. The conservative justices did not want to examine what Congress found. Instead, they sought to question whether Congress had any business reauthorizing the VRA at all. Listen to the *Northwest Austin* oral arguments today, and what jumps out at you is the eagerness of the conservative justices to substitute their wisdom for the work of Congress. When Scalia pushes Neal Katyal, principal deputy solicitor general (later he served as the acting solicitor general) representing the Department of Justice, on the need to make it easier for localities to bail out of preclearance, Katyal reminds him that Congress had considered, and rejected, precisely his argument in 2006. "The question is whether it's right, not whether Congress rejected it," replied Scalia, pushing aside his purported interest in textualism and original intent. The courtroom erupted in laughter, though Scalia did not crack a smile. This wasn't a joke. It was an opportunity that he, Thomas, and Roberts had awaited for decades.

Some justices to the right of Chief Justice John Roberts wanted the high court to move faster on the constitutional question posed by *Northwest Austin*. Roberts, however, saw no need for any sudden or overambitious movement. He had the votes. He had plenty of time. The chief justice understood that *Northwest Austin* provided the first opening for a patient master of the long game to address the big question raised by this small utility district. Roberts could move craftily and cannily, one strategic bite at a time.

NORTHWEST AUSTIN WOULD not be the Roberts Court's first major voting rights case. In 2008, the court upheld Indiana's new voter ID law, then the strictest in the nation. The law had passed on a party-line vote by Republicans at a time when Indiana remained competitive enough that Democrats could still win the state legislature. The bill's backers insisted that the new law safeguarded the integrity of the ballot, even though Indiana could not point to a single prosecution for in-person voter fraud. Its passage placed Indiana at the vanguard of this pesky modern barrier to the ballot box that most researchers agreed had the potential to block a small—but extraordinarily consequential in close states—percentage of largely Democratic-leaning voters from the polls. At the beginning of the twenty-first century, just eleven states required voters to show ID, and the most common check was a signature verification. But an onslaught of GOP state legislatures followed Indiana's lead.

Voter ID by itself is not discriminatory; it crosses the line, however, when states are caught curating acceptable forms of ID to those they find minority voters least likely to have, and then making it difficult or expensive for those voters to obtain them. Critics argue that voter ID not only fails to stop fraud, but that in-person voting fraud is so rare as to be nonexistent; conservative advocates of these laws insist that they are crucial to fighting fraud and protecting public confidence in election integrity. The U.S. Supreme Court, as it eroded the Voting Rights Act throughout the 2010s and 2020s, would essentially hand conservative lawmakers a blank check to pass any election laws they pleased if they could claim fighting fraud was the impetus—even though that fraud could never really be documented and existed primarily as a bogeyman to justify ever more suppressive laws.

Indeed, Roberts was not impressed when Paul Smith, once a fellow Supreme Court clerk alongside the future chief justice, argued that no one had been punished for this kind of voter fraud in America for decades. "It's a type of fraud that, because it's fraud, it's hard to detect," Roberts retorted.

Yet if that had actually been the case, at least one of the briefs supporting the Indiana law might have identified a single example of any fraudulent vote that the state's provision would have prevented from being cast. Of the four hundred million votes cast in the United States between 2000 and 2006, the law's supporters found one attempt at voter impersonation, and nine possible votes where impersonation might have taken place, but was not proven or prosecuted. None of those cases took place in Indiana.

Hundreds of thousands of Indiana voters, however, potentially lacked the kind of identification necessary to vote. The burden of the law's ID provisions fell disproportionately on minorities, the poor, the elderly, and others more likely to vote Democratic. Lower court judges such as Richard Posner, on the Seventh Circuit Court of Appeals, noted this glaring disparity, even as they found that the state still had the right to pass the law.

THESE PARTISAN EFFECTS are indeed the chief selling point of GOP-backed voter ID laws. And after the Roberts Court upheld them in *Crawford v. Marion County Election Board*, voter ID laws skyrocketed in red states during the 2000s and 2010s, providing one more advantage accruing for Republicans in close elections.

This reality later mugged Posner, one of the nation's most conservative judges at the time, who later publicly regretted and disavowed his decision in a memoir, *Reflections on Judging*. His court got it wrong, Posner conceded, writing that he "plead(s) guilty to having written the majority decision." Voter ID, he said, is "now widely regarded as a means of voter suppression rather than of fraud prevention." His decision did not foresee the consequences and effects, Posner wrote, adding that "We judges and lawyers, we don't know enough about the subject matters that we regulate, right?"

Justice Stevens, who wrote the controlling opinion for the high court, also later wished that he had made a different decision. It was, he said, a "fairly unfortunate decision." Like Posner, he regretted that he didn't have more and better information before him after the tide of new voter ID laws was unleashed. "I learned a lot of things outside the record that made me very concerned about that statute," Stevens said in a 2016 conversation with Justice Elena Kagan. "So I had the question: Should I rely on my own research or what's in the record?"

FOR THEIR PART, Justices David Souter, Stephen Breyer, and Ruth Bader Ginsburg expressed deep skepticism and suspicion of the utility district's case. "Preclearance is not affecting anything you're doing on a day-to-day basis, as I understand it," Souter told Coleman, who could only respond that deep in the minutes of one MUD board meeting was a brief reference to the possibility of someday changing election procedures.

"So between 2004 and 2009 the district has not sought preclearance?" Ginsburg asked, incredulously.

"That's correct," Coleman responded.

Souter and Breyer, meanwhile, pushed back on Coleman's argument that preclearance represented an extraordinary burden appropriate only for emergency circumstances, which could hardly exist in a nation that could elect a Black president.

"May I just raise a basic point here?" Souter asked Coleman, before rattling off a series of specific examples and statistics from the 2006 congressional report. "I don't understand, with a record like that, how you can maintain as a basis for this suit that things have radically changed. They may be better. But to say that they have radically changed to the point that this becomes an unconstitutional Section 5 exercise within Congress's judgment just seems to me to deny the empirical reality." Coleman insisted that the examples Congress discovered were either anecdotal or could be fixed through Section 2 litigation. Souter wasn't buying. "If the Section 5 safeguard is taken away, the pushback is going to start," he said presciently, quietly adding that "it has never stopped."

The real pushback began, however, when the two lawyers defending the VRA rose to make their case. Katyal represented the government, joined by Debo Adegbile, an NAACP litigator and onetime child actor on *Sesame Street,* now making his first argument before the high court. Perhaps in tribute to Snuffleupagus, the show's famed elephant-like Muppet who always seemed to disappear before adults could see him, Roberts wasted no time elevating conservative agitprop claims about the VRA. He first disparaged Katyal's argument that forcing covered localities to preclear election changes prevented many from trying to get away with racial inequities that would not pass DOJ muster.

"Well, that's like the old elephant whistle. You know, I have this whistle to keep away the elephants," said Roberts, dismissively. "There are no elephants, so it must work."

"Obviously no one doubts the history here," Roberts added. "But at what point does that history stop justifying action with respect to some jurisdictions but not with respect to others? . . . When do they have to stop?" Katyal explained that Congress had reauthorized the VRA for another twenty-five years, which meant that the national legislature wouldn't be reconsidering it before 2031. But Roberts, ignoring the near-unanimous verdict from Congress, expressed impatience that the job couldn't be declared finished already. "Well, they said five years originally and then another twenty years," the chief justice observed. "I mean, at some point it begins to look like the idea is that this is going to go on forever."

Kennedy, meanwhile, cited Coleman's own bogus billion-dollar figure as the cost of preclearance before himself making an argument that had little grounding in constitutional history. No state, Kennedy declared, ought to be treated differently by the federal government.

"The Congress has made a finding that the sovereignty of Georgia is less than the sovereign dignity of Ohio. The sovereignty of Alabama is less than the sovereign dignity of Michigan. And the governments in one are to be trusted less than the governments in the other," Kennedy maintained.

"I wouldn't put it at all in those terms," Katyal replied. "I would say what Congress found is that there is a historical amount of discrimination coupled with recent evidence and comparative data between covered and noncovered jurisdictions that justifies continuation of a remedy that states now overwhelmingly appreciate."

"This is a great disparity in treatment. The government of the United States is saying that our states must be treated differently. You have a very substantial burden if you're going to make that case," said Kennedy.

Katyal and Kennedy seemed to talk past each other.

When Adegbile took his turn, he tried flattering Kennedy rather than arguing with him. Adegbile praised Kennedy's decision in an earlier voting rights case that noted how Section 2 cases could often be "slow and inadequate to the task," in making the case for the continued need for preclearance. "I think that's absolutely right," Kennedy said, warming to the praise. "Section 2 cases are very expensive. They are very long. They are very efficient. I think this Section 5 preclearance device has been shown to be very, very successful."

Whatever progress Adegbile was making soon ground to a halt when Roberts interrupted with a charged question, one that he would repeat in similar form four years later in the *Shelby County* arguments. "Is it your position," the chief justice asked, "that today southerners are more likely to discriminate than northerners?" Adegbile tried to keep the focus on the congressional report. It's in those covered states, he told the chief justice, where "Congress found that the nature of the way discrimination is practiced, viewed through the lens of history, is that repetitive violations happened."

"So your answer is yes?" Roberts retorted.

Scalia, meanwhile, pointed to a practice in the Sanhedrin, the Israeli Supreme Court, which set aside any unanimous death penalty pronouncement on the principle that anything everyone agreed upon needed additional critical thought. The Voting Rights Act, which sailed through the

Senate 98–0, required the same skepticism. "Do you ever seriously expect Congress to vote against a re-extension of the Voting Rights Act?" he asked.

This Sanhedrin principle was not something Adegbile had studied or prepared for. "I wasn't familiar with it until he asked me about it at the podium, which is an uncomfortable way to learn," he ruefully recalls today.

Scalia's pseudo-question served a broader purpose. It was a claim that there was actually *too much* political support for the Voting Rights Act. Under this logic, it's the duty of the court, and courageous judges, to provide a corrective that politicians simply could not. "He's using the success of the vote and the overwhelming ratification as an argument against its constitutionality," Adegbile says, pointing out that the Senate's vote to confirm Scalia to the high court was also 98–0. "So to the extent that he actually believed in that principle, it should have been applied with equal vigor to his own confirmation, equally suspect under Scalia's version of the law."

IT'S DIFFICULT TO understand exactly what version of the law the justices ended up applying in the *Northwest Austin* decision. Judges are often accused of legislating from the bench when they issue an unpopular or disliked opinion, but *Northwest Austin* feels more like backroom horse-trading than judicious deliberating on the law.

In a decision that would have been unanimous, save a Clarence Thomas opinion that concurred in part and dissented in part, Roberts wrote an apparently unifying opinion for a court that appeared deeply divided during oral arguments. Everybody won, sort of. The utility district was allowed to bail out. Other small entities were also invited to apply for a preclearance reprieve. Section 5 survived, so the liberal justices also earned a reprieve and bought Congress time to potentially adjust the preclearance formula to meet the court's concerns.

Judges often deny that they are just politicians sitting on the bench, but *Northwest Austin* shows something closer to the reality. We won't know exactly how this decision came down unanimously for decades, until a deceased justice's papers become open to the public. Did the liberals side with Roberts, thinking that they needed to send a message to Congress to revise the VRA's preclearance formula before the court struck it down?

Did Roberts think the timing was wrong to strike down something as popular as the VRA? Or was he moving incrementally for strategic purposes—taking a short lead off first base as he prepared to steal second on the next pitch?

"They made a deal," says Blum.

"It's a compromise," says Adegbile.

For his part, Tatel offers blunt sarcasm: "It wasn't exactly a principled constitutional decision."

Roberts seemed to have done the impossible, and he won praise from the media and court watchers for "judicial statesmanship" and a common-sense solution that allowed the MUD to move its elections from a garage to a school without involving the federal government, but maintaining Section 5 for other localities where it was still needed. In opting to set aside the larger questions, the *New York Times* observed, the court made a "powerful statement" and "took a hard look at the current historical moment and decided that it has not yet come fully into focus."

None of this was exactly right. The court ducked the constitutional question, yes, but the Roberts decision—which every liberal justice signed onto—also ignores the clear text of the VRA and undermined the constitutional authority that the Reconstruction amendments awarded to Congress. Allowing the Northwest Austin MUD to bail out required Roberts to rewrite the Voting Rights Act in a way that he supported—but that Congress never intended, and in fact expressly opposed. When *Northwest Austin* first arrived at the district court, Tatel immediately understood the safest route would be to find a way to allow the utility board to escape preclearance and prevent the VRA issue from reaching the Supreme Court. "We actually said, if we can find a way for them to bail out, that avoids this whole thing, right? I tried to write it. I couldn't make it work. It doesn't work with the law. It's not right—but that didn't bother the court."

Liberals on the Supreme Court quietly claimed victory. Court insiders leaked to the *New Republic* that the liberal bloc saved the day, as Kennedy, the decisive swing vote, had been prepared to vote with Roberts and the conservative justices in a stunning 5–4 decision that would have struck down the VRA as unconstitutional. The liberals, according to the magazine, threatened a thunderous dissent that "would have accused the majority of misconstruing landmark precedents about congressional power." It was difficult to imagine the court's emboldened, precedent-defying conservative justices fearing a strongly worded dissent—but the Beltway-savvy *New Republic* nevertheless reported that either "Kennedy got cold feet" or "Roberts backed down."

If the liberal justices celebrated an imaginary win in an early skirmish, that was fine with the conservatives on the court. Roberts was busy digging a trench and setting a trap. Indeed, the liberal justices seemed to have scarcely noticed the actual language of the opinion they signed onto. "Things have changed in the South," Roberts declared, writing for nearly the full court. To make that implausible case, he cited voter turnout and registration rates that approach parity and what he called the rarity of "blatantly discriminatory evasions" of federal decrees. Those metrics, of course, could well support the case for extending the VRA—it clearly was working as a safeguard of fair ballot access in the former Jim Crow South. But Roberts insisted that the act's past success alone is not enough to justify its continuation. The Voting Rights Act, he wrote, "imposes current burdens and must be justified by current needs."

While liberals crowed to the *New Republic* over what was, at most, a holding-pattern consensus on the court, Roberts had suckered them into signing onto a much broader indictment, aimed at the future viability of the VRA. "The evil that Section 5 is meant to address may no longer be concentrated in the jurisdictions singled out for preclearance," he wrote for the court. "The statute's coverage formula is based on data that is now more than 35 years old, and there is considerable evidence that it fails to account for current political conditions."

Then Roberts made one additional stealth play that assured that the next challenge to the VRA would arise quickly and helped assure its success: an observation in his opinion known as a dicta—a comment in a case that might not be necessary to resolve it or even legally binding in the future, but that can be cited as a "persuasive authority" in future litigation. This is where Roberts gave birth to the fiction of "fundamental principle of equal sovereignty" among states. The trouble with this principle is that it doesn't exist. Roberts created it with an ellipsis and what can only be read as a deliberate misapplication of the law.

Here is what Roberts wrote in his decision:

> The Act also differentiates between the States, despite our historic tradition that all the States enjoy "equal sovereignty." Distinctions can be justified in some cases. "The doctrine of the equality of States . . . does not bar . . . remedies for local evils which have subsequently appeared." But a departure from the fundamental principle of equal sovereignty requires a showing that a statute's disparate geographic coverage is sufficiently related to the problem that it targets.

But before Roberts wrote this, there was no such principle—let alone a "fundamental" one. The cases that Roberts cites as authorities for the idea of equality among states actually concern the "equal footing doctrine." That is a very different principle, one securing equality among *newly admitted* states. It has nothing to do with voting rights or any other rights. No "fundamental principle" of equality among states governs the Fifteenth Amendment, which explicitly hands Congress the power to enact "appropriate legislation" to ensure equal treatment of *all voters* within states.

Southern states had made this claim before when they battled the constitutionality of Section 5. The first challenge, *South Carolina v. Katzenbach*, arrived in 1966, just one year after the VRA's passage. Then, an 8–1 court upheld the formula as "rational in both practice and theory." The one dissent, from Justice Hugo Black, a former Klansman, argued that it allowed the federal government to treat states unequally and like "conquered provinces."

In *Northwest Austin*, Roberts quietly lays the groundwork for Black's vision to triumph almost fifty years later. Precedent was not on the chief justice's side. Indeed, the Supreme Court itself rejected Roberts's cramped reading in *Katzenbach* when it upheld the constitutionality of the VRA—in the very sentence that Roberts uses to claim the opposite. How does he get away with turning up into down? He simply edited the court's precedent. He cut the clauses he didn't want, turned the ruling on its head, and called it law.

Compare what Roberts wrote above with the actual decision in *Katzenbach*:

> In acceptable legislative fashion, Congress chose to limit its attention to the geographic areas where immediate action seemed necessary. . . . The doctrine of the equality of States, invoked by South Carolina, does not bar this approach, for that doctrine applies only to the terms upon which States are admitted to the Union, and not to the remedies for local evils which have subsequently appeared.

The chief justice mischaracterized precedent and left out the parts he didn't like. Liberal justices either didn't notice the dicta or did not think that Roberts would be so brazen as to write it into law—citing his own invented precedent the next time a preclearance case came before the court. They underestimated both his chutzpah and hubris.

If the liberal justices lacked the foresight to understand Roberts's patient long game, or failed to understand his invitation for another locality to challenge preclearance—this time, one that the court could not simply bail out—one person most certainly did: Edward Blum.

"That's a fine first chop of the log," the master matchmaker said as he left the Supreme Court that morning. He knew where his axe would fall next: Shelby County, Alabama.

CHAPTER FIFTEEN

CALERA SITS AT the very heart of Alabama. Despite the best efforts of a new coffee shop, this two-stoplight downtown has seen better days. Train rides at the Heart of Dixie Railroad Museum are down to one day a week. The windows of the storefront Collectivus Church are papered black. Across the street, there's little evident demand for the South's Most Wanted Tattoos and Piercings.

Walk these eerily stagnant blocks today, and there's little sense that Calera, in 2008, had become the fastest-growing city in the state. Fewer than three thousand people lived here when the 2000s began, but over the next eight years the population multiplied to nearly twelve thousand. This burgeoning town, named after the Spanish word for lime, had been built on the dangerous work of extracting limestone and had a dark racial past. Lynchings continued here well past the dawn of the twentieth century. Many still remember separate water fountains for white and Black patrons at the ice cream parlor. The Confederate flag waved proudly outside the local historical society until a new director took it down in 1999, at the dawn of a new century.

Still, local officials preferred to think of Calera as part of the new South. Indeed, with its enviable three highway exits off I-65 and easy access to Birmingham and Montgomery, a development and population boom took hold. Cracker Barrel arrived alongside the interstate and became the favorite breakfast spot, and soon upmarket chain hotels, a trendy sports bar, a barbecue spot, and a gleaming, palatial Publix followed. In 2004, Calera's progress included electing a Black man, lifelong resident Ernest Montgomery, to the city council—just the second Black elected official in the city's history. Squint just the right way and you could almost see Calera as part of the changing South that Chief Justice John Roberts would reference when the U.S. Supreme Court ended preclearance in the 2013 *Shelby County* decision.

Yet the old South lay hidden underneath Calera's growth, unseeable to the eye but at the heart of the *Shelby County* case: the reworked border for Montgomery's council seat that officials authorized before the 2008 elections. As Calera boomed, it made 177 annexations between 1993 and 2006. These new stretches of the city included three upper-middle-class developments between Highways 22 and 31, with home after home of multipitched roofs, tightly cropped lawns, and giant SUVs parked in front. These land acquisitions added new, largely white subdivisions that emerged on the city's boundaries. Every change in the size or shape of a city, every decision about which neighborhood to annex and which to leave unincorporated, alters the voting strength of residents and minority groups. Calera's Black population grew from 13 percent to 16 percent during Montgomery's first term. But the reconstituted district, previously the city's only majority-minority jurisdiction, had been turned inside out. With the addition of those white neighborhoods, and the subtraction of a significant Black community Montgomery had represented, District Two went from 71 percent Black to just 30 percent, overnight. That August, Montgomery lost his seat—by two votes.

Since the annexations carried consequences for minority voters, they needed to be precleared under the VRA. There was one big problem: Calera's city fathers had failed to preclear the new maps. After Montgomery's historic victory, Calera's otherwise-white leadership decided that it was time to redistrict. Indeed, they'd simply forgotten, or not bothered, to preclear, as the VRA required, any of the 177 annexations over the previous fourteen years that increased the city's population and made the new maps necessary.

When the Department of Justice learned what was happening, it sent the city a blunt three-page letter and made it clear that no valid election could be held in Calera on an uncleared map. Calera ignored that warning. So the DOJ forced the city to run the race again, under the old maps—and this time Montgomery was elected by a commanding margin.

One might look at the Calera elections and conclude that preclearance did its job in Shelby County. The Voting Rights Act ultimately caught and prevented a subtle yet brazen effort that would have ensured an entirely white council. The VRA was working as lawmakers intended it to in 1965, protecting against continued discrimination in 2006.

But that's not how Edward Blum and Shelby County officials viewed things. When Blum discovered the DOJ's letter on its website early one morning from his desk in Maine, he recognized his dream test case. *Northwest Austin* had yet to be decided, but Blum understood what the Supreme Court was likely to do. As he read the DOJ correspondence, his mind already raced ahead to the next salvo, the next offering this savvy house cat could leave at the doorstop of 1 First Street NE. "Shelby County was attractive because it couldn't bail out," he told me. It was ineligible because of the numerous elections and annexations the county had overseen without preclearance. Yet for Blum's purposes, the county's dirty hands made it all the more appealing as a plaintiff.

"There had been objections in the county." That meant if Blum could help Shelby County challenge preclearance and the VRA formula, and if the case made it all the way to the U.S. Supreme Court, the justices would not be able to dodge the big constitutional issues as they had in *Northwest Austin*. There would be no way out: if Roberts and the conservative justices wanted the next chop as badly as Blum, the axe would be right there in front of them to question Section 5's constitutionality. "It was not hard to convince the county attorney in Shelby County," Blum says with a smile.

That attorney, Butch Ellis, represented both the county and many towns as their city attorney. "He hated Section 5," Blum recalls. He was angered over how hard it was, and how expensive it could be, to win preclearance." Ellis didn't have the resources to challenge the law. So when Blum offered to have his allies foot the bill, "[Ellis] was thrilled that I called."

Here was something of a Rashomon moment in the legal battles over the VRA: the same election, the same DOJ enforcement, viewed two completely different ways. Ultimately, as Blum foresaw, the U.S. Supreme Court would have the final word. Calera's redistricting set off a chain reaction that would result in new limits on the Voting Rights Act, and a rollback of civil rights protections for the first time in the nation's history.

If Selma is where the dream of a modern multiracial democracy was born, Calera, forty-three years later and some fifty-two miles northeast, is where it quietly began to wither away.

THE MOST CREATIVE and perhaps essential enforcement arm of the VRA, Section 5's preclearance regime, was born in Alabama as well. Following Bloody Sunday in Selma, when the nation then watched real-time horrors unfold in the South as state troopers met peaceful protesters with clubs, tear gas, and snarling dogs, Lyndon Johnson addressed Congress and the nation and demanded passage of the Voting Rights Act.

Yet, crucially, he also demanded that the VRA learn from the previous years of spotty gains under the Civil Rights Act of 1957 and 1960. Both laws were baby steps along the path to racial justice, requiring voting-related litigation to be heard in federal courts in the jurisdiction where the complaint was filed. This was a plainly unworkable oversight measure, since too many federal judges across the South, many of them segregationists themselves or otherwise unwilling to enforce the law, simply slow-walked trials and complaints arising from the two acts.

In Selma, for example, the federal judge for Dallas County protected segregationist sheriffs and regularly denied the DOJ's requests for records. He also stalled the scheduling of civil rights trials, sometimes for years. Politicians, meanwhile, would institute new barriers faster than Washington prosecutors could play voter-suppression whack-a-mole. The Justice Department first filed litigation in Dallas County in 1961, when only 1 percent of eligible Blacks were registered to vote. By 1965, the DOJ had won four years of voting rights "victories" but Black voter registration had only risen to 5 percent. Section 5 recognized that some localities with the worst track records could not be trusted to change—or even enforce the law—without supervision.

Those numbers were only a little better in Calera when Montgomery was born. In 1957, some 17 percent of Black residents were registered to vote. White and Black registration had come closer to parity by 2008 in Calera, as it had in much of the state. Registration, however, only tells part of the story—especially when redistricting and annexation, among other race neutral–looking strategies, could create the same results.

"This used to be the Montgomery district," says Reverend Kenneth Dukes, president of the local NAACP, as he guides us in his truck off Highway 31, away from the chain restaurants abutting the interstate, where we'd met at the Cracker Barrel for breakfast. "What happened in Shelby County is that they got tired of following the rules," says Dukes, one of the local activists who filed amicus briefs in *Shelby County*.

It's a bright February 2022 morning, and Dukes is now driving to the actual other side of Calera's railroad tracks, through some of the poorest neighborhoods in the county, to show me the redistricting changes that led to *Shelby County v. Holder*. "It's Black all the way down on this side of 31," Dukes says, "all on the other side of these tracks. They're very active, by the way." He takes me past the housing developments that sit next to the run-down Black elementary school, then several miles toward another impoverished Black community in the shadow of one of Calera's massive lime plants. "When they put these plants in, they put them in Black communities. That's just how it works," he says. "This reminds me of something you'd see in Punta Cana. See these trees? If there were any leaves on them, all the leaves would be white from the lime. People still have outhouses. Kids are born with asthma or birth defects."

We loop back toward Highway 31. "Let me show you what they did to the Montgomery district. First, they cut those Black neighborhoods out completely." We head up a hill and he takes a right turn into a gleaming new subdivision called Kinsale Gardens, new houses, tightly packed, trimmed lawns, as far as the eye can see. "Then they added this subdivision. They flipped the district. It had been 70 percent Black. As soon as they added this, it's 70 percent white."

The South had changed, and the South had stayed the same. "When they say things have changed in the South? Only one word has changed. Violence. If I go to the polls, I won't get beaten," Dukes says. "Intimidated, yes. Frustrated, yes. Just not beaten."

IN 2008, MONTGOMERY was determined that the new lines would not beat him. He wondered why his district needed to change so drastically, but the consultants and city demographers insisted this was the only map that worked. "Of course we ran anyway," Montgomery said. "We didn't like those numbers. But, you know, we thought that's the only way it could be." When Montgomery asked whether Washington had precleared the map, city officials replied as one: absolutely. That wasn't quite true.

It was true that the new maps had been sent to Washington. But when they arrived, DOJ officials discovered those 177 unapproved annexations. They had questions. On May 7, they asked for additional census data. It took the city six weeks to comply. They continued answering questions through August 18. The election was supposed to be held one week later.

Montgomery sat on the city council but had no idea any of this was happening. The soft-spoken, lifelong resident who works in a machine shop set out to campaign in the new subdivision, confident his public service and deep roots in the community would matter to Calera's new residents. He knew all the stories of racial discrimination in Calera. He knew what his parents lived through and what he had seen with his own eyes. But he wanted to believe Calera, and the South, had changed.

He didn't yet know that his own campaign was the latest chapter in Alabama's ignominious history. But as he knocked on doors, Montgomery heard the same refrain: these voters, almost entirely white, were backing his opponent, a newcomer who'd barely lived here more than a year. No one seemed willing to look him in the eye and tell him why. Montgomery yearned to believe better, but had no choice but to reach his own sad judgment. "They voted against me because of the color of my skin," he said.

The day before the election, Grace Chung Becker, an assistant attorney general with the DOJ, sent the city a stern warning. The annexations and the redistricting plan, she warned, "continue to be legally unenforceable." She noted that "[f]or 13 years, the city has failed to submit their adopted annexations for Section 5 review." The demographic data the city provided about population data, she said, "was unreliable." The city "failed to supply any reliable current population information" about the annexations. Calera's estimates of racial data, she noted, "[have] no basis." The city "appears to have failed to consider how the African-American population would be fairly reflected." DOJ called the geographer hired by the city, who told investigators "he was willing to provide information" about options that would have provided Black voters a "better opportunity" to elect a candidate of choice. The only problem, he explained, was that city officials "expressed no interest" in these alternatives. Becker made it clear that the council election would be unlawful. The council got its own advice, from city and county attorney Butch Ellis, and went ahead anyway. Montgomery lost to his white opponent—by those two votes.

Even the candidates didn't know anything was amiss until the following week, when the *Shelby County Recorder*—underneath a story about two cars being burned at an apartment complex—broke the news that "Calera's election may not be valid." The article quoted Ellis, who gave the paper a quote that sounded like he was just some flummoxed local attorney, as confused as anyone else. The new maps were simply intended to even out the population among districts, as the law requires, Ellis insisted—but the federal government wanted to make sure they were fair to minorities, he continued. "We are very confident that what we've done does not discriminate against anybody. But we've got to convince the Justice Department." Yet this was not Butch Ellis's, or Shelby County's, first dance with uncleared annexations.

FOURTEEN MILES AWAY in Alabaster, just north past the run-down strip mall churches dotting Highway 31, Bobby Lee Harris opened his *Birmingham News* and read ruefully about Ernest Montgomery's defeat in Calera. He recognized the situation: the backstage machinations and casual disregard for the Voting Rights Act by city and county officials mirrored his bitter election eight years earlier.

Alabaster's population at the time, just over 29,300, was nearly three times that of Calera, yet the two small cities had much in common. Both owed their founding to the limestone quarries that gave each city its name and the arrival of the Alabama & Tennessee Railroad. Both towns then blossomed into I-65 bedroom communities.

Both cities also had sizable Black populations who went many decades without representation on city boards and councils. That only began to change with the end of discriminatory at-large districts. Yet both continued tilting power toward white populations, anyway, simply not bothering to preclear dozens of annexations.

Harris chooses the local McDonald's to tell me his story. The election he describes sounds like it might have taken place in the 1950s, not in the twenty-first century. Court documents confirm all the bracing details—malfeasance and arrogance, corruption and privilege so breathtaking that it could only be the handiwork of people used to accruing power this way simply because it's the way folks here have always done things.

Harris represented Ward 1 on the seven-member Alabaster council—the only Black representative from a district drawn to ensure the city's sizable minority population had an opportunity to elect a councillor of their own choosing. The seat was created during the 1980s, after courts held that the Alabama legislature had "consistently enacted at-large systems for local government during periods when there was a substantial threat of Black participation in the political process."

It didn't take long for that Black majority seat to become threatened as well. Between March 1992 and March 2000, Alabaster—and Ward 1—began to change. During that time, the city expanded with 58 new annexations: 42 of them residential, 16 commercial. All those modifications needed to be cleared with the Justice Department. According to DOJ, none of them were. Two of those annexations, in 1994 and 1996 in a wealthy and nearly all-white development called Weatherly, were added to Ward 1. And as the August 2000 elections neared, Harris suddenly realized that it might be impossible for a Black candidate to win Alabaster's sole Black seat.

"They annexed Weatherly into my ward—but the city had failed to clear it with the Justice Department," Harris said. "And before we knew anything, the vote was here. It was time to vote—and Weatherly had diluted my district."

When Harris realized what had happened, he asked Alabaster's city attorney a basic question: Had the new wards been precleared? The flummoxed lawyer, one of Harris's former students, had to admit that no one had taken that required step. And so the city raced to come into compliance with the Voting Rights Act, after a decade of ignoring it. The council election was set for August 22, 2000. It wasn't until May 31 that the city requested DOJ's approval for a decade's worth of annexations and the new maps.

Officials in Washington needed until August 16 to finish their investigation. DOJ precleared the 16 commercial annexations and 40 of the 42 residential additions. But like Harris, they immediately noticed that the

two Weatherly annexations—99 percent white, according to voter registration records—would have transformed the city's only majority-Black
district to majority white. The DOJ also noticed that this wasn't necessary:
the city had the option of assigning the Weatherly neighborhoods to either
Ward 2 or Ward 6, both of which had fewer registered voters than Ward 1.
It would have been possible to preserve the Black-opportunity district,
had city officials made different choices. Instead, they chose to bleach the
ward white, without preapproval. The Justice Department spoke clearly:
Weatherly could become part of Alabaster. But it could not be attached
to Ward 1. They denied preclearance.

Alabaster officials scrambled. They had an election in six days. They'd
already printed the ballots, they told the DOJ, and it would be "extremely
difficult" to have new ones printed in time just for Weatherly. Panicked city
leaders who had failed to live up to their responsibility over the previous decade, who expressed more concern over preprinted ballots than following
the Voting Rights Act, accepted a compromise with the DOJ. They'd hold
the citywide mayoral election, and council races in the other six wards would
proceed as usual. Everyone would use the same ballots. But in Ward 1, residents of Weatherly would have their ballots tabulated separately. Harris's
election would take place under the previous map. Residents of the new
Weatherly neighborhood would be allowed to vote for mayor. However,
since Weatherly's addition to Ward 1 remained unapproved by the DOJ,
those voters would not be allowed to participate in the council election.

The following week, Harris won reelection, defeating Todd Goode, a
white challenger, by a certified vote of 326 to 287.

Harris owed his reelection to preclearance and the Voting Rights Act.
In Weatherly, 103 ballots were cast in the mayoral race. Even though those
voters would not have a voice in the council race, 101 of them nevertheless
marked the ballot. All 101 of them—every last vote—went for the white
candidate, Goode. If the election had gone off as Alabaster intended, Harris would have lost 388 to 326. If Harris had not spoken up, had DOJ not
intervened, Alabaster would have gotten away with annexing two entirely
white subdivisions, attaching them to a majority-Black ward, and ousting
the only Black council member.

"If it had not been for Section 5, I would have lost in 2000—on a map that had not been cleared, even though they knew that it had to be pre-cleared," said Harris. "That's why you need Section 5 today."

Today, a decade after preclearance's demise, Weatherly residents vote in Ward 1. The council has not had a Black member since. The road out-side this McDonald's has been renamed Bobby Harris Boulevard, in honor of the councillor whose vision helped develop two large shopping desti-nations off the interstate. Those developments in turn have helped fund new schools, a city hall, a senior center, and a public safety complex. Har-ris ran for a seat on the powerful county commission, but says the Black precincts were moved around at the last minute and his voters went home confused. The chief justice insists the South has changed, but Bobby Har-ris feels locked out and sees the same faces in power. Perhaps the schemes changed, but the result remained the same.

"All we've got is the ballot. Once you lose that, you don't have a voice, and that's what disgusts me today. We don't have a district today. Not a single district. And the question is *why?*

"Some things change. Other things remain the same."

IF CALERA STILL feels like *In the Heat of the Night*, Columbiana, Alabama, is *Gone with the Wind*. It's a South of ranches and plantations, where the downtown is home to fading murals painted on corner buildings advertis-ing overalls and nickel bottles of Coca-Cola. Across from a stately Renais-sance Revival courthouse sits the brick law office of Frank Ellis Jr. From a third-floor balcony where the eighty-two-year-old lawyer still takes his coffee before five most mornings, looking upon the quaint downtown and its well-appointed churches, Ellis, known as Butch, can survey a town his family has run for generations.

His father, Leven Handy Ellis, practiced law here as well, and served as Columbiana's mayor and state senator before becoming lieutenant governor of Alabama in the 1940s. Leven led the Alabama delegation to the 1948 Democratic National Convention, where they walked out in re-sponse to President Harry Truman and Senator Hubert Humphrey's calls to support civil rights in the party platform. Alabama delegates, he vowed, would "never cast their vote for any candidate associated with a civil rights program such as adopted by this convention." Along with other breakaway delegates from Mississippi, Louisiana, and South Carolina, they formed the "States' Rights" party that became known as the Dixiecrats and nominated segregationist Strom Thurmond for president in 1948.

Butch's son, Corley, served on the county commission before becoming a state representative. According to the *Washington Spectator*, Corley Ellis was the county commissioner who decided not to notify Ernest Montgomery that the commission was going to file suit against the Justice Department. Butch, who has represented Shelby County and nearly every town in it as city attorney for decades, duly proceeded to file the lawsuit and push it all the way to the U.S. Supreme Court. This is the way that you can connect Alabama's racial past to the current assault on the Voting Rights Act necessitated by that shameful history—all over the lifespan of a grandfather, a father, and son.

On the day I visit Butch Ellis in his office, he looks every bit the charming southern gentleman—silver-haired, honey-voiced, eyes as blue as the state's famed Lewis Smith Lake. He pours me a coffee and unwinds a story about how Shelby County has changed since 1965 and why the Voting Rights Act had become a relic of another time, much like those murals for nickel Coke and the Liberty Overalls sold at Eagle's Department Store.

"I was a county attorney when the Voting Rights Act passed. I really, truly believe that the Voting Rights Act in 1965 was justified. I support the Voting Rights Act, and I have, in my adult years. We did have a literacy test that required you to be able to read and write, and long story short we had less than 50 percent of the qualified voters registered in 1964, 1965 that would require preclearance. So it fit us. It properly fit us. But as the years went by, things changed. We don't have the prejudice that existed then."

Shelby County today, Ellis says, is still white, "heavily white, as you know," but it's a place where a Black man can be elected chairman of the county board of education ("our highest elected office") and where Black councilmen can be elected in cities that are 80 or 90 percent white. "There are just countless examples of that," he says, "and that's the way it has been for a number of years."

Despite Alabama's progress, Ellis says, the towns of Shelby County couldn't make the smallest changes to their election procedures. "We were still spending, literally, tens of thousands of dollars of taxpayer money that could be going to kids in school or providing public services. We were spending it on getting preclearance on every single thing we did." A small town wanted to form a fire district, Ellis says, but the petition sat so long with the Justice Department that time ran out to run the election under an Alabama state law.

Preclearance, Ellis says, was initially intended to sunset with the original Voting Rights Act in 1970. "Well, they extended it, and they extended, and they extended. Then they extended the last time, in 2006 for another twenty-five years. Our white voters were already electing Black candidates. And the Justice Department was being unreasonable about this stuff in a county, in a place in time, when we didn't have discrimination in the political place. We had, as I said, Black people beating white incumbents with white votes. Not with Black votes, with white votes. And it just was a different time."

Of course, it wasn't that different. In 1987, the Supreme Court held in *Dillard v. Crenshaw County* that "from the late 1800s through the present, Alabama has consistently erected barriers to keep black persons from full and equal participation in the social, economic, and political life of the state." The court ordered changes in more than 180 towns and counties, including Shelby County. Yet Shelby County and its largest towns entered into consent decrees, promised change, and never delivered. Calera, of course, annexed heavily white communities 177 times without seeking preclearance, then ran the 2008 election on unapproved maps despite the Justice Department's objection.

"Calera, we did have a difficult time with the Justice Department," Ellis admits. "I thought they were unfair and unreasonable, as we tried to work through it and get it done. They were smart-alecky about it."

Ellis would have the last laugh. In June 2009, he noticed the Supreme Court's decision in *Northwest Austin*, which contained Roberts's signal that a future test of the VRA's constitutionality was likely in order. "I read that case and knew that [preclearance] was unconstitutional. In my mind, I knew it," he said. Nevertheless, the county didn't have the extra cash to take a constitutional challenge to the Supreme Court.

"About that time, Ed Blum showed up," Ellis says.

CHAPTER SIXTEEN

JUST THREE YEARS after the Supreme Court decided 2009's *Northwest Austin*, Blum had the conservative court primed, exactly as he had imagined. Few could have delivered on this ambitious agenda, let alone this quickly. In the previous term, 8,952 cases knocked at the court's door and requested hearings. The justices heard oral arguments for just 79 of them, around 0.88 percent. A higher percentage of major-league baseball players have earned plaques in the Hall of Fame.

Yet in 2012, Blum managed to make history twice, capturing the justices' attention with *Fisher v. University of Texas*, an affirmative action case challenging the use of race in college admissions, and *Shelby County*. Blum and his lead Washington attorney, the veteran conservative insider Bert Rein, ticketed the case to the high court from the beginning. "I have the luxury of starting with what I want the Supreme Court opinion to read," Blum says, "and then working backward to the district court. Most lawyers don't have that latitude." Blum and his team understood that they would likely lose on the merits in the U.S. District Court in D.C. and then again in the U.S. Court of Appeals. They also understood that those defeats would not matter. They were simply the stepping stones leading to the U.S. Supreme Court and an audience of five conservatives they had every reason to expect receptive.

"The odds are always lousy," Rein told me. "But here there was a very good clue from the *NAMUDNO* case. The chief justice certainly had introduced a different mode of thinking—the so-called equality among the states. The court had thought about it once. Maybe they'd like to do it again?" Rein and Ellis filed with the U.S. District Court in Washington, they said, not because they expected a favorable ruling, "but because we knew that we would get noticed."

One person who noticed was the nation's first Black attorney general. Eric Holder kept a wary eye on the case. Holder believed that the new wave of voter ID laws were a direct response to the multiracial coalition that Obama assembled on his way to becoming the first Black president. "Their way of getting back at it was to somehow disenfranchise, disempower that coalition, using methods and a determination that I'd almost consigned to older, now-gone generations," Holder told me. Yet Holder, unlike Rein, never thought Roberts and the Supreme Court were actually ready to move.

"The Voting Rights Act? Which Congress just reauthorized 390 to almost nothing? You see the threat, but it's like 'Yeah, right,'" Holder said. "If this were to happen, it would be unbelievably bad and consequential. But the likelihood of that happening is not that great, you know?"

Holder did not yet realize his adversaries had hall-of-fame credentials. And he retained an institutionalist's faith that justices would call balls and strikes, not remake the law.

AS REIN AND Blum presumed, the district court sided against them, finding that the challenged provisions remained a "congruent and proportionality remedy" to the twenty-first-century problem of voting redistricting in the covered states and localities. Shelby County quickly brought the case to the U.S. Court of Appeals, where Judge David Tatel, for the second time in three years, stood between the Voting Rights Act and the U.S. Supreme Court.

Tatel immediately understood the stakes. The Supreme Court fired a warning shot toward Congress with *Northwest Austin*. Congress did not respond to the implied threat by revisiting the formula. When the Democrats controlled the House in 2009 and 2010, the focus was Obamacare. The ensuing backlash cost them the House and closed any window to take on the formula. Now Blum had returned with a plaintiff who forced the bigger questions.

In a 2–1 decision, Tatel and the Court of Appeals upheld the district court's ruling, again holding against Shelby County. The appeals court agreed that preclearance remained congruent, proportional, and constitutional. But Tatel knew that to be effective his ruling, yet again, would somehow need to persuade one person: Chief Justice Roberts.

This time it would not be enough to carefully summarize Congress's findings when it reauthorized the VRA, as he'd tried to do in *Northwest Austin*. Tatel told me he didn't believe that John Roberts was calling balls and strikes anymore; Tatel had to adjust his approach, or risk being over-turned. He would need to frame a decision that was responsive to the di-rection the court signaled in *Northwest Austin*. It would have to grapple with the "extraordinary federalism costs" of holding some states to a differ-ent standard as well as the genuine progress some parts of the South had made since 1965. At the same time, though, Tatel had to thread a needle to produce a viable interpretation of the law that fit that into the larger set of Supreme Court precedents.

If it's possible for an appeals court decision to sing, Tatel's sixty-three pages in his *Shelby County* ruling are a soaring "Hallelujah" chorus. It takes on Shelby County's claims through the lens of the concerns Rob-erts and the court set out in *Northwest Austin*. Chiefly it asks whether the burdens imposed by Section 5 can still be justified by current needs—and answers decisively that they can. There is no requirement for Congress to show "gamesmanship" for preclearance to be congruent and propor-tional. Tatel read every word of the congressional report and found that Sensenbrenner and Watt had gathered overwhelming evidence to support reauthorization.

The sixteen-thousand-page congressional record not only included twenty-one hearings and dozens of witnesses but also multiple academic studies and reports that evaluated equal access to the polls both nation-wide and specifically in the covered states. Again and again, experts showed why Section 5 remained necessary: between the 1982 and 2006 reauthorizations, Justice officials had brought 105 actions against cov-ered jurisdictions that went ahead and made changes without preclear-ance. During the same period federal observers were required to monitor elections on 622 occasions for constitutional issues in covered states and localities. Federal officials lodged upward of 700 objections to discrimina-tory voting schemes, while in another 800 instances, jurisdictions with-drew or modified plans to change electoral rules after Justice intervened.

Meanwhile, Ellen Katz, a law professor at the University of Michigan, studied all the Section 2 cases brought between 1982 and 2005 and found that the covered jurisdictions also made up 56 percent of those—even though they only contained a quarter of the nation's population, and even though Section 5 should have caught the most glaring violations well before a Section 2 case was brought.

Shelby County officials might look at that same evidence and believe there is "no longer systemic resistance" in covered jurisdictions that Section 2 could not handle. But they don't get to decide, Tatel wrote: "Congress, however, reached a different conclusion"—and "the County has offered no basis for thinking that Congress's judgment is either unreasonable or unsupported by probative evidence." Furthermore, the courts also had no business substituting their supposed wisdom on the subject for that of Congress. "These are quintessentially legislative judgments," he wrote.

Tatel's conclusion read like a direct message to the chief justice:

> The legislative record is by no means unambiguous. But Congress drew reasonable conclusions from the extensive evidence gathered and acted pursuant to the Fourteenth and Fifteenth Amendments, which entrust Congress with ensuring that the right to vote—surely among the most important guarantees of political liberty in the Constitution—is not abridged on account of race. In this context, we owe much deference to the considered judgment of the People's elected representatives.

This parting appeal would not be enough. "I probably shouldn't say anything about that," he now says, with a resigned sigh, but continues anyway. "You saw the extent to which I was trying to write *Shelby County* to satisfy this court. It was an audience of one. John Roberts. That was it. I wasn't writing that for anybody else."

Tatel may have been disappointed with the Supreme Court's decision in *Shelby County*, but he says he was "not surprised at all."

"I was writing for history. I did not expect to convince him. I really didn't. And that's because he wasn't convincible. He knew what he wanted to do. Congress hadn't responded. He was done. That was it."

Things had changed in the South. "Right. Of course, Congress didn't think so, right?" Tatel observes. "And the Fifteenth Amendment says this is up to Congress. They didn't give this decision to the Supreme Court. The Constitution gives it to Congress. You have the clear express textual delegation to the Congress in the Fifteenth Amendment. It's right there, right? It says *Congress*.

"Then you have a whole series of Supreme Court opinions not only sustaining the constitutionality of the act, but telling the courts when it comes to voting and race, Congress's decisions are what the courts have to follow. All that was gone in *Shelby County, Northwest Austin*. It just ignores it."

It all seems impossible to square. "That's because it's not square-able," Tatel says. "I mean, you're struggling with the fundamental problem of what our Supreme Court has become. I mean, there's no basis at all for the *Northwest Austin* decision or *Shelby County*. It's made up."

BERT REIN HAD never argued before the Supreme Court. But like John Roberts, Rein first arrived in Washington from Harvard Law and took up a prestigious position as a clerk at the U.S. Supreme Court during the 1966–67 term. Rein clerked for Justice John Marshall Harlan II, the grandson and namesake of the Supreme Court justice whose courageous, but lonely, dissent in *Plessy v. Ferguson* decried the injustice of "separate but equal." Harlan II was just as lonely, but also far less given to an expansive view of civil rights. He was often the sole dissenter from the Warren Court's landmark series of 1960s cases that established "one person, one vote."

Justice Harlan II maintained that the best way to handle malapportioned legislative districts was through the political process that malapportioned them in the first place—much as Roberts would conclude fifty years later in the infamous decision upholding partisan gerrymandering, *Rucho v. Common Cause*.

While Blum had spent years battling against racial preferences, Rein's specialty was antitrust litigation. As a young deputy assistant secretary of state under Richard Nixon, he focused on international aviation and telecommunications. Those fields, along with food and drug regulations, became his specialty once he entered private practice. He became an expert in guiding satellite makers and large airlines through the tangle of congressional and agency regulations.

This immersion in high-stakes regulatory law meant that Rein, like Roberts, played a careful long game. When Nixon campaign officials asked him to discuss his role in the 1972 reelection campaign, Rein's meetings coincided with one of Howard Hunt's appointments. When the young conservative lawyer met the CIA veteran who was just months away from his arrest in the Watergate break-ins, he felt a deep unease. Rein did not join the campaign, even though he knew he might be giving up the chance to run a federal agency at a young age. "Now, looking back, it was the best decision I ever made. It probably kept me out of jail."

Having wisely sidestepped a career-killing dalliance with Nixon's dirty-tricks team, Rein instead became a pillar of the Republican legal establishment and a Washington wise man, moving easily between political circles and the conservative legal world, tapped by the Reagan administration to help recommend candidates for the Department of Justice. By the early 1980s he'd founded his own firm, Wiley Rein & Fielding, alongside Fred Fielding, another principled survivor of the Nixon White House and later John Roberts mentor who'd become a well-known conservative legal rainmaker and elder statesman.

In the 1990s Rein led the Chamber of Commerce's aggressive and ambitious litigation efforts on behalf of business, just as Lewis Powell had urged back in 1971. But this was much less of a renegade mission, now that the courts were filling up with a new generation of business-friendly conservative judges, vetted by Powell's spiritual and intellectual descendants at the Federalist Society. In a long-game move that proved especially prescient, Fielding plucked a young Roberts from his DOJ job and brought him to the White House. At the time of Roberts's nomination, Rein enthusiastically testified to Roberts's conservative bona fides, telling NBC News that "I know he's conservative by talking with him about issues."

By contrast, when I pressed Rein on how well he knew Roberts before arguing *Shelby County*, he only claimed to hobnobbing with the chief justice "theoretically." Any insight, he said, "was more from what he had said on the bench. I knew he had thrown that idea of equal sovereignty among states into [*Northwest Austin*] and probably not just for the joy of saying,

'Hey, I want to say something about this.' You could tell the Section 5 formula was irksome to him."

Drawing on this valuable background, the lawyers for the *Shelby
County* plaintiffs hit upon a tightly focused strategy. They'd build an appeal around Roberts's concerns about equal sovereignty and whether the
preclearance formula still matched the modern needs of the communities governed by the VRA. Additionally, because Justice Kennedy had expressed worries about the costs of preclearance, and he always remained
a swing vote, they'd have a secondary argument that focused on the *literal* federalism costs. Like every other foe of the VRA, they'd seize on the
unsupported statistic Coleman seeded in the 2006 Senate hearings, and
cite it as an onerous $1 billion cost of compliance. All this meant ignoring
what had happened in Shelby County while claiming that the South had
changed. "Calera had a problem. But you can find dozens of examples in
other states that are like Calera," Rein said. In other words, if everyone is
breaking the law, you might as well rewrite it.

Of course that ignores a different reality: if everyone is breaking the
law, then nothing has actually changed.

IN DECEMBER 2012, the Judicial Education Project filed an amicus brief in
the *Shelby County* case that urged the Supreme Court to end preclearance. "The most recent reauthorization of the statute rested on outdated
assumptions and data that no longer support the extraordinary incursion
onto state sovereignty effected by the statute's broad and unequally appli-
cable preclearance requirements," the brief read in part. It had, of course,
been filed on behalf of one of the linchpins of the Leonard Leo empire, now
fronted by Carrie Severino, a former clerk for Clarence Thomas. The
amicus filing cited *Northwest Austin* prominently, but also twisted the argument of a law review article by the liberal law professor Richard Hasen,
who supported the VRA reauthorization but thought the formula should
have been modified because the court was likely to strike it down.

That citation was also straight out of the legal Right's playbook. This
was why, during the Senate Judiciary Committee hearings on the VRA's reauthorization, Hasen and other law professors supporting reauthorization

had been invited to testify. The goal was to create a documentary record ostensibly showing that even liberal legal thinkers doubted the constitutional soundness of the Act.

What was truly novel and unusual about the Judicial Education Project's involvement in *Shelby County* was that, many weeks before the group filed this amicus brief, as the *Washington Post* reported, it also silently funneled tens of thousands of dollars to Clarence Thomas's wife, Ginni, for work that remains unclear.

That January, Leo told Kellyanne Conway—the Republican pollster, and future Donald Trump campaign manager and senior counselor to the president—to pay Thomas "another $25k." The invoice vaguely lists the purpose as "Supplement for Constitution Polling and Opinion Consulting."

Leo did not want Thomas's name anywhere near the invoice. "No mention of Ginni, of course," he wrote.

Here's how the money traveled: Following Leo's instructions, Conway had her firm, the Polling Company, invoice the Judicial Education Project that very day for $25,000. The Polling Company then funneled the payment to the justice's wife through her firm, called Liberty Consulting.

This was not the first time Conway's firm contracted with Ginni Thomas. Between June 2011 and June 2012, the Polling Company sent $80,000 to Liberty Consulting. The documents show that the Polling Company planned to pay Thomas an additional $20,000 before the end of 2012.

In 2012, meanwhile, Thomas's own financial disclosure report valued payments from Liberty Consulting at somewhere between $1 and $15,000—even as Leo was arranging to "give" Ginni Thomas nearly twice that, and while Conway's payments approached six figures. Post–*Citizens United*, few of these groups are required to disclose their funding sources. And Supreme Court justices, unlike anyone else, fill out financial disclosure forms under an honor system without any actual checks or enforcement. All of which makes it virtual child's play for self-interested donors to dole out gifts to justices and their families, even when they have interests before the court, without oversight or consequences.

We don't know anything about the sort of work Ginni Thomas might have done for the Judicial Education Project. We don't know why Leo decided to involve Conway rather than pay the bill himself. We don't know how many other times Leo wanted to "give" money to the justice's wife. We don't know why Leo seems to have control of these dollars in the first place, or why there should be "No mention of Ginni, of course."

But here's what we do know: the Judicial Education Project brief aligned almost exactly with Clarence Thomas's concurrence in *Shelby County*.

The brief rested its argument on an odd notion: the equal sovereignty of states, which it called "a fundamental bedrock principle."

Thomas did not recuse himself based on the six figures gifted to his wife through Leonard Leo via an organization that had a crucial interest before the court. Instead, in the 5–4 case, his vote would prove decisive.

THE TASK OF defending the Voting Rights Act now moved to Donald Verrilli, the solicitor general of the United States, and a man who never shared the optimism of his boss, Eric Holder.

Verrilli spent the night before oral arguments pacing his room at a nearby boutique hotel. It was his ritual. A room on Capitol Hill, a short walk to 1 First Street NE in the morning, no unreliable transportation or parking anxieties required, a salmon dinner at the French bistro down-stairs. The nation's solicitor general had argued more than two dozen cases before the U.S. Supreme Court and had a well-earned reputation as both a John Roberts and Anthony Kennedy whisperer.

His understated, technical approach won cases even the smart set of court watchers thought he'd lost. When Verrilli made a subtle argument defending the Affordable Care Act's individual mandate by making a his-torical argument about the Constitution and taxation, CNN's Jeffrey Too-bin mocked it as "disastrous" and declared Obamacare good as gone. He was wrong. Verrilli had found the key that somehow brought the chief jus-tice along. As a result, he helped save the nation's health care program and preserved coverage for tens of millions of Americans. Three years later, in *Obergefell v. Hodges*, Verrilli would convince Kennedy and win same-sex marriage rights. He would then bring both Kennedy and Roberts along to strike down a Texas abortion law that had closed more than half the clinics in the state.

On the eve of arguments in *Shelby County*, the solicitor general knew he only had to persuade one of those two justices to join the four liberals and preserve the full protections of the Voting Rights Act. His team spent weeks in preparation. A lawyer arguing before the court might only get in two sentences before any justice interrupted with a question. Verrilli and other DOJ lawyers worked and reworked his opening lines, honing each word. They worked up the most demanding questions they could imagine a justice posing to Verrilli and spent hours practicing "moot court" arguments like they were still in law school. "It was the biggest challenge of my five years as solicitor general," Verrilli says, "because we knew that it was going to be extremely difficult if not impossible to get five votes. We knew we had four votes, for sure. But we had to get a fifth."

Verrilli developed two potential approaches. The first emphasized the historic nature of the VRA. He could raise the racial stakes and emphasize that the VRA's protections were the product of decades of toil by deeply committed activists, some of whom were killed along the way, arguing it was unthinkable to overturn something simply because it had some success in moving the country to a better place. "That's the 'Well, how dare you,' approach," Verrilli says. Such a moral challenge, Verrilli feared, might alienate two justices whose votes he needed, by making them feel like he was calling them racist if they didn't agree with him. "So that is not the approach I took."

Instead, he decided to emphasize what he calls "comparative institutional competence." This argument would set out to probe which branch of government had the best ability to make a decision this consequential. Congress had passed the VRA and repeatedly reauthorized it after rigorous fact-finding hearings. "The Constitution gave the Congress express authority to make the judgments about what was appropriate to enforce these constitutional guarantees," Verrilli says. "Congress has the institutional capacity to gather evidence and make policy judgments in the exercise of that authority. And the Court doesn't have that competence, therefore deference to the judgment of Congress was the right approach."

Yet as he nervously walked his room, his familiar rituals provided little comfort. All that prep had missed something. Verrilli had the nagging feeling that something unexpected awaited him.

CHAPTER SEVENTEEN

THREE YEARS AFTER that first call from Edward Blum to Butch Ellis, the Supreme Court heard oral arguments in *Shelby County v. Holder* in 2013 before a packed chamber filled with links to the nation's civil rights history.

On one side of the courtroom sat John Lewis and Ernest Montgomery. The lawyers included Rein, who clerked for one of two justices to dissent on a landmark Section 5 case before launching the career of the current chief justice by helping staff Reagan's DOJ; and Ellis, whose father helped launch the Dixiecrats movement.

The defendant was the first Black attorney general of the United States, whose sister-in-law, Vivian Malone Jones, desegregated the University of Alabama in 1963, two years before the passage of the Voting Rights Act, over the defiance of Governor George Wallace, who vowed to defend against the "oppression of the rights, privileges and sovereignty of this State."

Wallace's heated invocation of state sovereignty would have an eerie echo fifty years later. Chief Justice John Roberts used the same language while perversely insisting that things had changed in the South.

Justice Sonia Sotomayor stared down Rein and the Shelby County legal team at the very beginning of oral arguments. "Assuming I accept your premise, and there's some question about that, that some portions of the South have changed, your county pretty much hasn't," she said. "In the period we're talking about, it has many more discriminating—240 discriminatory—voting laws that were blocked by Section 5 objections. There were numerous remedied by Section 2 litigation. You may be the wrong party bringing this.

"Why," she asked, "would we vote in favor of a county whose record is the epitome of what caused the passage of this law to start with?"

Rein's careful reply turned the *Northwest Austin* case right back on the liberal justices: "When I said the South has changed," he noted, "that is the statement that is made by the eight justices in the *Northwest Austin* case." This would be the first time that the liberal justices' compromise three years earlier boomeranged back at them. It would hardly be the last.

Justice Elena Kagan took the next shot. "You're objecting to a formula, but under any formula that Congress could devise, it would capture Alabama. If Congress were to write a formula that looked to the number of successful Section 2 suits per million residents, Alabama would be the number one state on the list. If you use the number of Section 5 enforcement actions, Alabama would be number two."

Rein did not shrink away. "We are here to challenge this formula," he said, "because in and of itself it speaks to old data. It isn't probative with respect to the kinds of discrimination that Congress was focusing on and it is an inappropriate vehicle to sort out the sovereignty of individual states."

Then it was Ruth Bader Ginsburg's turn. "Mr. Rein, you keep emphasizing over and over again in your brief, registration, and you said it a couple of times this morning. Congress was well aware that registration was no longer the problem. This legislative record is replete with what they call second-generation devices. Congress said up front: we know that the registration is fine. That is no longer the problem. But the discrimination continues in other forms."

Rein had prepared for this thrust as well, and he knew how to turn what liberals saw as the primary flaw of his case into a secret strength. Here, he'd tack toward the textual originalists. The specific problem the VRA had been intended to counter—unequal registration rates—had been remedied, he argued. The extraordinary problem that required an extraordinary piece of legislation and federal oversight of states had been cured. If Congress wanted to address a different, contemporary problem, it needed different, contemporary legislation. "I think your question shows it's a very different situation," Rein said. "Congress is not continuing its efforts initiated in 1975 to allow people—"

Sotomayor cut in, trying to refocus on the moral harm the VRA aimed to cure. She appealed to the ever-shifting nature of voter suppression, the old poisons in new bottles. "What Congress said is it continues, not in terms of voter numbers, but in terms of examples of other ways to disenfranchise voters, like moving a voting booth from a convenient location for all voters to a place that historically has been known for discrimination," she said. "This Court or some may think that secondary is not important. But the form of discrimination is still discrimination if Congress has found it to be so."

"When Congress is addressing a new evil, it needs then—and assuming it can find this evil to a level justifying the extraordinary remedy . . . never before and never after invoked by the Congress, putting States into a prior restraint in the exercise of their core sovereign functions," said Rein. "I'm not questioning whether Congress did its best," he said, referring to the substantial sixteen-thousand-page record. "The question is whether what Congress found was adequate to invoke this unusual remedy."

During oral arguments, Rein told the court that Blacks had equal access to the polls in the South. "You look at the registration, you look at the voting. That problem is solved on an absolute as well as a relative basis."

"Well, Mr. Rein," interrupted Justice Kagan, "that is the question, isn't it? You said the problem has been solved. But who gets to make that judgment, really? Is it you? Is it the court? Or is it Congress?"

When Rein answered that while Congress could weigh in, the court got the final word, Kagan had a droll response. "Well, that's a big new power that you are giving us, that we have the power now to decide whether racial discrimination has been solved. I did not think that that fell within our bailiwick."

It was the rueful sarcasm of someone who knew she was about to lose. This was Rein's first-ever appearance before the court. And with the Voting Rights Act on the line, the Supreme Court's liberal lions couldn't lay a glove on him.

THE DAY DID not go as smoothly for the veteran litigator Verrilli. When the solicitor general approached the lectern, he immediately realized his unease was more than warranted. Verrilli anticipated the objections he would hear from the conservative justices and tried to take them on in his opening remarks. But he was on the defensive from the beginning, and the justices were better prepared with numbers—even though the statistics were sometimes misleading at best. It took Roberts mere moments to lower the boom. From then on, Verrilli found himself on the wrong end of a series of queries from the bench seeking to dismantle the foundations of his argument. His interrogators included a chief justice who had been working toward dismantling the VRA ever since he arrived in Washington. John Roberts was more than ready for this moment.

Verrilli opened by emphasizing the "substantial record" built by Congress during the 2006 reauthorization, while also conceding that Section 5 worked more as a deterrent than an actual enforcement tool. The chief justice promptly sandbagged the solicitor general with a well-rehearsed question of his own: "Do you know which state has the worst ratio of white voter turnout to African American voter turnout?" Verrilli had to admit that he did not.

"Massachusetts," answered the chief justice.

"Do you know what has the best, where African American turnout actually exceeds white turnout?" Roberts did not even wait for an answer, perhaps a small consolation to the government's lawyer, who did not have one anyway. "Mississippi," the chief justice thundered.

"But Congress recognized that expressly in the findings when it reauthorized the act in 2006. It said that the first-generation problems had been largely dealt with but there persisted significant . . ."

The chief justice did not want to hear about the 2006 reauthorization. He had another trick question teed up: "Which state has the greatest disparity in registration between white and African Americans?" he interrupted.

"I do not know that," Verrilli had to admit, again.

"Massachusetts. Third is Mississippi, where again the African American registration rate is higher than the white registration rate."

Roberts's cherry-picked stats didn't hold up to scrutiny. Fact-checkers struggled to find any studies that corresponded to his numbers. NPR's down-the-middle law correspondent Nina Totenberg charged that Roberts had "misconstrued" the facts. In the *New York Times*, a young data journalist named Nate Silver debunked the chief justice's "dubious" use and comprehension of statistics. William Galvin, Massachusetts's outraged secretary of state, said Roberts relied on "clearly erroneous data" and generated his numbers only by including Black noncitizens, who, of course, cannot vote. "It's deceptive and it's a slur on Black voters," charged Galvin.

When reporters asked the court to document Roberts's numbers, his spokespeople refused. At that point, it didn't really matter, anyway—the damage had been done. The government's lawyer was on his heels and wobbling. What do you do when the chief justice hits you with phony statistics in the middle of oral argument?

Verrilli, his head swimming, tried to calmly pivot to his main point: whether it was the job of Congress or the Supreme Court to decide when racial equity had been achieved. "I tried my best to transition away from those attack questions," he told me. There was no escape. The chief justice, his prey wriggling, peered down from the bench and moved in for the kill.

"General," Roberts began, "is it the government's submission that the citizens in the South are more racist than citizens in the North?"

Verrilli took a deep breath. "It is not, and I do not know the answer to that, Your Honor, but I do think it was reasonable for Congress—"

"You said it is not, and you don't know the answer to it," interrupted an understandably confused Roberts.

"It's not our submission," he clarified. "As an objective matter, I don't know the answer to that question." Verrilli tried to transition back to Congress, again, without any more luck than he had before. "What I do know is that Congress had before it evidence that there was a continuing need based on Section 5 objections, based on the purpose-based character of those objections, based on the disparate Section 2 rate, based on the persistence of polarized voting, and based on a gigantic wealth of jurisdiction-specific and anecdotal evidence."

Roberts interrupted: "A need to do what?"

"To maintain the deterrent and constraining effect of the Section 5 preclearance process in the covered jurisdictions."

"And not impose it on everyone else?" Roberts asked, convinced, sincerely or not, that Massachusetts needed preclearance as badly as a state like Mississippi. Roberts apparently didn't know or care that officials using Section 5's preclearance provisions in Mississippi had just a few years earlier helped stop officials from canceling an election that a Black candidate was about to win, with the blessing of the state courts. Massachusetts had elected the first Black senator to win his seat via the popular vote, Edward Brooke, a Republican, in 1966 and 1972. Mississippi had yet to elect a Black candidate statewide ever.

Verrilli's answer only played into the hands of a chief justice who had already given the impression—wrongly—that the statistics from noncovered states like Massachusetts told a different story, and that he knew those numbers better than the solicitor general. Nothing improved for Verrilli when Alito took his turn assailing the government's case. Alito also wanted to know why Congress didn't update the Section 5 formula during the 2006 reauthorization.

His question had been asked and answered: the formula had been addressed on multiple occasions and new "bail-in" and "bail-out" mechanisms added during previous reauthorizations provided additional flexibility to cover states where new problems emerged, or to recuse states and localities that showed improvement.

But perhaps because the beleaguered solicitor general was already on the defensive, or perhaps because Alito framed his question as a misleading gotcha—asking "Suppose Congress in 1965 had based the coverage formula on voting statistics from 1919, forty-six years earlier?," as if the 1970s updates just never happened—Verrilli kept stumbling into traps. Verrilli's response to Alito's ill-formed chronological hypothetical just set up Justice Kennedy's next question, which suggested the government had reverse-engineered a formula to cover the states it desired. When the solicitor general replied that the court had upheld the formula four different times, Kennedy swatted him away.

"Well, the Marshall Plan was very good, too. The Morrill Act. The Northwest Ordinance," said Kennedy, suggesting the VRA had become as irrelevant as the effort to rebuild Europe after the Second World War, the plans to charter land-grant colleges during the Civil War, and the governing authority over the land west of Ohio during the 1780s. "Times change."

Verrilli's head kept spinning. He kept pointing to the exhaustive congressional record that had been built during the nearly unanimous 2006 reauthorization. But every time he did, he was either told that times had changed, the law was outdated, or things were worse elsewhere. He was told that Congress had measured the wrong things—but he was then asked to explain why the problem Congress said was worse in Alabama wasn't just as bad in Tennessee. The questions came from justices who seemed to have their minds made up based on little more than a feeling or a smattering of statistics that didn't hold water.

Speaking with me nearly ten years later, Verrilli still sounds shaken over an encounter unlike any other over a career spent arguing some one hundred cases before the Supreme Court. "The facts?" Verrilli said to me, in disbelief. "The facts were irrelevant to them. We saw from the *Northwest Austin* decision that the conservative majority was broadcasting very clearly that they planned to strike down the coverage formula. The fix was in on this from the beginning."

Before this relentless judicial rope-a-dope assault could come to a merciful conclusion, Justice Scalia—with a long question that seemed much more like a comment—proposed that the purpose and goals behind the Voting Rights Act could not be trusted because it was too popular in Congress. Congress, Scalia suggested, must have passed the VRA with such large margins because politicians didn't believe they could vote against it—and therefore it would require brave, unelected judges to strike it down.

Every time the Voting Rights Act had been reauthorized in the Senate, Scalia observed, fewer people voted against it. Back when the VRA was first passed, he noted, there were double-digits against it in 1965 and 1970. Now? No one. Scalia interpreted this as groupthink for the court to remedy, not as progress, or an indication that fewer southerners with views on race that dated back to the Morrill Act served in Congress.

Scalia went as far as to call the VRA a "racial entitlement." That drive-by characterization was hardly a surprise to anyone who remembered his *Washington University Law Quarterly* article three decades earlier, suggesting the court's special mandate was to quash such race-conscious boondoggles because politicians who needed to face actual voters would never do it themselves.

"I think it is attributable, very likely attributable, to a phenomenon that is called perpetuation of racial entitlement," Scalia continued in the same vein. "Whenever a society adopts racial entitlements, it is very difficult to get out of them through the normal political processes. I don't think there is anything to be gained by any senator to vote against continuation of this act. And I am fairly confident it will be reenacted in perpetuity unless— unless a court can say it does not comport with the Constitution."

When Scalia mentioned racial entitlements, Verrilli says, much of the courtroom gasped. "That was one of the most stunning moments in my tenure as solicitor general," he says. "But take a step back and think about that for a minute. One of the great principles of the constitutional conservatives is you take the words of the Congress at face value. You don't look behind them for their motives or anything else. And then you apply them as they were enacted. Here you have justices saying that we're going to not just discount but essentially ignore an almost unanimous vote in the United States Congress in favor of reauthorization because we know what they were up to. *We know that they weren't genuinely concerned about protecting voting rights.* Good grief!"

Yet Scalia insisted that "[y]ou have to show, when you are treating different states differently, that there's a good reason for it. That's the concern that those of us who have some questions about this statute have. It's a concern that this is not the kind of a question you can leave to Congress," said Scalia. The great irony here, of course, was that the court's foremost apostle of textual originalism was completely ignoring that the text of the Reconstruction amendments leaves this job specifically to Congress. "Even the name of it is wonderful," he sneered. "*The Voting Rights Act.* Who is going to vote against that in the future?"

Scalia's question may have been rhetorical, but the answer was clear: the five conservatives on the U.S. Supreme Court.

THE LAST OPPORTUNITY to persuade the justices that things had yet to change in the South fell to Debo Adegbile. Adegbile was the only lawyer who argued *Northwest Austin* as well as *Shelby County*, and he thought carefully about how to approach his case. The conservative justices wanted to focus on the unfairness of specific states receiving different treatment from others due to sins from another time. Adegbile wanted them to understand what it was still like to live in those states right now.

Section 5 wasn't unfair to the state of Alabama, compared to the state of Tennessee. It created fairness for the people of Calera. And to remove it because Tennessee and Alabama ought to be treated equally only hurt the people of Calera. Adegbile also wanted to emphasize scholarship that showed Section 2 and Section 5 worked best *together* in the covered states, sustaining victories, especially in small southern localities where racial prejudice had proven toughest to root out and precinct changes or other chicanery could be most virulent.

"Do you think all of the noncovered states are worse in that regard than the nine covered states?" Scalia demanded, as Adegbile presented the numbers. "Every one of them is worse."

"It's a fair question . . ." he began.

"It's not just a fair one, it's the crucial question. Congress has selected these nine states. Now, is there some good reason for selecting these nine?"

It took Justice Breyer here, in his meandering manner, to underline Scalia's question. Breyer's questioning also highlighted Adegbile's concerns about the court's history in handling matters of race—a consistent pattern of wanting to fast-forward to the ending, and asking how much longer these special protections (or entitlements, in Scalia's charged phrasing) might be necessary.

Adegbile had a story to tell. He wanted to shake the court's confidence about how much progress had actually been made in the South. He had a powerful example, also from Alabama, about a state senator named Scott Beason. Beason had worn a wire for the FBI during an investigation into Capitol corruption and recorded conversations with his colleagues. In one of those recorded conversations, Beason and two other Republican members discussed economic development in a largely Black county where a casino and racetrack were among the largest employers.

"That's y'all's Indians," said one member, Representative Benjamin Lewis.

"They're aborigines, but they're not Indians," replied Beason.

Later, Beason agreed with his GOP colleagues who suggested growth at the casino could backfire by bringing in a new cohort of "illiterate" Black voters. In that scenario, he said, "there would be a big turnout by Black voters because casino owners would offer free buffets and gambling credits to attract Black customers and then bus them to the polls."

Beason chaired the powerful Senate Rules Committee in the Alabama legislature. He knew he was wearing a wire. The conversation was recorded at the Capitol. "He's caught on tape, on his own tape, on his own wire. One way to understand it is," Adegbile says, "he's not caught. This is just how he talks.

"Yes, the South has changed and made progress, but some things remain stubbornly the same," Adegbile told the court. Adegbile says today that he hoped to show the justices how Alabama lawmakers talked about Black voters even when one of them knew others were listening. "I wasn't reading something from 1960. I wasn't reading something from 1950. *2011."*

Roberts, however, appeared unimpressed. He returned to his theme: enough progress had been made over fifty years so that all states could be treated the same. "Have there been episodes, egregious episodes, of the kind you are talking about in states that are not covered?" When Adegbile replied that there had been, Roberts twisted the knife. "Well, then it doesn't seem to help you make the point that the differential between covered and noncovered continues to be justified."

"But the great weight of evidence!" Adegbile began. "This statute is in part about our march through history to keep promises that our Constitution says for too long were unmet."

Roberts, however, had already pulled back his chair. He glanced at the clock. Adegbile's time had run out. The chief justice politely moved on. None of the conservative justices had posed a question about Calera, about Ernest Montgomery's seat, about the realities on the ground. They were not interested in learning more about Alabama in 2013. The time for any march through history had come and gone.

Donald Verrilli stopped by Eric Holder's office at the Department of Justice that afternoon and told his boss that arguments had gone poorly. He warned the attorney general that the court was going after the entirety of preclearance and intended to eviscerate the VRA. Holder still couldn't believe that was possible. "*The Voting Rights Act?* Come on," Holder said. But to the solicitor general, the writing was on the wall.

"I walked out of that courtroom certain that's what was going to happen," Verrilli told me. "I was never optimistic at all."

CHAPTER EIGHTEEN

DONALD VERRILLI'S PESSIMISM was abundantly justified.

On June 25, 2013, in a 5–4 decision written by John Roberts, the Supreme Court struck down one of the most crucial parts of the Voting Rights Act as unconstitutional. The preclearance formula that Congress reenacted in 2006, Roberts held, had become outdated and did not consider "current conditions" of discrimination in the states and localities it covered. And singling out those states for disparate treatment, Roberts wrote, failed to accord each state its "equal sovereignty."

Roberts didn't end preclearance itself. He paralyzed it by striking down the formula that governed it. Then he sent it back to a gridlocked and polarized Congress to fix—an all-but-impossible task under the best conditions, harder still given new political incentives as well as the stringent constitutional standards the decision imposed.

"Congress, if it is to divide the States, must identify those jurisdictions to be singled out on a basis that makes sense in light of current conditions," Roberts wrote for the majority. "It cannot simply rely on the past." The formula, he held, was "based on 40-year-old facts having no logical relation to the present day."

He effectively brushed away the thousands of pages in the congressional record supporting the 2006 reauthorization of the VRA as irrelevant. "History," he wrote, "did not end in 1965," though he showed no inclination to grapple with it. He knocked down the idea that Section 5 deterred bad behavior in the states with the deepest history of discrimination. "Under that theory," he wrote, Section 5 "would be effectively immune from scrutiny" and all but permanent. "The argument could always be made that it was the deterrence that accounted for the good behavior."

Perhaps most significantly, the preclearance formula violated what Roberts called "equal sovereignty" principles. While Texas, Alabama, and other covered states might wait "months or years and expend funds" to enact a law, New Mexico, Tennessee, and other neighboring states "can typically put the same law into effect immediately."

Roberts coated the court's decision in faux modesty, acting as if Congress had regretfully backed it into a corner. Though overturning an act of Congress is "the gravest and most delicate duty that this Court is called on to perform," Roberts noted, almost sadly, Congress "leaves us today with no choice."

This was a classic Roberts rhetorical play: It sounded ever so reasonable. *Of course, 2013 is not 1965.* It appeared ever so respectful of Congress, adopting the voice of a patient yet disappointed parent. *Your mom and I don't want to take this away, but really, we did warn you, so what else could we possibly do?*

This feigned humility was pure misdirection. The *Shelby County* decision is a deeply radical one, dressed in modest garb. It usurps powers the Constitution specifically awards Congress. It uses an imaginary conception of "equal sovereignty" among states as its basis—an entirely fictional principle Roberts invented just four years earlier. Back then he summoned it to life with a dishonestly edited dicta in the *Northwest Austin* case, and here he granted it the status of hallowed doctrine. Roberts's opinion playacts as if it is not overturning preclearance—in dismayed parent mode, he suggests the court is merely sending the formula back to Congress to recheck its homework. At the same time, though, *Shelby County* sets a much higher constitutional standard for any legislative action on voting rights. Any headway Congress might make was almost guaranteed to fail the court's review, even if lawmakers managed to try again and successfully overcome its polarization on voting rights—something Roberts certainly knew would be all but impossible.

"No one," he wrote, "can fairly say that the record shows anything approaching the pervasive, flagrant, widespread, and rampant discrimination that faced Congress in 1965."

No one? Ernest Montgomery, Mary Young, and Bobby Lee Harris might like a word. Roberts left no indication that he had heard their names at all;

his short, twenty-four-page decision makes no mention of the discriminatory events in Calera or Alabaster. The recent chicanery in Shelby County
is dismissed with a couple sentences, and in the most insulting manner. To
say that Shelby County lacked the moral standard to escape preclearance
because DOJ kept catching its localities devising new ways to discriminate based on race, Roberts wrote, "is like saying that a driver pulled over
pursuant to a policy of stopping all redheads cannot complain about that
policy, if it turns out his license has expired." The extra level of scrutiny, he
said, would just be random. An incredulous Ruth Bader Ginsburg, in her
dissent, observed that Shelby County is "no redhead."

Why was it suddenly the new consensus on the court that discrimination must be rampant or flagrant for Congress to take it on? Roberts's explanation was as baby-simple as it was unconvincing: *things had changed
in the South*. That the past hadn't really ended in Shelby County—that the
methods had changed but the results in places like Calera were drearily the
same—didn't bother Roberts at all. The calendar had turned.

One of the largest and fastest-growing cities within Shelby County had
defied the Voting Rights Act—annexing land and redrawing districts, without the necessary preapproval. The predictable result was a diminution of
the power of Black voters. But the court disregarded all that, electing to
worry about Alabama's sovereignty and dignity instead. The South, and
indeed the nation, had elected Black officials and now a Black president.
Perhaps in the long-ago time of 1965, Roberts held, it made sense to divide
states that had histories of literacy tests and lower minority registration
from those that did not. But that distinction no longer existed, the court
ruled. "Today the Nation is no longer divided along those lines, yet the
Voting Rights Act continues to treat it as if it were."

Here yet again, Roberts was a very long way away from calling balls
and strikes. He was remaking the game from scratch, ignoring history,
and accepting fifty years of arguments hurled against the VRA from
southern states that previous courts had rejected. He was also pointedly
brushing aside thousands of pages of congressional hearings and fact-
finding showing that Black and other minority voters desperately needed
those protections. Ignoring the record and looking at little more than the

calendar, the chief justice of the U.S. Supreme Court declared a new day of racial equality across the South.

The triumph belonged as much to Lewis Powell, Michael J. Horowitz, and the conservative funders who realized the courts provided the best opportunity to move the country to the right. Powell, the genteel Virginia segregationist, imagined a judiciary that allowed wealthy elites to maintain control over American elections despite growing diversity and calls for change. Horowitz narrowed that vision to incubating conservative thinkers in law schools and the academy. Right-wing foundations and megadonors invested for the long term and patiently funded the Federalist Society, litigation projects like Blum's, and the firms that would do the lawyering and write supportive amicus briefs. FedSoc alumni and officials joined GOP administrations and ensured that fellow travelers won key appointments to the high court and the federal bench. Yet *Citizens United* and *Shelby County* delivered victories Powell could have only imagined, victories that demonstrated the power of handpicked conservative judges to overturn the will of the people and the judgment of Congress, and impose an antidemocratic agenda that advantaged conservatives at all levels of American politics.

Just as they had built the outlandish arguments in *Citizens United* from a fantastical framework in *Wisconsin Right to Life*, the Supreme Court's five-vote conservative majority had ushered in a new age of radical legislating from the bench to upend Congress's past five decades of work on voting rights, guiding the nation, and the law, toward outcomes that benefited their conservative views—and pushed the nation toward minority rule.

THE NATION'S CONFIDENCE in the Supreme Court has never been lower. Nearly two-thirds of Americans have not very much or no confidence at all in the high court, according to an April 2023 Gallup poll. But when pollsters dig deeper, they find that large majorities see the nine justices as partisan proxies, viewing the law through whatever political lens might create victory for the policy preferences of their side. That's a perfectly fair conclusion to reach, given the intense partisan polarization on the court, and the hundreds of millions of dollars both parties have spent to install justices into lifetime appointments.

But what many Americans still don't suspect is that the justices might just be *making the law up as they go along*. That the emperors have no clothes at all. That their opinions carry footnotes and the force of law but stand on air. That it is all about political power, and fancy-sounding legal doctrines lend cover. That five—and now six—of them can get away with this because they make up a majority ideological bloc, accountable to no one.

That's the real story behind John Roberts's opinion in *Shelby County*: the chief justice of the United States obliterated the most successful and important civil rights legislation this nation has ever seen, the act that made us a multiracial democracy for the first time, not just on flimsy crite-ria but on none at all. He simply made it up.

"It's made up," agreed the conservative judge and law professor Michael McConnell, a George W. Bush appointee to the U.S. Court of Appeals, on NPR. "There's no requirement in the Constitution to treat all states the same. It might be an attractive principle, but it doesn't seem to be in the Constitution."

"This is a principle of constitutional law of which I had never heard," the conservative judge and legal scholar Richard Posner famously con-curred, "for the excellent reason that . . . there is no such principle. . . . In order to overturn that, the court just made up a principle of constitutional law, this idea of the equal sovereign status of the states. That's just made up. It really made its appearance for the first time in anything like this context in the *Northwest Austin* decision."

"Yes, that's right," says Leah Litman, a law professor at the University of Michigan and a Supreme Court clerk during the 2011–12 session. "There are passing references to the idea of equal sovereignty. But if you pause and think about them for more than like a second, it's clear that [Roberts] made the doctrine into something that it just wasn't before *Shelby County*."

Litman is the national authority on equal sovereignty. In 2016, she wrote a searching and complete sixty-seven-page history of what Roberts called a "fundamental principle" and "historic tradition." Her conclusion?

Roberts manufactured it for his own purposes. It is, she writes, "an invented tradition," invented by John Roberts, now cited by John Roberts.

"As we made clear in *Northwest Austin*," Roberts wrote in the *Shelby County* decision, "the fundamental principle of equal sovereignty remains highly pertinent in assessing subsequent disparate treatment of States." You have to go back more than a century to find the other cases Roberts cites as justification—the former law clerk must have required his own clerks to scour hundreds of dusty casebooks—but those precedents simply don't match up to what Roberts is claiming here. They don't say what he wants them to say. They don't apply to this issue.

Litman makes it clear that the actual history of equal sovereignty has to do solely with the admission of new states. The principle exists only to prevent Congress from imposing admission standards that might violate other constitutional rules. And even then, it's been ignored in the breach, she notes: when Utah, for example, gained admission to the Union, it had to abolish the practice of polygamy as a condition. As Litman decorously concludes, equal sovereignty "allegedly stands from long-standing observation," but "turns out to be somewhat recent in origin." She writes that "the doctrinal basis of the equal sovereignty principle is far less compelling than these statements suggest." Run that through the law-review-to-English translator and it comes back with a cow and a poop emoji.

In her dissent, Justice Ginsburg called out this sleight of hand as "unprecedented" and wondered whether Roberts was silently overruling precedent with no discussion, by extending equal sovereignty beyond the admission of new states. This notion had been thrown out by Roberts as mere dicta in *Northwest Austin*, she wrote—an unnecessary observation within that opinion with no legal authority or binding whatsoever. Now, she charged, Roberts "ratchets up" that dicta, "attributing breadth" to the equal sovereignty principle.

Even these spot-on appeals to precedent and history, however, miss the point, which like everything having to do with the Roberts Court's record is political: Roberts wanted this real-world outcome. He'd promoted it as far as back as that December 1981 memo in which he maintained that Voting Rights Act violations "should not be made too easy to prove, since they provide a basis for the most intrusive interference imaginable by federal courts into state and local processes." If it took him forty years to get there, and if he needed time to gin up a reactionary and regressive agenda as a sonorous-sounding doctrine, so be it. It was all in a day's work in one of the signature undertakings of the conservative movement remaking the Supreme Court into a reliable ideological delivery system for the GOP policy agenda.

WHAT ROBERTS DIDN'T make up in his opinion, he simply got factually wrong.

Roberts based much of his sense that things had changed in the South on voter registration statistics that, to him, showed that Blacks and whites had achieved something close to parity—and that in some states, Blacks had even surpassed whites. His opinion even included a chart documenting how registration rates had improved in the states covered by Section 5 between 1965 and 2004.

Here the same basic objection that discredits the suddenly urgent mandate of equal sovereignty applies: garbage in, garbage out. Roberts had the statistics backward. They did not show what he said they did. In many cases, the actual numbers showed the opposite.

Roberts used the numbers from the Senate Judiciary Report—the one that Republicans who voted for the VRA reauthorization generated after the bill's passage with the purpose of generating precisely this outcome. GOP lawmakers wanted this record to furnish the basis for the litigation to undermine a bill they supposedly supported—and presto: here was the chief justice himself citing it.

But somehow—intentionally or otherwise—the committee got it all wrong.

What happened? Roberts and the Senate committee overstated white registration numbers, giving an artificial sense that Blacks and whites had achieved parity.

Roberts's chart counted Hispanics as whites—even those who were not U.S. citizens and therefore remained ineligible to vote. That basic error instantly threw all subsequent demographic comparisons off, badly.

In Georgia, for example, Roberts claimed that Black registration had risen to 64.2 percent, and white registration had fallen behind at 63.5. But without the Hispanic numbers, white registration grew to 68 percent. That's still, of course, an improvement from 1965. But it's not an example of Black registration outpacing white.

In Virginia, meanwhile, Roberts argued that the gap between whites and Blacks had narrowed to just 10 percent. Except in reality, it was more than 14 percent.

Roberts, and GOP staffers on the Senate committee, simply didn't understand how the census reported race numbers. The U.S. Census Bureau treats race and ethnicity differently. Hispanics are counted as an ethnicity, and then usually included under white. The chief justice and the committee should have instead used the data for "white non-Hispanic."

When reporters asked Roberts to explain how he could have gotten something so crucial to his argument so backward, and whether the shoddy data he relied on affected his decision, the chief justice declined to answer any questions. A spokesman replied that the court "does not comment on its opinions, which speak for themselves."

"THIS WAS CONGRESS'S decision to make," former solicitor general Verrilli insists. "Section 2 of the Fifteenth Amendment, Section 5 of the Fourteenth Amendment in the Constitution itself expressly gives to Congress the power to enforce these constitutional guarantees by appropriate legislation. And it's a rare thing in the Constitution that Congress is given express power to enforce constitutional guarantees. That was not the case about the original Bill of Rights, for example."

The formula still worked. Yet because Congress did not change it, Roberts wrote, nothing else mattered. "We are not ignoring the record," he wrote. "We are simply recognizing that it played no role in shaping the statutory formula before us today."

Litman says that's simply a nonsensical position. The court had no basis to assume that Congress had ignored the record when it decided to maintain the current formula. Indeed, the record, she points out, is among the reasons why Congress thought the formula needed to continue. She notes further that the Supreme Court had never previously struck down

a law on the basis that it was too antiquated to remain constitutional. Indeed, she says, Congress uses decades-old facts all the time when crafting
legislation—such as the Clean Air Act's reliance on vehicle emissions over
time. "The constitutional violation in *Shelby County* was about the kind
of decades-old data on which Congress had relied," she writes, "data that
evinced the states' ugly histories of racial discrimination—and the purpose
it was used for—predicting that states were likely to discriminate on the
basis of race."

The court's impatience with the past, its eagerness to declare the job
complete, the nation whole, echoed back through history for Adegbile. He
had studied *United States v. Cruikshank* and the *Civil Rights Cases* and
remembered the rulings where justices insisted that Blacks must "cease to
be the special favorites of the law" even as freed slaves still carried the scars
of the bondage.

"I think the thing that people didn't fully appreciate is that *Shelby
County* is a bad decision, not only because it misconstrues the law, and
ignores the record, and breaks with precedent, and substitutes what looks
like a political judgment for the political judgment of Congress—that we
amended the Constitution to vest with the power to enforce this right—
that the court in the Reconstruction era had not adequately protected," he
says. "Some of the reason that we needed these amendments was because
the court itself had failed to protect folks."

If you fast-forward from the Reconstruction era to the Roberts Court,
he says, the indelible throughline is a resistance to the full sweep of the
Reconstruction amendments. "It's just the continued resistance to the
commitment to make the country whole, and to be an inclusive democracy," Adegbile notes. "And it's being dressed up in sophisticated legal arguments. It's not that we're actually past anything. It's that we now are at
a point where we have the power to decide that we're going to vary from
the mission, create a situation where voters are exposed, and where we're
going to advantage the manipulations of state actors and local actors to
impose barriers."

Adegbile mourns the loss of the preclearance tool, but also the deterrent protection. "*Shelby* is important because it sends a signaling effect. It

announces a federal retreat from the minority protection principle. That's what sends the barbarians to the gate to attack voting rights. It's open season."

Holder still stammers in disbelief. "Okay, Mr. Chief Justice, you say that America has changed. OK. And what's your basis for saying that, as opposed to Congress holding hearings, thousands of pages of testimony, hundreds of exhibits that say America has changed some, but not enough? You're saying, *No, Congress, essentially you're wrong. The coverage formula is wrong.* They were in essence making a factual determination that what Congress did was inadequate, wrong, not reflective of this 'changed America.' OK. Then where were your researchers?"

Holder has spent the decade since he left the Obama administration working to end partisan gerrymandering; he's well aware that the problems extend nationwide, to Ohio and Wisconsin and Utah. "But that's not a basis to throw away a statute that was working," he says. "Especially when you see what happens once the statute is removed. In those places that were covered, the issues that Roberts calls inappropriately second-generational went right back to being first-generation, immediately. The polling places that were closed are disproportionately in places that were once covered by the act. The voter purges were disproportionately in places that were covered by the act.

"There was still a difference. As bad as Wisconsin and some of those northern states were, there was still a difference sweeping from Texas all the way to North Carolina that justified the Act's continued existence."

RUTH BADER GINSBURG is now revered as a modern-day "Great Dissenter." Her most famous dissent, and her most prescient line, came in *Shelby County*. "Throwing out preclearance when it has worked and is continuing to work to stop discriminatory changes," she wrote, "is like throwing away your umbrella in a rainstorm because you are not getting wet."

Ginsburg predicted what would happen just as soon as covered states no longer needed to endure preclearance: throw the umbrella aside, and everyone gets drenched.

Preclearance, noted Ginsburg, arose for that very reason. Congress and the courts grew weary of playing whack-a-mole with jurisdictions that would persistently replace one vile barrier with another just as soon as litigation caught up with them. Laws that banned particular barriers proved inadequate, because "[e]arly attempts to cope with this vile infection resembled battling the Hydra. Whenever one form of voting discrimination was identified and prohibited, others sprang up in its place."

Roberts, Ginsburg charged, believed that since the VRA helped put an end to the specific barriers from 1965, that preclearance could end and be celebrated as a success. "With that belief, and the argument derived from it, history repeats itself," she writes. "The same assumption—that the problem could be solved when particular methods of voting discrimination are identified and eliminated—was indulged and proved wrong repeatedly prior to the VRA's enactment."

Again and again she tried, as did Judge Tatel in the lower court decision, to push Roberts to engage with the congressional record. She wanted Roberts to see that second-generation barriers were exactly what Congress had designed preclearance to stop—precisely because it had proven too difficult to guess where future restrictions would surface.

But to Roberts, none of these examples mattered. It wasn't just that these examples didn't match the horror of the days before 1965. It was that the chief justice thought these were entirely different issues. "The dissent relies on 'second-generation barriers,' which are not impediments to the casting of ballots, but rather electoral arrangements that affect the weight of minority votes," he wrote. Here, Roberts made the same argument that he did during the 1982 reauthorization fight. He was viewing *Shelby County* through the exact lens he brought to the battle over Section 2 four decades earlier. To the chief justice, the purpose of the Voting Rights Act was to raise Black registration rates. It was to ensure access to the polls. It wasn't to guard against the effects of any more sophisticated, sub rosa schemes that white officials might then enact to prevent Black voters from gaining any actual political power along with the franchise.

And once the registration numbers had achieved parity, everything in the South appeared sunny to John Roberts. He did not see the threat of rain at all.

DAYS AFTER THE Supreme Court's ruling in *Shelby County*, Adegbile went to Selma, Alabama, for the annual re-creation of the march across the Pettus Bridge. He saw John Lewis and walked over and tapped him on the shoulder. "Look, I tried to speak truth to power," he told the congressman, who had nearly died for voting rights on that bridge. Lewis grabbed him and wrapped him in a bear hug. "You did," he said. "You did."

Eric Holder winces visibly when the case is referenced by its full name, *Shelby County v. Holder*. The former attorney general is still unable to accept the horror of having his name on a case that gutted such historic legislation. He cites two days as the worst of his tenure as attorney general: the day that he accompanied President Obama to console the parents of children slain during the Sandy Hook school massacre, and "the other one was to hear from the Supreme Court that the Voting Rights Act of 1965 was, in substantial ways, murdered."

Holder called the press into his office, but advisers counseled him not to say what was really on his mind. He wishes that he had ignored them and really sounded the alarm. "Had I been allowed to express what I was truly feeling," he told me, "I would've taken the court to task for what it did, the cavalier way in which it did it and also to predict that what happened next was going to happen."

Nevertheless, Holder was shocked by how quickly the southern states enacted new restrictions. "I have to admit, I didn't think it would be that fast. I thought you would see attacks on the right to vote over a few years. But Texas is within a couple of hours. Then you start to see these bills, these rollbacks, these new processes that we clearly would have stopped. We would have stopped.

"Nothing had changed in the South," Holder said. "The only thing that changed was the personnel on the U.S. Supreme Court."

Holder didn't tell anyone, but he made another decision that day. The attorney general traditionally argues one case before the high court. It was something Holder had dreamed of since his days as a young summer associate four decades earlier, sent to the court to file paperwork. Now the court was tainted in his eyes. He did not want to honor it, or its traditions. "Not after *Shelby County*," he told me. "I just decided no. No."

Donald Verrilli speaks quietly and sadly, an institutionalist, a man who has dedicated his career to justice. Verrilli still replays this crushing case in his head, again after again, wondering if there was anything else he could have done to guard the promise of the Voting Rights Act against its implacable ideological foes. "I wish I could tell you, David, that I have stopped doing that, but I have not. It haunts me to this day." He slows and wipes his eyes; it's clear he's fighting back tears, and unsuccessfully. A decade later, the distinguished litigator is still overcome by it all.

"I think all the time about what I might have done differently, because it was a devastating defeat and it had huge consequences. I take solace in the thought that I really don't think there's anything I could have done differently. But that only makes it marginally less powerful."

Verrilli wipes his eyes once more, politely excuses himself, and walks slowly away.

PART III

THINGS HAVEN'T CHANGED

CHAPTER NINETEEN

THE ONE ARGUMENT Roberts had in his favor in Shelby County—the narrowing gap between white and Black voter turnout over the decades since the VRA's passage—dissolved upon his decision. In March 2024, the Brennan Center released a study on growing racial turnout disparities. The results were discouraging but not shocking: The difference in voting rates between white and nonwhite voters grew steadily over a dozen years, and fastest in the states where the chief justice removed federal oversight.

Between 2010 and 2022, Brennan found the turnout gap between white voters and voters of color grew by five percentage points, to eighteen. The gap between white and Black voters leapt by eight percentage points, to sixteen. In the states and localities where preclearance had been in effect, the turnout gap doubled compared to the rest of the nation. "*Shelby County* cost hundreds of thousands of votes from voters of color in formerly covered counties in the 2022 midterm election," the researchers concluded.

Yet it didn't take more than a decade of study to confirm what happened next. The aftershocks began immediately. The consequences of *Citizens United* and *Shelby County* quickly became clear to everyone. Republican lawmakers were prepped and ready. Just as soon as the U.S. Supreme Court made clear that it would no longer stand on the side of voters in defense of meaningful and fair elections, states under GOP control leapt into action.

"The guard was taken away from the gates of the prison," Representative James Sensenbrenner says. "And they all ran out."

In remarkably short order, the nation learned that John Roberts had created a vast, inviting playground for a whole new generation of right-wing political strategists determined to suppress the votes of Black and minority Americans. *Shelby County* and *Citizens United* signaled to the Right that the U.S. Supreme Court would not stand in the way of their most extreme agendas. Indeed, the court not only enabled but unleashed them and made America's worsening antidemocratic crisis possible.

These decisions—coupled with the most extreme gerrymanders in the nation's history (themselves soon to be blessed by the Roberts Court) and a growing Federalist Society influence within the judiciary—left the Right on the verge of a victory Lewis Powell dreamed of but could scarcely imagine: a permanent antidemocratic structure that enables the few to rule the many, unchecked and nearly undefeatable.

Texas may have ditched its umbrella and gotten soaked first, but it didn't take long for dark clouds to spread over all the formerly covered states.

Within minutes of the *Shelby County* decision, then Texas attorney general Greg Abbott tweeted that the state's voter ID law, the most stringent in the nation—passed prior to *Shelby County*, but blocked by a unanimous three-judge federal panel that found it would "disenfranchise minorities and the poor"—would go into effect immediately.

Things had changed in the South? The new Texas law disproportionately affected Latinos, not only the fastest-growing population in the state but also the largest contingent among the 795,955 registered voters that an official Texas study estimated would lack the necessary documentation to cast a ballot. The new law demanded that voters present either a driver's license, a gun license, a military ID, or a U.S. passport or naturalization papers. Gun licenses made the list, but college IDs did not.

"Texas has been a laboratory for this," says former Texas congressman Beto O'Rourke, who represented El Paso. "It's devastatingly effective. On the eve of the 2018 election, Texas was either fiftieth, or near fiftieth, in voter turnout. It is 100 percent not an accident and not for love of democracy, but 100 percent by design."

When lawmakers passed the voter ID measure in 2011, as "emergency legislation," they insisted it was simply a safeguard against voter fraud. The ensuing legislative debate presented no evidence that such fraud existed.

What Texas did produce, however, was data that showed 10.8 percent of registered Hispanic voters—not noncitizens, but legally registered voters—lacked the newly required state ID. That was more than double the rate of 4.9 percent of non-Hispanic voters (including both white and Black voters) who lacked the ID. When a federal court denied preclearance, it noted that many Texas counties lacked a driver's license office or had one open only a handful of hours each month. The court also observed that many Latino and Black voters faced a two-hundred-mile round trip to obtain the ID, and that the legislature had consistently rejected amendments that might have mitigated the disproportionate effect by expanding the permissible IDs and alleviating the cost of transportation and underlying documents.

Eric Holder watched helplessly from DOJ as *Shelby County* "took away control that allowed us to keep under control to some extent that which has been for too long a part of this nation. You look at the redistricting that followed the election of 2010. That, coupled with the *Shelby County* decision—those are the things that pulled that lid off, pulled that control away and allowed it to spill out, gave air, gave oxygen to these darker forces that have always been a part of our nation."

Those dark forces then set about reshaping the nation in their image—by systematically disenfranchising anyone not like them. These states had not changed. They were now allowed to be their true selves once more. For Roberts and the conservatives on the court, the principle might have been state sovereignty. For Blum and his allies, it may have been honoring the goal of a color-blind nation that they believed to be at the heart of the civil rights movement. The legislative sessions that followed *Shelby County* showed it all to be a deep and grievous folly. State by state, Republican lawmakers became ever more brazen: this was a court-enabled opportunity to seize power. What legislators did not claim themselves, lower federal courts and state supreme courts under the influence of the Federalist Society and the right-wing dark money machine would grab for them.

The consequences would be immediate and long-lasting, and felt everywhere.

THINGS MIGHT BE bigger in Texas, but this was only the vanguard of the new voter suppression surge. States previously covered by preclearance—along with other states under one-party Republican control in the wake of the 2010 census—moved with astounding speed to pass new laws that locked in their advantages. They built a twenty-first-century labyrinth designed to keep students, young people, African Americans, Latinos, and other demographic groups potentially sympathetic to Democratic candidates from voting.

Alabama and Mississippi also activated voter ID bills that had been passed in anticipation of the court ending preclearance—still another sign the conservative justices ignored that things were not so different in the South. Alabama legislators, well aware that their law would not pass muster, never bothered submitting it for preclearance; they waited and announced implementation plans after the *Shelby County* decision arrived. It required a driver's license or another state-issued photo ID in order to cast a ballot, and it eliminated birth certificates, Social Security cards, utility bills, and other forms of previously acceptable identification. Alabama's secretary of state estimated that as many as five hundred thousand registered Alabama voters—20 percent of all voters statewide—lacked the necessary ID. That included a ninety-two-year-old great-grandmother who tried to cast a ballot on Election Day 2014 with her state-issued public housing ID only to be turned away. Voter participation overall plunged to 41 percent in this first election after *Shelby County*—the first time turnout dipped below 50 percent in Alabama since 1986.

By the following election, Alabama moved to make it even harder for Black voters. In September 2015, Alabama closed thirty-one of its sixty-seven Department of Motor Vehicles offices. The burden would be borne by Black voters, and across the state's impoverished Black Belt counties. Eight of the ten counties with the highest percentage of nonwhite voters had their DMV offices shuttered. All five of the counties where Democrats performed best in 2012 had their locations closed.

The chief justice's opinion in *Shelby County* maintained that "[i]n 1965, the States could be divided into two groups: those with a recent history of voting tests and low voter registration and turnout, and those without those characteristics. Today the Nation is no longer divided along those lines, yet the Voting Rights Act continues to treat it as if it were." The recklessness of Roberts's opinion looked more blatantly disastrous as state after state embraced policies that disproportionately harmed minority voters—and immediately saw voter turnout plummet. In Virginia, which enacted a new ID bill before the 2014 midterms, turnout dropped from nearly 45 percent in the previous two midterms to just over 36 percent.

But it wasn't just voter ID efforts that picked up steam. Voter roll purges soared nationwide between 2014 and 2016: Some four million additional names were erased from the voting rolls during those two years than between 2006 and 2008. Almost sixteen million Americans were removed from the voting lists between 2014 and 2016, and another sixteen million between 2016 and 2018, according to research by the Brennan Center for Justice. Not every removal, of course, is voter suppression: as people die or move, states need to update their lists. At the same time, the process can be political and prone to errors—and not infrequently to racial targeting: names and matching data can be similar and confused. Other times, states have focused on common Black and Latino surnames.

The Brennan Center found still more disturbing results inside these numbers: the states that had been covered by preclearance purged voters at a "significantly higher" rate than the others. Florida, which had been sued by the Department of Justice and blocked by a federal court from continuing a deeply flawed 2012 voter roll purge that mistakenly identified tens of thousands of Floridians as noncitizen voters, without preapproval, started the program up again post-*Shelby*. Ron DeSantis then won a tight 2018 gubernatorial election by fewer than 33,000 votes. Texas removed 363,000 more voters in the election cycle following *Shelby County* than it did in the cycle preceding it.

Georgia went even further: it took 1.5 million voters off the books between 2012 and 2016, twice as many as those erased between 2008 and 2012. Then in 2018, Georgia secretary of state Brian Kemp ran for governor while simultaneously looking to purge some 300,000 voters from the rolls and pausing an additional 53,000 registrations. Nearly 80 percent of those paused were Blacks and other minorities.

Georgia was also among the top three states in reducing the number of voting precincts. (Texas finished first with 750, followed by Arizona with 320 and Georgia at 214.) Between 2012 and 2018, states that had previously needed to bring these changes to the federal government could shutter precincts as they pleased. They did. The transformation was radical: the formerly precleared states closed at least 1,688 polling places, often at the very last minute and with little, if any, public notice.

The *Shelby County* decision paved the way, and Georgia's secretary of state made sure that county election officials knew that they now had free rein. In a February 2015 memo to county election boards, Kemp suggested that officials act quickly to consolidate precincts, noting—twice, and in bold—that "as a result of the *Shelby vs Holder* Supreme Court decisions," counties are "no longer required to submit polling place changes to the Department of Justice for preclearance." One-third of Georgia's counties took Kemp up on his invitation.

The *Atlanta Journal Constitution* then determined that precinct closures so dramatically increased the average distance between voters' homes and the polls that they prevented anywhere from 54,000 to 85,000 voters from casting a ballot in 2018. That decline, the paper calculated, made it 20 percent more likely that Black voters would miss the election. That fall, Kemp defeated Democratic gubernatorial candidate Stacey Abrams by fewer than 55,000 votes.

IF JOHN ROBERTS was correct and things had actually changed in the South, state lawmakers in North Carolina might not have spent the weeks preceding the court's decision meticulously researching racial data. That research supplied the demographic mandate for Republicans to launch a new voter ID bill that required very specific documentation and promulgated dozens of pages of new restrictions on early voting, out-of-precinct voting, and voter registration—as well as hundreds of new precinct closures.

In April 2013, Ray Starling, a general counsel and top adviser to North Carolina House Speaker Thom Tillis, emailed the state election board for a "breakdown, by race, of those registered voters in your database that do not have a driver's license number."

As lawmakers considered whether to end out-of-precinct voting, the *Washington Post* and others reported, they requested additional information that broke it down by race. One GOP member sent an email in March 2013 that asked "Is there no category for 'Hispanic' voter?" That followed an email from a GOP legislative staffer who wondered "Is there any way to get a breakdown of the 2008 voter turnout, by race (white and black) and type of vote (early and Election Day)?"

These lawmakers, who included David Lewis and future House Speaker Tim Moore, were launching very granular inquiries. In addition to seeking data on how Black and white voters used early voting, they wanted to know the specific racial designations of state residents who might be registered to vote and which kinds of state identification they might have. They were curious about how white and Black voters used same-day registration—and were moved by something more than idle curiosity to discover how many sixteen- and seventeen-year-olds, by race, took advantage of the opportunity to preregister in civics class prior to their eighteenth birthday.

GOP lawmakers and their staffers were keenly interested in students—and Black students in particular. Lewis forwarded a peculiar request to the University of North Carolina system. He sent officials an email "about the number of Student ID cards that are created and the % of those who are African American." The college administrator told his team that Lewis's email needed to be considered urgent. "He needs it in 2 hours or less."

Meanwhile, North Carolina's election board provided legislators with the driver's license data—and Republican data crunchers matched the driver's license database against the statewide voter file. They determined that as many as 612,955 registered voters seemed to lack a driver's license or official DMV identification card. They also discovered that a higher percentage of registered Black voters lacked a license compared to whites.

Then, after analyzing all this data, Republicans assembled a bill to require a license. It started in the state general assembly, where it passed along party lines in April 2013. The bill stalled before heading to the state senate but this was no accident. Lawmakers knew the *Shelby County* decision neared. When it arrived, the assembly's bill was suddenly replaced with one almost five times as long—a measure that even Republican lawmakers referred to as "the monster." It was a fifty-seven-page bill itemizing new voting restrictions that affected voting and registration in many myriad ways, all of which disproportionately affected Black voters.

The state senator who chaired the rules committee, Tom Apodaca, admitted to reporters that the impending Supreme Court decision stalled the original bill, and then freed lawmakers to go even further. He told reporters when the "monster" was introduced that, with the "legal headache" of preclearance removed, "now we can go with the full bill."

The "monster" boasted four dozen restrictions on ballot access. Almost none of them would have been possible prior to the Roberts decision.

"It was voter suppression on steroids because they knew that they didn't have to deal with preclearance," says Reverend William Barber II, who as president of the state NAACP led a lawsuit against the bill under Section 2 of the Voting Rights Act.

The monster from North Carolina was eventually overturned by a federal court—but three years later, after all the state and local elections that occurred during that time. This is what voting rights advocates warned about during the *Shelby County* case: the difference between stopping race-based restrictions before they start, or spending three years and multiple election cycles on expensive, time-consuming legislation trying to catch up with them. Roberts assured the nation that Section 2 would work just fine. But it didn't. Then again, Roberts had also assured the nation that these laws belonged to another time, that history had not stopped in 1965.

Lawmakers immediately proved him wrong. The racial data showed lawmakers that more than 60 percent of Black voters cast an early ballot in 2008 and 64 percent did so in 2012 (compared to just 44.5 and 49.4 percent for whites). It also revealed that Blacks disproportionately preferred to use the first seven days of early voting. So the bill eliminated that entire week.

Black voters also disproportionately used same-day registration, in part because they tended to move between counties more often, necessitating reregistration. After racial data confirmed that, the bill ended same-day registration as well. Race data also indicated that Black voters, perhaps again because they moved more often, disproportionately voted in the right county but in the wrong precinct. The bill then ended out-of-precinct voting. And following up on Lewis's urgent queries, the North Carolina GOP's research showed that Black high school students took disproportionate advantage of registering to vote early at school. Once more the legislature abolished it.

Yet the most blatant example of how little had changed in the South was this: after the *Shelby County* decision, the North Caroline legislature went back into the bill and rewrote the voter ID provisions using the race data. That's right: post–*Shelby County*, with that race data in hand, they eliminated the nondriver's-license alternatives from the bill, intentionally excluding the forms of ID Black voters were most likely to possess and retaining those that whites were more likely to use.

A three-judge federal panel ultimately struck the bill down in July 2016. The judges called it "the most restrictive voting law North Carolina has seen since the era of Jim Crow." They accused GOP lawmakers of targeting and suppressing the votes of Black North Carolinians "with almost surgical precision."

The legislators who drove these new restrictions insisted—as those who would suppress the vote have since the nation's founding—that their only motivation was to protect election integrity. If that had been the case, however, instead of requesting detailed racial breakdowns from the state election board, the white North Carolina Republicans could have asked for something else—say, the number of in-person voter fraud cases brought to a district attorney over the previous dozen years. The board of elections had that data, as well.

But of course, lawmakers didn't bother to ask for data supporting the ostensible rationale for the monster voter-suppression bill. If they had, they would have seen a report that showed some forty million votes had been cast in North Carolina between 2000 and 2012. The number of voter fraud cases? Just two.

THE *SHELBY COUNTY* decision invited Congress to try again and draft a new formula. "Congress, if it is to continue to divide the states, must identify jurisdictions to be singled out on a basis that makes sense under current conditions." Yet as Roberts well understood, the current political conditions in Congress made that impossible. The conservative justices, after all, had just handed them the very policy outcome that many had sought over the previous forty years. They were more than happy to delegate the task of eviscerating the Voting Rights Act to the Supreme Court. It posed no special threat to their future electoral prospects to confirm judges to whom they could outsource the dirty work.

Republicans who had voted for the VRA reauthorization in 2006 now applauded the decision that gutted it. "As a South Carolinian, I'm glad we will no longer be singled out and treated differently than our sister states," said Senator Lindsey Graham.

Georgia GOP representative Lynn Westmoreland, who led the anti-reauthorization forces in 2006, had suggested then that a fair alternative to the old preclearance regime would be a national system enforcing the VRA with equal intensity. Now that the Supreme Court had rejected the formula, however, Westmoreland dropped the notion, exposing the whole proposal as nothing more than a legislative diversionary tactic.

"That's right," Westmoreland says today. "At that point in time, it was like we're not going to update this at all. The court sent it back to Congress and says you can do this if you want to"—and here the former congressman laughs—"but I think everybody was so relieved that the court had ruled on it. Look, this was something that nobody even wanted to debate on the floor. People weren't just jumping up to argue against the Voting Rights Act."

Roberts had done all these VRA opponents a huge favor, by taking on the wrecking project that they were too cowardly to discuss on the House floor. With that windfall in hand, those members had no interest at all in Roberts's invitation to find a fix. Roberts had just gotten them *out* of the fix.

Sensenbrenner had been bitterly frustrated that the court ignored his committee's extensive research demonstrating the continuing need for preclearance. But with more than three decades in Congress, he was also an institutionalist to the core. So he embraced the implicit challenge in *Shelby* for Congress to try again.

Sensenbrenner and Representative John Lewis crafted a compromise that included a national preclearance trigger—not just one for the South—and updated the formula to take into account the large Black turnout for Obama in 2008 and 2012. But thanks in no small part to the recursive logic of gerrymandering and voter suppression, Congress had become far more ideologically extreme. Speaker John Boehner and Representative

Paul Ryan, says Sensenbrenner, wanted to get something done—only now the Speaker no longer controlled his caucus, which relied extensively on redistricting to hold its majority.

The new chairman of the Judiciary Committee was Bob Goodlatte from Virginia, "and he didn't like the Voting Rights Act either, again, because of his state's history," Sensenbrenner says. "Basically, I was told to go pound sand," he says, adding that Westmoreland promised primaries against Republicans who would dare back a new Voting Rights Act. "Westmoreland was particularly adept at saying that he would be able to turn the forces of evil loose to anybody that wanted to do that."

David Price, a Democratic congressman from North Carolina, watched Congress paralyze itself into inaction while GOP state lawmakers back home ran wild with the new freedom Roberts had awarded them.

"The history of this is uniquely affected by that misbegotten Supreme Court decision," Price says. "Once the court ended it, then it becomes much harder to put it back together than it was to sustain it. The utter cluelessness of that decision, by the way—clueless in the sense of having no sense of what it would mean on the ground in this state. Voter ID, the restriction of early voting, the entire list of suppression measures—that Supreme Court decision was just the green light to go ahead with this. And that was true across the country."

CHAPTER TWENTY

IT WAS THE gerrymander that everyone except John Roberts and his allies on the U.S. Supreme Court could see.

Rucho v. Common Cause arrived at the high court in 2019 with a confession: North Carolina Republicans never bothered to mask their intent to award themselves ten of the state's thirteen seats in Congress.

State Representative David Lewis, a cochair of the legislature's redistricting committee (and also an architect of the state's "monster" suppression bill), openly admitted in a legislative session that lawmakers drew the 10–3 map in this closely contested state because "I think electing Republicans is better than electing Democrats" and "I do not believe it's possible to draw a map with eleven Republicans and two Democrats." He knew this to be true, of course, because GOP strategists had tried. Indeed, the new map also came bearing a mountain of DNA evidence that revealed exactly how the gerrymander was created and functioned.

That helped convince a bipartisan lower court—in the first ever ruling by a federal court to block a congressional map as an unconstitutional gerrymander—that the new maps violated the equal protection and "one person, one vote" guarantees embedded in the Fourteenth Amendment.

There would even be a devastating smoking gun: tens of thousands of documents from the hard drive of master GOP mapmaker Thomas Hofeller that included spreadsheet after spreadsheet filled with racial and partisan data and hundreds of sample maps that showed how precisely Hofeller drew each district to secure maximum GOP advantage.

The fierce rebuke in federal court by Judge James A. Wynn Jr., which ran to nearly two hundred pages, sought to restore balance to a formerly competitive state. North Carolina's congressional races had become so one-sided that an influential report from Harvard compared the integrity of the state's electoral boundaries, unfavorably, with the uniparty balloting in Venezuela and Iran. Wynn called the congressional map an "invidious" and "discriminatory" gerrymander that "insulates Representatives from having to respond to the popular will."

Just as was the case with Judge Tatel's decisions in *Northwest Austin* and *Shelby County*, Wynn had crafted his opinion with a small yet influential target audience in Washington, D.C.: the conservative justices on the U.S. Supreme Court. In past election-map cases, this five-vote bloc had voiced its mistrust of modern statistics and social-science research methods. They would also be the arbiters of *Rucho v. Common Cause*.

If only one of them could be persuaded, Wynn reasoned, then perhaps the Supreme Court would, for the first time, establish national standards that ended the scourge of partisan gerrymanders forever. It was an outcome that any supporter of America's beleaguered formal democracy should devoutly hope for, as the most effective, durable gerrymanders in the nation's history had reshaped the battle for the U.S. House and reshaped John Adams's formulation that it should be an exact replica of the people, in miniature. The new electoral order launched with *Citizens United*, worsened by the dark money influx that fueled the crucial 2010 midterms, and magnified by *Shelby County* finishing off preclearance unleashed gerrymanders the likes of which the nation had never seen. New technology, big data, and unlimited dark money added up to the installation of one-party minority rule in state after state, a firewall impervious to electoral waves and the will of the people. This was, in many ways, the pinnacle of the GOP's fifty-year effort to rewire the rules of the game, first by taking control of the rulebook and then by installing the referees.

Voters looked back to the courts for help. Would the Roberts Court stand up for voters—or would *Rucho* be added to the cases in which the court willfully closed its eyes and locked in huge advantages for Republicans?

The basic question was the same one that framed *Northwest Austin*, *Shelby County*, and the high court's other voting rights decisions: Would it defend representative democracy, or defend the partisan interests of those who put them on the bench? The grim verdict turned out to be the same here.

IT'S IMPOSSIBLE TO grasp the shameful, shambolic state of our politics without first understanding the impact of REDMAP. The all-too-apt acronym stands for the Redistricting Majority Project, implemented during the 2010 midterm cycle, and fated to deform the prospects for genuinely competitive two-party rivalries in many key districts and states for decades ahead.

The present scorched-earth profile of partisan rivalry doesn't lack for big explanations. Some suggest that it's due to the emotional and tribal appeals of party fealty in an otherwise fragmenting digital age. Others argue for "the Big Sort"—the idea that Americans of varying ideological persuasions have voluntarily segregated themselves into blue cities and red rural areas and outer suburbs to surround themselves with like-minded thinkers. Still others point to the moment in 2015 when Donald Trump descended the escalator at Trump Tower and launched his presidential campaign. But these forces are chiefly symptoms, not the cause. Our country is bitterly divided today in no small part because conservative political strategists have gerrymandered it to be that way.

REDMAP, and the rampant gerrymandering of congressional districts and state legislative maps that followed in its wake, is the true original sin. In 2008 when majorities in Michigan, Wisconsin, Ohio, Pennsylvania, Florida, and North Carolina voted for Democratic candidates at the top of the ticket, Democrats could also earn majorities in those states' legislatures and congressional delegations. By 2012, that was no longer the case. In Pennsylvania, for example, the statewide congressional vote favored Democrats in 2008 and 2012 by roughly similar margins. The balloting in 2008 produced twelve Democrats and seven Republicans. But in 2012, a nearly mirror image margin of victory delivered seats to thirteen Republicans and just five Democrats. There is no evidence that all the Democrats in the state moved to Philadelphia and Pittsburgh to be closer to other Democrats who appreciate vegetarian Thai food. They were *sorted* but not of their own volition—they'd been strategically repatriated throughout the state's district maps via redistricting, after Republicans flipped the state legislature and seized control of the process.

I wrote an earlier book called *Ratf**ked: Why Your Vote Doesn't Count* about the REDMAP strategy. But the problem only deepened as citizens across gerrymandered states used the few remaining tools available to them to battle back, only to come up against courts and conservative judges who had been placed in these very positions because of their commitment to GOP partisan politics. *Citizens United* helped fund the 2010 gerrymanders. The ensuing maps locked in Republican control. Republicans then moved brazenly to create enduring advantages for themselves through new voter ID rules and other suppression rules, which the Supreme Court enabled in *Shelby County*.

This transformation tracks the fallout from three elections, starting in 2008. With Barack Obama's election, it seemed that a new American majority was beginning to take shape, even producing a Democratic supermajority in the U.S. Senate. Republicans, searching for a path back to power, hit upon a bold countervailing strategy: a sweep of key swing-state legislatures in 2010, they reckoned, could be quietly more consequential on the eve of the decennial redistricting that follows the census. In the *Wall Street Journal* that March, just weeks after the *Citizens United* decision, no less an eminence than Karl Rove outlined the REDMAP strategy, which would be led by former RNC chairman Ed Gillespie and Chris Jankowski, a veteran GOP strategist able to devise such an audacious play because he focused largely on elections that build state power. It would be funded with $30 million kicked in by Fortune 500 megaplayers like Walmart, Reynolds American, Pfizer, AT&T, and Citigroup, together with mainline GOP stalwarts including the U.S. Chamber of Commerce—now a fully engaged power broker decades after the Powell Memo—and Blue Cross Blue Shield. "There are 18 state legislative chambers that have four or fewer seats separating the two parties that are important for redistricting," Rove wrote. "Seven of these are controlled by Republicans and the other 11 are controlled by Democrats, including the lower houses in Ohio, Wisconsin, Indiana and Pennsylvania." They swept the chambers. All fell red.

The consequences were swift. As Rove noted, "Winning these seats would give (Republicans) control of drawing district lines for nearly 190 congressional seats." The actual number neared 200. It only requires 218 for a majority in the U.S. House.

GOP majorities in these critical states were thus empowered to redraw congressional district maps to pack as many Black and Democratic voters into as few districts as possible, creating a wholesale political resegregation along both sides of the Mason-Dixon line. We think of the 2010 election as the Tea Party's ascendancy, but its far more momentous and lasting impact was to unleash the partisan and racial gerrymanders that played a vital role in creating the Trump electorate.

Then in 2012, the nation reelected Obama and handed Democratic congressional candidates 1.4 million more votes than their Republican rivals. But the numbers showed that, in down-ballot races, this truly was a rigged election. Courtesy of the newly gerrymandered playing field that the census and the state legislatures had created, GOP strategists had successfully built a red firewall allowing them to retain a thirty-three-seat majority in the U.S. House, along with oversize and unrepresentative majorities in those formerly purple state legislatures. REDMAP and *Shelby County* acted as accelerants on each other, creating optimal conditions for rampant polarization and restrictive voting rules written to limit the power of minority and Democratic voters.

Those gerrymanders have proved rock-solid over the past decade-plus of general political upheaval. By 2020, more than fifty million Americans—nearly one in five of us—lived in a state in which one or both chambers of the legislature are controlled by Republicans, even though they won fewer votes. Democrats win more votes. Republicans hold power.

Redistricting created vast swaths of GOP minority rule. The ingenuity of the high-tech gerrymanders launched after the 2010 cycle had broken down battlegrounds like Wisconsin and North Carolina into districts utterly unrepresentative of their constituencies. Those noncompetitive districts moved all the action to GOP primaries, which created all manner of perverse incentives for alt-right ideologues, white nationalists, and conspiracy theorists to move into maximum influence—and at times, elective office. The party was hijacked because its leaders chose, consciously and at every turn, to place barriers before voters they believe do not support them, rather than persuade those citizens to join their side.

"We had a path to convince, say, Latino and Black citizens that conservatism would work for them," admits Bob Inglis, a former Republican congressman from South Carolina. "The path taken has been this raw grab for power. It really becomes an apartheid system."

Emboldened by the most precise partisan and racial gerrymanders this nation has ever seen, Republican vote suppressors moved on to new quarry. They enacted punishing voter ID laws, oversaw mass purges of voting rolls that disenfranchised minority and other Democratic-leaning voting blocs, closed precincts and polling stations, approved draconian new restrictions on registration, and even instituted modern-day poll taxes.

Entrenched, untouchable legislators at the state and federal levels adopted these antidemocratic measures in the hope that a parallel new cohort of activist conservative judges would move in unison with them to further cement their power. "First we're going to gerrymander. Then we're going to suppress the votes in inner cities. Then we're going to discredit mail-in voting," says William Kristol, with the rueful sadness of a veteran conservative kingmaker who could no longer stomach how his party chose to win and exercise power.

Democrats didn't see REDMAP coming. To be sure, they had other demands on their time and attention beyond monitoring state legislative races in Round Rock, Texas. Not long after Obama's 2012 reelection, Eric Holder told me, he and the president spent a confused evening at the White House, looking over the results and trying to understand why Republicans still held the House and so much power in state capitals. "We thought we had done well in terms of the raw vote, but it wasn't at all reflected in the number of representatives we had at both the state and federal level," Holder said. "REDMAP had been a small part of my consciousness before the 2012 election. . . . Then we saw the election results."

IT TURNED OUT that the president and his attorney general were not the only ones frustrated and bewildered by the 2012 results; the GOP, after jury-rigging the outcomes in so many state and congressional races, was flummoxed by the party's failure to win the presidency. Having just lost the popular vote for the presidency for the fifth time in the previous six elections, dating all the way back to Bill Clinton's first victory in 1992, Republicans surveyed more than twenty-six hundred party officials, experts, voters, and more for a report officially dubbed the *Growth and Opportunity Project* but known among party operatives as the Autopsy.

The diagnosis was blunt: The party had become synonymous with "stuffy old men." It was "talking to itself." Republicans had lost their way with young voters who were "increasingly rolling their eyes at what the Party represents." They didn't know how to talk to minorities, who now "think that Republicans do not like them or want them in the country." Onetime GOP supporters now used words like *scary* and *out of touch*. The key recommendation to start reversing these glum trends was for the party to embrace a multiracial nation, else the GOP's "appeal will continue to shrink to its core constituencies only."

The Autopsy was dead on arrival; indeed, it had already been smothered by the same people who commissioned the report. Republicans had chosen their strategy two years earlier, even if they didn't fully realize it: they'd chosen REDMAP. "The redistricting changed the dynamic on the ground," Michael Steele, the former chairman of the Republican National Committee (RNC), told me. "The type of person who would then get out and run for those seats was a very different breed of person. When they amassed in the Congress, they weren't Tea Party anymore. They were now the Freedom Caucus."

The transformation would have been all too plain had party leaders only looked a bit more closely. As Obama and Holder pondered 2012's mysterious outcomes, and the Republican establishment tried to retool its sales pitch to recapture the White House, the proprietor of a small-town sandwich shop called Aunt D's prepared to take a seat in Congress. Mark Meadows would represent the conservative mountain towns of western North Carolina, and exactly half of Asheville, the region's largest city, in the newly redrawn Eleventh Congressional District.

Republicans had a free hand to draw the state's maps after REDMAP helped the party claim both chambers of the legislature. They wasted no time before making use of the opportunity. Thomas Hofeller, the GOP's

Zelig-like redistricting mastermind, managed always to be on hand when Republicans sought to bend the spirit of the Voting Rights Act's provisions on majority-minority districts and pack as many Black voters as possible into the fewest possible districts. When North Carolina's legislature got down to drawing new district maps, Hofeller was tasked with redrawing ten of the state's thirteen districts for Republican control. It worked. North Carolina would send ten Republicans and three Democrats to Congress for almost the entire decade ahead, scoring more than 70 percent of the seats even in years when Democrats won more votes. One Hofeller masterstroke made it possible. Artists, independent spirits, and environmentalists have traditionally flocked to the hippie enclave of Asheville, surrounded by conservative hill towns, for the majestic Blue Ridge Mountains, thriving local brewpubs, vegan cafés, and independent bookstores.

A decade ago, North Carolina's Eleventh District, with Asheville at its heart, was among the nation's most competitive congressional districts, seesawing with shifting political winds. It favored Republicans during the two elections that followed the September 11 attacks, then veered toward Democrats beginning in 2006 as the Iraq war stagnated and stock market tumbled.

Hofeller cracked Asheville in half and scattered the region's biggest city and most significant concentration of liberals harmlessly across two districts they didn't have any chance to win.

Then incumbent Heath Shuler, perhaps the most conservative Democrat in Congress, took one look at Hofeller's handiwork and promptly launched a far more stable career as an energy lobbyist. Meadows, meanwhile, read the temperature of the district, recognized the only election he needed to win was the GOP primary, and outbirthered the entire field. When his closest competitor provided a long-winded answer at a Tea Party rally to a question about whether he would pursue an investigation into Obama's citizenship, Meadows provided a direct answer: "Yes." Then he smirked as the crowd laughed its approval. "You know what? We'll send him back home to Kenya or wherever it is."

In that moment, Donald Trump's future chief of staff was on his path to real political power.

NC-11 wasn't the only district that had a new face in the post–2012

Congress, and precious few members of this insurgent class on the right resembled the changing nation. If the demographic change driving American politics at the national level was an electorate that was becoming younger, more urban, and multiracial, Republicans decided to abolish it and create an electorate of their own. The Republicans drew themselves a fantasy nation where their base gained power even as it shrunk—a land where the Right's America became whiter and more conservative even as the exact opposite dynamic had taken hold in the rest of the country.

Donald Trump didn't do this. Trump just swept up the pieces.

Today, there's real anger, and real regret, in Steele's voice as he outlines the shift in strategy that happened in part on his RNC watch. "We gave up on our ideas. We gave up on our values. All we had left was just to game the system against the voter. . . . When you do that, you get voter ID laws, you get voter restrictions on the number of days when people can vote early, where they can vote, and requirements that are damn near close to what Jim Crow laws were in the South. There's very little difference between having a bowl of jelly beans on a counter that you ask the voter to count before they get allowed to vote and having them come in for an ID at some god-awful hour at a location in Alabama that's thirty miles from their home."

THOMAS HOFELLER, MEANWHILE, not only perfected the maps, but helped sell the strategy.

Hofeller's handiwork is perhaps best seen in North Carolina, viewed through the prism of the line that divides Asheville—and one other surreal district boundary containing perhaps the ugliest gerrymander in North Carolina or in the entire nation. It's the congressional-district line that cuts in half the nation's largest historically Black college, North Carolina A&T State University, in Greensboro. The district line divided this majority-minority campus—and the city—so precisely that it all but guarantees it will be represented in Congress by two Republicans for years to come.

North Carolina Republicans have long denied that this line, between the state's Sixth and Thirteenth Congressional Districts, was intentionally drawn to dilute Black voting power, which would be a violation of the constitutional prohibition against racial gerrymandering.

But when I obtained eighteen hard drives and tens of thousands of documents from Hofeller's private files, becoming the first journalist to obtain this treasure trove that tells the story of the last decade, I found proof that Hofeller knew exactly what he was doing. His hard drives included giant databases he'd created that detailed the racial makeup, voting patterns, and residence halls of more than a thousand North Carolina A&T students. He also collected similar data that tracked the race, voting patterns, and addresses of tens of thousands of other North Carolina college students. Some spreadsheets have more than fifty different fields with precise racial, gender, and geographic details on thousands of college voters.

A spreadsheet named "NC College Voters for ZIP ID" contains voter data for more than 23,100 North Carolina university students, including thousands in Greensboro. The detail for the North Carolina A&T students is precise: students are sorted by residence hall. That means that Hofeller knew which A&T students lived in Aggie Village, on the north side of campus, and which resided in Morrow or Vanstory Halls, on the south side—along with a detailed racial breakdown and information about their voting status. As Hofeller sought to create two reliably Republican congressional districts, his computer contained information on the precise voting tendencies of one of the largest concentrations of Black voters in the area.

And if Hofeller cross-referenced that spreadsheet against another included on his hard drive, this one saved as "80 pct College Voters on Non-Match List"—which identified 5,429 North Carolina college students who appeared to lack the necessary ID required to cast a ballot at the time he drew the congressional maps—he could have crafted this line along Laurel Street, with even greater specificity about who would and would not be likely to vote.

He appears to have gathered much of this information after the state NAACP challenged North Carolina's stringent voter ID law, part of the monster package that the legislature passed once the Roberts Court ruled in *Shelby County*. Hofeller worked with the Republican legal team that was defending the law. (The team included Thomas Farr, whom Donald Trump would later nominate for an appointment to the federal bench.) In February 2014, Hofeller wrote to a Republican attorney about an effort to match North Carolina's master voter-registration file against the driver's-license database to see which voters might be affected by the ID law. The team also looked to compare that information against that of the closest Department of Motor Vehicles offices.

That's critical real-time evidence showing the many ways how *Shelby County* and the aggressive redistricting campaigns in Republican state legislatures worked hand in glove to cement and secure minority rule.

THE U.S. SUPREME Court heard two cases in late 2017 that offered an opportunity to establish real limits on partisan gerrymandering, and to do so in nonpartisan fashion. *Gill v. Whitford* challenged the constitutionality of Wisconsin's state assembly map, drawn so punishingly that even when Democrats won nearly 55 percent of the statewide vote, they barely won a third of the seats. *Benisek v. Lamone* took on the most egregious Democratic gerrymander of the 2010 cycle, a Maryland congressional seat that lawmakers turned inside out to give themselves a 7–1 edge. Both maps insulted voters and democracy itself and rendered a decade's worth of elections essentially immaterial.

Yet as lawyers in both challenges worked to convince Justice Kennedy that an array of new metrics provided courts the tools they needed to find a map guilty of excessive partisanship, someone else was actively pushing Kennedy the other direction: John Roberts.

During oral arguments, Roberts suggested that these new approaches—all of them simple, all of which pointed overwhelmingly in one direction—were so confusing as to be "sociological gobbledygook." The Harvard-educated chief justice pretended it was all just beyond his understanding. "It may simply be my educational background," he said, predicting that if the court injected itself into the process, citizens would just believe politics guided the decision.

"Why did the Democrats win?" Roberts imagined an "intelligent man on the street" asking. "The answer is going to be because EG was greater than 7 percent, where EG is the sigma of party X wasted votes minus the sigma of party Y wasted votes over the sigma of party X votes plus party Y votes." That man on the street, Roberts concluded, "is going to say that's a bunch of baloney."

Supreme Court insiders, multiple members of the congressional leadership, and another member of Congress who regularly saw Kennedy and other justices socially told me that Roberts had played his usual savvy long game. Roberts did not want the federal courts giving a thumbs-up or thumbs-down to every congressional map—but he also knew that Kennedy sought a solution. He knew as well that Kennedy was nearing retirement. Roberts simply needed to prevent Kennedy from siding with the liberal wing one more time, then await a more conservative justice the following year. The chief justice's focus on the supposed recondite calculations behind the gerrymander findings appeared to be simply to confuse an eighty-one-year-old justice into thinking that ninth-grade math was as impossible to solve as the Van der Waerden conjecture. (Which provides an estimate of how many polynomials have interchangeable root numbers, of course.)

Roberts carried the day. In a result not unlike *Northwest Austin*, the chief justice worked out what, at a glance, looked to be a political compromise. The Wisconsin case would be punted back to the lower courts on technical grounds. The Maryland case would be dismissed for being filed too late. The larger questions about justiciability would wait for another day. The liberal wing lacked the votes to rein in partisan gerrymanders, but the issue remained open to renewed scrutiny from the high court, and the federal courts could continue hearing future claims. Kennedy, however, retired sooner than the liberals imagined, announcing that he would step down just days after the court issued its opinion. For the chief justice, the sidestep in the state gerrymander cases reprised his classic feint: as anyone who watched him during *Wisconsin Right to Life* or *Northwest Austin* remembered, Roberts happily took his time on big questions of voting rights and democracy. The patient chief justice knew he would always have the votes next time to get his way.

A MORE CONSERVATIVE replacement for Kennedy arrived the next year in the form of Neil Gorsuch, along with the next opportunity for Roberts to finally earn his desired outcome in *Rucho v. Common Cause*.

Judge Wynn, writing for the lower federal court, had tailored his opinion to win the assent of Roberts, just as Tatel had in the *Northwest Austin* and *Shelby County* cases. But his attempt to demystify statistics and the math of gerrymandering, in order to assure the chief justice that the case's underlying social science was both valid and tested, would fall on deaf ears. Wynn experienced the same frustrating outcome as Tatel when he tried to craft an opinion that would confront Roberts with the reality of the full congressional record ahead of the 2006 VRA reauthorization.

"There is no constitutional basis for dismissing" a partisan gerrymandering claim, Wynn wrote, "simply because they rely on new, sophisticated empirical methods." Wynn then offered a clear-eyed explanation of three new metrics that can reveal gerrymandering, and an easy-to-understand discussion of what the numbers showed about North Carolina maps. In the end, Wynn explained, it's not that any individual metric suggests that these maps are unfair or statistical outliers—it's the collective weight of evidence when *all* of them do. This was a point especially easy for judges to understand, since it referenced their own interpretation of the cumulative weight of evidence during every trial they supervised.

Or it might have been. Instead, Roberts's opinion for a 5–4 majority in *Rucho* was a tour de force of intellectual dishonesty. The Supreme Court's election jurisprudence took another hard right turn in favor of pure power and partisanship. The *Rucho* opinion misrepresented the constitutional basis of the plaintiff's claims, pretending—over several pages—that the case was about proportional representation when the plaintiffs specifically dismissed that as an argument. It ignored the findings of the lower courts. It redefined Supreme Court precedent as it pleased. It feigned ignorance of the difference between a gerrymander drawn based on available technology in 1981 compared to the sophisticated computer power of 2016. It pretended that voters can simply fix gerrymandering by tossing their officials out of office—a pseudo-remedy that completely failed to take into account how gerrymandering actually works. Just at the moment in which federal courts nationwide, and judges appointed by presidents of both parties, agreed that they did have the clear and manageable tools needed to strike down egregious gerrymanders, Roberts wiped that possibility away and closed the federal courts to future claims.

"Federal judges have no license to reallocate political power between the two major political parties," Roberts wrote, "with no plausible grant of authority in the Constitution, and no legal standards to limit and direct their decisions." Which is to say: once politicians of his party had snatched that political power and locked themselves in office, the Supreme Court justices appointed by that party would do nothing to stop an assault on the basic tenets of representative democracy.

Justice Kagan read her withering dissent from the bench. "For the first time ever, this court refuses to remedy a constitutional violation because it thinks the task beyond judicial capabilities," she wrote. "The partisan gerrymanders in these cases deprived citizens of the most fundamental of their constitutional rights: the rights to participate equally in the political process, to join with others to advance political beliefs, and to choose their political representatives. In so doing, the partisan gerrymanders here debased and dishonored our democracy, turning upside-down the core American idea that all governmental power derives from the people."

As was the case with *Shelby*, the real-world consequences of Roberts's *Rucho* opinion were swift, devastating, and entirely predictable. Freed from any restraint and given a green light to gerrymander at will, lawmakers from both parties hit the gas. Hard. From Texas to New York, Florida to Utah, New Mexico to Tennessee, and Oklahoma to Utah, lawmakers cracked and packed districts with giddy enthusiasm. They were keenly aware that in a nation this divided, control of the U.S. House could be decided through redistricting, well before voters cast a single ballot. Without any national standards of scrutiny in place, conservative state courts in Florida and North Carolina rubber-stamped gerrymanders designed to keep Republicans in office. Meanwhile, liberal state courts in New York and Maryland followed the law and basic fairness and rejected extreme Democratic gerrymanders, also helping Republicans. When one brave GOP justice on Ohio's state supreme court stood up for the state constitution and rejected GOP gerrymanders time and again, the legislature and governor lawlessly ignored the court's decision.

In John Roberts's America, it's heads Republicans win, tails Democrats lose—and anyone who thinks rules, fairness, or math matter is nothing but a sucker.

LUXURY CABANAS ATOP Austin's JW Marriott kept state legislators cool poolside as August-in-Texas temperatures soared above 103 degrees during each day of the American Legislative Exchange Council's (ALEC) 2019 annual meeting. The gathered Republican officials could enjoy a $14 rooftop Peppered Paloma cocktail with Patrón silver, housemade grapefruit poblano soda, and Chilean salt, all while gazing over Lady Bird Lake and the nearby state Capitol, or catching a ball game on the cabana's fifty-five-inch private TV.

Downstairs, meanwhile, weeks after John Roberts extended the life of GOP gerrymanders another decade in *Rucho*, five of the GOP's most seasoned redistricting minds and überlawyers would teach legislators the finer points of tilting maps and drawing districts that would allow them to retain the spoils of minority rule into perpetuity.

I obtained an exclusive audio recording of the closed-door panel called "How to Survive Redistricting," moderated by influential Republican lawyer Cleta Mitchell with four expert guests—Hans von Spakovsky of the Heritage Foundation, North Carolina election lawyer Thomas Farr, former Georgia representative Lynn Westmoreland, and Texas state representative Phil King.

Leonard Leo wasn't in the room, but his money certainly was. Mitchell is the chairwoman of the Public Interest Legal Foundation, where Von Spakovsky is also a director. PILF has been funded by the Leo-tied 85 Fund. Its chief financial officer is Neil Corkery. Von Spakovsky and Jason Snead, who now runs the Honest Elections Project, another group with deep ties to Leo and his network, developed a voter fraud database for the Heritage Foundation. (It's perhaps most notable for managing to identify far fewer than two thousand alleged incidents since the early 1980s, the tiniest percentage of the billions of votes cast over that time.)

During this session, the legislators were advised by Westmoreland to treat redistricting as "political adult blood sport," trash potential evidence before it can be discovered through litigation, avoid the word *gerrymander*, and make deals with Black and Latino legislators that guarantee them easy reelections by packing as many minority voters as possible into their districts, thereby making the rest of the map whiter and more conservative.

"You are going to be sued. Let's start with that," Mitchell told a packed room at the ALEC gathering, attended by more than fourteen hundred people, including Trump administration officials and top conservative lawmakers, thinkers, donors, and activists. Mitchell—who a year later would become infamous as one of the leading proponents of the "Big Lie" that the 2020 election had been stolen from Donald Trump—made light of ALEC's reputation as a conveyor belt for cookie-cutter conservative legislation enacted by state after state. "Mindless state legislators, we're just pouring in information and we're indoctrinating you, pouring into your empty skulls!" she said, sarcastically. "We're going to teach you how to gerrymander."

And then she did. "Let us begin with the fact that, probably, your notes from this conference, and this workshop, will be part of a discovery demand," Mitchell said on the recording, dropping the sarcasm. "My advice to you is: if you don't want it turned over in discovery, you probably ought to get rid of it before you go home."

As Farr and Westmoreland taught lawmakers to conceal the true intent of their maps and appear to play by the rules, Von Spakovsky envisioned a longer game to change the rules of redistricting entirely. Von Spakovsky, a member of the Trump-Kris Kobach "election fraud" commission, urged GOP lawmakers to use citizenship data to redistrict state legislatures rather than count the total populations of districts, the latter being the constitutional standard for U.S. House districts and the longtime norm for states, as well.

Now the Roberts Court and the network that put them there had infiltrated everything from the Supreme Court to state legislatures, working to install minority rule and knock over anything—even the basic precept of "one person, one vote" that stood in its way.

CHAPTER TWENTY-ONE

THE BEST WAY to understand the influence of Leonard Leo is to listen to what his closest allies say about him—especially when they speak candidly before movement friends, secure in the supposition that no one else is listening.

Rebekah Mercer, the billionaire heiress widely viewed as the most powerful woman in Republican politics, delivered one such encomium when she introduced Leo as a speaker at a 2020 gathering of the secretive and influential Council for National Policy—where wealthy donors and industrialists, movement leaders, and media moguls plot the direction of the Right behind closed doors. In audio obtained by the *Washington Post*, she underlined Leo's role in assembling the list of preapproved originalist judges that Donald Trump agreed to elevate to the Supreme Court.

"Leonard Leo has been doing this for years. He is one of us," she said. "He understands that elections may come and go, but judges with lifetime appointments are going to be here for a long time." Mercer called the right-wing makeover of the high court Trump's most lasting legacy, "but he's doing it based on a lot of the work by Leonard Leo."

Mercer was mostly echoing the growing consensus on the right: Leonard Leo was no deferential institutionalist, in the mold of many past legal intellectuals; he was a revolutionary world-builder. "No one," wrote the conservative legal activist Ed Whelan, in 2016, "has been more dedicated to the enterprise of building a supreme court that will overturn *Roe v. Wade* than the Federalist Society's Leonard Leo."

Clarence Thomas's wife, Ginni—a longtime Leo crony and a far-right activist who, emails and other records show, pressured state lawmakers to overturn Joe Biden's victory and had involvement with John Eastman and others strategizing how to appoint alternate electors—kicked Mercer's panegyric up a notch when she introduced Leo at an awards ceremony she created for a group called United in Purpose. Before this crowd of true-believing right-wing activists, she boasted that Leo "is the reason there is a conservative legal movement across the country that has lawyers and judges who find their way to sessions where they learn things and where they get elevated." Leo, she said, "has single-handedly changed the face of the judiciary." She also admiringly noted that Leo wears many hats in the game of brokering power in Washington.

"He doesn't really tell all that he does," she concluded, in a nod-and-wink acknowledgment of Leo's devotion to behind-the-scenes networking. "But I know enough to know the man is a force of nature."

Justice Thomas has seconded his wife's grateful appreciation of the great man of power. In conversation with Leo at a 2018 Federalist Society meeting, the longest-serving Supreme Court justice laughed as he praised Leo as "the third most powerful person in the world."

"God help us," Leo replied, straightening his tie. "God help us."

That's the sort of faux-humble raillery that powerful men can indulge as they hold forth before the revolution's foot soldiers. But when they assume their more solemn role as strategists and ideological prophets, the false modesty melts away. Here, for example, is Leo addressing a room full of wealthy donors and movement leaders at the same Council for National Policy retreat, in a secret audio obtained by the *Washington Post*: "We stand at the threshold of an exciting moment in our republic, the revival of our structural constitution by the U.S. Supreme Court."

"I don't think this has really happened since probably before the New Deal," Leo continued, "which means no one in this room has probably experienced the kind of transformation that I think we are beginning to see."

The rapt audience at the CNP confab concurred and delivered their own grateful appraisals of Leo's handiwork. During the Q-and-A session following Leo's talk, one man told him that "I don't know of any time in history when a person's had as much trust and responsibility for such a third branch of government as you have at this time. . . . I was in a dinner with him"—and here he referred to President Trump—"and you, and I saw the way he deferred to your counsel. We're delighted that he does."

———

GINNI THOMAS IS right: Leonard Leo does wear many hats. Leo spent decades as a vice president at the Federalist Society, bouncing between the high-powered constitutional deliberations of the so-called conservative debate club and the messaging demands of conservative movement politics whenever there was a Supreme Court nomination to help manage.

As he refined his leadership skills in both arenas, Leo helped build the ultimate conservative credentialing and vetting machine. He transformed the Federalist Society from another right-wing conclave in the legal academy into perhaps the most powerful engine of the conservative revolution in the real world. If *Citizens United* drowned American politics in right-wing dark money, and *Shelby County* and extreme gerrymanders cemented GOP control of elections, Leo's operation provided the all-important third leg: the judges who would lock it all in place, while also driving extreme agendas on guns, voting, reproductive rights, and the regulatory state, victory after victory that could not have been won through the political process.

By the time Trump ascended to the presidency, the Federalist Society was the conservative movement's premier manufacturer of ideological discipline and professional prestige—roughly what Yale's Skull and Bones Society had been to an earlier cohort of conservative leaders bred in the bosom of the WASP aristocracy. But where that Ivied bastion of secretive privilege was clubby and selective, what Leo built with the Federalist Society as its engine was a model of how to wield power on the right via the fabled canons of the American meritocracy. It may have started as a simple pipeline to make sure conservative administrations selected conservative judges, but it has metastasized into something far more insidious and dangerous—in its complexity, its funding, its reach, and its goals.

Post–*Citizens United*, Leo used the Federalist Society as the intellectual motor that powered an interlocking set of lavishly funded front groups that gave him and the organization more power over the judiciary and our democracy than anyone could have imagined. Those judges, in turn, have all but guaranteed that the gerrymanders they craft and the voter ID bills they pass will remain intact.

Gene Meyer, Steve Calabresi, and other leaders worked hard to present or preserve the Federalist Society as an intellectual home for conservative-leaning scholarship and debate. They insisted that the Society took no position on issues or cases and emphasized the diversity of thought across the conservative and libertarian spectrum. From their perspective inside the legal academy, that might even be true. (Although in November 2022, co-founder Calabresi responded to an article in the *Yale Daily News* that suggested ties between Federalist Society donors and anti–affirmative action litigation. Calabresi declared his support for affirmative action in admissions and campus hiring. Days later, the Board of Directors clipped his wings. Calabresi told Nina Totenberg that the Federalist Society board voted that he ask any journalist he spoke with not to identify him either as a cofounder of the organization or cochair of the Board of Directors.)

Yet the organization's role vetting judges, and Leo's position as Federalist Society executive and also an outside, Oz-like puppet master, made it look like something different: that if members aligned themselves as reliable thinkers on specific doctrines and approaches, the right doors could open. By the early aughts, the Federalist Society had blossomed from campus debate club into exactly what Michael J. Horowitz, Ed Meese, and the Society's right-wing institutional funders hoped it would: the intellectual gateway and proving ground through which any ambitious conservative lawyer or judge proceeded to have any hope of advancement within GOP circles. "The people I met at student conferences a decade ago are now sitting federal judges," Josh Blackman, a law professor at South Texas College and regular Federalist Society speaker, told *Politico*. "The people you meet here and the networks you build up over years—they're very, very important."

BUT THAT GATEKEEPING function entails a great deal of additional movement discipline. To begin with, Leo and his allies at the Federalist Society leveraged their influence to wield de facto veto power over GOP judiciary selections. During the Reagan and Bush administrations, FedSoc alums in prominent positions in the White House and DOJ worked to select reliable judges from the limited pool of conservatives. They crossed their fingers that they would remain conservatives once safely ensconced on the bench.

Now the operation was something entirely more powerful. FedSoc alums were no longer hopeful ideologues. They ran the show, start to finish. Gatherings such as the CNP confab, the Federalist Society's annual soirees in Washington, D.C., or private parties held at Leo's lavish home in Maine are all testament to a vision that took Lewis Powell's memo and operationalized it with hundreds of millions of dollars. Leo—the intern who heard Hatch's vow that Democrats would never mistreat another GOP judicial nominee—built the complicated but astonishingly well-oiled billion-dollar machine that did much more than solidify right-wing control of the Supreme Court for generations. It made him the ultimate power broker, the puppet master of a nation changed by *Citizens United, Shelby County*, and *Rucho*, and now by a judiciary beholden to no law but its own.

Yes, Leo advised and executed the plans to place Roberts, Thomas, and Alito on the Supreme Court, and then developed the list that Trump used to select Kavanaugh, Gorsuch, and Barrett. But he also knew that even that level of control was insufficient for his extreme, antidemocratic crusade on voting, elections, reproductive rights, guns, and the regulatory state. To get all the wheels of his judiciary-capture contraption spinning in the same direction, he used his perch from the Federalist Society—and the dark money madness unleashed by *Citizens United*—to create the network that funded the campaigns that placed these justices on the court— and then he ensured that, once they were seated, they would be given the right sort of cases, courtroom arguments, and sympathetic briefs to review. Leo is more responsible than anyone for the current look of the Supreme Court, but he has also stacked and packed the judiciary at all levels, using Federalist Society allies and intel. Drew Tipton, the district court judge in the southern district of Texas who effectively took control of the Immigrations and Customs Enforcement (ICE) and restarted deportations after President Biden installed a temporary pause? Federalist Society. Thomas Hardiman, who has undone gun regulations and called for a return to the eighteenth-century notion of "cruel and unusual punishment" rather than a contemporary moral understanding? Federalist Society.

It's the tie that links the most extreme Trump judges and the most head-scratching, ahistoric, and judges-as-culture-warrior decisions that have emerged over the past decade. And all that required funding the organizations that elected state attorneys general, state supreme courts, conservative litigation centers—all devoted, in one way or another, to advancing the legal doctrines that the conservative law firms would lean on in court.

The *Washington Post* columnist Ruth Marcus calls the Federalist Society "a one-stop shopping network" for promoting and credentialing conservative lawyers, confirming their ideological bona fides, and placing them on the fast track to the judiciary. But what Leo has built is something even bigger: to borrow the analysis of sociologist Max Weber, he's successfully institutionalized the charisma of the right-wing legal movement. The result has remade the Federalist Society and Leo World into an all-expenses-paid resort for supporting lawyers and judges, while also generating the cases that they will decide. Recent reporting has shown that it's not some hyperbolic turn of phrase to call the Leo network and the Federalist Society a resort—key movement figures such as Ginni and Clarence Thomas and Samuel Alito are commonly awarded with high-end getaways and other perks.

Trump, himself a close student of the role of baksheesh in cultivating political loyalty, clearly recognized Leonard Leo as a kindred spirit in his hour of need, en route to his election in 2016. Trump also likely deferred to Leo as a fellow brand ambassador and empire builder: political power may come and go, but the billion-dollar institutional networks controlled and ideologically purified by Leo last forever.

Leo, in turn, understood the transactional benefits of his alliance with Trump. Together with his lieutenant Donald McGahn, Leo pulled together the Federalist Society's dream list of Supreme Court appointees as the insurgent GOP nominee was seeking to shore up support among the traditional conservative-movement faithful. For an evangelical corps of rank-and-file GOP voters who had long felt taken for granted by the party establishment, the new legal-cum-social contract proffered by the Trump campaign was reassuringly clear and straightforward: they'd sign on to support a New York businessman with no religious faith, a documented history of sexual assault and multiple divorces—and an inconvenient history of donating to Democratic political campaigns. He'd get the GOP nomination and a chance to rent the White House. Leo and the

Federalist Society would claim the Holy Grail: the permanent power of the courts.

"We're going to have great judges, conservative, all picked by the Federalist Society," Trump promised in a 2016 interview on the deeply conservative Breitbart Radio Network. The more traditional members of the Federalist Society who still hold to its roots as a debate club must have winced, but Trump's right-wing radio audience knew exactly what a promise to install Federalist Society judges meant.

Trump adviser Sam Nunberg first had the idea to broker a deal between Trump and Leo. During a meeting at the Conservative Political Action Conference (CPAC) in 2015, Nunberg told Leo—whom he knew from his days as Federalist Society chair at Touro Law School on Long Island, a sign of how deeply connected and traveled Leo is—that Trump could well be the nominee and that the two ought to meet. Nunberg told me that his pitch to Leo was simple: "Donald was aware of Fed Society's work and policies and in agreement." Leo, noncommittal, didn't seem to take Trump's path to the nomination seriously. Leo never imagined this would end with three picks for the court, quips Nunberg, "until 8 P.M. on election night when returns started coming in."

Leo appears to have understood that loaning the Federalist Society's imprimatur to Trump would be great for the candidate's brand. When Trump handed Leo and McGahn the keys to the court, and wrapped the Federalist Society in a bear hug so that its conservative cred rubbed off on him, the die was cast. The only way forward for conservative judges was to win Leo's full-throated approval—even though the Federalist Society kept insisting the group remained nothing more than a humble debate club, independent from partisan politics and positions on issues.

If anyone had ever believed this, no one could even pretend any longer. Certainly Trump knew better, as did conservative judicial aspirants, and all the wealthiest donors on the American right.

"I think the Federalist Society crossed a line when Leo worked with Trump to develop that list of Supreme Court nominees," says author and scholar Amanda Hollis-Brusky. "Leo was working openly with a candidate for the Republican Party to say, 'We have given our stamp of approval to this list. If you vote for him, you vote for us.' He's always been doing his power broker thing, but he's largely been working behind the scenes. That was the moment where the Federalist Society really did cross the line—with Leo kind of continuing to work in the White House and Trump just giving the whole process over to him."

LEO HAD POSTPONED his start at the Federalist Society in 1990 to help prepare his friend Clarence Thomas for his bruising confirmation hearings. Fifteen years later, he took leaves of absence to help coordinate the selections and nominations of Roberts and Alito. Leo ran both justices' nominations proceedings in the Senate like a political campaign, dedicating a cool $15 million toward a war room, outreach to reporters, TV advertisements, focus groups, polling, and telemarketing. The Roberts and Alito campaigns had served as a critical proof-of-concept test for Leo's vision of a new network captained by the Federalist Society that would call all the shots in the politics of the law, and in treating judicial nominations as sophisticated political campaigns.

When George W. Bush won reelection in 2004, Leo and a handful of longtime friends first began talking about launching a nonprofit that might aid the two nominees who were expected to fall to Bush in his second term. The Judicial Confirmation Network—the fledgling organization that helped secure both Roberts's and Alito's nominations—had its roots in a buoyant celebratory dinner for conservative legal activists at an Italian restaurant in Washington. Leo was there, of course, along with conservative real estate developer and megadonor Robin Arkley II and longtime Leo partners Neil and Ann Corkery (often listed on official filing documents as the treasurer or officers of organizations Leo runs himself or helps direct from a close distance). Also in attendance was Justice Antonin Scalia, a sign of how even the justices backed this revolutionary ideological project.

The informal group soon became a fixture in Washington's conservative influence-peddling scene. As *Politico* has reported, to maintain some distance from the Federalist Society, and preserve the talking point that FedSoc did not take political stances, Leo's networks changed names and addresses like they were trying to stay a step ahead of hot pursuit. Leo and his partners renamed JCN from the Judicial Confirmation Network to the Judicial Crisis Network after Obama's election changed its mission. They listed its headquarters in nonprofit filings as the Corkerys' well-appointed Virginia home. But JCN would do its real work in the same downtown Washington, D.C., office building—indeed the same hallway—where the Federalist Society is housed. (The ties between the two groups are at once obvious yet legally distinct. JCN was run for years by longtime Leo confidante Carrie Severino, herself a former Supreme Court clerk for Thomas. When the *Washington Post* stopped by JCN in 2019, and no one answered the phone, a security guard called over to the Federalist Society office, who sent someone down to bring the *Post*'s Robert O'Harrow Jr. and Shawn Boburg over to JCN. The actual distance between the organizations was a corridor.)

The newly chartered JCN had its work cut out for it in 2008. The confirmation opportunity under Bush became a confirmation crisis after Democrats took over Washington that year. With the specter of a new slate of Democratic nominees across the federal judiciary, the JCN supercharged its funding and changed strategies. The group focused first on a key strength of the Federalist Society: movement discipline. JCN officials worked to keep Republicans united against Obama judiciary selections. They also made it painfully clear to any GOP lawmakers tempted by the siren song of bipartisan compromise that crossing JCN came with a steep price. When New Hampshire Republican candidate Kelly Ayotte said that she would have voted to confirm Sonia Sotomayor, JCN hit her with a barrage of attack ads and nearly tipped the primary election to her insurgent challenger. In 2016, when Ayotte was up for reelection, she toed the party line, supporting Mitch McConnell's scorched-earth blockade of Merrick Garland's nomination to succeed Scalia on the high court. According to *ProPublica*, Leo even threatened a Republican governor that any defiance of his selection for a state court judgeship would be met with "fury from the conservative base," at an intensity that "(you) have never seen."

Meanwhile, with federal appointments out of their control, JCN shifted focus, spending millions to influence state attorney general and judicial elections. This was an extension of the Right's successful strategy to capture statehouses and legislatures in the 2010 midterms, and to employ this new power base to unleash a wave of gerrymanders and voter-suppression strategies throughout the states, taking full advantage of the political opportunities delivered by *Citizens United*, *Shelby County*, and the 2010 elections. State courts were a key linchpin of this effort: they were necessary to defend policy gains—and often the maps themselves—against litigation.

As a de facto campaign arm of the Federalist Society and the Leo network, JCN drew its funds from the same cohort of right-wing donors Leo had corralled behind the ideological capture of the federal judiciary. Millions flowed in from a dark money group called the Wellspring Committee, led by close Leo ally Ann Corkery and founded in 2008 not long after JCN as part of the Koch Brothers network. Thanks to Roberts's outlandish 2010 ruling in *Citizens United*, it became increasingly difficult to track the money as it flowed from the conservative billionaires and other wealthy benefactors into one dark money waystation after another.

The Wellspring Committee, listed as a nonprofit based in Virginia, was a sluice gate for dark money in right-wing campaigns, and soon became a key funder of the JNC; under the see-no-evil provisions of *Citizens United*, millions in donor cash could bounce back and forth between Wellspring and the JCN, which then distributed it to state groups in Wisconsin, North Carolina, Michigan, Ohio, and elsewhere for state judiciary candidates. Alternately, JCN could pump millions of Wellspring dosh into the Republican Attorneys General Association and the Republican State Leadership Committee to pick up new allies. These newly flush outfits, and others like them, would later go on to bring challenges to *Roe v. Wade*, the Biden administration's student-loan and immigration plans, and virtually any other litigation material that the conservative supermajority on the Supreme Court could translate into conservative victories.

Many of those same donors, such as Arkley and Paul Singer, had been longtime, and big-ticket, funders of the Federalist Society. This was the other enormous opportunity taking shape as Leo eagerly assumed the role of legal consigliere to the Trump campaign in 2016: he could harness this robust network of cash and influence to immediately leverage Barack

Obama's stalled nomination of Merrick Garland to the Court into an instant win for the conservative legal movement should Trump manage to win the presidency.

So just a few doors down from the Federalist Society, JCN coordinated the multimillion-dollar efforts to embolden GOP senators to blockade Obama's selection of Merrick Garland. Had Garland replaced Scalia on the court, after all, it's all but certain that the *Rucho* decision on partisan gerrymandering, along with other 5–4 voting rights cases, would have been decided the other way. The Leo network was raising and spending hundreds of millions of dollars, nearly all of it secretly and without any need for disclosure, on a campaign to lock in control over the judiciary and, in turn, over state and federal policy nationwide, just as soon as it had a pliant Republican president.

Much was on the line, and much of the work was done by a group called Creative Response Concepts, or CRC—an organization regularly furnishing logistical and financial support to Leo's various front groups.

The key players were conservative activists who had toiled for years in right-wing gutter politics and mastered the dark arts of manipulating elections' toxic lies. CRC and its president, Greg Mueller, a longtime Leo friend, made its name with the "Swift Boat" ads that torpedoed John Kerry's presidential campaign in 2004 with unsubstantiated rumors that the Democratic nominee had lied about his heroism in Vietnam. CRC would then go on to work for the Federalist Society. (In 2018, during Brett Kavanaugh's explosive nomination hearings, CRC and longtime conservative activist Ed Whelan worked together to advance the preposterous notion that the sexual assault alleged by Christine Blasey Ford had been committed by a Kavanaugh doppelgänger.)

Less than four weeks after Trump's victory, the president-elect turned to the Supreme Court pick that would now be his—or rather, Leonard Leo and Donald McGahn's—to make.

The nominee, Neil Gorsuch, did not learn about his selection from the president. The third most powerful person in the world reached out to him instead. "On or about December 2, 2016, I was contacted by Leonard Leo," Gorsuch wrote in answer to congressional questions about the selection process.

Once Gorsuch's nomination was announced, JCN swung into action. The group channeled $10 million into supporting Gorsuch's nomination. Before a single hearing had been convened, JCN had mobilized $17 million to land Gorsuch his seat—first to keep it warm, and then to ensure his occupancy. JCN called it "the most robust operation in the history of confirmation battles." Its principal client in the Leo network, CRC, claimed that the materials it created on behalf of Gorsuch, from online memes to op-eds to ads, had yielded 1.2 billion engagements. During Gorsuch's confirmation hearings, Rhode Island Democratic senator Sheldon Whitehouse, the leading voice in the U.S. Senate on judicial ethics and campaign finance, asked Gorsuch what this group saw in him that made that price tag worthwhile.

"You would have to ask them," he replied.

"I cannot," Whitehouse replied, "because I do not know who they are. It's just a front group."

Whitehouse went on to explain to Gorsuch how the groups supported his nomination work. "They set up an array of benign-sounding front groups to both organize and conceal their manipulation of our politics. And Supreme Court justices socialize with this small group, and then they go and they tender—render decisions that give that small group immense political advantage, particularly the ability to hide the political expenditure of their money.

"Does that look right to you?" Whitehouse asked.

"Senator," Gorsuch said, almost sadly, "I have no information about anything you have just described. I do not know about that."

THE PUTSCH BEHIND Gorsuch's nomination was a preview of coming attractions. Leonard Leo and his allies were simply getting warmed up for the main event: the ideological capture of the high court, for generations. Leo and his allies were raising staggering amounts of money in the post–*Citizens United* world they'd created, funneling hundreds of millions of dollars through an ever-expanding network of front groups, with the goal of influencing—from the shadows—every major decision delivered by the judiciary, whether Americans liked it or not.

During 2016, as the *Washington Post* and *New York Times* have reported, Leo set up four new organizations—the for-profit BH Group,
and three nonprofits, the BH Fund, America Engaged, and the Freedom
and Opportunity Fund. CRC came on board to handle all the media. The
BH Group launched itself with a seven-figure gift to the new president
who made it all possible, via the Trump Inaugural Committee.

These four new groups landed in the center of an already tangled
consortium of interlocking directorates and overlapping funders choreographed under Leo's direction. That's why mapping Leonard Leo's influence at its peak is like sketching an octopus orgy: there are arms and
legs everywhere, relationships are reciprocal and intertwined, names and
strategic alliances change, but the faces remain the same.

According to a landmark investigative report by the *Washington Post*,
Leo's new nonprofits pulled in $33 million in 2016 and 2017 alone, includ-
ing some $24.2 million from a single donor later identified as billionaire
Chicago industrialist Barre Seid. (When Seid later turned his entire company over to Leo's network in a billion-dollar bequest, the key broker of
the deal was Chris Jankowski, the REDMAP mastermind, in a moment
that brought together the generational capture of state legislatures and the
courts.) The groups began, in classic Leo-led (and Roberts-enabled) fashion, to transfer the cash back and forth among themselves: BH Fund sent
over just about $3 million to the other three nonprofits launched along-
side it.

The Center for Responsive Politics and MapLight managed to track
where much of that money went: right back into Supreme Court nomination battles and into CRC's pockets. Four million went to a group called
Independent Women's Voice, which coordinated an astroturf campaign
of women leaping to the defense of Brett Kavanaugh when sexual assault
allegations arose during his confirmation hearings. Heather Higgins,
IWV's president, says the group branded itself to appear nonpartisan and
objective while actually being ideologically aligned with the GOP. "Being branded as neutral," she said in a 2015 speech, "but actually having
the people who know, know that you're actually conservative puts us in a
unique position."

America Engaged shipped $1 million to the National Rifle Association, which then promptly launched a $1 million ad campaign to back Gorsuch on Second Amendment grounds.

Another nonprofit, the Rule of Law Trust, nestled itself into the Leo network in 2018. This group was created by Neil Corkery with Leo as its only listed trustee. Its coffers immediately filled with $80 million. Investigators said that this massive outlay came from as few as one or as many as three wealthy donors, all of it gifted with no disclosure requirements at all.

When the indefatigable researcher and former Senate Judiciary Committee counsel Lisa Graves testified before Congress in 2020, she listed at least nine different named entities that Leo and his network operate under. This combination of front groups and advocacy shops formed "the hub of a secretive scheme to capture the courts and remake our laws," Graves said. Between 2014 and 2018, she said the dark money network controlled a combined income upward of $400 million. Now it sits at more than $2 billion.

In 2020, when Leo shifted from executive vice president to cochairman of the Federalist Society, he launched yet another new company called CRC Advisors—with CRC's Greg Mueller as CEO and another Federalist Society vice president, Jonathan Bunch, as executive director. (Carrie Severino, from JCN, assumed some of Leo's old responsibilities at the Federalist Society.)

Perhaps just for misdirection, or perhaps to attempt a clean slate with the media and public, the Judicial Crisis Network and the Judicial Education Project, meanwhile, rebranded themselves as the 85 Fund and the Concord Fund. The Concord Fund then registered its name in Virginia as the Honest Elections Project. This group soon made its name as the legal vanguard of election denialism on the right, propagating spurious claims of voter fraud, and then advocating for very restrictive new election laws to address the voter fraud that its lawyers have failed to document anywhere. "Twinned 501(c3)s operating out of the same office with the same staff under multiple fictitious names," Whitehouse told me. "It's the same operation, trying very hard to convince people otherwise."

The 85 Fund is now listed as doing business from suite 268 at 3220 N. St. NW in Washington. It turns out that's a UPS Store on the edge of Georgetown; there are no suites, just mailboxes.

The Wellspring Committee continued to shift money across the great Leo octopus orgy until late 2018. It was launched by the Corkerys in 2008 and collected $28 million from one donor soon after Scalia's death. It then turned around and funneled $38 million to JCN during the Garland and Gorsuch battles. By the time Wellspring shuttered, not long after Kavanaugh took his lifetime appointment, the money hub had shipped more than $58 million to the JCN.

Neil Corkery opened the Rule of Law Trust not long after Wellspring ended; Graves reports that almost all its expenditures go to reimburse the BH Group. It did award at least one other grant in 2019: $895,000 to Leo's America Engaged, which has passed money between at least one Koch-related group in addition to the funds that went into the NRA's Gorsuch support.

In 2020, the serious cash money arrived: as mentioned earlier, Leo scored what's believed to be the largest political donation ever, $1.6 billion from the Chicago businessman Barre Seid. In what now appears to be a conditioned reflex, he deposited it with a new nonprofit that he called the Marble Freedom Trust.

According to its IRS records, obtained by the Center for Media and Democracy, Marble spent $182 million to build right-wing institutions between May 1, 2021, and April 30, 2022, alone.

Which institutions, where? Thanks to the Leo court's decision in *Citizens United*, that's really hard to say. We know that $153 million went to the Schwab Charitable Fund—but that's a donor-advised fund whose entire purpose is to keep investigators off the trail of who is giving what to whom.

But the Marble filing did turn up one other major cash beneficiary: the Concord Fund, which took in $29 million. The Concord Fund then promptly shifted $12 million in fees to CRC Advisors.

A HANDFUL OF emails and grant reports discovered when hackers released internal documents from the conservative Bradley Foundation in 2016 show just how Leo conducts his network to generate such resonant harmonies. Bradley has long been one of the Federalist Society's most generous donors, shipping millions to help run the operation—toting up as much as $3 million in a single year. The Federalist Society founders and some of the lawyers and thinkers most closely aligned with the organization have also received multiple Bradley Prizes, each one accompanied with a $250,000 cash gift.

But in 2014, Leonard Leo needed a little more money from Bradley. Two important cases, nurtured by Federalist Society legal brainpower and funded by the movement's wealthy network, had arrived at the U.S. Supreme Court. One case, *Friedrichs v. California Teachers Association*, looked to defund unions by making dues collection more difficult; the other, *King v. Burwell*, aimed to unravel the Affordable Care Act and eliminate health coverage for millions through a complicated technicality designed, in part, by Federalist Society–aligned thinkers.

Bradley had already ponied up to help support the litigation. But Leo needed extra support in the form of two amicus briefs he wanted to be certain that the high court considered. Each brief would cost up to $250,000. Bradley's grant officer, Michael Hartmann, immediately recognized the value, since the foundation had already backed the cases in their early stages. The request, Hartmann noted, had been "initiated by Bradley Prize recipient Leonard Leo of the Federalist Society for Law and Public Policy Studies." (The official contact, however, was Neil Corkery, through his address at the UPS Store.)

Hartmann recommended a grant of $150,000. "At this highest of legal levels, it is often very important to orchestrate high-caliber amicus efforts that showcase respected high-profile parties who are represented by the very best lawyers with strong ties to the Court," he wrote. "Such is the case here, with *King* and *Friedrichs*, even given Bradley's previous philanthropic investments in the actual, underlying legal actions." The additional briefs, the proposal noted, would also carry the names of former Supreme Court clerks now with major conservative D.C. law firms—one more example of the Federalist Society pipeline and influence-gathering machine at work.

Once the additional funds had been approved, Hartmann had questions about how the money drop would work. He knew who to ask.

"Leonard, is there a 501(c)(3) nonprofit to which Bradley could direct any support of the two Supreme Court amicus projects other than Donors-Trust?" he wrote in a December 16, 2014, email to Leo.

"Yes," Leo replied from his Federalist Society email account later that afternoon, "Judicial Education Project could take and allocate."

"Can you get us a contact person there, or have someone send us a letter with their tax-exempt status, board, and budget?" Hartmann wrote.

Leo, again from his Federalist Society account, quickly looped in his pal Neil Corkery.

The Judicial Education Project brief ended up carrying the names of eight law professors, all of them with long-standing relationships to the Society, including cofounder Calabresi. In the end, Bradley not only backed both sets of plaintiffs in *Friedrichs* but a dozen different amicus briefs, many filtered through the Leo network, funded by dark money, powered by Federalist Society attorneys. Many of those lawyers were in turn connected to powerful judges through clerkships attained through Federalist Society connections, aimed at influencing justices installed with the help of Leo and his network.

YET IT STILL wasn't enough. Roberts failed to provide the necessary vote to scuttle Obamacare. And an eight-member court after Scalia's death would deadlock at four on *Friedrichs*. So when he made a call on February 13, 2016, to notify Mitch McConnell, the Senate majority leader, that Scalia had passed, Leo knew the judicial crisis on the right was at a new tipping point. The conservative judicial project hung by the tiniest thread: if Obama replaced Scalia, the balance of power would shift dramatically.

The forces of movement conservatism had to return to the larger project of fortifying the court's conservative majority. The only hope: a McConnell-led stonewall that declined to consider any Democratic nominee, and rolling the dice on a Republican president winning election in the fall. The guiding strategy had to be worked out immediately: Republican presidential candidates would debate that evening. Everyone needed to be on the same page. And the Senate blockade needed to look like McConnell's idea, rather than a proposal from a less credible figure inside the GOP caucus, such as conservative bomb-thrower Ted Cruz.

Once again, the Federalist Society network operated at the highest, and most secretive, levels of American politics. As the veteran *New York Times* reporter Carl Hulse details in his terrific book *Confirmation Bias*, Leo and McConnell worked out a detailed plan, unprecedented in modern times, to deny a president's nominee to the Supreme Court for the nearly nine months before an election without any fair hearing at all.

As Leo had taken on his new court-shaping role, there was a frenzied behind-the-scenes scrum among D.C.'s conservative legal elite to win his favor. But you could glimpse its telltale aftereffects, if you knew where to look.

Leo wanted to win the next *Friedrichs* case and reward his donors with a big policy victory. The largesse of Bradley and other foundations and donors kept the network alive. These outfits wanted to clock game-changing wins at the high court for their investment, not prestigious amicus briefs to frame. That required more justices who would deliver them.

"When Brett Kavanaugh's clerks were trying to make sure he got on Donald Trump's list to be on the Supreme Court, they made a pilgrimage to the Federalist Society to see Leonard Leo" and "kiss his ring," Ruth Marcus, the court watcher at the *Washington Post*, told NPR.

But the way to impress Leo wasn't through mere flattery or courtly displays of deference. You won entry into the Federalist Society's inner circle by authoring opinions that delivered victories to the movement billionaires who funded Leo's network. And you furnished the intellectual firepower for such victories by advancing the wild-eyed theorems concocted in the originalist and textualist laboratories of Federalist Society conferences and movement-funded law schools and journals.

Neil Gorsuch aced his audition for the high court by signaling that he would take on the administrative state. The court's precedent known as *Chevron* deference grants latitude to federal agencies to take necessary action to fulfill their regulatory mandates. It had thus long been a target of conservatives who wanted to rein the agencies in, and corporations who bristled under their regulations. In a dissent in *Gutierrez-Brizuela v. Lynch*, Gorsuch made it clear that if tapped for the Supreme Court he would not flinch from a key conservative goal, arguing *Chevron* "permit[s] executive bureaucracies to swallow huge amounts of core judicial and legislative power and concentrate federal power in a way that seems more than a little difficult to square with the Constitution of the framers' design." Just in case anyone missed his meaning, he added: "Maybe the time has come to face the behemoth."

Kavanaugh, for his part, had padded his own résumé for Federalist Society review by endorsing the fanciful "major questions" doctrine when he dissented in a D.C. Circuit Court of Appeals decision that upheld the Federal Communications Commission's rules on net neutrality. His dissent also hinged on the originalist claim that Congress had not expressly delegated this authority to the agency.

Kavanaugh also embraced something called the unitary executive theory in a dissent in *PHH Corp v. Consumer Financial Protection Bureau.* Elizabeth Warren worked to establish this agency after the 2008 economic collapse and housing meltdown. PHH, a mortgage lender, had been fined $109 million for alleged kickbacks to insurers—precisely the kind of risky behavior that led to the CFPB's creation in the first place.

Kavanaugh's objection was that the CFPB had a single director—in order to protect it from political interference—but the independence of its director also flew in the face of the unitary executive doctrine that right-wing originalists deployed as a blunt instrument to fatally weaken agencies from the inside. "Independent agencies pose a significant threat to liberty," Kavanaugh offered in a dissent that dropped the word *liberty* a dozen times. Then, in a footnote, Kavanaugh targeted the Supreme Court's *Chevron* precedent, citing "significant criticism" within the legal world, which of course was right-wing judicial code for the work of Federalist Society–aligned professors. Still, for all his indignant appeals to imperiled liberties, Kavanaugh had to acknowledge he wasn't in a position—yet—to be making new court precedent: "In any event, it is not our job to decide" whether *Chevron* should be overturned, he wrote ruefully; that solemn responsibility fell to the justices on the high court.

The footnote, together with the entire text of the dissent, served as a wink and a job application. If this was what conservatives wanted, Associate Supreme Court Justice Kavanaugh would get it done.

Kavanaugh hadn't made the original Leo-McGahn list. But with these shows of ideological brio, he earned his way into their circle of trust, which amounted to the same thing. For the seat opened by the retirement of Justice Anthony Kennedy in 2019, Trump "picked somebody who wasn't on the list—and there's not a whisper of complaint," marvels Senator Whitehouse, "because somehow the system knew that Kavanaugh had worked Leo, the signal had been given, that this was okay, and he was going to be a good guy."

Amy Coney Barrett, meanwhile, whom Trump nominated near the end of his term to replace the deceased Ruth Bader Ginsburg, had practically been grown in the FedSoc and Leo network laboratory. She had trained at one of the most conservative law schools in the nation, Notre Dame, and then kept working the elite nexus of the right-wing legal movement. After graduation, she clerked with Scalia (who rarely looked at a résumé outside the Ivy League elites). She then won a perch in the legal academy with the aid of a fellowship from the Olin Foundation, which worked with the Federalist Society to identify and support a new generation of conservative academics. Barrett's Olin fellowship included not only a generous stipend but also office support at a law school and mentorship from established conservative academics.

As the trio of Trump's right-wing justices took their places on the court, the legal Right was lining up behind a case that would allow the court to revisit the union issues at the heart of *Friedrichs* in a case called *Janus v. American Federation of State, County, and Municipal Employees, Council 31*. The plaintiff's legal team—which was challenging the collection of membership dues in public-sector unions—was again generously funded by Bradley, and their filing was bedecked with another dozen amicus briefs, also funded by Bradley.

The inviolable new conservative majority on the Roberts Court would also get a do-over on regulatory law and the sacrosanct unitary executive theory—sanctioned, in turn, by the major questions doctrine, in the 2022 case *EPA v. West Virginia*. Now Neil Gorsuch was primed to take his next shot at the administrative state—and he wouldn't miss. The court relied on the jury-rigged major questions doctrine to roll back the EPA's power to regulate greenhouse gases and battle climate change, arguing that Congress—which established the EPA more than five decades earlier—needs to spell out each power the agency possesses in forensic detail.

Change the justices, change the law. But perhaps more important is an emerging new modus operandi for the legal Right: change the justices and shift power. After all, what the vague major questions doctrine really does is undermine Congress, federal agencies, and the White House anytime that the Supreme Court decides something "major" or "controversial" is afoot. It awards whatever power to the court that the court would like to wield. Major questions really means minority rule.

LEO'S SUCCESS IN transforming the U.S. Supreme Court—together with his intricate knowledge of lawyers and judges at all levels of the conservative legal hierarchy—has also made him a natural candidate to remake state supreme courts and push them in a decidedly more conservative direction.

From well behind the scenes, Leo and his constellation of judicial advocacy groups have helped guide selection of Federalist Society–approved favorites as judicial nominees and fund their way to the bench in Ohio, Michigan, Wisconsin, and North Carolina. But perhaps his most consequential involvement comes from Florida, where Governor Ron DeSantis— himself a Federalist Society member at Harvard Law School who met Leo during his student years in Cambridge—invited Leo to lead an off-the-books committee to vet the conservative bona fides of finalists for the state supreme court.

This is not the way state supreme court appointments had worked in Florida. Previously, nonpartisan commissions selected by the governor and the state bar association made recommendations to appoint candidates to state judgeships. The state supreme court, however, did not reliably rubber-stamp conservative legislation; indeed, in 2015 and 2016, state judges painstakingly unraveled an unconstitutional partisan gerrymander of Florida's congressional map that one judge compared to a wild conspiracy out of an espionage thriller. The court directed the legislature to draw a new map ahead of the 2016 elections that produced a delegation that more closely matched Florida's overall partisan breakdown.

DeSantis and Leo tossed that practice aside in a quest for a state supreme court that would line up with their conservative ideologies. Representative Matt Gaetz, the Florida congressman who guided DeSantis's transition team, says that DeSantis wanted Leo to run a "concierge screening process" to determine which of the eleven finalists ought to get three positions that would come open immediately as three liberal justices reached retirement age.

"It was just Ron and the FedSoc crew, and they made it clear they didn't need any other help," Gaetz told the *Washington Post*.

The nonpartisan commission's meetings had been advertised and open to the media and the public. This secret questioning stayed behind closed doors. According to the *Post*, Leo and his team asked candidates detailed questions about originalism, textualism, and whether they interpreted the Constitution based on "original intent." DeSantis has now named five of the seven members of the state supreme court. All of them are members of the Federalist Society.

Then, in 2022, after DeSantis made clear he wanted Florida's legislature to produce a congressional map with a larger GOP advantage—in violation of state constitutional provisions that specifically outlaw partisan gerrymandering—the state supreme court handpicked by the governor and Leonard Leo allowed the map to stand. It tore apart a historically Black district and attached pieces of it to several surrounding districts, all of which now elected Republicans. It handed the GOP three additional seats in the House—a staggering twenty of Florida's twenty-eight seats in a state DeSantis carried in 2018 by fewer than thirty-three thousand votes. Florida's gerrymandered congressional delegation was enough to supply the deciding margin that tipped control of the U.S. House to the Republicans in the 2022 midterms.

LEONARD LEO'S ELEVEN-BEDROOM New England summer home isn't the only thing you can buy when you become this wealthy and influential, and control this much money.

In March 2016—just as Trump offered to sign onto a list of Supreme Court nominees with Leo-approved constitutionalist views during a meeting with Leo and McGahn at the D.C. law firm Jones Day—Leonard Leo also bought a law school.

That's right: Leo, the Federalist Society, and wealthy conservative

interests now brandish the keys to the Supreme Court and the George Mason Law School across the river in Arlington. The price tag: $30 million.
The check procured naming rights to the school—but more than that, it
laid the groundwork to transform the former commuter law school into
an institutional bastion of the permanent legal revolution on the right. In
recognition of this mission, the law school would now carry the name of
Antonin Scalia, the Federalist Society's first faculty adviser before his as-
cent to the Supreme Court.

Two donors provided the cash. Leo brokered both deals. The first
$10 million arrived from the Charles Koch Foundation. The other donor,
who put forth the remaining $20 million, wished to remain anonymous. It
took a year before persistent Freedom of Information Act requests from a
recent alumna, Allison Pienta, revealed the donor's identity. It was another
Leonard Leo satellite group, the for-profit BH Fund.

Pienta found the BH Fund registered in the state of Virginia with two
officers listed on the incorporation forms: President Leonard Leo and
Secretary-Treasurer Jonathan Bunch, better known as a vice president of
the Federalist Society. The fund had been launched with a secret $24 mil-
lion donation from a single donor—which additional FOIA sleuthing determined to be Barre Seid, the midwestern surge protector magnate who
parked $1.6 billion of his fortune at the Marble Freedom Trust. (Leo and
Seid had been introduced by Federalist Society cofounder Gene Meyer.)

"The Federalist Society network has billions now because they've been
cultivating these people for fifty years," says Bruce Bartlett, the former
Reagan economic adviser. "They've written them into their wills. Now
the payoffs are coming." (Bartlett left the GOP over the party's Trumpian
transformation. His new allies on the left, he adds, "are way, way behind
the Right on messaging, building institutions, and finding donors to finance these things.")

Leo started directing dark money to the George Mason Law School
when Henry Butler took over as dean in 2015 and realized it was in deep
trouble. The northern Virginia school, housed in a former Arlington department store, was struggling to attract top students and sinking in the
prestigious *U.S. News* law school rankings.

After some initial talks with Leo, Butler developed a five-year plan to revive the school's fortunes. Charles Koch and other conservatives had invested deeply in the Mercatus Institute, a libertarian think tank dedicated to deregulation, and other free-market economic programs on campus. Why not recast George Mason as a conservative hothouse for legal scholarship as well? Butler sent Leo a formal pitch in mid-September, which university officials have since heavily redacted. What remains legible is a clear overture to rebrand the Mason school as a premier ideological battlement for the legal Right. Leo wanted in. "There are a number of questions that came up. We should schedule a call," Leo wrote the dean from his Federalist Society email account. That call took place four days later, on September 25, and Butler followed up immediately. "I very much appreciate your wise counsel," he replied.

That counsel bore rapid fruit, at least as measured by cash transfers. Early in the morning on February 26, 2016, Butler texted Janet Bingham, the president of the George Mason University Foundation, that a "$30,000,000 deal came together last night. The Justice Antonin Scalta [sic] School of Law. Confidential for noW. Onward and Upwadl [sic] Henry $20 [million] from anonymous donor from [redacted] and $10 [million] from K." The K stood for Koch. The redacted donor was Leo's billion-dollar benefactor.

"A game changer for Mason Law," Butler wrote provost David Wu. "Off to Cabo for a week of R&R." From the beach, Butler emailed Leo that the university should hire several of Scalia's former clerks as professors. "Jonathan Mitchell is an obvious target," he wrote—a signature appointment for any institution extending the hard-Right judicial legacy of Antonin Scalia.

Mitchell, who clerked for Scalia during the 2002–03 term, wrote the Texas law that tried to undercut abortion rights by requiring all providers to have admitting privileges at hospitals. When the U.S. Supreme Court struck the law down in 2016 in a 5–3 ruling, Mitchell struck back. He crafted another law—one that not only banned all abortions around six weeks into a pregnancy, but also turned neighbors into bounty hunters and enabled citizens to sue anyone they suspected of being party to an illegal abortion. "The audacious legislative structure," observed the *New York Times*, "flummoxed lower courts" and sent "supporters of abortion rights scrambling for some way to stop it."

The courtship of Mitchell was just the beginning. A review of thousands of pages of George Mason emails and documents—many detailing the relationships among Leo, the Federalist Society, conservative donors, faculty members, and the Trump administration—shows how deep and coordinated the ideological rebranding of the George Mason Law School was. Documents show that George Mason officials who insisted that the entire Leo-brokered $30 million gift would go to scholarships, with no ideological preconditions, were being less than truthful.

The grant agreement with BH Fund furnished the law school with $4 million annually over the next five years—with extensive strings attached. And Leonard Leo would be the person pulling them. The law school needed to document that it was meeting a "Mission," as defined by Leo. Regular status reports had to show that the school had not strayed from that mission. Leo would review them. The school needed to retain its focus on law and economics—a key conservative field of scholarship—while developing "additional related areas of concentration and intellectual leadership such as . . . constitutional studies, administrative law, and the relationship between law and liberty." That meant launching two new centers of study at the school: the Center for the Study of the Administrative State and the Liberty & Law Center. One of Butler's progress reports to Koch and Leo—under the heading "Cash Is King (scholarships are cash)"—stated that CSAS had been funded with $400,000 of "naming-gifts scholarship revenue."

The first director of the CSAS was a Federalist Society protégé whom right-wing advocates would add to their list of potential Supreme Court justices. Neomi Rao indeed quickly leveraged her new post into a key position of political influence, serving as the Trump White House's Office of Information and Regulatory Affairs administrator. This post is known informally as the federal "regulatory czar" and carries with it extensive powers to strike down agency rulings and remake regulatory law. When Rao came on board, one of her principal mandates was to help GOP donors flout safety regulations.

Henry Butler's emails show that the dean tried to lure her back, requesting $1.5 million from one donor "to entice Neomi to return home to Scalia Law after she dismantles the administrative state." But Leo had bigger plans for her. As the White House's gatekeeper to the judiciary, Leo scored Rao a seat on what's often referred to as the second-highest court in the land, the D.C. Circuit Court of Appeals, in 2018, even though she had never served as a judge, let alone tried a single case. Later, *Balls and Strikes*, a law publication named after Roberts's famous pronouncement, would call her "The Worst Trump Judge in America" for decision after decision that protected Trump from various investigations and congressional fact-finding.

Leo's fingerprints would not end there. The Mason-Scalia emails show how Leo and the Federalist Society became intimately involved in some of the most routine academic and administrative operations of the school. Leo and his allies recommended candidates for faculty appointments, coordinated fundraising for the school, and connected conservative students with conservative judges for clerkships. They also put forward candidates for positions at the new centers, listed students for admission, and launched new programs to educate attorneys general and federal judges on free-market, antiregulation initiatives. Leo even planned menus and catering agreements ("that I will be approving, and, as we discussed, paying for") for a Union Station gala to honor Scalia. Butler sent Leo several options for "save the date" postcards to be approved.

In other emails, Leo suggested adjunct professors and other potential full-time hires, forwarding résumés directly to Butler. "We're on it!" the dean enthusiastically replied. Butler also kept Leo apprised of efforts to add Rachel Brand to the faculty, a Trump DOJ assistant attorney general who was also on the GOP team during *Bush v. Gore*. She had also worked with Leo to vet Roberts and Alito for the Supreme Court. "Unanimous," Butler wrote Leo of the decision to offer the job. "Thanks for all your help."

Leo forwarded Butler a potential student whose "father is a senior executive at [redacted]." A professor, J.W. Verret, wrote to Bunch, "We are hoping to place Scalia Law Alumni who are current members of our Fed Soc student chapter, alumni who were active in Fed Soc, and other Scalia Law conservative and libertarian alums in federal clerkships." Professor Verret especially wanted the "opportunity to get such candidates in front of judges incoming under the new administration."

Michael Greve, the former Smith Richardson program officer who now teaches at Scalia Law, says students come to George Mason with the expectation that they'll be fast-tracked into influential and prominent posts in the conservative legal revolution. "Once upon a time they competed to be on the law review," Greve told me. "Now they compete to be the next incoming president of the Federalist Society. Wow. And they're quite conscious of it. Come study with us," he says, adding, "as hard as Scalia Law competes for incoming students, we work even harder at placing them and connecting them."

It became even easier to get in front of Supreme Court justices when Scalia Law hired three of them for well-paid and cushy visiting professor gigs. These sinecures bring the justices close to maxing out what they are allowed to earn in outside income, as they lead leisurely seminars in Europe over the summer months when the court is out of session. Kavanaugh came on board in March 2019 as a distinguished visiting professor and taught a two-week course in Runnymede, England, three summers running, on the Creation of the Constitution. Gorsuch's classes have met in Iceland and Italy. The law school involved Gorsuch in selecting the Italian city where he would be the coprofessor of a two-week course on national security and separation of powers. The school made clear that the justice would not have to work that hard, that his role would be done by noon, and that there would be excursions to Florence and Bologna.

"Fantastico!" Gorsuch replied. You could almost hear the summery Aperol spritz cocktails being mixed in the background.

THE PICTURE WAS as strangely beautiful as it was disconcerting: a photorealistic painting of five central figures in the campaign to push the courts to the right. It hangs at billionaire conservative real estate developer Harlan Crow's massive lakeside resort in Upstate New York's Adirondacks. The painting depicts five men—Crow, Clarence Thomas, Leonard Leo, Mark Paoletta (Ginny Thomas's lawyer and Donald Trump's general counsel in the Office of Management and Budget), and University of Georgia School of Law dean Peter Rutledge. The men are relaxed, surrounded by lush trees, seated in rustic rocking chairs. Crow wears a gingham shirt and khaki shorts. He and Thomas smoke cigars. A statue of a bare-chested Native American, reaching toward the skies, towers over them.

The portrait reflects yet another of Leo's jobs: making sure the Supreme Court supermajority he engineered holds together for the long term.

Remember, when that gathering took place, Republican presidents had appointed thirteen of the last seventeen Supreme Court justices dating back to 1970. Yet the court's current Republican supermajority took decades to congeal ideologically because many of the GOP appointees drifted toward the center, and even the left. Nixon appointee Harry Blackmun and Ford appointee John Paul Stevens blossomed into reliable liberals. Reagan appointees Anthony Kennedy and Sandra Day O'Connor provided many important votes for Republican interests—including *Bush v. Gore*—but could not be counted on to overturn abortion rights, for example. George H. W. Bush practically gave the Federalist Society its mantra—"No more Souters!"—when he appointed a jurist who wouldn't budge from the center.

So while Leo's top priority might be the ideological vetting of true believers, he quickly understood that maintaining the key relationships that have created and sustained the Right's takeover of the legal system means a lot of face time among the fabulously wealthy. That means spending a lot of time in Harlan Crow country: providing a chummy social scene of like-minded elites. The background changes, depending on the core demographics of the client list—it can be a Union Station reception, or a law school donors' reception, or a tour of high court doctrine and history in picturesque Italian towns during the court's summer break. It can be a gracious assembly of ideological comrades in arms on a billionaire's yacht or Adirondacks compound.

Conservatives had long bemoaned the tendency of their selections to the high court to drift toward the center over time. They even had a name for it. They called it the Greenhouse Effect, named after Linda Greenhouse, the *New York Times* reporter who covered the Supreme Court for decades (and still writes one of the most insightful columns on the law in the paper of record). Conservatives postulated that in clubby confines of Washington, D.C., some justices could be pried from their ideological outlooks because they valued affirmation from Greenhouse and the re-spect of the Georgetown social set.

So Leo and his Federalist Society allies understood that it wouldn't be enough for them to nurture young conservatives from the first week of law school, through clerkships, and into careers in courtrooms and on the bench. They also had to create a new social milieu for their recruits to net-work and thrive in—places where they felt rewarded and appreciated, even cosseted. Crow lavishly funded the Federalist Society and other Leo efforts to transform the courts. His disclosed payments cover more than $10 mil-lion; the undisclosed dark money, he has suggested, could be higher by several degrees of magnitude. But it's his hospitality—long Indonesian cruises on a superyacht, two decades of summer vacations in Crow's lodge overlooking Upper St. Regis Lake, six-figure payments to help put Thom-as's grandnephew through private school, buying Thomas's mother's house in Savannah and allowing her to live in it rent-free—that might matter just as much.

Alito and Leo, meanwhile, according to eye-opening reporting from *ProPublica*, enjoyed a luxury junket at the behest of the billionaire hedge fund mogul Paul Singer—another prominent donor to both the Federalist Society and the Leo network—not long after Leo helped Alito win con-firmation to the bench in 2007. The flight on Singer's private plane was valued at upward of $100,000, each night at the Alaska fishing lodge cost over $3,000, and the men reportedly drank wine that cost four figures per bottle. (Alito recalls the accommodations as "comfortable but rustic" and denies that the wine cost that much.) The lodge was owned by JCN megadonor Arkley. Singer had regular business before the court. Alito never recused himself or reported the trips on his financial disclosure forms. (In the *Wall Street Journal*, Alito sniffed that the six-figures flight was inconsequential because if he hadn't sat there it "would have otherwise been vacant.")

In other words, Leonard Leo's empire extends to five-star fishing cab-ins in Alaska.

Leo also could not ensure that his supermajority he engineered in part to help the Right downplay or deny the reality of the greenhouse effect in climate change would be immune from the Linda Greenhouse Effect—

unless and until he'd created a counterestablishment version of the same respectability politics, funded and secured by an ideological corps of interested billionaires.

Not long before Thomas and Alito made headlines for accepting extravagant gifts, private flights, and swanky vacations, another story revealed how big money donors worked every imaginable angle to ingratiate themselves into the conservative justices' social circles. The aim of these gatherings was as transparent as their luxury trappings: to stiffen the right-wing majority's resolve to deliver conservative opinions, especially on abortion and other cases of interest to the religious right.

Reverend Robert Schenck—a longtime antiabortion activist who broke with the Right—revealed before Congress that he raised $30 million between 2000 and 2018 for a nonprofit called Faith and Action that had one special hidden mission: Operation Higher Court, a furtive and shockingly successful effort to build friendships with conservative justices and reward them with dinners, trips, and other emollients.

As part of that operation, which Schenck also dubbed the "Ministry of Emboldenment," the reverend arranged for forty top donors to the Council for National Policy—the even more secretive consortium of right-wing megadonors where Leo had been feted by Rebekah Mercer—to become "stealth missionaries." In that capacity, they were charged to meet and mingle with Alito, Scalia, Thomas, and others at a gala to benefit the Supreme Court Historical Society. Private trips ensued—to vacation homes in Jackson Hole and elsewhere, along with private dinners where the justices felt so comfortable they let their guard down. Indeed, the mood there was so collegial and convivial, Schenck maintains, that Alito tipped off his new friends to a forthcoming decision he had written in the landmark 2014 Hobby Lobby case that exempted private corporations from government mandates they had a religious objection to, such as the contraception mandate in the Affordable Care Act. (Alito denies leaking the opinion early.)

Schenck testified that Alito and Thomas especially understood and appreciated these efforts, both in grateful emails and in person.

"Keep up the work you are doing," Schenck says Thomas told him in one such exchange. "It is making a difference."

CHAPTER TWENTY-TWO

THE FALLOUT FROM John Roberts and the conservative court's blessing of extreme partisan gerrymanders was swift and far-reaching, and could be felt almost everywhere that Americans tried to persuade their own representatives into taking action that majorities demanded.

Perhaps one of the clearest examples could be seen in Tennessee in the days following a deadly March 2023 school shooting in Nashville. The days following this horror followed an all-too-familiar arc of bewilderment and despair. A Vanderbilt University survey found that 70.5 percent believed schools would be safer if a background check had to be performed before every gun sale.

Pleas and polls meant nothing to Tennessee lawmakers. Members of the state legislature's hard-Right GOP majority were entrenched in such safely gerrymandered districts that rendered them bulletproof. Republicans only broke Democratic control of the state house in 2008, but the GOP rapidly unleashed its patented array of vote-suppressing tactics to secure a permanent majority: redistricting, partisan and racial gerrymandering, the criminalizing of voter registration drives, and other measures. In 2022, lawmakers eviscerated a longtime blue district in Nashville by cracking the city in half and attaching the remaining pieces to rural communities hundreds of miles away. Then the state legislature took aim at the city itself. It worked to cut the number of seats on Nashville's city council in half, eliminated community oversight commissions that monitored the conduct of the police department, and worked to wrest control of the airport, local tourism dollars, and the metro sports authority.

That's what insurmountable, gerrymandered supermajority power can do: give the GOP eight of Tennessee's nine seats in Congress, as well as a 27–6 GOP edge in the state senate (82 percent of the seats) and a 75–24 advantage in the state house (with 76 percent of the seats). Tennessee is red but not that red. Donald Trump carried the state in 2016 and 2020 with 60 percent of the vote, but Republicans held nearly 80 percent of all legislative seats by overwhelmingly uncompetitive margins. Even fighting against it was a fool's errand. Half of all Republicans in the state legislature had no opponent in 2022. Of the thirty-eight who did face a challenger, their reelection was all but foreordained: thirty-four of them won with upward of 60 percent of the vote.

And so Tennessee's state legislature, mere weeks after the school shooting, began to consider measures that would do the opposite of what voters desired. As thousands of protesters amassed outside demanding reform, lawmakers moved to weaken the state's permit requirements and scale back required firearms training.

This seemed backward to three of the state's house Democrats, Representatives Justin Jones, Justin Pearson, and Gloria Johnson. The three lawmakers took advantage of a brief recess to approach the podium with a megaphone, orchestrating chants such as "Gun control now!" together with citizens seated in the balcony. The protest certainly goaded Tennessee Republicans into swift action. Within a week, they'd used their supermajority power to expel Jones and Pearson, both Black, from the chamber; Johnson, a white woman, avoided removal by a single vote. Republicans maintained that the actions of the protesting Democrats flaunted House rules. The GOP speaker, Cameron Sexton, compared the trio's actions to the January 6 insurrection at the U.S. Capitol, except "maybe worse." The expulsions, just the fourth and fifth in Tennessee since 1867, left some 140,000 people in their majority Black districts in Nashville and Memphis without any representation in the state house.

Tennessee's raw power grab is just one of the latest fronts in the war for minority rule, enabled by the Roberts Court's democracy decisions. Latest, of course, doesn't mean new: many of these tactics have long and ugly histories that stretch back to Reconstruction. But once your opponents have been gerrymandered into irrelevance, and the courts have removed the protections that held the worst instincts of politicians in check, then it's open season on ethics, decorum, tradition, guardrails—and anything else that stands in the way of perpetual one-party rule.

Once the legislature has been captured—and cannot reasonably be lost—it becomes the fount of all power. If citizens try to use their right to vote and mount a constitutional initiative to introduce change, lawmakers raise the bar to block them. If voters elect a governor of the opposite party, the legislature erodes that executive's power. If the courts look to enforce state constitutional protections that defend free and fair elections, conservatives create and embrace a made-up theory that gives the legislature primacy with everything having to do with election law and procedure. They will then couch it in phony "originalism," and push it through the courts they control. If prosecutors investigate police or seek criminal justice reform, lawmakers can either remove them from office or strike at their powers. If blue cities in red states look to enact their own policies, legislatures will either just seize more governing authority there, or else entirely rescind that right. And if representatives from the other side step out of line, or otherwise give offense, their irate colleagues can simply expel them from their seats.

This is what checkmate looks like in a competitive autocracy enabled and maintained by the court's decisions in *Citizens United*, *Shelby County*, *Brnovich v. DNC*, and *Rucho*. It's what purplish states, including Wisconsin, North Carolina, and Ohio, have already become, in a dress rehearsal that is now primed to roll out nationwide. These states still hold elections. Citizens can still turn out and vote. But the results are preordained—and any outcomes that the legislature doesn't like, whether at the ballot box or from the courts, might well be overridden or simply ignored. It's ruthless, ingenious, and brutally efficient. It turns protections against tyranny of the majority into something much more sinister and antidemocratic.

MUCH OF THE GOP minority rule playbook was perfected in North Carolina. From there, it steadily migrated to other states where Republicans used a gerrymandered legislature as a base to consolidate control everywhere. When Roy Cooper, a Democrat, defeated incumbent governor Pat McCrory in 2016, McCrory used the devastation unleashed by Hurricane Matthew and Great Smoky Mountains wildfires as cover for inflicting harm on the incoming chief executive. McCrory called a special lame-duck session of the state legislature, mere days before Cooper would be inaugurated, ostensibly to aid those battered by the hurricane. Then, well after midnight, the gerrymandered legislature walloped Democrats instead. "We never saw it coming," said then-state senator Jeff Jackson, now a member of Congress. "They started filing bills that were forty pages long. To pull off an ambush like that, all the Republicans had to be on it. They had been working on this for weeks."

Republicans whacked the number of political appointees Cooper could make from fifteen hundred down to just under four hundred, taking away all the extra positions they'd awarded McCrory when he was elected. Cabinet officials now had to be confirmed by the GOP-controlled Senate—a requirement that awarded Republicans near-veto power over the smaller number of appointments Cooper was still allowed. Republicans also reworked the state and county board of elections, previously led by the governor's party, so that now both parties had an equal number of seats. But they also stipulated that Republicans had tie-breaker control in even-number years—when elections were actually held—and Democrats took over in the odd years, when they were not. The chicanery did not end there. Elections for the state supreme court, previously nonpartisan, would now clearly pit Republican justices against Democratic ones. And since Democrats currently controlled the state supreme court, Republicans made it more difficult and time-consuming for cases to get to there, mandating that they first be heard by the state court of appeals, which, yes, they happened to control.

Other GOP-led states turned this playbook into the minority-rule bible. Few states proved quite so ambitious in their embrace of minority rule as Wisconsin, where the 2011 GOP gerrymander of the state assembly and senate proved the most impenetrable in the nation. Wisconsin remains one of the most closely divided states in the nation at the presidential level and during statewide elections. That was once true in the state legislature, as well. Democrats and Republicans swapped control of the state senate five times between 1992 and 2006; but the senate has not budged since the GOP flipped it in 2010 and remade the map. Now the GOP holds a 22–11 supermajority there. The assembly is even less responsive to voters. Republicans have held between 60 and 64 seats every year since the post-2010 lines went into effect—even in years when Democratic candidates won hundreds of thousands more votes.

Perhaps the best example of how Wisconsin legislators made themselves impervious to the ballot box arrived in 2018, right after the Roberts Court declined to come to the rescue of voters in the *Whitford* case. In that year's election, voters reelected a Democrat to the U.S. Senate, defeated incumbent Republican governor Scott Walker, awarded Democrats every statewide office, and favored Democratic assembly candidates by 203,000 votes. Republicans won a 63–36 majority, anyway—nearly two-thirds of the seats—with less than 46 percent of the vote. Then, following the North Carolina playbook, a legislative majority that lacked popular support proceeded to limit the power of the leaders the voters actually elected.

Tony Evers and Josh Kaul, the new governor and attorney general, campaigned on a pledge to withdraw the state from litigation challenging the constitutionality of the Affordable Care Act. The legislature, as part of its lame-duck power grab, limited Evers's ability to pull out of litigation and granted that power instead to the GOP-controlled senate finance committee. Then, lawmakers granted themselves the right to intervene in any litigation they desired, even if the attorney general's office chose otherwise. This maneuver effectively gave the Wisconsin GOP uncontested standing to pursue any litigation at taxpayers' expense to protect its own political interests. The Republican majority then hamstrung Evers's ability to expand Medicaid, stripped his powers to appoint key members of commissions, and blocked any efforts to enact his own policies on economic development and health care. Then, for good measure, they gave themselves the power to block any regulations written by the administrative agencies under the governor's control.

"This was a new front in the war on democracy in Wisconsin," says Gordon Hintz, the former Democratic minority leader in the state senate. Hintz faced the Sisyphean task of leading a caucus that could not win against a GOP majority led by Speaker Robin Vos that would do anything to preserve power. "This went to a new place. This said we're willing to change the powers of the governor and attorney general who were elected to use those powers, before they even started. This was an assault on the voting public."

The League of Women Voters led a coalition of organizations that tried to block the lame-duck power grab in state courts. The coalition's suit claimed that the session itself was unconstitutional under the plain text of the Wisconsin state constitution that controls when the legislature can meet. But the state supreme court, itself in GOP hands, upheld the session and the laws on a 4–3 vote that fell along partisan lines. "The Legislature remains accountable to the people of Wisconsin for any failure to follow its self-imposed statutory or procedural rules," the majority ruled, in the latest flagrant example of a GOP court blinding itself to the reality of modern gerrymandering. Then, abruptly reversing direction, they threw up their hands, disavowing any effective oversight on the legislature: "The judiciary serves as a check on the Legislature's actions only to the extent necessary to ensure the people's elected lawmakers comply with our constitution. . . . The constitution confers no power on the judiciary to enjoin or invalidate laws as a consequence for deficiencies in the implementation of internally-imposed legislative procedures."

Voters had nowhere to appeal but to the courts for relief from runaway lawmakers rewriting the rules of democracy to lock themselves in power. The GOP-controlled court then pretended there was nothing they could do and shifted the burden back to voters to throw the offending legislators out of office. This isn't originalism or federalism. Nor is it democracy. When a constitutional system of checks and balances has been hijacked to ensure that it does neither, but rather reinforces a self-perpetuating loop of one-party dominance and minority rule, that's an autocracy.

Wisconsin's GOP putsch immediately made itself felt in urgent questions of public policy. When Evers, acting with widespread popular support, demanded special sessions on gun violence, Covid voting protocols, and the status of an abortion ban from 1849 that went back into effect when the U.S. Supreme Court reversed *Roe v. Wade*, the legislature gaveled in and out in mere seconds. Soon, the state supreme court made it even more difficult for Evers to replace political appointees from the previous Republican administration. When the GOP legislature simply refused to confirm hundreds of the new governor's appointees, some of the former officials then refused to leave office, even after their term had expired. Without the confirmation of a replacement, the court ruled, along 4–3 partisan lines, the official could not be removed—even once his or her term was up.

Hintz noticed how the gerrymander changed the nature of the GOP caucus. All those uncompetitive districts meant the elections that mattered most in Wisconsin became GOP legislative primaries, sleepy and low-turnout races that favored the most extreme candidates. One by one, he notes, small-town "Waukesha Chamber of Commerce types" were replaced by representatives who embraced conspiracy theories and election denialism, and had otherwise gone "full QAnon."

Wisconsin's judiciary experienced a similar sudden transformation. Veteran judges watched with dismay, and then disbelief. Richard Niess spent two decades representing insurance companies in civil cases—"A very conservative side of the law," he says—and served on GOP governor Tommy Thompson's committee on judicial appointments before he was named to the Dane County circuit court bench himself in 2004.

Suddenly, constitutional questions that Niess and his colleagues had never seen over generations seemed to arrive one after the other. And when Niess scrupulously applied precedent, the text of the law, and its original intent to reach a careful decision, a disturbing pattern emerged. The decisions that went against Wisconsin conservatives were all overturned by a state supreme court that had swung decisively to the right. When Niess struck down the lame-duck session, he says, "I wrote a decision which is as strict constructionist, historical, and precedent-based as you can find, because I knew I would be pitching it to the supreme court and the prevailing world of strict construction. My decision was originalist. And boom, they went against it."

"Now that I'm off the bench [I] can speak freely," Niess tells me. "That's when I became quite concerned that this whole idea of strict construction, historical antecedent, all of that—it's largely a ruse to cover up pure, raw, political power."

The Wisconsin court had changed—in the same fashion that the U.S. Supreme Court had changed. One justice at a time, it had been remade by the Federalist Society in its own image. Lifetime institutionalists like

Niess weren't running the process any longer. Walker's judicial appointments were protégés of Michael Brennan, who founded the Federalist Society chapter in Milwaukee. Walker's two appointees, Rebecca Bradley and Daniel Kelly, both served as past presidents of the Milwaukee chapter. The Bradley appointment left Niess and others mystified, since membership in the Federalist Society seemed to be the sum total of her experience, both in Milwaukee and in law school—except for one year as a judge handling juvenile cases. The largest outside funder of Bradley's campaign, meanwhile, was an entity new to Wisconsin, called the Wisconsin Alliance for Reform. WAR spent $2.6 million to install Bradley on the state's high court for a full term. More than half of WAR's spending—$1.4 million—arrived in a single donation from the Leonard Leo–backed Judicial Crisis Network. The Republican State Leadership Committee (RSLC) stepped up with an advertising blitz on Bradley's behalf that pushed well into six figures.

By 2019, the price tag in state judicial elections soared dramatically. To place Brian Hagedorn, another Federalist Society member and former chapter president (and Walker's chief counsel) on the Wisconsin Supreme Court, different legs of the Leo octopus funneled some $5 million into his April election. The expenditures included well over a million dollars in advertising into tiny Wisconsin media markets over the final days of the race—spots that dominated the airwaves and drowned his middle-of-the-road opponent in an ocean of negative messaging.

The RSLC, which orchestrated the REDMAP strategy that flipped state legislatures like Wisconsin's and then gerrymandered them to ensure a decade of control, also played a major role in ensuring that state courts would be a bastion of GOP minority rule. The organization opened an internal shop called the Judicial Fairness Initiative focused on winning state supreme courts. The return on investment for state legislatures had proven incalculable for the big-money Right. Now it discovered that state supreme courts could be won just as cheaply, and it would be a crucial ally in fending off legal challenges to gerrymandered district maps and lending support to legislation passed by captured chambers.

All the usual major Leo-affiliated players swung into action. Leo's Judicial Crisis Network routed more than $3 million to the RSLC in 2018.

In 2019, two weeks before the Hagedorn election, it sent another $1 million. Immediately after that cash infusion arrived, according to RSLC documents, the group internally shifted $1.2 million over to the Judicial Fairness Initiative. Then, according to research by True North, the RSLC dropped another $1.2 million into Wisconsin over the last two weeks of the race, none of which had to be disclosed until the day of the election itself.

"It has turned into a very toxic stew," Niess says.

The legislature and the conservatives on the court then worked to undermine the 2020 election results in Wisconsin, which Biden carried by fewer than 21,000 votes. Trump's attorneys sought to disqualify more than 221,000 votes cast in the state's most heavily Democratic-leaning counties, particularly votes cast early and via absentee ballot. They lost at Wisconsin's state supreme court but it was frighteningly close, a 4–3 decision after one conservative justice sided with the liberals and ruled that Trump's challenge came too late. Nevertheless, three other justices ruled in Trump's favor, reviving fears of voter fraud that legislators first fueled without any evidence.

That didn't put the issue to rest. Vos, the assembly speaker, retained the former chief justice of the Wisconsin court, Michael Gableman, to lead an investigation into voter fraud in Wisconsin, even though there were no credible allegations of such fraud. Gableman, who had already called the election stolen, couldn't find any either—despite spending almost $700,000 in taxpayer money on his fruitless Keystone Kops quest.

Nevertheless, in March 2022 he issued a report calling for the decertification of the state's 2020 electoral votes. Never mind that this was legally impossible even in his former court; Gableman was just warming up—he also recommended that the state disband the bipartisan Wisconsin Elections Commission. In April 2023, meanwhile, groups with ties to Leo and billionaire conservative funder Richard Uihlein funneled millions toward the campaign of the former justice Daniel Kelly, who after leaving the court worked with Republicans on a scheme to direct Wisconsin's 2020 electoral votes to Donald Trump. He lost. But the threat has hardly receded.

"Speaker Vos made the same calculation that Republicans who backed Trump did," says Hintz, the former minority leader. "They went along with the crazy as long as it gave them power." The original lame-duck power grab, he says, was a grim indication of just how far the GOP was willing to go. "I think you lose your way when you start dismantling the infrastructure of our country. You realize how fragile democracy is," he says. "They are going to try to give themselves the power to administer the elections and overturn the results of an election if they don't like them."

So what happens in 2024 if Wisconsin, once again, tips the Electoral College balance? Would the Wisconsin legislature seek to overturn the election then?

"Yes," he said, then repeated it: "Yes. They are telling us what they are going to do. We should listen. We should be terrified."

STATE COURTS, STATE constitutions, and even large majorities of citizens provide little protection against determined minority rule. When a state legislature decides to go rogue—joined by the governor, secretary of state, and other elected officials willing to trash the oaths they swore to uphold the state constitution—even the most courageous state supreme court can be steamrolled, leaving voters defenseless.

"It is hard to recognize Ohio," former governor Bob Taft, a Republican who served from 1999 through 2007, tells me. "The consequences of extreme gerrymandering have been obvious here. The districts are skewed so much one way or the other that the primary election, when turnout is light, becomes more important than the general. The main constituency becomes the primary voter, when, in theory, representatives should serve everyone. Everyone is concerned about their right flank. No one wants to get out of line."

Ohio voters have grown frustrated with gerrymanders that turned a moderate Republican state into an extreme one—and disgusted with lawmakers so brazen and corrupt that the Ohio House speaker and the chairman of the state Republican Party were indicted (and ultimately convicted) in a $61 million bribery and racketeering case. So they've tried to reclaim their government with two sets of reforms. In 2015, upward of 71 percent of voters overwhelmingly approved an amendment to the state constitution to repair redistricting for the state legislature—a process that had been routinely captured and abused by partisans. They expanded the number of players involved in drawing new districts, created new criteria to encourage bipartisan consensus, and required the final maps to approximate the state's partisan balance, roughly 54 percent Republican and 46 percent Democratic. In 2018, voters extended those reforms to the state's congressional map, which had locked the state into an unproportional 12–4 GOP delegation. Both houses of the state legislature ratified the amendments.

Then, when redistricting arrived next, in 2021, state GOP lawmakers blew right past it, as if the state constitution wasn't there at all.

Maureen O'Connor, the state's former chief justice, a lifelong Republican and former lieutenant governor, is still staggered by the sheer lawlessness of the power grab. When a moderate and veteran institutionalist sounds a warning that likens the political order in a purple state to the putsches that created Nazi Germany, it behooves all of us to pay close attention.

"They had a supermajority. And the president of the senate made a comment and said, 'We can pretty much do whatever we want,'" O'Connor tells me. She's providing an all-too accurate paraphrase of the position advanced by Matt Huffman, the senate GOP leader who served on the commission. "When you couple what happened with the commission with that statement, it's so clear what gerrymandering can produce: this attitude that we've got the numbers, we can do whatever we want.

"They don't care," O'Connor marvels. "Those are the philosophies of dictatorships and not democracies."

O'Connor says now that she knew the fix was in when Republicans submitted their first maps in 2021 and awarded themselves more than 80 percent of the state legislative seats. Republicans claimed that this redistricting plan was actually in line with the state's partisan balance—a misreading of the relevant statute that's nothing short of perverse. Under the new GOP orthodoxy, it wasn't the 54–46 result in the most recent Ohio election cycle that mattered; it was that the GOP had captured thirteen of the sixteen last statewide races. So the new commission, dominated 5–2 by Republicans, miserably failed to come anywhere close to its mandate to bolster fair conditions of two-party competition.

The power grab worked splendidly to the Republicans' advantage.

The GOP ultimately secured itself a 63–36 edge in the state house and a 23–10 edge in the state senate. Governor Mike DeWine, a Republican, pronounced himself "very, very sorry," and conceded that the maps could have been "more clearly constitutional." Still, he endorsed the party-line vote to adopt the clearly unconstitutional maps. "More clearly constitutional," O'Connor snorts now. "It's constitutional, or it's not constitutional. It's like a little bit pregnant."

O'Connor and the state supreme court rejected the maps in a 4–3 vote, with the Republican chief justice joining three Democrats in finding them unconstitutional. (One of the three conservative votes in favor of the maps came from Justice Patrick DeWine, the governor's son, who chose not to recuse himself.) The court ordered the commission to try again. It would not be the last time. The commission then effectively ignored the court. That would not be the last time, either.

The GOP operated in defiance of the court not twice, not three times, but seven times—five times on the state legislative maps, and twice again on the congressional map. The same 4–3 majority told the commission again and again that it had failed to honor its responsibilities. And all seven times, the commission's GOP majority—including the governor, secretary of state, auditor, and two legislative leaders—barely budged. On several occasions, they refused to even meet at all.

Every time, they ignored the court's orders to follow the bipartisan process. Sometimes they resubmitted the same maps the court had already rejected. Another time they met in public but stalled until the court's deadline nearly expired. At that point the GOP leaders realized that they just happened to have a finished map that favored them all set—you know, just in case the process happened to break down. In the middle of all this flagrant disregard of the law, the legislature and state officials discussed impeaching O'Connor and removing her as chief justice for the grave sin of defying the party's will. One member of the commission, Secretary of State Frank LaRose, played to the GOP base by supporting O'Connor's impeachment even as he privately conceded the whole ploy was baseless and lawless. "I should vote no," he wrote in an email to his chief of staff, even calling GOP arguments "asinine." A cowed LaRose voted yes instead.

O'Connor, however, was not cowed—not by impeachment, not by seven tortuous rulings, not by the federal courts. She told the Associated Press that the lawmakers backing the gerrymandered maps should go back to fourth-grade civics and study the Constitution. Then, she added, "maybe, just maybe, review what it was like in Germany when Hitler intimidated the judiciary and passed those laws that allowed for the treatment of the Jewish population."

Ohio Republicans could get away with all this because an Ohio pro-life group found two federal judges—both Trump appointees, both Federalist Society members and on Leonard Leo's approved list of nominees—to deliver a curious ruling that allowed the GOP to run out the clock and have their way. As the Ohio GOP stonewalled the state supreme court and refused to draw constitutional maps, the right-to-life group was pursuing parallel litigation to uphold the gerrymanders in federal court before the Federalist Society judges. The plaintiffs insisted that with primaries approaching, *something* had to be finalized so elections could proceed.

Of course, they were crying wolf—no map had been finalized because Republicans had stiff-armed the state supreme court—but the conservative judges gave the old fable a different ending. Via a 2–1 vote, a three-judge panel imposed a late May 2022 deadline for the sides to agree—or else, they said, they would be forced to impose the latest GOP map for the 2022 elections. If voters disagreed, the court wrote, apparently with a straight face, they would need to deliver their verdict on Election Day—on maps a state court repeatedly found unconstitutional, but the FedSoc federal judges forced on the state anyway. "We must presume state actors will work together to reach homegrown solutions," the majority wrote. "And if they fail, then it is up to the voters to punish them if they so choose."

The dissent got it right: in making this decision, Algenon L. Marbley wrote, "the majority tables a watershed constitutional referendum, abrogates controlling decisions of the state Supreme Court, and unwittingly rewards the Commission's brinkmanship over the rights of Ohio voters." Indeed, with zero incentive to act, the GOP commissioners never even bothered trying to craft a fifth plan that the state supreme court might find constitutional. Now they knew that all they needed to do was wait a month, and the federal court's decision would deliver the maps they wanted right into their laps. It was an open invitation to gerrymander, and the commission happily accepted.

The GOP majority leader in the state house, Bill Seitz, celebrated on Twitter. "Too bad so sad. We win again," he wrote. "Now I know it's been a tough night for all you libs. Pour yourself a glass of warm milk and you will sleep better. The game is over and you lost. . . . Turn out the light. The party's over."

A bitterly frustrated O'Connor, the Republican chief justice, knew that this was not a party worth attending. The federal court, she said, reassured state GOP leaders that their delays and inactions would be rewarded and "engaged in a stunning rebuke of the rule of law." Speaking to me, she still sounded furious. Members of the federal judiciary, she says, still reach out to her and apologize for a decision that she says none of them can comprehend or justify. "Where do you think the incentive was to come up with a constitutional map? None. They knew they had it in the bag. They knew they could run out the clock and get the maps they wanted. So that's what they did. And then the election of 2022 for both Congress and our General Assembly were run on gerrymandered, unconstitutional maps."

Unsurprisingly, those maps handed the GOP supermajorities. All the seats the Republicans claimed were competitive toss-ups were won—again unsurprisingly—by the GOP. Republicans captured just over 57 percent of the statewide legislative vote. But they won 68 percent of the state house seats and 79 percent of the state senate.

"This was the plan all along," O'Connor says. "They were counting on the Sixth Circuit and then the ability to take it to the U.S. Supreme Court. It isn't the way it's supposed to be. And, you know, we soundly criticize elections that happen in Russia or other countries. They have elections. But they're not meaningful elections. There's no choice. Are we far from that?"

CHAPTER TWENTY-THREE

HERE IN AMARILLO, Texas, just minutes from the Palo Duro Canyon where Indiana Jones's *Last Crusade* ends with a sip from the cup Jesus drank from during the Last Supper, the conservative and religious Right's quest for its own Holy Grail continues unabated. One headquarters is a law office on the ninth floor of the sleek, triangular Amarillo National Bank towers that arise above Amarillo's otherwise dusty, historic downtown. Take the elevator next to Ebby's Edibles & Getables up to the Morgan Williamson firm, and that's where Leah Davis works as an attorney. Her office, in turn, doubles as the national headquarters for something called the Alliance for Hippocratic Medicine—a coalition of antiabortion religious organizations whose mailing address is 1,230 miles away in Bristol, Tennessee.

So why, on August 5, 2022, barely six weeks after the *Dobbs* decision overturned *Roe v. Wade*, did Davis register her law office as the street address for an organization that gets its mail an eighteen-hour drive east? That has everything to do with a judge named Matthew J. Kacsmaryk, who sits on the U.S. District Court for the Northern District of Texas. When the Alliance for Hippocratic Medicine decided to sue the Food and Drug Administration over its approval of the abortion-inducing drug mifepristone, the group looked to file before the friendliest judge possible. Kacsmaryk is the only federal judge in Amarillo. So if you file a case here, there is a near-perfect chance that it will come before him. Appeals go straight to the Trumpiest court in America, the Fifth Circuit, sometimes called the "blown fuse of American jurisprudence," and from there they can quickly end up before the U.S. Supreme Court.

Call it the Kacsmaryk-Fifth Circuit conservative raceway, where the finish line is the conservative supermajority at SCOTUS. The antidemocratic horrors unleashed by circuit courts stocked by Donald Trump with Federalist Society acolytes represent one of the greatest growing dangers to free and fair elections, and a frightfully successful effort to give conservative courts such unfettered power as to render elections and local control meaningless, even in blue cities and blue states. This is why the Alliance for Hippocratic Medicine established an outpost in Amarillo: it represented the quickest, surest path to getting a ban on the abortion pill mifepristone before the high court. Kacsmaryk delivered it in April 2022, the very week the Black Tennessee Democrats were expelled from the legislature.

The Kacsmaryk raceway had become well-traveled for conservative activists. When Texas sued over the Biden administration's immigration policy, Kacsmaryk reinstated Donald Trump's "Remain in Mexico" procedures. When Biden looked to extend workplace protections to the LBGTQ community, Kacsmaryk blocked them, as well as federal Title X protections that had helped teens obtain birth control without parental permission.

Kacsmaryk's religious and political beliefs are well known to all; they're the reason why he was placed on the federal bench in the first place. Kacsmaryk cofounded the Federalist Society's chapter in Fort Worth. He has spoken at a dozen Federalist Society events. And before Trump appointed him as a federal judge, working from a list of Leo-approved nominees and Federalist Society members, Kacsmaryk worked as an attorney at a Texas-based religious nonprofit legal group called First Liberty. (According to research conducted for Senator Sheldon Whitehouse and the Senate Judiciary Committee, nearly 90 percent of Trump's appellate court picks were members of the Federalist Society.)

First Liberty is an associate member of the State Policy Network—a well-funded group of coordinated right-wing organizations that advance deeply conservative policy outcomes in state legislatures and courts. It receives much of its eight-figure annual budget through DonorsTrust and other big-ticket conservative foundations. First Liberty then funnels some of its money back to a private corporation held by Leonard Leo. Immediately after Trump nominated Kacsmaryk to the federal bench in 2017, documents from the IRS and other agencies showed that First Liberty had recently begun the first of several six-figure payments to Leo's CRC

Advisors. In both 2018 and 2019, as *Jezebel* and the *Washington Post* have reported, First Liberty paid CRC just under $140,000 a year.

First Liberty, in turn, shares its president and CEO with the Council for National Policy (CNP), a deeply secretive and influential hub for conservative activists founded in 1981 by Morton Blackwell, Richard Viguerie, and Phyllis Schlafly. The CNP now serves as a critical clearinghouse for Leonard Leo, Ginni Thomas, and others on the right who have raised billions in their efforts to remake the federal judiciary in their image. Kelly Shackelford, the First Liberty leader, who is also the chairman of CNP Action and a vice president of CNP, set out the whole pay-to-play arrangement in a behind-closed-doors speech in 2020 captured by the *Washington Post*. "Some of us literally opened a whole operation on judicial nominations and vetting," he said. "We poured millions of dollars into this to make sure the president has good information, he picks the best judges."

That's how Amarillo suddenly became known less for its proximity to the end of *The Last Crusade* than for its role in launching the next one: a red-state mission to move the entire nation to the right with the help of GOP and Federalist Society judges on the federal bench. It doesn't always work; sometimes the Fifth Circuit goes too far even for the conservative high court. In many ways, these federal circuit courts have moved so hard to the right, and so quickly, that the U.S. Supreme Court has struggled to keep control. (And if the court's conservative majority does sometimes slap down the out-of-control courts, they win media praise for reasonableness.) Circuit courts have forced the issue on abortion, voting rights, and the regulatory state. These decisions matter everywhere: a radical ruling from a circuit court in Texas on reproductive rights, for example, can pause the accessibility of abortion pills in blue states where they had been perfectly legal.

This is what happens when the fallout from *Citizens United* and *Shelby County* moves into blue states and blue cities, expanding the power of the extreme Right and allowing it to reach nearly everywhere, all based on control of the courts. The lead strategists in this holy struggle are also investing hundreds of millions to place conservatives on state supreme courts and support gerrymandered state legislatures. This state-driven campaign serves as a critical bulwark for the legal Right's national objectives: it's all arranged to ratify and uphold preemption laws that prevent blue cities in red states from passing their own laws on guns, education, voting rights, electoral reforms such as ranked choice voting, and the minimum wage. Much of this preemption, such as efforts by Florida and Arizona to ban ranked choice voting anywhere in the state, likely would not have been possible prior to *Shelby County* ending preclearance. The New Preemption has been made possible, in part, by the Right's smothering of the Old Preclearance.

KACSMARYK MIGHT BE the best-known exponent of the movement we might call the New Preemption, but he's hardly an outlier.

Preemption works in two basic ways. Preempt *up* and you create the infrastructure in which red states, conservative attorneys general, and friendly judges can conspire to block federal action or change federal law. The *Dobbs* decision, for example, grew from a challenge to Mississippi's fifteen-week abortion ban that the state attorney general transformed into a vehicle for the conservative high court to take down *Roe v. Wade* nationwide.

The second method is to preempt *down*. This makes it possible for red state legislatures to block policies enacted by blue cities—or even laws that red legislatures think blue cities might someday pass. That explains why liberal Austin, Ann Arbor, Columbus, Chapel Hill, Nashville, Philadelphia, St. Louis, and Madison, among others, cannot raise their local minimum wage. It's also the reason why Detroit, Cleveland, and Atlanta can't mandate paid leave or fair scheduling laws. Gerrymandered legislatures have simply forbidden such actions.

The New Preemption makes the key right-wing tactics of gerrymandering and court capture worse; it multiplies one dangerous thing by another in order to enmesh a massively larger population subject to minority rule. Taken together, the Old Suppression and the New Preemption add up to an audacious play to seize the political agenda everywhere and change the rules under which all Americans must live. It's working. And there's no easy way to stop it.

During the Trump administration, conservatives confirmed 226 judges to the federal bench during just one term—a pace that dwarfs what Obama,

Bush, and Clinton each managed to achieve in two. Just as important, Trump named 54 federal appellate judges to lifetime appointments. That's just one fewer than the number Obama appointed over eight years. Those judges tipped three of the nation's thirteen appellate courts—which operate just one rung below the Supreme Court—from liberal to conservative. Meanwhile, Leo and his allied groups spent tens of millions in dark money, funneled through local foundations and nonprofits, electing Federalist Society acolytes to seats on state supreme courts in Ohio, Wisconsin, North Carolina, Michigan, and many other states. Those judges would rule on any litigation involving redistricting and gerrymandering, and well understood just what sort of decisions they'd be expected to deliver. They can be counted on to entrench extreme lawmakers from whiter, rural districts that don't look like the population centers of most states in their ideological mission to impose their social and cultural values on disenfranchised majorities.

"State legislatures enjoy near-absolute power to reconfigure local governments, at least so far as federal law is concerned," writes Nicholas Goldrosen in the *University of Illinois Law Review.* "Local municipalities enjoy no sovereignty of their own but are subsidiaries of the state, which the state can create, regulate, and destroy as it pleases."

DESTROY AS IT *pleases.* Sometimes the legislators who passed a given preemption law are engaged in culture war chest-beating and hoping to catch the attention of a Fox News prime-time panel. That was the case, for example, when a clutch of red state legislatures prohibited communities concerned about the environment from banning plastic bags. Other times, they're undertaking a bald racist power grab.

That's the clear upshot of the measures that rural red-state GOP lawmakers passed to choke off power and authority from multiracial cities. In Tennessee, for example, 93 percent of the state might be rural, but two-thirds of the state's 6.5 million people live in cities. Nevertheless, the white, conservative supermajorities in the state legislature have conducted a coordinated power play against Tennessee's major cities, stripping their councils of half their seats, gutting their police oversight commissions, reining in local prosecutors, then expelling Black members from Nashville and Memphis on the flimsiest grounds.

The clear racial implications of such actions should automatically trigger the intervention of the federal government, as the Voting Rights Act mandates. After all, preemption and the expulsion tactics in Tennessee are simply the latest innovations in a long line of discriminatory tactics designed to erode Black political power.

But the U.S. Supreme Court put an end to any expansive reading of the VRA in a little-known 1992 decision, *Presley v. Etowah County Commission*. It's well worth revisiting this ruling in detail because it effectively blessed so much of the behavior state legislatures get away with today. It gets to the heart of the most crucial question in our democracy today: Is it enough to have the right to vote, or must that vote be meaningful? In other words, is the right to vote purely symbolic, or can lawmakers and judges sever it from the substantive exercise of political power? The court's cramped decision in *Presley*, written by Justice Kennedy, tragically endorsed the latter position.

The *Presley* case went back to 1986, when two similar things happened in Alabama's Etowah and Russell Counties. Each county entered into consent decrees with the Department of Justice and replaced at-large elections that had produced all-white county commissions for as long as anyone could remember with district elections. That fall, voters in both counties elected the first Black members of those commissions in modern times. Etowah added two new districts and agreed that the new commissioners would share "all the rights, privileges and duties" of the others. That did not last long.

Mere months after the election of the first Black member, Lawrence Presley, the Etowah County Commission made a major change to its most important power: allocating funds for road construction and other maintenance. Before Presley's arrival, each commissioner controlled the budget, the road crew, the shop, and the equipment in his area. The new rules kept that power with the same white incumbents, while also shifting countywide spending to a majority vote of the full commission. Presley would still be permitted to serve—he just wouldn't be able to spend any money on projects in his district.

Black voters had a seat on the commission. But by changing the rules, the white majority ensured they wouldn't have influence. Essentially, they found a way to add the districts while keeping the old at-large system in place when it came to the actual exercise of power. Russell County made a similar move with the same effect, shifting budgetary power away from the commission to a single veteran white official.

In his majority opinion, Kennedy appeared unconcerned by the coincidence of these changes taking place so quickly after the first Black members joined the commissions. He insisted that the reconfigured governments in each county had no "direct relation to voting itself," and "affected only the allocation of power among governmental officials." Neither change, Kennedy ruled, required a new voting qualification, standard, practice, or procedure. It was not a grandfather clause, a poll tax, or a literacy test, in other words, so under Kennedy's understanding of the text and purpose of the VRA, there was nothing to see here.

Instead, the justice asserted that the changes wrought in both county governments were just an example of how "constant minor adjustments in the allocation of power among state and local officials" allow federalism to operate "as a practical system of government and not a mere poetic ideal."

Justice Stevens, in his dissent, suggested a commonsense compromise that Kennedy refused. Stevens argued that the courts or the Justice Department should examine any reallocation of powers that followed the election of a Black candidate after a new consent decree went into effect. Otherwise, he wrote, "The lesson is clear for jurisdictions that want to limit minority influence: If you cannot dilute the votes of black citizens themselves, you can simply dilute the vote of the representative they elect."

State legislatures would quickly master the maneuver Stevens described— not in the service of any "poetic ideal" of American federalism, but in the service of the familiar mandate to secure maximum protection of political power for GOP officials.

IN EARLY FALL 2022, Jaylen Lewis, twenty-five, and his girlfriend went for a drive on a Saturday evening in Jackson, Mississippi. But as Lewis and his date, both Black, approached the funky cultural district of largely white

Fondren—four blocks of creative barbecue, Prohibition-era cocktails, and wood-fired Biloxi snapper served with garlic chile sauce—he worried that an unmarked car might be following them. Sure enough, at the next red light, a man emerged from the car behind Lewis and approached the driver's-side window. He was a Capitol Police officer, though the state Capitol was some three miles to the south. Lewis reached for his phone to shoot a video but as he turned to look at the man, all he viewed outside his car window was a gun pointed at his head. The officer fired. And just after 9 P.M., the young man died in his car while his girlfriend howled in disbelief and despair. It was the fourth shooting by the Capitol Police in less than five months.

Jackson has the largest proportion of Black residents in the nation, at 83 percent. Yet it is also a city within a city. In much of Jackson, you cannot drink the water—and the state, over decades, has failed to fund infrastructure repair necessary to keep basic necessities of life such as water and power widely available and safe. Drive just a couple blocks away, however, and you might enjoy the $59 cowboy rib eye with maître d' butter in the wood-paneled southern sanctuary of Char's. If you're especially flush, you can purchase a $1.2 million Fondren home in a gated private hideaway with wrought-iron railings, spiral staircases, and French doors overlooking the patio and swimming pool.

To secure these disparities for the white minority, Mississippi's gerrymandered state legislature voted in 2022 and 2023 to erect new political walls around the city's white neighborhoods. The move drains resources away from the rest of Jackson and creates a separate and unequal enclave with its own police and judicial system, all while expanding the jurisdiction of the aggressive Capitol Police further throughout the city. "It reminds me of apartheid," said Jackson's mayor, Chokwe Antar Lumumba, as he watched the House vote to approve the new system. "They are looking to colonize Jackson, not only in terms of them putting their military force over Jackson, but also dictating who has province over decision-making."

Every other county court system in the state is elected by local citizens or appointed by local officials. Judges and other officials in the Capitol Complex Improvement District court will be appointed by the state's conservative, white chief justice. And the Capitol Police—whose job had largely entailed protecting state buildings, providing security for lawmakers, and running the metal detectors at entrances—now patrol a growing stretch of the city.

That's a dramatic change in responsibilities, so perhaps those four shootings between July and September 2022—the most anywhere in Mississippi—could have been foreseen. But the Capitol Police's lethal track record in its new role has done nothing to dampen the legislature's enthusiasm for creating what is essentially a second police department and justice system in Jackson. This system is not accountable to the majority-Black council or the people, but rather to state officials. And those officials are already making plans to increase the Capitol Force to 170 officers and expand its ability to patrol citywide. That would create a police department nearly the size of Jackson's current force—but one that will be in no way answerable to any elected local leadership.

"That terrifies me. It also angers me," said Arkela Lewis, Jaylen's mom.

It's not only Tennessee and Mississippi where gerrymandered, one-party legislatures have moved to take away local control and oversight over police departments in blue and often majority-Black cities. When "defund the police" became a slogan on the left after the killing of George Floyd by Minneapolis police, state legislatures in gerrymandered Florida, Georgia, and Texas passed laws that prohibited localities from cutting police budgets. Meanwhile Missouri's legislature—which citizens tried to release from lopsided GOP gerrymanders via a statewide initiative in 2018, only to have lawmakers reimpose partisan districting—advanced a bill to take over the St. Louis Police Department in 2023, which passed the House along partisan, and largely racial, lines.

Nor are red-state legislatures only preempting policing power in blue cities. As cities have elected progressive prosecutors with criminal-justice reform agendas, state legislatures have looked to remove them from office or cut them off at the knees. Seventeen states have introduced thirty-seven bills since 2017 that would allow conservative legislatures to usurp the powers of democratically elected prosecutors in blue cities.

The alarming trend line is clear. In Texas, for example, the legislature has looked to limit the long-standing discretion of district and county attorneys to decide which cases to bring and proposed handing the power to prosecute cases involving abortion access and other culture-war crusades to any prosecutor in the state—or to the state attorney general—if a local official declined to prosecute. Georgia's state legislature established an oversight board, governed by state officials, that can recommend the ouster of county prosecutors they disfavor. Similar measures have been introduced or passed, in rigged legislatures in Georgia, Florida, Ohio, Pennsylvania, Tennessee, and Indiana. There is little that Philadelphia, Austin, or Nashville can do in response.

Such is life under the one-party oligarchy that imposes its will on cities unlucky enough to find themselves in red states. For anyone following the high court's assault on self-government, it was an outcome long foreseen by *Shelby County*, the removal of preclearance, and the next wave of uncontrolled gerrymandering that created a new generation of power-mad state legislatures across the country.

BACK IN AMARILLO, meanwhile, Texas attorney general Ken Paxton continues wearing a path to Judge Kacsmaryk's chambers. During the first two years of the Biden administration, Paxton filed twenty-six lawsuits seeking to roll back the Democratic administration's top priorities on immigration, federal regulation, abortion, Covid mandates, student loan relief, and much more. He filed seven of those lawsuits before Kacsmaryk, and another seven in Victoria, before another ideological ally and Federalist Society member, Drew Tipton. Others went to Wichita Falls and still another hard-Right federal jurist, Reed O'Connor.

Like the abortion challenges mounted by the Alliance for Hippocratic Medicine, none of these cases had any compelling reason to be filed in these jurisdictions. Indeed, a Paxton case challenging the Labor Department over pension trusts has no actual tie to Amarillo at all. But Paxton has worked the loophole to get his signature legal challenges before the judges he wants. It's an easy call, since the Federalist Society turnstile has put them on the bench for this very reason.

Paxton's challenges are joined by other red state prosecutors recruited as field marshals in the right-wing putsch for legal power—fellow members of the Republican Attorneys General Association (RAGA). RAGA is still another organization funded by the great impresario of the conservative takeover of the bench, Leonard Leo. The Concord Fund and Judicial Crisis Network, both groups controlled by Leo's various entities, are the leading donors to RAGA. That trend continued during the first half of 2023 as action on abortion, voting, public education, and so many hot-button issues raged in state legislatures and state courts. The Concord Fund donated $1 million to RAGA during the first six months of 2023, nearly four times the second-leading donor, according to research by the Center for Media and Democracy. That lifted Concord's overall giving to RAGA up to $16.8 million since 2014. RAGA, in turn, sends $7,500 a month in consulting fees back to CRC Advisors, as it has since 2020.

THUS STATE LEGAL officials on the right can thwart a Democratic president's priorities by procuring funding for extreme challenges and placing them before judges that Leo's network nurtured and promoted. State legislatures, often with the help of the same judges and the same network of funders, have pushed social policies far to the right on reproductive rights, how history is taught in public schools, and other galvanizing culture-war issues on the right. These measures are all opposed by large majorities in those states, but the Leo-financed court machinery charged with notional oversight of the legislatures has ensured that such opposition simply doesn't matter.

The Last Crusade ends with a realization: Indiana Jones drops the Holy Grail that he has been chasing, knowing that his obsession will lead to certain death. "Let it go," instructs his father, who spent a lifetime seeking the chalice himself. Today's legal Right would deride the Joneses as weak-kneed liberals; they know that the whole point of a holy crusade is to lock up all the raw power you can.

CHAPTER TWENTY-FOUR

IN A TINY, tasteful kitchen in San Luis, Arizona, Guillermina Fuentes prepares lunch, much like any other Latina grandmother. There's homemade guacamole and her dazzling orange hot sauce, ready to cover plates of burritos and pupusas—fried pancakes made from cabbage and onion. There's only one clue that Fuentes has become the face of voter fraud in America: a high-tech security center mounted above the refrigerator showing views from four different outdoor cameras.

The lifelong community organizer and first female mayor of this remote border town in Arizona's farthest southwest corner never needed home security before. Now she routinely monitors any activity outside her house for one simple reason: a hazy snatch of video footage of her made a brief appearance in conservative muckraker Dinesh D'Souza's widely debunked film *2000 Mules*. D'Souza's movie is nonetheless an urtext among the die-hard adherents of the election-denying "Stop the Steal" movement that alleges Joe Biden wrested the presidency from Donald Trump in 2020 thanks to widespread voter fraud.

The footage that upended Fuentes's life shows nothing remotely like voter fraud. It's simply a shot of someone handing four mail-in ballots to Fuentes as the former mayor worked a voter information table outside the Cesar Chavez Cultural Center in the days before Arizona's August primary. That's right: it's not even related to the presidential balloting in November, but that makes no difference to the fan base for *2000 Mules*. Nor does it matter to the videographer who filmed the handoff—Gary Snyder, a local conservative gadfly who'd battled with her for years.

San Luis is a farming community, nestled in the region where most of the lettuce Americans eat all winter is grown. Fields of organic romaine, green leaf, red leaf, and iceberg stretch toward the horizon, along with acre after acre of broccoli, cauliflower, spinach, and kale. Most people here walk with the hunch farmworkers get after they've spent years doing the back-breaking work of planting, tending, and harvesting these fields under an unforgiving western sun. In 1993, Cesar Chavez died here while fighting for farmworkers' rights against agribusiness giants in an Arizona court-room.

But the steady demand for farmwork has attracted laborers for genera-tions. Between 1990 and 2000, San Luis—not thriving Phoenix or a retiree hotbed like Scottsdale—grew faster than any city in Arizona, save one. Just over 4,200 people lived here in 1990; that exploded to 37,333 by 2021. Those numbers swell every morning as day laborers arrive from Mexico. Cross the pedestrian bridge from Mexico today and you're greeted by dozens of parking lots filled with school buses with attached port-a-potties that whisk arriving day laborers from the border to the fields.

When Fuentes, the second of twelve children, arrived in San Luis from San Luis Rio Colorado, Sonora, with her family at sixteen, she alternated high school with days in the lettuce fields. It might have been a distance of only a few miles, but it felt like another world. She spoke such poor English that school, such a comfort in Mexico, felt impossible, while fieldwork seemed familiar and known. It was only in her twenties, with two children to support on her own, that she sought a different life. She mastered En-glish, earned a degree at night school, and finally achieved citizenship. She began to volunteer at the San Luis community center, helping residents who also struggle with English with legal services, unemployment insur-ance, and food stamp applications. In a small and tight-knit community, Fuentes became someone everyone trusted and depended upon for help that the government seemed unwilling to provide.

After all these years of community service, including helping new cit-izens negotiate the challenge of voting for the first time, Fuentes seemed like a natural person for locals to ask for help with a mail-in ballot during the pandemic. Arizona was already conducting most of its voting by mail. San Luis, however, is one of the many rural Arizona communities that does not have mail service at home. Instead, there's a single post office, on the edge of town in view of the border, filled with row after row of post office boxes, 16,350 to be exact.

Without mail service or public transportation, in a poor community with many non–English speakers, senior citizens, and families without cars, voting by mail in San Luis is anything but simple. Many residents are hard-pressed to contend with the process's multiple forms, mail-in envelopes, and mandated signatures.

Those challenges multiplied after Arizona's legislature, newly empowered to enact changes to election laws after *Shelby County* freed it from preclearance, passed new restrictions on Arizona's long—and entirely fraud-free—tradition of third-party ballot collection. Then, in 2021, in *Brnovich v. DNC*, the Supreme Court allowed these onerous restrictions to stand, despite abundant evidence that they were passed with racial intent and had the clear effect of hindering minority voters. The *Brnovich* majority went further still—narrowing Section 2 of the VRA and rewriting its text in ways diametrically opposed to congressional intent.

Then, one August morning, in broad daylight outside the Cesar Chavez Cultural Center, four neighbors handed Fuentes their ballots. She checked them over and helped one voter add a missing address. The quartet of voters then insisted she drop them at the post office for them. As Snyder's video camera captured jittery footage from the parking lot, Fuentes accepted the ballots and agreed. In the eyes of Arizona law, Fuentes had become a "ballot harvester." And in an exchange that lasted no more than forty-five seconds, the U.S. Supreme Court helped turn a border-town grandmother into a felon.

THE VOTING RIGHTS Act was of course intended to police the laws passed by state legislatures like Arizona's, not to imprison senior citizens working to ensure equal access to the ballot box. Yet the Supreme Court's decision in *Brnovich* all but strips it of that purpose. As Justice Elena Kagan wrote in her passionate dissent, it "mostly inhabits a law-free zone."

Congress and previous courts long ago recognized that one of the Voting Rights Act's key functions would be to shield minority voters from new voting rules that appear neutral on paper but discriminate in practice. As long as politicians have worked to tinker with election laws and procedures, they've dressed up racial discriminatory policies in the flexible mandate of fraud prevention. Officials once claimed that the poll tax "preserved the purity of the ballot box" and "facilitated honest elections." *Old poison in new bottles*, Justice David Souter called this in a 2000 voting rights case.

Even practices we take for granted today, such as voting ourselves, alone and in private with a secret ballot, initially abridged the franchise for poor Black and white citizens who could not read a ballot on their own. The secret ballot was an Australian innovation that didn't gain wide usage in America until the 1890s, just as many southern constitutions looked for race-neutral end arounds to skirt the Reconstruction amendments. It could often be difficult to tell whether the new processes protected election integrity or looked to suppress votes—though at other times, it was dismayingly easy. One 1892 song from Arkansas, for instance, proudly proclaimed that "The Arkansas Ballot works like a charm / It makes them think and scratch / And when a Negro gets a ballot / He has certainly got his match." Historians now report that the introduction of the Australian-style secret ballot led to a drop in white participation between 8 and 28 percent across the South—and a decline among Black voters from between 15 to 45 percent.

These days, of course, lawmakers have only gotten better at creating ostensibly race-neutral pretexts for voter suppression, and they rarely confess their racial intent by bursting into song. That's why Congress amended the VRA in 1982, over John Roberts's plentiful objections, to instruct courts to focus on the consequences of a law—its effects—rather than the legislature's claimed motivation or intent. The new Section 2 made it clear when a state or locality was in violation. The key test was whether, based on the "totality of circumstances," access to the ballot box was "not equally open" to all, and if members of a minority group had "less opportunity" to participate. If Blacks, Latinos, Native Americans, and other racial minorities had equal access and equal opportunity but turned out at different percentages, that's fine. But when laws create conditions that disadvantage one group over another—if it's harder, say, for Latinos or Native Americans to vote than others—that's when Section 2 goes to work.

Consider the two Arizona laws the U.S. Supreme Court upheld in *Brnovich*, after a federal appeals court struck them down as unconstitutional. One, the ballot collection ban, makes voting much harder for rural Latinos like those in San Luis, who lack home mail service, as well as Native Americans, who are more likely to lack vehicles *and* might have to travel hours to the nearest post office. The other, a policy that throws out any ballot cast accidentally in the wrong precinct, disenfranchises Black and Latino voters who are nearly twice as likely to cast such ballots as whites, in part because Arizona closes and relocates precincts serving minority communities with startling regularity, sometimes more than once a year.

Perhaps no state in America has closer elections: the court's ruling in *Brnovich* came just seven months after an election in which a mere 10,457 votes—0.3 percent—separated Joe Biden and Donald Trump in Arizona, and Republicans held both houses of the state legislature by the narrowest possible margin: 16–14 in the senate and 31–29 in the house. A handful of votes could tip a chamber, or even the presidency. So any new regulations that affect thousands of votes can change the outcomes of races. If you were looking to skim a few thousand votes here and another few thousand there, a ban on third-party ballot collection and a practice of discarding out-of-precinct ballots would be weapons you'd want in your arsenal. According to the text of Section 2 as passed by Congress and signed by the president, both would be textbook violations of the Voting Rights Act. And yet, as Kagan wrote in her *Brnovich* dissent, "the majority reaches the opposite conclusion because it closes its eyes to the facts on the ground."

And in Arizona, where lawmakers played the age-old game of claiming they were protecting election integrity while systematically making it more difficult for minority voters to cast ballots, the facts on the ground are straightforward and difficult to deny.

"It's a shame," Fuentes tells me, "because we're going back to those years when minorities weren't supposed to speak up, when minorities weren't supposed to vote."

In Arizona, those years didn't end until the passage of the Voting Rights Act and the extension of preclearance statewide. Even then, the state battled to make it harder—or even impossible—for its large minority communities to participate in elections. For decades, they did so in open defiance of the law. When Congress finally extended the vote to Native Americans with the Indian Citizenship Act of 1924, Arizona and others responded with new poll taxes, literacy tests, and intimidation tactics designed to prevent the Native vote—more than 14 percent of the statewide population, and a majority in many major counties—from counting at all. The literacy tests kept Latinos and Blacks from voting as well.

Rural schools, as well as schools on tribal land, were severely under-resourced; upward of 80 to 90 percent of Native Americans, for example, could not read in 1948. So a test that required anyone who wanted to vote to read the U.S. Constitution aloud proved remarkably successful at keeping minorities from the polls. When Congress reaffirmed Native American voting rights with legislation in 1940, Arizona responded by tightening its literacy test—and otherwise ensuring that Native Americans and other minorities might have the franchise on paper, but not in reality. Even when Native Americans on tribal land in Arizona returned after fighting in World War 2, the state fought them all the way to the U.S. Supreme Court when they sued for the right to vote at home after protecting freedom abroad. Arizona lost, but continued to use the literacy test until Congress banned it in 1970—and after Arizona's appeal to continue using it failed at the Supreme Court in 1972.

Those efforts faded but never ended; Arizona fielded twenty-two DOJ preclearance objections under Section 5, including for statewide redistricting plans in the 1980s, 1990s, and 2000s that limited minority voting power. Nearly half of Arizona's counties received objections from DOJ for local changes, as well. In 2006, the Department of Justice reported instances of harassment and voter intimidation by polling officials against members of the Navajo Nation. On tribal land statewide, local county recorders impermissibly purged voters because of the county's own confusion around address issues, or assigned Native American voters to the wrong precinct, and then rejected the provisional ballots cast by those voters. In 2012, Apache, Navajo, and Coconino Counties experienced the highest rate of rejected provisional ballots for all counties in the state of Arizona. In 2012, officials in Maricopa County repeatedly mistranslated materials for Spanish-language voters, even incorrectly listing Election

Day as November 8, and not November 6, on two different sets of voter outreach forms. The mistake did not occur on the English-only versions.

Then, in 2016, Maricopa County, home to 60 percent of Arizona's voters, reduced the number of polling places by more than 70 percent. The new closures forced Latino and Black voters, on average, to travel more than twice the distance to vote than white voters did. The impact of the poll closures fell deepest on minority communities—and the new voting locations, often placed on precinct boundaries, proved confusing. They often re-precincted minority voters not to the polling places closest to their homes, but to ones much farther away. Tough new restrictions on out-of-precinct voting then meant voters who cast a ballot in the wrong precinct, often through no fault of their own, had their ballots discarded entirely. This burden also fell hardest on minority communities.

Arizona's Republican-led state legislature never identified any actual fraud as lawmakers worked to pass one new restriction after another. Sometimes, foreshadowing arguments that would be heard in state legislatures nationwide after the 2020 election, they claimed that these laws were necessary to protect election integrity from nebulous doubts and fears about fraud. But in the case of third-party ballot collection, there was no proof of a single case of fraud or abuse throughout its long history in Arizona. "I used to be a role model for people who wanted to participate. Now I am a ballot harvester," Fuentes says, practically spitting out the words. "Now those people saw me go to jail and they're afraid. They're afraid to go to the polls, afraid to vote by mail, and that's what they're trying to do. They intimidate us openly."

BALLOT HARVESTING. 2000 *Mules.* It's no accident that those looking to criminalize these methods of making it easier to vote in Arizona's heavily Latino rural areas, or vast Native American reservations with only a handful of post offices scattered across land larger than some eastern states, use the language of drug-running and organ theft. But proponents of these laws have to make the practices sound scary because they've been unable to prove any instance of actual fraud. Fuentes served thirty days in prison for her actions, locked into a dark cell with a single threadbare blanket, even though a subsequent investigation that included a rigorous handwriting analysis of the four ballots she returned proved that each of them was filled out and signed by the legal citizen to whom the ballot belonged. Tracey Kay McKee, meanwhile, a sixty-four-year-old white woman from Scottsdale, received probation and no jail time for casting her dead mother's mail-in ballot for Donald Trump in 2020.

Arizona Republicans spent five years and multiple legislative sessions passing several versions of bills cracking down on third-party ballot delivery. What they couldn't do over that time is document a single case of actual fraud. The effort began with a state senator from Yuma named Don Shooter, a Republican whose district included San Luis. A district court quickly identified his motivation: a desire to eliminate an effective get-out-the-vote campaign in San Luis and other Latino communities that resulted in Shooter winning his seat by a closer-than-expected margin. His victory, with 53 percent of the vote, came with 83 percent of the white vote and just 20 percent from Latinos.

The Department of Justice recognized the intent and potential effect of Arizona's third-party restrictions as well. The ban on third-party collection was part of a wider package of election reforms; when the new laws were submitted for preclearance, the DOJ allowed them all, with the ballot-collection measure as the sole exception. Officials asked for more information about how the new ballot-collection rules might affect minority communities. It didn't help the state's case that Arizona's elections director, who helped draft the provision, admitted to the Justice Department that the provisions were "targeted at voting practices in predominantly Hispanic areas in the southern portion of the state near the Arizona border." The legislature, likely recognizing that it lacked the information necessary to satisfy the Justice Department, decided to withdraw the law.

Then they waited. Like Texas and other states that had been subject to preclearance, Arizona anticipated the Supreme Court's decision to strike it down in *Shelby County* by adopting new restrictions on third-party ballot collection yet again. This time, the state's GOP lawmakers knew they might not need the approval of the federal government. So in June 2013 in the final hours of the state legislative session and just four days before the *Shelby County* decision arrived, Arizona banned partisan ballot collection and installed new restrictions on nonpartisan efforts. Both measures passed on a party-line vote.

Voters howled. Almost immediately, citizens circulated petitions to repeal these new laws via the ballot initiative. More than 140,000 Arizona voters signed petitions to force the statewide vote, which, if successful, would have also prevented the legislature from passing any similar legislation without supermajority support. The legislature stood down for a second time, but refused to change course. In the next session, lawmakers simply broke the larger package of restrictions apart, passed the provisions à la carte, and dared citizens to circulate petitions and fight each battle individually.

With the threat of preclearance removed, and with little fear that citizens could stop them, Arizona lawmakers revealed their true motivation again and again: they claimed to tackle voter fraud that courts later found to be "unverified," "farfetched," and even "demonstrably false" with restrictions that they were told, in nearly pleading terms, would devastate the voice of Latino and Native communities across Arizona.

Supporters of these new laws didn't just ignore those pleas; they snickered. Only 18 percent of Native American voters in Arizona's rural counties have home mail service, compared to 86 percent of white voters in the exact same counties. When Representative Charlene Fernandez, a Democrat representing rural southwest Arizona including San Luis, begged her colleagues to consider "what it's like to live in a rural, rural area, sometimes 40 miles away from the nearest post office box," and that "over 10,000" of her voters could be disenfranchised without help from third-party collectors, lawmakers openly laughed on the House floor. She continued on, nonetheless, trying to explain that a minor burden for some could be an insurmountable obstacle for others. "The convenience of walking to a post office is not afforded to everybody. The fact that you can open your front door and leave mail there and somebody will pick it up is not afforded to everybody. Please understand that it's so different."

Instead, Republican lawmakers cited a blog post and video from A.J. LaFaro, the chairman of the Maricopa County GOP, which became known simply as the LaFaro video. LaFaro filmed a Latino man he claimed was trying to deliver ballots, a man he repeatedly called a "thug." There was no illegal act depicted in the video. There was no proof that the allegations in the video's narration or in the blog post were true. Lawmakers latched on to it, anyway; during the ensuing campaign they repeatedly cited "videos we've all seen," as if this purported evidence proved anything. The Republican candidate for secretary of state in 2016, then a state senator, even included the footage in one of her television ads.

Don Shooter, meanwhile, the senator from Yuma and San Luis, told one distortion after another as he testified in support of his bill. At one point, he even claimed that third-party collectors turned in five thousand ballots right at the deadline during his 2010 election. In actuality, there had been some five thousand ordinary requests for early ballots in the district, made over many weeks.

Meanwhile, in addition to this wealth of evidence showing racial intent around ballot collection, studies showed that Arizona's precinct closures and new out-of-precinct voting rules had the disparate impact that community leaders feared. Jonathan Rodden, a Stanford political scientist who studied the new rules, called them "a dizzying array of precinct and polling-place schemes that change from one month to the next." The net effect was to require voters to expend "significant effort" simply to keep up. It was a vicious one-two combination. First, Arizona shifted precincts with great frequency—affecting all groups, but Blacks and Latinos twice as much as white voters, according to the Rodden report. Then, if voters showed up at the wrong precinct, they could be given a provisional ballot to fill out—which was then most likely discarded. Arizona's provisional voting rate hit 18 percent in 2014, the highest rate in the nation. Arizona also rejected more provisional ballots than any other state. Indeed, Rodden reports, "no other state comes close." In 2012, only thirty-five thousand nationwide were thrown out for being cast in the wrong precinct. Nearly one-third of them, just under eleven thousand, were from Arizona.

The racial inequity here is dizzying, as well: ballots cast by minority voters were far more likely to be discarded. In 2016, the discard rate was 131 percent higher for Latinos, 74 percent higher for Blacks, and 39 percent higher for Native Americans than for whites. Some 60 percent of all votes in Arizona come from Maricopa County. Latinos there were 110 percent more likely to have their ballots discarded, while Blacks were 80 percent more likely, and Native Americans were 74 percent more likely to be disenfranchised.

Moreover, the rate of out-of-precinct voting was also 65 percent higher for Democrats than Republicans in Maricopa County, and 56 percent higher in Pima. None of this confusion was the voters' fault. Suspiciously, one-quarter of out-of-precinct voters went to the wrong place, but that balloting site was actually closer to their home than the polling place they were assigned. "Hispanics and Native Americans are more likely to live farther from their assigned polling places," Rodden found, "and Hispanics are more likely to live in proximity to multiple proximate polling places to which they are not assigned."

But without Section 5, Arizona lawmakers had a free hand to use unfounded claims of fraud to complicate voting for minority groups. They were equally free to proceed to discard tens of thousands of ballots in a closely divided and rapidly changing state where those votes could easily have shifted outcomes from one candidate to another. Preclearance would have prevented these changes from affecting elections. Now, the burden of proof has shifted. Lawmakers could pass new restrictions, reap the benefits over several electoral cycles, and wait for time-consuming litigation to unfold under Section 2. That calculation meant, for example, that when a federal appeals court declared both laws unconstitutional, the proponents of minority rule remained aware—just as they were during *Shelby County*—that the lower courts hardly mattered. The ultimate arbiter of the fate of ballot access in Arizona would once more be the hand-selected conservative majority on the U.S. Supreme Court.

A SUPREME COURT that focused on the simple text of a statute would not have placed the Voting Rights Act in jeopardy merely by taking up the *Brnovich* case, but a court where such claims veer between false modesty and rank hypocrisy is something else entirely. Indeed, many voting rights advocates and election law experts such as Richard Hasen warned against bringing the *Brnovich* complaint in the first place, believing it was "overreach" and, as it pitted the Republican and Democratic National Committees against each other, dangerously partisan. They worried it would provide a "vehicle to eviscerate what remains of the crown jewel of the civil rights movement." Unfortunately, their fears were not misplaced.

As the Supreme Court held the two-hour, online oral argument in March 2021, American democracy looked its most rickety. It was just ten weeks after the January 6 insurrection at the Capitol, Donald Trump's mob assault on the peaceful transfer of power fueled by repeated false claims about nonexistent voter fraud and a stolen election. Meanwhile, state legislatures fueled by these baseless allegations hustled to pass new voting restrictions. Georgia's GOP legislature, for example, signed off on a ninety-plus-page law that looked to end absentee balloting for young voters, and forced voters into longer lines where it would become a crime to hand them water. When Governor Brian Kemp signed the measure into law, he sat before a portrait of the Callaway Plantation in Washington, Georgia, where generations of slaves picked cotton.

Against this backdrop, the court's conservatives again acted to promote voter suppression and further weaken voting rights protections—all the while denying they were doing any of this at all. They thus further empowered GOP lawmakers who claimed without any proof at all that they passed these laws because they just needed to prevent, yes, nonexistent voter fraud.

Why, asked Justice Neil Gorsuch, isn't preventing voter fraud a valid state interest? "Does Arizona have to wait for fraud to occur in Arizona, using a practice, before it can outlaw it?" he asked. Chief Justice John Roberts had a similar concern, citing a 2005 report from a bipartisan commission that recommended eliminating the practice of allowing candidates or party officials from collecting ballots.

Perhaps the most truthful answers were given by Michael Carvin, the lawyer representing the RNC, and Roberts's youthful colleague in the DOJ Civil Rights Division all those years ago. As Kagan tested Carvin with hypothetical examples that almost seemed ripped from the Georgia law, it was clear that she was trying to signal how worrisome things could become if the court narrowed Section 2 and allowed laws like these to pass constitutional muster. "A state has long had two weeks of early voting and then the state decides that it's going to get rid of Sunday voting on those two weeks, and leave everything else in place." Would that violate the Voting Rights Act? Kagan asked. Carvin said no and sounded incredulous that he was fielding the query at all.

"These are all hypotheticals that have never existed in the real world," he said.

"This doesn't seem so fanciful to me," Kagan replied.

Carvin felt so confident of the ultimate outcome in *Brnovich* that he freely admitted that the entire case was really about partisan advantage. When Justice Amy Coney Barrett asked Carvin why the Republican Party was involved in the case, and why they cared about "keeping, say, the out-of-precinct voter ballot disqualification rules on the books," he said the quiet part out loud. The appeals court decision, he explained, "puts us at a competitive disadvantage relative to Democrats."

Politics, Carvin added, "is a zero-sum game." Every "extra vote they get," he said, "hurts us."

WHILE CARVIN FRANKLY disclosed how significant these votes could be in determining winners and losers, the Supreme Court's 6–3 decision upholding these laws, written by Alito, brushed aside any burden they might pose to voters. Indeed, it turned Section 2's guarantee that all voters would have the same opportunity to cast a ballot inside out, mangling the clear language that prohibited any "standard, practice or procedure" that results in any "denial or abridgement" of the right to vote. Alito hollowed out the transformational promise of an electoral process that is "equally open" to all.

More than that, Alito—a conservative justice who has long proclaimed himself a strict textualist—actually rewrote the statute itself. The conservative majority simply invented new standards, modified the words of Congress as they—not the people's elected representatives—saw fit, and stood the Voting Rights Act on its head. "The mere fact there is some disparity in impact does not necessarily mean that a system is not equally open or that it does not give everyone an equal opportunity to vote," Alito wrote. This, of course, is exactly the opposite of what Congress intended when it refashioned Section 2 during the 1982 reauthorization and turned aside the arguments of Roberts and the DOJ.

Roberts and Carvin lost the battle that year, but thirty-nine years later, they won the war. They'd long desired to rework Section 2 in a way that would benefit Republicans and limit the influence of minority voters. Congress thought otherwise. But now it only took five votes—and Roberts and Alito had two of them. And with Amy Coney Barrett's recent ascension to the court, the conservatives even had a vote to spare. This was the first major decision handed down by the 6–3 supermajority. It could not have been more consequential.

Brnovich made it easier for states to enact restrictive measures if they believed they were preventing fraud. The court endorsed this finding even if the states in question could not demonstrate that fraud existed or presented any actual dangers. It also made it more difficult for minority voters to fight such laws. Alito presented what he called five guideposts, none of which appeared in the actual text of the VRA, for future claims. In reality, these were more roadblocks than guideposts and created an almost unreachable bar for future plaintiffs to meet. At the same time, the court was making it easier than ever for lawmakers to enact any suppressive measure they desired under the guise of preventing fraud.

Alito arbitrarily set the state of play with the 1982 VRA reauthorization as the benchmark standard for legality, reasoning, inscrutably, that any law in place in 1982 could not have been discriminatory. In turning back the clock, however, Alito returned voters to a time when there was far less absentee voting, voting by mail, and early voting. The decision therefore makes it possible for states to roll back the practice of early voting on Sundays under the reasoning that such voting did not take place in 1982, and Black voters could take advantage of other days. The decision, which upheld restrictions on third-party ballot collection on tribal land that lacked accessible post offices or home mail delivery as a "usual burden of voting," did not even mention the words *Native Americans*.

This 1982 benchmark can't be found in the text. It can't be found in the legislative history. It can't be found anywhere in any congressional report. It was not passed by Congress, and it was not considered by Congress. Moreover, Congress crafted the entire statute reauthorizing the VRA in

1982 making it perfectly clear that it was seeking to prevent both racial intent and effects in response to *Mobile v. Bolden*. The intent of Congress could not have been any more direct. But there would be no deference to Congress. Alito simply scribbled over the Voting Rights Act, rewriting a congressional statute the way he wanted it to appear.

"The majority fears that the statute Congress wrote is too 'radical,' that it will invalidate too many state voting laws. So the majority writes its own set of rules," Kagan wrote in dissent. "What is tragic here is that the court has (yet again) rewritten—in order to weaken—a statute that stands as a monument to America's greatness and protects against its basest impulses."

In its disastrous 2013 ruling in *Shelby County*, the Supreme Court gutted preclearance provisions by fashioning a fictitious "equal sovereignty doctrine" from whole cloth. Roberts, writing for the court's conservative majority, had assured Americans back then that things had changed in the South—but also that Section 2 would be there for anyone who needed it. Now, eight years later, the court turned Section 2 into something all but unrecognizable. Such are the victories possible with a patient, antidemocratic long game to unwind the VRA.

BACK IN SAN Luis, Arizona, where these decisions matter most, Luis Marquez shakes his head sadly. Election Day here used to be a party, says the decorated, retired police officer and longtime member of the board of education. It felt like a street festival, he says, with music and locals carrying sizzling plates of carne asada. "The last two years, it has been very quiet," says Marquez. "People were not asking for help. They were not. And then whoever could help didn't want to help because they were afraid. When Guillermina got jail, everybody was nervous."

At the local Baptist church, two congregants, Tere Varela and Maria Robles, usually volunteer translation services for retirees for whom Spanish is their first language. This year, however, both felt far too nervous to have anything to do with assisting with the vote.

"We don't want to help," Robles told the *New York Times*. "We're afraid."

"Is that the purpose of this?" Varela asked. "To keep us from voting?"

Meanwhile, thanks to *2000 Mules*, conservative activists continue to descend on San Luis. The film is based on research by a group called True the Vote, whose outlandish claims have been repeatedly debunked by fact-checkers and government investigators, as the *Texas Tribune* and others have reported. But the lies it has sanctioned have moved into the national bloodstream—in part because it has been amplified by so many state legislators and conservative media outlets. A group like True the Vote might seem to exist on the far fringe of the election-denying ecosystem, but like so many other formerly fringe factions, tendencies, and organizations on the right, actually it's wired right into the heart of the conservative establishment.

True the Vote debuted in Wisconsin in 2011, thanks to a $35,000 grant from the Bradley Foundation. It has dispatched its team around the country to speak at meetings hosted by Americans for Prosperity—one of the largest tentacles within the Koch Brothers' conservative octopus. And its lawyer on at least one case, according to court records, is James Bopp—the right-wing legal mastermind who helped win the *Citizens United* decision. True the Vote is "having a real impact on the way lawmakers and states are governing elections and on the concerns we have on what may happen in the upcoming elections," Sean Morales-Doyle, the acting director of voting rights at the Brennan Center for Justice, a nonpartisan think tank, told the *New York Times*.

In her tiny living room, surrounded by photos of children and grandchildren, and a framed flag flown in her honor at an American military base in Afghanistan, Fuentes sighs wearily. "But they say I'm running a ballot-harvesting Mafia."

She is on probation for two years and cannot vote.

CHAPTER TWENTY-FIVE

IN 2022, THE Supreme Court heard two cases deeply rooted in John Roberts's younger days. One echoed his career-shaping tour as a Republican lawyer in the Reagan-era Justice Department. The other recalled his work as a key member of the legal team that helped deliver Florida, and the presidency, to George W. Bush in 2000.

Merrill v. Milligan (now *Allen v. Milligan*), from Alabama, reunited Roberts with Section 2 of the Voting Rights Act. A three-judge district court panel, including two Trump appointees, ruled that Alabama needed to redraw its congressional map and create a second Black opportunity district. It was a textbook case: Alabama is more than 27 percent Black, but lawmakers drew one overwhelmingly Black district in its total delegation of seven, and ensured white Republicans would win the other six.

Alabama Republicans appealed to the Supreme Court, which blocked the lower court's decision until the case could be briefed and argued before the justices. That delay heightened the stakes for the Voting Rights Act challenge, while also allowing Alabama to hold the 2022 congressional elections on a map that a federal court had deemed racially discriminatory.

Alabama's attorneys teed the case up for Roberts to pull the plug on any role for Section 2 as a check against invidious redistricting. They showed themselves well-acquainted with Roberts's memos during the 1982 reauthorization fight, when he formulated DOJ's arguments on behalf of making claims more difficult to prove. "Alabamians will suffer the constitutional harm of being assigned to racially segregated districts, irreconcilable with the Fourteenth Amendment, the Fifteenth Amendment, and the VRA as initially conceived," the attorneys argued. They could have only

intended the phrase *as initially conceived* as an echo of Roberts's own crusade against Section 2.

John Roberts: This Is Your Life rolled on with *Moore v. Harper*—an
audacious challenge from embittered Republican legislators in North Carolina who argued that the state supreme court exceeded its authority when
it struck down their congressional map as a partisan gerrymander. They
based their claim on a radical theory known as the independent state legislature (ISL) doctrine, which, under its most extreme reading, asserts that
the word *legislature* in the Elections Clause hands all power for election-
related procedures to state legislative bodies. Much like the unitary executive doctrine or the major questions doctrine, ISL emerged from the
conservative legal movement with the goal that its judges and justices
would enshrine it into law, to be cited whenever it would benefit the Republican Party. The lawmaker plaintiffs in *Moore v. Harper* believed that
under the ISL doctrine they were free to make election law in their own
preferred image, free from any checks and balances ordinarily provided by
a state constitution, state supreme court, or gubernatorial veto.

The claims in *Moore v. Harper* terrified the nation's top historians of
the Revolutionary era, who called it "historically implausible," and argued
that there is "no evidence that anyone at the time expressed the view." It
terrified the national association of state supreme court chief justices,
who stood together as Democrats and Republicans to insist the "Elections
Clause does not bar state court review of state laws governing federal elections under state constitutional provisions." It went too far for even Ben
Ginsberg, the GOP election lawyer who built a long and brilliant career
on exploiting every loophole in the law for his side. In an amicus brief,
he called the ISL doctrine "wrong as a matter of law" and warned that it
would "increase the odds that state legislatures replace the popular vote
with their own political preferences."

This discredited nineteenth-century notion is indeed a work of fiction.
One of the key documents it is based on is widely believed to be a forgery.
But GOP lawyers dusted it off during *Bush v. Gore* looking to prevent the
recount of votes in several Florida counties ordered by the state supreme
court. They also tried using it to protect the state legislature's assertion
that it could award the state's Electoral College votes to Bush.

Then, in a 2015 case from Arizona testing the constitutionality of an independent redistricting commission established by voters eager to take mapmaking power away from a legislature that regularly abused it, Roberts gave the bogus principle new life. He embraced an early variant of the independent legislature doctrine in a dissent that might be the most caustic and furious he's ever handed down. In *Arizona State Legislature v. Arizona Independent Redistricting Commission*, a 5–4 court found in favor of the voters who established the Arizona commission. Yet Roberts clearly believed the authority rested solely with state legislatures.

"What chumps!" he thundered about those who worked a century earlier to amend the Constitution to elect U.S. senators via statewide popular vote rather than having them be chosen by the legislature.

"Didn't they realize that all they had to do was interpret the constitutional term 'the Legislature' to mean 'the people'?" the chief justice asked sarcastically.

In both *Moore v. Harper* and *Allen v. Milligan*, the stakes could not have been any higher. How John Roberts would decide to play these two cases had the potential to alter elections well into the future. *Milligan* could well award Republicans the U.S. House for likely the rest of the decade. And *Moore* could award all but abolish any unfettered power over elections to gerrymandered legislatures in states like Wisconsin, Arizona, Michigan, Georgia, and Pennsylvania, at a time when GOP majorities in those chambers had fallen under the sway of election deniers. The 2024 election stood in the balance. So did all the elections that would follow.

THE MODERN REVIVAL of the ISL theory began with pure desperation during *Bush v. Gore*, as the brightest legal minds flung makeshift constitutional spitballs to see what might stick. They were seeking to turn an election in the GOP's favor during a moment unlike any other in modern American politics. With the help of three future conservative justices, a 5–4 conservative court, in an unsigned opinion following drearily predictable partisan lines, awarded the presidency to Bush. The GOP majority did not embrace the novel interpretation of the Elections Clause. Instead, it ended the recount under the equal protection provision in the U.S. Constitution, on the grounds that only some of Florida would be recounted and not all of it. Then the court admitted the speciousness of its reasoning by declaring the decision a one-off and not binding precedent.

Three of the conservative justices found the state legislature argument more alluring. Chief Justice Rehnquist, along with Thomas and Scalia—who scoffed at the reasoning that carried the day with the colorful private declaration that it was, "as we say in Brooklyn, a piece of shit"—also signed onto a Rehnquist-penned concurrence. There the chief justice contended that "there are a few exceptional cases in which the Constitution imposes a duty or confers a power on a particular branch of a State's government. This is one of them."

"In most cases," Rehnquist wrote, "comity and respect for federalism compel us to defer to the decisions of state courts on issues of state law. That practice reflects our understanding that the decisions of state courts are definitive pronouncements of the will of the States as sovereigns." But not always. The U.S. Constitution, Rehnquist explained, provides that "Each State shall appoint, in such Manner as the *Legislature* thereof may direct," electors for president and vice president. He italicized the word *legislature* for extra emphasis.

His concurrence would lay dormant for decades. It would not, however, be forgotten.

WHEN THE SUPREME Court froze preclearance in *Shelby County*, it insisted that Section 2 would hold strong for those who needed it. Yet that debate never seemed to settle at all. In February 2022 it grew ominous, when the Supreme Court blocked the creation of a new Alabama congressional map as ordered by a lower court on the grounds that the redrawn map would arrive too close to November's elections. Roberts, intriguingly, was in the minority that would have allowed a new map and a second Black district to be established in 2022. Yet his dissent carried a dark undertone. Roberts suggested that the court take another look at the test that governs Section 2 in redistricting: the *Gingles* test, which requires minority groups to show that they reside in a "sufficiently large and geographically compact" manner to constitute a majority. The test, Roberts suggested, had

"engendered considerable disagreement and uncertainty." The invitation
to revisit *Gingles* seemed to augur danger for what remained of Section 2.

The news broke as I was in Calera, where Roberts had ignored the facts
on the ground as he ripped the heart out of Section 5 in *Shelby County*.
If Section 2 now stood on thin ice, this being Alabama, it never took too
long to check out the latest threat to the Voting Rights Act in person. I
drove south to inspect the boundaries of Alabama's Seventh District—a
60 percent Black-majority seat based in the state's west-central Black Belt
counties while stretching north toward Birmingham and east to Montgomery. The boundaries of Alabama's Seventh District largely respected
county lines except for these two cities.

What I found was startling but not surprising: these lines neatly trace,
and perpetuate, Alabama's long history of racial injustice. The district
carves out a sliver of Montgomery County—which corresponds almost exactly to the city's racial divide. It gathers up the Black neighborhoods still
recovering from decades of racist redlining practices on one side, while
saving nearby wealthy, white communities like Pike Road for the second.
The ZIP codes with the Whole Foods stores slide into the white district.
The streets where Rosa Parks refused to stand for a white bus rider remain
separate and unequal.

If the Seventh District is packed with Black voters, the Black voters
living in counties just east of Montgomery have been cracked in half. The
straight line just east of Montgomery bisects the Black voters in Macon
(also home to Tuskegee, still gerrymandered today more than six decades
after the court tried to put an end to its racial gerrymander in the 1960
case *Gomillion v. Lightfoot*). Very little has changed in this corner of the
South, either. This county is home to one of the largest concentrations of
Black voters on this side of the state, but the lines make it impossible for
them to play any part in electing a U.S. House member of their choosing.
They've been gerrymandered into irrelevance in the Third District: severed from the Black Belt, whacked in half again for good measure, and
added to counties that are more than 90 percent white.

This is the dreary legacy of both *Shelby County* and *Rucho*. That one-
two judicial punch ended up doing damage to far more than just Democrats and communities of color, however. It pushed our politics toward

deeper and more unrepresentative extremes and provided Americans with fewer tools to pull it back toward common sense and decency.

THE *MOORE V. HARPER* case also was rooted in the original sin of redistricting. But on top of that, it boasted generous complements of Federalist Society scholarship and high-profile boosters amplified by tens of millions of dollars from Leonard Leo's dark money networks. In 2022, North Carolina's state supreme court overturned the state's GOP-approved congressional map as an unconstitutional partisan gerrymander. Sophisticated computer modeling showed that it would almost always award ten of the state's fourteen seats to Republicans. A coalition of voting rights organizations took the case all the way to the state supreme court, which agreed, ruling in a 4–3 decision, that the state constitution guarantees that "all elections shall be free." The court ultimately adopted a map drawn by the respected political scientist Bernie Grofman, which produced seven Republican-leaning seats, six favoring Democrats, and one toss-up. In 2022, it created a responsive and proportional 7–7 map.

Republican state legislators, however, looked to test the conservative justices' growing interest in the independent state legislature theory. "If a redistricting process more violative of the U.S. Constitution exists, it is hard to imagine it," argued North Carolina GOP legislators in their emergency application to the Supreme Court. This line of argument suggested a certain lack of creativity, given that the plaintiffs' own maps had been struck down multiple times in the previous decade. But what the complainants lacked in originality they made up for in ingenuity. "The federal constitution expressly provides that the manner of federal elections shall 'be prescribed in each State by the Legislature thereof,'" the lawmakers wrote. They asked the court to "put a stop to the North Carolina judiciary's usurpation of the General Assembly's specifically enumerated constitutional authority to regulate the manner of congressional elections," or else reward "judicial activism of the most brazen kind."

Evidently, we'd all been doing the Constitution wrong all these years. This is not an argument that the Supreme Court had ever accepted—and for good reason. The court's notion of "legislature" had long been established to mean whatever the lawmaking process in the state allows. It's not how the balance of power between the federal courts and the state courts ever worked. But that's not really the point here: the advocates of the ISL theory see it as the latest appealing blunt instrument that they can wield to win effectively unfettered power for state legislatures to remake maps and completely revise election laws, procedures, and certifications. It is, in short, a manifestly terrible idea—as is clear to anyone who's not part of Leonard Leo's network or on his payroll.

If this doctrine of the independent legislature has a modern father, it's Michael Morley, a well-respected law professor at Florida State. In 2015, he published an online law review article arguing that "the term legislature should be interpreted in accordance with its plain meaning." In Morley's view, that meant "solely and exclusively to the multimember body of representatives within each state generally responsible for enacting its laws." The hook for Morley's piece was the 2015 argument in the *Arizona Independent Redistricting Commission* case. Roberts cited Morley's paper in his stinging, sarcastic dissent when the court, by a 5–4 vote, upheld the commission's constitutionality and threw cold water on the independent legislature theory. Justice Ginsburg, for the majority, wrote that "we conclude that the Arizona Legislature does not have the exclusive, constitutionally guarded role it asserts."

Yet that decision didn't derail this zombie-style phony constitutionalism—it only pushed back its next day in court. Roberts's citation also elevated Morley's stature. He made at least eight speaking appearances at Federalist Society events. The Federalist Society even helped Morley revise and update his piece; a new version was published in the *Georgia Law Review*, "with the help of the Young Legal Scholars panel at the 22nd Annual Federalist Society Faculty Conference."

Other conservative justices soon shared Roberts's budding infatuations with the independent legislature theory. In the run-up to the 2020 presidential election, a lower federal court extended Wisconsin's deadline for mail-in ballots to be received by six days. The ruling required election officials to count any vote that had been postmarked by Election Day even if its arrival had been slowed by the mail or a dramatic increase in pandemic mail-in voting. The court had extended the same grace period during the April primary, and an additional 79,000 properly postmarked ballots arrived during those extra six days. That's more than three times the 22,748-vote margin that handed Trump the Badger State in 2016.

In the court's decision, Kavanaugh and Gorsuch used separate concurrences to endorse the ISL theory. The Supreme Court, Kavanaugh wrote, may overrule a state supreme court if it defies "the clearly expressed intent of the legislature" in an election law case. Gorsuch was even more forceful. "The Constitution provides that state legislatures—not federal judges, not state judges, not state governors, not other state officials—bear primary responsibility for setting election rules."

Alito and Thomas expressed their interest when they joined Gorsuch in a dissent when the court denied the emergency stay in *Moore v. Harper*, prior to hearing the full case. They described this theory that was not grounded in any credible history or law as "an exceptionally important and recurring question of constitutional law." (So much, yet again, for the strict and unstinting historical inquiry of the originalist school.) Kavanaugh agreed in his own concurrence. "The issue is almost certain to keep arising until the court definitively resolves it," he wrote.

The issue was only certain to keep arising because it was reverberating around the echo chamber of the legal Right. Conservative thinkers, Federalist Society lawyers, Leonard Leo–funded organizations pushing unproven claims of voter fraud, and Republican-appointed justices had dusted off a makeshift, justly forgotten relic of speculative nineteenth-century law and dressed it up as an urgent new question in constitutional jurisprudence. None of it was sustained either by the plain text of the Constitution or the intent of the Founders—yet here it was, claiming status as an "exceptionally important" question that the court suddenly needed to resolve. It was a roiling hurricane, gaining power, even though it had been largely manufactured for political purposes, with Leonard Leo's network of legal enforcers manufacturing the heat energy to accelerate the storm.

Yet the conservative justices were right about this: the independent legislature doctrine wasn't going away. It was, after all, at the heart of Federalist Society member John Eastman's two-page memo to Mike Pence's aides—later known as the "coup memo." In his delirium of phantom election theft, Eastman had asserted that state legislatures alone can determine their slates of electors, and he suggested that the vice president had the authority to throw out electors if the states sent competing slates. The Big Lie that the 2020 election had been stolen from Trump, and the effort to overturn the election that led to the January 6 insurrection, could not have been possible without the ISL theory.

The doctrine was also central to briefs filed after the 2020 election in highly dubious cases by the Honest Elections Project, the group closely linked to the Federalist Society's Leo through alternate names such as the 85 Fund and Judicial Education Network. The reason the group kept re-branding itself was almost certainly to disguise its origins and intent, as it pushed arguments that would have been dismissed as coming from the far discredited fringe just years earlier. But now that these efforts were tightly aligned with the same network that installed the Supreme Court's new conservative majority, "fringe" and "mainstream" now referred to a distinction without a difference on the legal right.

Honest Elections filed a brief that pushed the independent legislature theory in a Pennsylvania case in which state Republicans battled a state court ruling permitting a three-day extension for properly postmarked ballots to be counted due to the pandemic and mail-delivery slowdowns. In its amicus brief to the court, the Honest Elections Project maintained that this decision arrogated the power over elections that the U.S. Constitution exclusively granted to the legislature.

The brief asked the Supreme Court not only to rule in favor of the Republicans, but to take the opportunity to embrace the independent legislature theory. "State legislatures are vested with plenary authority that cannot be divested by state constitution to determine the times, places, and manner of presidential and congressional elections," the group wrote. "This case provides a timely opportunity to put these questions to rest."

This isn't "something that we just stumbled across to advance a particular political agenda," Jason Snead, the executive director of Honest Elections Project, claimed in an interview with NPR. It gets to "the very core of what it is to have a free election."

"When the Constitution says legislatures write the laws that govern our democracy," he asked, "is that what it means, or does it mean something else?"

The watchdog group Accountable.US did the difficult work of following the money as it sloshed through the interconnected Leo network, Donors-Trust, and the big-ticket foundation donors on the legal right. Five groups that filed amicus briefs in support of the independent legislature theory—Honest Elections, ALEC, the Public Interest Legal Foundation, Claremont Institute, and America's Future—received more than $90 million between 2016 and 2022. Much of that money—more than $70.4 million—was funneled through DonorsTrust. More than $6 million came from Bradley, another $3.6 million from Scaife, and an additional $2 million from Searle, among other donors.

These same groups, active first with the Federalist Society and Leo on the fight to push the courts to the right, were now funding efforts to remake democracy via those same judges. And they had now moved on to spend tens of millions funding organizations that spread the Big Lie and stoked insurrection.

DonorsTrust gave the 85 Fund more than $48 million in 2020. Also in 2020, it gave at least $28,135,539 to some forty organizations that have backed the January 6 rioters or perpetuated the voter fraud allegations that fueled the failed coup. The Fund has also helped fund organizations that challenged elections results in five states and another that sent eighty buses to the January 6 rally in Washington, D.C.; the Bradley Foundation, meanwhile, helped bankroll the conservative lawyer Cleta Mitchell, a Federalist Society member who fought to overturn the 2020 results in Georgia, and pushed more than $9 million into that insurrectionist ecosphere.

Leo and his allies had engineered a capture of the courts. Now they hoped to reap the rewards, using the combination of gerrymandered state legislatures and the new 6–3 supermajority to build enduring dominance that no one would have the power to block.

CHAPTER TWENTY-SIX

THE TWO VICTORIES for voting rights at the end of the Supreme Court's 2022–23 session caught almost everyone by surprise.

In a pair of decisions both written by Roberts, the U.S. Supreme Court pushed aside the most extreme reading of the independent state legislature doctrine. It also applied Section 2 of the Voting Rights Act to the case featuring textbook violations of it in Alabama, ordering the legislature to draw a second congressional district where Black voters would have an opportunity to elect a member of their choosing.

It was a marked contrast to the 2021–22 session, when the conservative supermajority seemed to pull a beleaguered Roberts farther and faster than he wanted to go, most notably in its sweeping rejection of *Roe v. Wade*. This time, Roberts won two conservatives to his position. Kavanaugh joined the 5–4 majority in *Allen v. Milligan*, and Kavanaugh and Barrett signed on with Roberts and the progressives on *Moore v. Harper*.

Court watchers and op-ed pages exulted as the surprising crosspartisan coalitions seemed to restore Roberts to the center of the court. A year earlier, CNN, *Politico*, and the *New York Times* had all bemoaned that Roberts had "lost control" of his court, calling him "the lonely chief" or, more tragically still, "the chief justice who wasn't." Now, Roberts appeared neither sidelined nor irrelevant. He was the master umpire, controlling balls and strikes behind home plate once more. "John Roberts, conservative statesman," cheered the *New York Times*. "Chief Justice takes back the reins," NPR rejoiced. "Democracy survives another day," a relieved *Washington Post* exhaled. *Slate* appeared dumbfounded, marveling that "John Roberts and Brett Kavanaugh really did just save the Voting Rights Act."

But all the hosannahs were premature. Supreme Court analysts, perhaps eager to believe that reasonable adults were in charge again, lost track of the Roberts modus operandi on high-profile cases involving voting and democracy. The Roberts pattern is always to take a small step before the big leap.

"Democracy Saved!" might be a more satisfying headline than "Democracy Saved, Today, Sort Of, But Look Out." Yet a closer examination of both decisions shows no cause for even the tiniest sigh of relief. Roberts and his allies have again embedded time bombs in both cases: open invitations to conservatives to try again, along slightly different legal arguments, which the Right's justices conveniently set forth.

Moore v. Harper and *Allen v. Milligan* aren't the end of the line. They merely establish the next theaters of engagement. These cases have the same DNA as *Wisconsin Right to Life*, *Northwest Austin*, and *Whitford*. In those cases, recall, Roberts appeared to be the winner from all angles—securing what were described as reasonable victories for court institutionalists while simultaneously laying the groundwork for the bomb-throwing insurgents. Despite the mainstream press's hallelujah chorus in these two most recent rulings, they are unlikely to stand as any sort of lasting precedent. Just as in Roberts's closely calibrated earlier rulings on similar cases, the conservative majority will return to wreak fresh havoc, in its own good time.

In this one tactical sense, Roberts does indeed have the reins of the court back in his hands. *Allen v. Milligan* was, in short, nearly the identical play Roberts made in *Wisconsin Right to Life*, which had been the first measured step toward *Citizens United*. Of course at the time, court watchers mistakenly took *Wisconsin Right to Life* to be a reasoned, incremental glide toward First Amendment speech rights for corporations, rather than a sudden lurch away from democratically conducted elections.

It was also the go-to strategy in *Northwest Austin*: building an apparent left-right coalition on paper, and disingenuously inviting Congress to fix the preclearance formula itself. All the while, Roberts was painstakingly setting up the grounds he would use to decide *Shelby County*—taking care to ensure the liberal justices went along with a decision declaring the formula ripe for deeper review as the price for not blowing up the Voting Rights Act straightaway. Roberts adopted the same slippery strategy yet again in *Whitford*, the redistricting case that the court punted until the chief justice stalled on the pretense of a standing technicality, waiting until he had the court he wanted. Once Kennedy retired and Kavanaugh arrived, Roberts reliably delivered the result that locked in GOP gerrymanders in red states and purple ones where Leo had created FedSoc majorities on state supreme courts.

It's true that in the Supreme Court's 2022–23 term, the conservative majority chose not to detonate these particular cases. Instead, they've set themselves up to do so down the line—in both cases through short, clever invitations in Kavanaugh's brief concurrences.

In *Allen*, Roberts and Kavanaugh appeared to be offended by Alabama's insistence that the court jettison decades of Voting Rights Act precedents. Alabama overreached—clumsily, but not without good reason after *Brnovich* and *Dobbs*—assuming that the supermajority might be anxious to act on "race neutrality." They also reckoned—again, not unreasonably—that Roberts would want to finish the decades-long wrecking job on Section 2 that he launched back in the Reagan Justice Department.

Roberts declined this opportunity—but he did help see to it that the last remaining safeguards within Section 2 remain on shaky ground. That's because the Kavanaugh concurrence appears to offer a blueprint for the next case. While Kavanaugh provided the fifth swing vote, he suggested that a different argument might have won him over—and then helpfully explained what it would be for future litigants. Perhaps, he suggested, Section 2's redistricting protections have an expiration date. His concurrence carried an eerie whiff of *Shelby County*: *Things have changed in the South* and the old refrain of *This cannot continue forever*.

"[E]ven if Congress in 1982 could constitutionally authorize race-based redistricting under Section 2 for some period of time, the authority to conduct race-based redistricting cannot extend indefinitely into the future," Kavanaugh wrote. "But Alabama did not raise that temporal argument in this Court, and I therefore would not consider it at this time."

At this time: a more easily devoured trail hasn't been laid out since Hansel scattered breadcrumbs in the forest. It was a curious argument: a decision finding that Alabama legislators had passed an unconstitutional, racially discriminatory map seems like an odd place to suggest that maybe the time had also come to declare protections against official discrimination no longer necessary.

It might have been the place to realize that Alabama would still benefit from preclearance. Perhaps things had not changed in the South after all. Alabama immediately defied the court, passing a new map that did not include the second Black opportunity district, furnishing in the process yet another example of why preclearance mattered. The Republican mapmakers dared the court to uphold its own ruling. Even under court order, they enacted a map showcasing the same resistance to multiracial democracy that Alabama had mastered for decades.

Had preclearance still been in effect to protect against Alabama's determined racial gerrymanders, the state's discriminatory map would have been struck down during the winter of 2021. The state would have then prepared a new one to go into effect before the 2022 elections, ensuring representative elections that fall. Instead, Alabama received a free pass to hold at least one election on a discriminatory map—as did Louisiana, Georgia, and Texas—providing Republicans with a clutch of safe seats equal to their new majority in the U.S. House. The line from *Shelby County* to the current slender GOP majority in the House is straighter and more direct than most Alabama districts.

The *New York Times* did half the math—and as a result, the paper of record gullibly swallowed the Roberts spin whole. "If Democrats win back the House, they will have John Roberts to thank," the *Times* proclaimed, suggesting for good measure that the Alabama decision could also unwind discriminatory maps in several other states with Black Democrats replacing white Republicans.

Roberts and Kavanaugh, however, had almost certainly done the rest of the equation. Even if Democrats gained a seat in Alabama, fresh GOP gerrymanders in Ohio and North Carolina would more than make up for it.

More importantly, *Milligan* provided the road map for the next challenge (much like *Northwest Austin* contained the key for *Shelby County*), and Louisiana, Georgia, and Texas could follow it perhaps without ever having to draw a compliant map. Kavanaugh's mind-reeling suggestion that what racial gerrymandering needed was a deadline after which it would just go away fit neatly into the court's long-stated and disgraceful desire, ever since Reconstruction, to simply decree a new day of justice and harmony. Instead, most every time, it launched a new era of inequity and injustice.

Louisiana recognized the invitation and quickly RSVP'd. Days after the court's holding, Louisiana lawmakers, showing themselves to be slightly more strategically minded than their counterparts in Alabama, cited the Kavanaugh decision as they fought against a new map at the Fifth Circuit Court of Appeals. They merrily suggested that the time had come to sunset race-based redistricting. Such an outcome might seem at first glance to be contrary to the essence of the *Milligan* decision—unless, that is, *Milligan* was really just a delaying tactic.

Indeed, in the same rush of late-term decisions, as Roberts was still being feted as a savior of democracy and champion of the court's credibility, the long-awaited decision regarding the use of race in college admissions arrived. Here, the court awarded Edward Blum the victory he'd spent two decades—and endless millions in dark-money foundation donations—battling to achieve. Roberts managed to end the use of race in higher education admissions and telegraph the future retirement of protections for minority voters during redistricting negotiations, all the while winning accolades for safeguarding democracy.

Somehow, the chief justice managed to be lionized even as he brazenly umpired the game to the benefit of his own side. That's not just calling balls and strikes—it's delivering a World Series to a gambling cartel while an entire retinue of sports reporters are covering a completely different and wholly imaginary ball game.

WHEN *MOORE V. HARPER*—the case from North Carolina involving the ISL theory—was swatted away by a 6–3 majority, the Roberts-penned decision sparked another round of backslapping. Progressive activist groups such as Common Cause hailed a total victory and a "historic pro-democracy decision." Even liberal outlets such as *Mother Jones*, MSNBC, the *Washington Post*, Democracy Docket, and the Center for American Progress claimed that the court had "rejected" the independent state legislature theory.

"When state legislatures prescribe the rules concerning federal elections, they remain subject to the ordinary exercise of state judicial review," Roberts wrote for the majority. "The Elections Clause does not insulate state legislatures from the ordinary exercise of state judicial review."

That was indeed comforting to hear from this court, and worthy of a sigh of relief. State legislatures, Roberts emphasized, have no "exclusive and independent authority when setting the rules governing federal elections." The mass exhalation from liberal commentators was grounded in the hope that the *Moore* ruling would wipe some of 2020's nightmare scenarios off the table. By rights, Roberts's opinion ought to prevent extreme lawmakers from pushing slates of fake electors, or declaring that "voter fraud" marred a close election in order to set themselves up as the final arbiters of the outcome in the name of "election integrity."

And if the decision had indeed stopped there, it would have been fair to characterize it as a rejection of the independent legislature theory and perhaps even real grounds for celebration. But Roberts—in what smells like another negotiated behind-the-scenes compromise to build a six-vote coalition, while also taking his first step to the right—did not stop there.

Indeed, *Moore v. Harper* actually takes a partial step *toward* the ISL theory. In a clear echo of *Northwest Austin*, the price for rejecting the most wild-eyed version of the theory was inducing the liberal justices to sign on to a decision that adopted a milder version of the doctrine.

You might call it the independent legislature-lite approach with half the lunacy, but all the danger of the U.S. Supreme Court overriding state courts and determining election outcomes itself. What could go wrong? Ask the liberal justices who signed onto *Northwest Austin*, thinking they were forestalling the worst but actually only enabling *Shelby County*. Or if you really want to lie awake with night terrors, just imagine a 2024 or 2028 version of *Bush v. Gore*.

That's because buried within the details of this decision, as well as a short concurrence by Kavanaugh, are the seeds of future cases to come. *Moore* is hardly the silver-bullet antidote to take out this dangerous zombie notion once and for all. Instead, it's John Roberts working yet again in stealth mode, taking the modest step to the right before the leap that inevitably follows. Yes, the court may have batted down the craziest version of the independent legislature theory—whose best supporting evidence is a set of 1787 documents, referred to as the Pinckney Plan, every reputable historian considers forged. But the lite version of the theory remains very much a going concern, thanks to the court curated and cultivated by the Right over generations to ensure outcomes and drive power.

The court's decision not only makes it clear that the Elections Clause does not liberate state legislatures from state constitutions and state law, but also stipulates that federal courts must not abandon their duty to exercise judicial review. "This Court has an obligation to ensure that state court interpretations of state law do not evade federal law," Roberts writes. "State courts do not have free rein."

Furthermore, Roberts holds that state courts must "not transgress the ordinary bounds of judicial review such that they arrogate to themselves the power vested in state legislatures to regulate federal elections."

What exactly does that mean? The court doesn't tell us. It's a reversion to the core precept of the independent legislature school of outcome-driven oversight that serves as a recipe for chaos. It would be an all-purpose license for a court badly damaged in the eyes of the public to play Calvinball—the Calvin and Hobbes game in which the players define and alter the rules during the contest itself—and make those standards up as they go along, in cases that could tip a presidential election.

As the New York University law professor Rick Pildes has pointed out, *Moore* does not adopt any standard at all as far as what "ordinary bounds" might be. Nor does the decision set any boundaries whatsoever to guide state courts or identify when federal courts might jump in and override. Indeed, Pildes notes, Roberts did not even rule on whether the North Carolina state court exceeded its role when it overturned the wildly gerrymandered maps at the heart of this case. We don't have any idea what the conservative majority on the court might consider transgressive. We might not know until the court informs us. And that could arrive in the heat of a disputed presidential election.

Perhaps the court did not assess the merits of this case because Republicans captured the North Carolina Supreme Court in 2022, and immediately undid the previous court's decision, allowing their legislative comrades free rein to enact a newly gerrymandered map. But what happens if Wisconsin's newly progressive majority undoes that GOP gerrymander and Badger State Republicans look to the high court for relief on the grounds that the state supreme court has transgressed its bounds? Given that every major decision that the Roberts Court has made on voting rights and democracy has aligned with the political interests of the GOP, it's dismayingly easy to imagine that the standard will become yet another dressed-up version of heads Republicans win, tails Democrats lose.

Likewise, we are now heading into the 2024 presidential election cycle without any sense of what the federal courts believe to be an appropriate and nontransgressive role for state courts to play.

That means the most important lines from the decision might be from Kavanaugh's short concurrence, which cites *Bush v. Gore*, a case decided via such shoddy reasoning that the justices who installed George W. Bush in the White House refused to put their names to it and insisted that it be nonbinding as precedent. "In other words, the Court has recognized and articulated a general principle for federal court review of state court decisions in federal election cases," Kavanaugh wrote, blithely disregarding the bright red disclaimer on *Bush v. Gore*. "In the future, the Court should and presumably will distill that general principle into a more specific standard such as the one advanced by Chief Justice Rehnquist."

That Rehnquist approach would have helped engineer Bush's victory. Now a court conservative majority that includes three lawyers who helped develop and argue Bush's case has announced that it can put its thumb on the scale in a future election, without defining the standard for that action in advance. This would be a heavy ask even for a court with a sterling reputation. From this court, so thoroughly outsourced to the Federalist Society, GOP operatives, and billionaire oligarchs, it's truly terrifying.

A court that has already proven, time and again, its willingness to alter process, invent doctrines, and predetermine outcomes for its own side in landmark rulings on the proper conduct of democracy in America shouldn't be afforded the benefit of the doubt when it sets out to conjure up a new doctrine of election oversight on the fly. Kavanaugh's detour into the independent state legislature debate in *Bush v. Gore* sets the stage for a new era of high court Calvinball. The Roberts Court is positioning itself to decide the next battery of ideologically driven challenges to democratic process with no clear standard at all. Vibes will evidently carry the day, on a case-by-case basis, as the individual justices will be empowered to rule on the basis of how they feel about that state supreme court's interpretation. With all due respect to John Roberts's new cheering section in the press, this is a harrowing position for a deeply partisan court to set out to address challenges arising from the next presidential election—especially with election deniers holding key positions in decisive swing states.

INDEED, JUST AS in Kavanaugh's concurrence in the Alabama redistricting case, the clear message of *Moore* to right-wing litigants is to keep trying. The next wave of independent legislature challenges will arrive in the days after the 2024 presidential election. And they could prove crucial in deeply gerrymandered Georgia, Wisconsin, and Arizona. These three extraordinarily close states provided President Biden's electoral college victory in 2020 with the slenderest of margins—and they were also the sites of militant challenges from election deniers, some in the state legislature that sought to overturn the results of free and fair balloting in the raw pursuit of power.

It's easy to imagine what these controversies might look like after the 2024 balloting. If the court adopted the Rehnquist standard, per Kavanaugh's suggestion, it would resume the work begun in *Bush v. Gore* and make itself the ultimate arbiter of any recount.

Let's say that the 2024 election comes down to the state of Wisconsin. Long lines in Milwaukee lead the state supreme court to keep polls open several additional hours to ensure that every vote is counted. Or maybe a deluged U.S. Postal Service in the Badger State has a backlog of ballots postmarked on or before Election Day but has not been able to deliver them all. Then, just as it did in 2020, the state supreme court provides additional time for any ballot sent prior to the deadline to arrive. Republicans duly appeal both state rulings to the U.S. Supreme Court, which would then decide whether potentially thousands of likely Democratic votes would count in a state where margins in 2016 and 2020 have been razor-thin.

Here's another possibility. Imagine what happens if the fictional, yet frighteningly plausible, plot from the final episodes of HBO's *Succession* became real life. On that show about family machinations inside a conservative media empire quite like Rupert Murdoch's at Fox News, a suspicious fire breaks out at a Milwaukee vote-counting center on election night. Wisconsin will determine the presidency. Yet some 100,000 ballots in a Democratic-leaning area—more than enough to tip the balance in either 2016 or 2020—are destroyed. The state supreme court orders extraordinary relief to find a way to count those votes. The U.S. Supreme Court shuts it down, effectively picking the next president.

Outlandish? Ridiculous? The stuff of prestige TV and not reality? Perhaps. But no more so than Florida in 2000, when a handful of hanging chads, a poorly designed butterfly ballot, abortive recounts—and finally an abysmally reasoned decision from the U.S. Supreme Court—determined the winner.

Someone, of course, needs to decide when elections go haywire. But when the standard is not clear in advance, and when that authority ultimately falls to a court that might as well be wearing red and blue robes rather than black ones, no one should feel reassured about the prospects for American democracy. That skepticism is exponentially more justified when the recent history of the court's rightward direction is taken into account—when the self-appointed referees in a bitter partisan scrum for power have been tapped to determine outcomes for one partisan side in advance. Adding in the steady devolution of the court's methods, reasoning, and spurious appeals to history into a glorified form of Calvinball, it's simply not credible to suppose that it could be relied on for anything more than rubber-stamping the critical operations of our democracy to the perpetual minoritarian advantage of Team Red.

This descent into opportunist hackery is the real legacy of the Roberts Court. As the justices on the inviolate right-wing majority are cheered by Federalist Society crowds and feted by politicians, as they vacation on superyachts and spend summers junketeering in Italy, they still fail to understand why they're seen as partisan actors. Or perhaps more accurately, and far worse, they just don't care.

The ultimate message of *Moore v. Harper* is that it's the U.S. Supreme Court—and John Roberts—who will make these decisions going forward. In the system that John Roberts has created, the decisions over control of our elections all begin, and end, with him.

CONCLUSION

ON A WEEKDAY morning in June 2022, I walked up Anthony Kennedy's driveway in McLean, Virginia, a modest home in a wealthy suburban D.C. enclave. I had a question I hoped he would answer.

The neocon thinker Irving Kristol once suggested that a conservative is a liberal who has been mugged by reality. American democracy had certainly been roughed up by the Supreme Court's combination of *Citizens United*, *Shelby County*, and *Rucho*. The evidence had become hard to dispute: The impact of unlimited dark money had remade our elections. Partisan gerrymanders had turned purple states into bright red ones where voters had no meaningful voice. And even if one believed in all good faith that things had changed in the South by 2013, the accumulated weight of a decade of racial gerrymanders, precinct closures, voter ID laws aimed at minorities with "surgical precision," and the blatant chicanery unleashed by state legislatures seemed more than enough for a reasonable person to take a second look.

I wondered whether reality had mugged a centrist conservative who joined the majority in two of those cases and whose sudden retirement enabled the third viewed the American democracy he had helped create from retirement. Did Anthony Kennedy open the newspaper each morning and wonder whether any of those cases, with hindsight, should have gone the other way? Did his confidence that allowing unfettered outside funds on elections would not lead to corruption or cause Americans to lose faith in elected leaders now seem misplaced? Did he, too, wonder whether preclearance might have needed a longer run? Did he wish that he'd looked a little deeper into those new statistical methods of measuring gerrymanders in the *Whitford* case, instead of accepting the standing dodge?

Nearly every neighbor seemed to have construction or landscaping crews in their yard, but as I rang his doorbell, I could see the retired justice inside at the sink washing his own breakfast dishes. I smiled and waved. He wasn't expecting a visitor but opened the door, still holding a dish towel.

When I posed the question to him—Did the last decade give him any reason to regret his vote in *Shelby County?*—an eclipse came over Kennedy's face and his mood darkened.

"Regrets? No!" he practically barked, then repeated it again. "No. What is there to regret?"

As I started to mention some of the actions by legislatures in the states formerly covered by preclearance, Kennedy quickly closed his door and latched it. "No regrets," he said again, slamming the door shut for emphasis.

Indeed, when it comes to regrets about voting rights, few conservative members of the court—current or former—seem to have them. As 2024 dawned, Leonard Leo and Federalist Society judges showed little interest in slowing down the assault on the Voting Rights Act. It looked to tighten the conservative grasp on American elections.

When Black voters joined with the NAACP in Arkansas to challenge a 2021 state house redistricting plan that underrepresented minority voters—taking the U.S. Supreme Court at its word that Section 2 of the VRA protected everyone nationwide—Lee Rudofsky, a U.S. district judge appointed by Trump and a longtime Federalist Society member, found a novel way to dismiss the case by creating his very own faux-originalist technicality.

Rudofsky ruled in February 2022 that citizens had no private right of action under the Voting Rights Act. A Section 2 claim, he ruled, could only be brought by the U.S. attorney general. This, of course, would effectively freeze most VRA enforcement. The DOJ can't spot every local issue; individuals and groups see them first. And some Departments of Justice simply might not have any interest in enforcing the VRA.

Six decades of precedent that established that private citizens and organizations had this right, as well as the statute itself and clear original intent of Congress, did not stand in Rudofsky's way.

The U.S. Supreme Court had affirmed this right for as far back as 1969, in *Allen v. State Board of Election*, when it held that "the achievement of the Act's laudable goal could be severely hampered . . . if each citizen were required to depend solely on litigation instituted at the discretion of the Attorney General." It said it again in 1996's *Morse v. Republican Party of Virginia*, writing that the "the existence of the private right of action under Section 2 has been clearly intended by Congress since 1965."

Then there's the text of the VRA itself, which clearly explains that a case can be brought by the attorney general "or an aggrieved person under any statute." During the 1982 reauthorization, both the U.S. House and Senate Judiciary Committee reports explicitly reaffirmed the intent of Congress. The House report clearly states that "citizens have a private right of action to enforce their rights under Section 2," and the Senate also wrote to "reiterate the existence of the private right of action under Section 2." Indeed, the NAACP, League of Women Voters, Common Cause, and the ACLU brought and prevailed in the vast majority of Section 2 cases; only 15 of 182 successful Section 2 challenges had been brought by the attorney general since the 1982 reauthorization.

Given that clear language and long-standing precedent, Rudofsky's decision seemed unlikely to stand on appeal—except that it drew a three-judge panel on the U.S. Court of Appeals with two Federalist Society members included on Leo's master list of preapproved potential Supreme Court justices. In his decision in late 2023, Trump appointee David Stras insisted that the VRA itself "is silent on the existence of a private right of action," and that he did not see a "single word or phrase" in the VRA to support any conclusion that it existed at all.

The Leo/FedSoc network left fingerprints everywhere. Stras had clerked for Clarence Thomas at the Supreme Court at the same time as Carrie Severino, Leo's handpicked leader of the Judicial Confirmation Network, who later assumed many of his duties at the Federalist Society. Stras may have even owed his seat on the appeals court to JCN: Severino directed the group's six-figure TV ad buy in support of Stras's nomination when Democratic senators in his home state of Minnesota tried to derail him.

Meanwhile, the Honest Elections Project—itself founded by Leo in 2020 and funded through the Concord Fund—filed an amicus brief signaling the conservative legal movement's interest in the case. The brief twisted the facts, the purpose of the VRA, and even the suggestion by

Rudofsky that the Black voters may have had a strong case on the merits had he believed that they had standing to bring the lawsuit. Instead, they argued that it was Section 2 claims—not likely racial gerrymanders—that undermine voters' confidence in elections and the integrity of our electoral processes. Congress, the Leo-front group argued, "never intended for Section 2 to be used by litigation groups as a vehicle to undermine basic laws that improve election integrity."

To make their case, they cited a line that Justice Gorsuch dropped into his concurrence in the *Brnovich* case from Arizona "to flag one thing." Gorsuch wanted to suggest that the private right to action might be an "open question." No matter that precedent, textualism, and original intent said the opposite. Just as *Wisconsin Right to Life* bred *Citizens United*, and *Northwest Austin* pointed to *Shelby County*, just as a Rehnquist footnote in *Bush v. Gore* inspired *Moore v. Harper*, Federalist Society–approved federal judges picked up the melody from the opening notes played by a Trump high court appointee selected from Leonard Leo's own short list. If it seems as if they're all singing from the same hymnal—conservative judges placed on the bench to enact wild-eyed theories, all funded and vetted by the same people—it's because the harmonies are too pristine to believe otherwise.

FAR TOO MANY explanations for the perilous state of American democracy begin with Donald Trump's gilded descent on a Trump Tower escalator in June 2015 as the celebrity businessman announced his candidacy for the Republican nomination for president, then quickly bested a field of governors, senators, and GOP royalty and bent the party to his image.

This narrative is too convenient and begins too late. John Roberts and Leonard Leo helped set the stage. *Citizens United, Shelby County,* REDMAP, partisan gerrymanders in North Carolina, Wisconsin, Michigan, and Pennsylvania—all this preceded Donald Trump's arrival on the scene. The Roberts Court sent us down this path. The heart of all Republican political power is its supermajority on the Supreme Court. It's the Supreme Court that has played the greatest role in undermining free and fair elections, creating an enduring minority rule in much of the country, and eviscerating voting rights in ways that lined up with the interests of the Republican Party every time.

An unelected supermajority of six people—the masterfully achieved goal of five decades of conservative scheming, bought and paid for by billionaires, wielding its power swiftly and steadily on behalf of wealthy donors, the religious Right, and, most importantly, the Republican Party—has created an existential crisis for representative democracy and majority rule as we know it.

The American public understands this. A July 2023 poll found that 62 percent of Americans believe that "the court is increasingly corrupted and faces a legitimacy crisis." A Pew Research poll that same month found the court's favorability at its lowest point in three decades of opinion surveys dating back to the mid-1980s. A solid majority of Americans view the court unfavorably. The court's approval ratings have collapsed by 26 percentage points since just 2020.

The conservative justices, meanwhile, playact befuddlement over any question of the Supreme Court's legitimacy and seem unconcerned that majorities of Americans disapprove of transparent partisan rulings dressed up in constitutional garb. In interviews, Alito and Thomas have suggested the only thing partisan about their rulings is this critique that they are partisan, rather than simply following the Constitution and the law. Meanwhile, the justices brush aside the avalanche of 2023 stories from *ProPublica*, the *Washington Post*, the *New York Times*, and elsewhere about hidden, cozy financial relationships with right-wing donors. Seats on private planes, private school tuition, luxury vacations, European junkets, real estate deals—all of it unseemly at best, unethical if the court bothered to subject itself to the most basic professional standards, at worst in violation of the extraordinarily limited disclosures required by law—are passed off as mere kindness between friends. After all, who hasn't had a pal buy his mom's house for a more than fair price, then allowed her to continue living there, rent-free?

The conservative justices, in their rare public remarks, usually before friendly crowds or under gentle questioning from another federal judge at a gathering of colleagues, have dismissed questions of the court's legitimacy as mere disagreement with its rulings. They pretend that their critics, in other words, are the ones playing politics, while they reach neutral, inevitable, and nonpartisan decisions of law. The news media should strip the justices of this veneer by identifying them as the Republicans and Democrats that they are.

"I don't understand the connection between opinions people disagree with and the legitimacy of the court," Roberts said in September 2022, before a judicial conference in Colorado. "You don't want the political branches telling you what the law is. And you don't want public opinion to be the guide of what the appropriate decision is."

The chief justice, of course, is not that obtuse. In this moment of victory, naturally, the justices would rather not admit that this has been a political project at all. They are mere umpires, logging balls and strikes, with no difference between Trump judges or Obama judges. Yet the conservative legal project had the purpose of winning the courts to win outcomes too unpopular to be won via the political process. Certainly the supermajority, armed with the votes to do so, would like to impose those out-of-the-mainstream, and sometimes deeply unpopular, views and have Americans accept them as objective readings of the law rather than a political verdict they cannot effect delivered by ideologues in red robes.

Thomas suggested critics of the courts were whiny children, "destroying our institutions because they don't give us what we want, when we want it." Amy Coney Barrett, a year after her confirmation, defended the impartiality of the court and its adherence to the law. "This court is not comprised of a bunch of partisan hacks," she insisted. "Judicial philosophies are not the same as political parties." She delivered this insistent speech at the University of Louisville's McConnell Center, named, yes, in honor of Mitch McConnell.

Barrett is welcome to make this claim. We do not have to believe it. We can trust our eyes. After all, we watched in 2016 as McConnell and his GOP colleagues invented the inviolable principle that Supreme Court nominations should not be considered during a presidential election year, at least when a Democratic president makes the selection. We then watched in fall 2020 as Donald Trump nominated Barrett after the death of Ruth Bader Ginsburg, and McConnell and his allies rushed her onto the court with record speed even with early voting for the president underway.

"If there's a new member of a court and all of a sudden everything is up for grabs," Kagan said in 2022, "all of a sudden very fundamental principles of law are being overthrown, are being replaced, then people have a right to say: What's going on there? That doesn't seem very law-like."

In short, we can see that the Supreme Court is not acting like a court, but rather like a tribunal of nine, a final arbiter on every question—major or otherwise—that operates as if it's above our system of checks and balances, rather than one piece of it. It is a court that has been stacked in a manner unbefitting of a democracy. And we can see the arrogance of a supermajority that doesn't seem even slightly concerned with the public's lack of faith. The justices are wrong when they think their current standing with the public is about mere disagreement over decisions. It's about a democracy in which a handful of unaccountable justices wield power above and beyond what anyone should hold.

Samuel Alito, in an interview published in the *Wall Street Journal* in July 2023, derided any attempt by Congress to enact a code of ethics for justices. "I know this is a controversial view, but I'm willing to say it," he said. "No provision in the Constitution gives them the authority to regulate the Supreme Court—period." Most constitutional scholars disagree. The Constitution establishes the Supreme Court. It awards Congress the power to organize it. Among other things, Congress controls its budget, the building where it meets, and the number of justices. It sets their pay. It mandates that a new session begins on the first Monday in October. It has much control over its jurisdiction and the kind of cases the court can hear. It requires recusal when a justice has a conflict of interest, and the filing of certain financial disclosure forms. Alito wishes to enforce checks and balances without having them apply to him. His words had the feel of a warning to anyone who imagines that bold, necessary structural reforms could rein in this court and restore majority rule: Just try. You'll never get it past us.

But what was so breathtaking about Alito's bold pronouncement—weighing in on the constitutionality of a bill before Congress even enacts it—was the interview itself. Alito granted four hours of interview time to David B. Rivkin Jr., a well-known Federalist Society and conservative lawyer who has represented Leonard Leo and, in July 2023, sent a letter on his behalf to the Senate committee considering the Supreme Court ethics package. The Senate committee wanted to understand Leo's role in facilitating relationships between justices and donors.

That wasn't Rivkin's only tie to the Supreme Court: he also represents a couple whose federal income tax dispute will be heard by the high court during the 2023–24 session. Alito spent four hours—in his chambers and also the *Wall Street Journal*'s New York offices—with an attorney with specific interests before the justices, who then praised him in a national newspaper as the "Supreme Court's plain-spoken defender." The article alone practically makes the case that Congress needs to pass an ethics standard.

It is the justices' own actions, again and again, that have precipitated the court's staggering disapproval ratings and created a legitimacy crisis. The supermajority wants it both ways: to act in ways that delegitimize itself, while then calling talk of their illegitimacy dangerous.

A gulf exists between the admirable and restrained court that Roberts says he desires and the actual court that he has led for the last eighteen years. According to a 2019 study, during Roberts's first fourteen years as chief, the Supreme Court overturned precedents in 21 cases—and Roberts voted with the majority 17 times, the second most of any justice. In 15 cases that overturned precedents with clear partisan implications, he voted for conservative outcomes 14 times.

As Linda Greenhouse observed in the *New York Times*, court watchers have a tendency to assess winners and losers, and the larger state of play, at the end of each session. That misses the bigger picture, she suggests, in which Roberts, while maintaining his faux-modest garb, has created "a profoundly different constitutional world, a world transformed, term by term and case by case, at the Supreme Court's hand."

The conservative judicial project, after all, bore limited fruit during the Burger and even the Rehnquist Courts. The Right's goals, Greenhouse writes—an end to abortion, stronger Second Amendment gun rights, an end to affirmative actions in college admissions, reining in the regulatory state, enhancing the rights of the religious—had gone nowhere under Rehnquist. *Roe v. Wade*, arguably, had even been *strengthened*. Greenhouse does not mention *Citizens United*, *Shelby County*, *Rucho*, or *Brnovich*, but they only make this case stronger. On every significant question about voting rights and democracy that reached the Supreme Court before this last term, Roberts led a party-line vote that benefited the Republican Party each time. By 2023, she writes, "every goal on the conservative wish list had been achieved. All of it. To miss that remarkable fact is to miss the story of the Roberts court."

THE SYSTEM IS "in deep trouble," and "the hour is late," warned Lewis Powell in the 1971 memorandum that preceded his nomination to the Supreme Court. All these decades later, the complete victory by the conservative legal movement that he helped birth and inspire gives those words an even more ominous undertone. Political science studies have suggested that the Republican hammerlock on the Supreme Court will continue until at least 2065; that's our lifetime and perhaps much of our children's lifetimes. The dark reality as the court enters its imperial, supermajority phase, not only rearranging constitutional rights as it pleases but centralizing more and more power within itself, the least democratic branch of our government, is that things will get worse before they get better.

Meanwhile, the nation stands at a crossroads. The question before America is whether an increasingly multiracial nation can ever become a multiracial democracy. The debate over whether 1619 or 1776 should be seen as America's founding is a contentious one. But there can be little argument over the date when America finally blossomed under its professed ideals: 1965, when the Voting Rights Act and other civil rights legislation reanimated the Reconstruction amendments, long ago snuffed by the nineteenth and early twentieth-century U.S. Supreme Court; established the principle of "one person, one vote"; and broke down Jim Crow barriers to make that dream real.

That project was the mission of the activist Warren Court that the conservative legal movement rose in opposition against. The NAACP and other civil rights organizations used the courts in similar ways—cultivating plaintiffs, backing lawsuits, placing them before courts they believed to be friendly. One could say that all courts are activists, and that there is little difference between liberal or conservative activism, only a rooting interest for one side or the other. There is an important difference, however. Those 1960s cases decided by the Warren Court sought to break down segregation and breathe full life into the Reconstruction amendments. They were not looking for new rights. They were asking the courts to finally enforce constitutional protections that had lain dormant for nearly a century. This was activism that sought to protect those that the law had otherwise seen fit to meet with dogs, clubs, and bullets when they demanded only the right to vote.

The Roberts Court—with a majority of justices appointed by presidents who have lost the popular vote, affirmed by a Senate itself built on minority rule, and with two members confirmed under dubious circumstances—has done the opposite. Whether gutting the Voting Rights Act, enshrining gerrymanders that enhanced the power of Republicans, or allowing a tsunami of corporate money to drown our elections, this court's project has been the determined dismantling of democracy, and the birth of a nation where your rights and your access to the ballot box depend on where you live and, once more, the color of your skin. Our most antidemocratic institution seems determined on creating and enforcing antidemocratic results, while denying that it is a political institution or activist at all.

We're faced with two options: reforming the court, or yielding to its GOP supermajority for a generation or longer. Reform might be difficult, especially in this moment of extreme partisanship. This is not the place for a complete discussion, yet there are many commonsense fixes with broad support, including term limits, allowing each president to appoint two justices, and strong new ethics requirements. Other structural fixes, all constitutional and within the power of Congress, would tackle the actual issue: expanding the number of justices, limiting the scope of what the Supreme Court can review, requiring larger majorities to override congressional legislation, even reorienting a justice's job altogether and drawing panels of federal judges to hear cases rather than handing each case to the same nine. It is time for Congress to stand and fight for the role of the people, or else the nightmare Abraham Lincoln envisioned in his first inaugural will have come true, and "the people will have ceased to be their own rulers."

Perhaps we can at least conquer partisanship to agree on this: In any republic or representative democracy, no nine people should hold this much power for life. And in any nation where the people rule, no legal movement, whether aligned with the Democratic Party or the Republican Party, should be able to capture generational power by locking in unelected, lifetime appointees and then having them bend the rules to their side's liking. We will only undo our antidemocratic present with more democracy.

ACKNOWLEDGMENTS

Jen Marshall, a force of nature and a brilliant agent, believed in this book and my work in a moment where that confidence meant everything. She brought me to Aevitas Creative Management and delivered me to the spectacular Jane von Mehren, a true partner and literary mastermind who shaped an idea into life over many months and shepherded it to reality. I am deeply fortunate to have two sensational friends and dynamic pros by my side, and grateful for their rejuvenating faith, genius, and kindness.

Jane, in turn, united me with the finest editor in Matt Harper at Mariner. Matt is any author's dream: he identified the larger story here that went far beyond *Shelby County*, and placed Roberts and the Supreme Court at the heart of our nation's antidemocratic crisis. Matt's enthusiasm, insightful guidance, perfect instincts, and rigorous edits sharpened and improved the arguments and narrative every step of the way. Each conversation pointed toward important new questions; his passion for democracy and this project was sustaining and unequaled. His deep editorial vision is matched only by his great humanity and generosity. This book is as much his as it is mine.

Chris Lehmann, a one-of-a-kind intellect and my masterful editor at the *New Republic*, the *African American Policy Forum*, and the *Nation*, helped focus and refine this book and my thinking. He was the first reader of almost all of these chapters, and I'm very thankful for his hard work, and his unrivaled mix of clarity and genius.

Dr. Sam Wang, a tireless democracy warrior and true friend, not only turned the Princeton Gerrymandering Project into a second home, but arranged a lengthy writing retreat in Princeton that allowed me to finish the final chapters. Thank you to Teri Boyd and Aleksandar Hemon, who generously loaned me their Princeton home for two weeks, a magical gift of time and space.

FairVote has been my professional home for seven years, over which time we've seen ranked choice voting and our nonpartisan electoral reforms move from the margin to the mainstream. The deep commitment and integrity of this entire team to building a more perfect union is an everyday inspiration. They've made so much of my work possible. Thank you: Rob Richie, Lan Nguyen, Ashley Houghton, Brian Cannon, Will Mantell (my daily sounding-board and sanity-check), Deb Otis, Danielle Allen, Meredith Sumpter, and all of my colleagues, past and present.

I'm grateful to everyone who read and commented on various chapter drafts along the way: Rose Aguilar, Alli Arbib, Stephanie Neely Aude, Adam Eichen, David Faris, Caroline Frederickson, Amy MacKinnon, Mike O'Neil, Eric Segall, Erin Geiger Smith, Bert Thurber, Brian Weinberg, and Jim Wilson.

Thank you to everyone who spoke to me for this book, on and off the record, on all sides of the political and legal spectrum. I'm especially grateful to the conservatives who kindly took the time to talk, especially Edward Blum, Michael Horowitz, Michael Carvin, Stephen Markman, Bruce Fein, Michael Greve, Mit Spears, Butch Ellis, and Edwin Meese, among so many others.

Thank you to everyone at Mariner for your enthusiasm, hard work and belief in this book, especially Maureen Cole, Jen McGuire, Beth Silfin, Ivy Givens, Amy Reeve, and Laurie McGee. Thank you, Nicole Stockburger and Maggie Cooper from ACM.

Thank you to all of the brilliant authors, thinkers, scholars, and colleagues on the democracy, Supreme Court, and voting beats from whom I've learned so much and on whose shoulders this book stands. I am fortunate to call many of them friends. I'm especially grateful to Carol Anderson, Ari Berman, Joan Biskupic, Emmet Bondurant, Conyers Davis, Pete Dominick, Katie Fahey, Gaby Goldstein, Chris Geidner. Linda Greenhouse, Rick Hasen, Santita Jackson, Kira Lerner, Sam Levine, Michael Li, Nancy MacLean, Jane Mayer, Ruth Marcus, Norm Ornstein, Doug Poland, Heather Cox Richardson, Adam Serwer, Mark Joseph Stern, Steven

Teles, Michael Tomasky, Jeffrey Toobin, Michael Waldman, and Wendy Weiser.

Thank you, Ann Southworth, for the holy grail of the Horowitz Report; Ralph Neas for hours of wonderful conversation; Bill Kristol; Judge David Tatel for welcoming me into your chambers; everyone in Calera who showed me around town and spent days explaining the roots and consequences of *Shelby County*; the Reverend Jesse Jackson for the honor of crossing the Edmund Pettus Bridge in Selma at your side; Oliver Houck; Amanda Hollis-Brusky. Eric Holder, Donald Verrilli, and Debo Adegbile spent hours generously reliving a Supreme Court defeat whose sting still lingers.

None of this is possible without the enduring love, patience, and support of my family, Jennifer Smedes and Wyatt Hudson, as well as my mom, Toby Daley.

Thank you, Alice Martell. Royal Easthampton and our captain Lloyd Cole. Paige Casey, Bertis Downs, Kristen Fabiszewski, Sara Macro Forrest, Panio Gianopoulos, Kristine Gual, Beth Hamilton, Paul Hogan, Meaghan Mulholland Hutson, Erin Keane, Jack McFadden, Tom Navin, Lisa Noller, Jen Rhodes, Molly Ringwald. The DBs. Kate Smedes and Kristen Murray. The Williamsburg Fire Department. Ann Novick, Sharon Esdale, Amanda Turk. Elizabeth Riley, everything and beyond.

It's been more than twenty-five years since I've written anything that Scott Timberg hasn't read, mocked slightly, then helped improve. Scott, we love you and miss you every day.

RESOURCES

THIS BOOK IS the product of almost a decade of writing and reporting on how our elections have been broken, intentionally, by those who seek to block a flourishing multiracial democracy and install an entrenched one-party rule instead. It builds on my previous two books on the threats posed by partisan gerrymandering and battles over the right to vote at the state level.

Antidemocratic began as a history of the *Shelby County* decision but it soon became clear that the Shelby County story could not be fully told without a broader lens on how the courts evolved from the 1960s-era fair apportionment and "one person, one vote" revolution under Chief Justice Earl Warren into a Supreme Court that, in decisions involving those looking to make elections more equal and just, and those who would rig maps and place additional barriers between some citizens and the ballot box, embrace the latter every time, awarding political advantages to the Republicans who placed them on the bench. The book needed to look backward from *Shelby County* and explore the Warren Court backlash that helped spawn the birth of originalism, the Federalist Society, and the efforts to place reliable conservatives on the bench. And then it needed to explain the threats to free and fair elections that the *Shelby County* decision, along with other antidemocratic decisions, unleashed on our elections.

Extensive endnotes for this book can be found online at davedaley.net, but since they are not included here, I wanted to provide some background on the reporting and research process. The backbone of *Antidemocratic* is more than one hundred interviews, both on and off the record, with key participants in these events at every level. These interviews include multiple U.S. attorneys general, solicitors general, the lawyers who argued these cases on both sides before the U.S. Supreme Court, federal judges, top Justice Department officials, veterans of the Ronald Reagan administration, conservative funders and litigators, members of Congress, governors, state legislators, state supreme court justices, voting rights activists, law professors and scholars, local officials, and many, many others. I am deeply grateful to everyone who spoke to me, especially those on the conservative side who may disagree with the conclusions I have drawn, but who took the time to help me better understand their perspective and important historic events.

I have tried to indicate whenever an interview is with me by saying so within the text on first reference, or if not, crediting the source on the page. When an interview is drawn from another source, I have worked to credit it within the text or to cite it online. My thanks as well to so many of the librarians and archivists who guided me through boxes of papers, both in person and online. Lewis Powell's papers are at Washington and Lee University. The memos between Potter Stewart and Lewis Powell were discovered in the Stewart papers in Yale University's Special Collections. The National Archives were a tremendous help on boxes of John Roberts's memos, and many other documents were obtained through the Ronald Reagan Presidential Library and Edwin Meese's papers at Stanford University's Hoover Institution. The oral history with Representative Don Edwards was furnished by the libraries at the University of North Carolina at Chapel Hill.

This book wouldn't exist without other writers and researchers who have been covering these topics for many years, sometimes even decades, both as journalists and scholars, in popular publications and academic presses and journals. I'm very grateful for that work as well, and for the opportunity to integrate their scholarship and thinking into this narrative to present a fuller portrait of the last five-plus decades than I would have been able to otherwise. Two books from more than fifteen years ago remain crucial. Ann Southworth's *Lawyers of the Right*, published by the University of Chicago Press and Steven M. Teles's *The Rise of the Conservative Legal Movement*, published by Princeton University Press in 2008, are the most serious and thoughtful looks at this important history. Their work informs so much of the background and thinking of the early chapters. Teles's brilliant paper "Transformative Bureaucracy: Reagan's Lawyers and the Dynamics of Political Investment," published in 2009 by Cambridge University Press, was also crucial for connecting the dots between the growth of the legal movement and the purposeful ways ideas were put to work in the Meese Justice Department to bring about lasting, revolutionary change. After months of sleuthing, Ann Southworth provided me with what might be the only complete copy of the Horowitz Report available anywhere. I greatly appreciate her collegiality and generosity. Amanda Hollis-Brusky is a scholar who is also a brilliant reporter and has done masterful work on the Federalist Society. Her book *Ideas with Consequences: The Federalist Society and the Conservative Counter-revolution* was absolutely essential and guided me through the thicket of how FedSoc ideas, journals, and conferences helped lead to the *Citizens United* decision. What she captured, perhaps for the first time, is the way that the conservative legal movement effectively cornered every market: developing legal theories, helping them gain currency and credibility, then launching cases in which those theories could be tested, placed before judges they'd prevetted for the bench.

Noah Feldman's audiobook *Takeover* is tremendous on the birth of the Federalist Society. Just as important was a 2007 thesis by Jonathan Riehl, a doctoral student at the University of North Carolina, called "The Federalist Society and Movement Conservatism: How a Fractious Coalition on the Right Is Changing Constitutional Law and the Way We Talk and Think About It." Riehl recognized the group's importance more than fifteen years ago and talked to all the significant players at great length and depth, and many opened up to him in ways that they will not before reporters today. It's a tremendous resource and work. Another terrific graduate student, Patrick Gallagher at the University of Chicago, uncovered key memos on originalism and pointed me deeper into the papers of the Office of Legal Policy. His thesis, "The Conservative Incubator of Originalism," is top-notch. Calvin TerBeek's masterful work on originalism should lead to a wholesale reconsideration of its racial roots and underpinnings. Prior to the reauthorization of the VRA in 2006, the University of Southern California's Gould School of Law published a series of in-depth studies of Voting Rights Act violations across the states covered by preclearance, written by top experts. They were extraordinarily helpful in directing me toward stories that were otherwise uncovered and undertold.

Stephen Markman not only worked in the middle of the 1982 reauthorization fight but also wrote a remarkable legislative history of it for the *Washington and Lee Law Review*, with Thomas Boyd, in fall 1983. Gary May's *Bending Toward Justice*; Charles S. Bullock III, Ronald Keith Gaddie, and Justin J. Wert's *The Rise and Fall of the Voting Rights Act*; and *Winning While Losing*, edited by Kenneth Osgood and Derrick E. White, offered compelling histories of the VRA's long life and also Reagan's Washington. Jeffrey Toobin's reporting in the *New Yorker* was critical on the Federalist Society's influence in Washington, the role of John Roberts, and the *Citizens United* and *Shelby County* cases. Jesse H. Rhodes's *Ballot Blocked* turned around the way I saw the 2006 reauthorization, from the last moment when the VRA was bipartisan to the first step in its erosion behind closed doors and in the courts.

A number of recent books on the court were invaluable in offering history, context, behind closed-door detail, and so much more: Joan Biskupic's biography *The Chief* is masterful on Roberts's early days, his time at DOJ, and *Shelby County*. No one does this better than Linda Greenhouse, and *Justice on the Brink* is another brilliant book. Michael Waldman not only runs the Brennan Center for Justice but authored *The Supermajority*. Carl Hulse's *Confirmation Bias*, the great Ruth Marcus's *Supreme Ambition*, and *Dissent* by Jackie Calmes focused on recent confirmation battles but pulled back to brilliantly narrate the larger history. Adam Cohen's *Supreme Inequality* wonderfully shows how the court has undermined fairness not only on voting issues but across the board.

No one follows the money like Jane Mayer in *Dark Money*, which was crucial on the background of the conservative foundations. Senator Sheldon Whitehouse tied much of the money and Leo network together in *The Scheme*. The great historian and thinker Nancy MacLean untangled the deep roots of the Koch network and the Right's long-standing plans for minority rule in her masterful *Democracy in Chains*. The indefatigable Lisa Graves has compiled report after report tracking the funders on the right; it's extraordinarily difficult and painstaking work and anyone writing on this owes her a giant debt.

Virtuoso investigative reporters have tracked and unraveled huge pieces of the Leo octopus, and I've also relied on Heidi Przybyla at *Politico*; Robert O'Harrow Jr. and Shawn Boburg of the *Washington Post*; Andy Kroll, Andrea Bernstein, and Ilya Marritz at *ProPublica*; Nick Surgey of *Documented*; and Steve Eder, Jo Becker, Shane Goldmacher, and Kenneth P. Vogel at the *New York Times*.

Adam Serwer of *The Atlantic*, Jay Willis and the team at *Balls and Strikes*, and Mark Joseph Stern and Dahlia Lithwick of *Slate* should be hailed as national heroes for the astute and relentless eye they bring to their analysis of the court's work.

My friend Ari Berman and I seem to share a mind in how we look at these cases and history, and we approach these topics in very similar ways. His 2016 book, *Give Us the Ballot*, remains the most incisive and wonderfully narrated story of the modern struggle to protect the vote; sometimes I would think I had something new in Roberts's papers only to realize Ari's eye got there first. Ari's look at the '82 fight and Roberts's long history is nothing less than terrific.

My apologies to any of the brilliant thinkers I have missed here. The online notes will have greater detail, links to articles and archives wherever possible, and line up with each place in the text.

David Daley

February 9, 2024

INDEX

Mueller, Greg, 290, 293
municipal utility districts (MUDs),
    186–94, 198–201

Nader, Ralph, 5, 9, 30, 33, 34
napalm, 4–5
Nashville school shooting of 2023,
    310–11
National Association for the
    Advancement of Colored People
    (NAACP), 76, 159, 199, 210, 260,
    273, 372, 373, 379
National Legal Center for the Public
    Interest, 30
National Review, 14, 16–17, 92, 94, 115
National Rifle Association, 292–93
National Right to Life Committee,
    166–67
National Urban League, 82
Neas, Ralph, 68, 72–73, 83, 84
Neshoba County Fair, 67
"Neutral Principles and Some First
    Amendment Problems" (Bork),
    11–15
New Deal, 4, 18–19, 281
New Left, 4, 26
New Preemption, 327–34
New Republic, 17, 202, 203
New Yorker, 119, 120, 121
New York Times, 8, 19, 20, 29, 62, 65,
    72, 77, 78–79, 82, 91, 95, 102, 164,
    179, 191, 202, 231, 292, 297, 303,
    307, 349, 350, 361, 364, 375, 378
New York University, 367
Niess, Richard, 316–17
Nixon, Richard, xviii, 51, 97, 222–23
    Blue Ribbon Defense Panel, 6, 7
    election of 1968, 3, 11
    election of 1972, 11, 145, 223
    Powell Memo, 7, 8–9
    State of the Union (1970), 5
    Supreme Court nominations, 11, 18, 60
    Voting Rights Act and, 67
Nixonland (Perlstein), 167
noblesse oblige, 6, 72

Nofziger, Lyn, 72
North Carolina, 258–61, 264–65, 266,
    268, 271–74, 312–13, 356, 367
North Carolina A&T State University,
    272, 273
Northwest Austin Municipal v. Holder,
    195–205, 208, 265, 366
    arguments and opinion, 195–96,
    198–205, 217, 235
    background, 191–94, 275
    impact, 196–98, 201–5, 218–20, 222,
    223–24, 229, 234, 239, 243, 276,
    362, 364, 374
Norton, Eleanor Holmes, 26
Notre Dame University, 55, 299
Nunberg, Sam, 286

Obama, Barack, 183, 195, 219, 249,
    289–90
    election of 2008, 176, 267
    election of 2012, 268, 269–70
    election of 2016, 288
    judicial nominations, 328
Obamacare (Affordable Care Act), 69,
    219, 226, 295, 296, 309, 314
Obergefell v. Hodges, 226
O'Connor, Maureen, 320–23
O'Connor, Reed, 333
O'Connor, Sandra Day, 71, 76, 120,
    147–48, 168, 181, 307
Office of Legal Policy, 100–101, 118–19
Office of Management and Budget
    (OMB), 35–36
O'Harrow, Robert, Jr., 288
Ohio, 266, 319–23, 333
Olin, John, 20, 24–25, 29, 30, 36, 37
Olin Foundation, 37, 94, 96, 299
Oliver, Karl, 132–33
Olson, Ted, 90, 93, 95, 124, 159, 171
O'Neill, Michael, 154
"one person, one vote," xviii, 3, 11, 13, 42,
    52–53, 222, 264, 279, 379
Operation Eagle Eye, 59–60
Operation Higher Court, 309
Operation Originalism, 106

ABOUT

MARINER BOOKS

MARINER BOOKS traces its beginnings to 1832 when William Ticknor cofounded the Old Corner Bookstore in Boston, from which he would run the legendary firm Ticknor and Fields, publisher of Ralph Waldo Emerson, Harriet Beecher Stowe, Nathaniel Hawthorne, and Henry David Thoreau. Following Ticknor's death, Henry Oscar Houghton acquired Ticknor and Fields and, in 1880, formed Houghton Mifflin, which later merged with venerable Harcourt Publishing to form Houghton Mifflin Harcourt. HarperCollins purchased HMH's trade publishing business in 2021 and reestablished their storied lists and editorial team under the name Mariner Books.

Uniting the legacies of Houghton Mifflin, Harcourt Brace, and Ticknor and Fields, Mariner Books continues one of the great traditions in American bookselling. Our imprints have introduced an incomparable roster of enduring classics, including Hawthorne's *The Scarlet Letter*, Thoreau's *Walden*, Willa Cather's *O Pioneers!*, Virginia Woolf's *To the Lighthouse*, W.E.B. Du Bois's *Black Reconstruction*, J.R.R. Tolkien's *The Lord of the Rings*, Carson McCullers's *The Heart Is a Lonely Hunter*, Ann Petry's *The Narrows*, George Orwell's *Animal Farm* and *Nineteen Eighty-Four*, Rachel Carson's *Silent Spring*, Margaret Walker's *Jubilee*, Italo Calvino's *Invisible Cities*, Alice Walker's *The Color Purple*, Margaret Atwood's *The Handmaid's Tale*, Tim O'Brien's *The Things They Carried*, Philip Roth's *The Plot Against America*, Jhumpa Lahiri's *Interpreter of Maladies*, and many others. Today Mariner Books remains proudly committed to the craft of fine publishing established nearly two centuries ago at the Old Corner Bookstore.